explorations

A Navigator's Guide to Quantitative Research in Canadian Political Science

Keith Archer
The University of Calgary

Roger Gibbins
The University of Calgary

Loleen Youngman
The University of Calgary

 I(T)P Nelson

an International Thomson Publishing company

Toronto • Albany • Bonn • Boston • Cincinnati • Detroit • London • Madrid
Melbourne • Mexico City • New York • Pacific Grove • Paris • San Francisco
Singapore • Tokyo • Washington

THOMSON

™

NELSON

ISBN 0-17-617519-9

Consists of:

Explorations
Archer/Gibbins/Youngman
ISBN 0-17-605663-7, © 1998

Contents

Introduction *viii*

PART 1   OVERVIEW TOPICS

1. The Scientific Approach to Politics *2*

- Empirical and Normative Analysis *5*
- What Is Science? *10*
- Hard and Soft Sciences *10*
- Postulates of Science *14*
- The Methodology of Science *20*
    Steps in the Scientific Method *21*
- Criticisms and Limitations of the Scientific Approach to Politics *31*
- Working as a Team *33*
- Self-Study *34*

2. Theory-Oriented Research and the Issue of Causality *35*

- Quantitative and Qualitative Approaches to Empirical Research *36*
- Basic and Applied Research *37*
    Theory: Relationships between Concepts *40*
- Developing and Testing Theories *45*
- Hypothesis-Testing *47*
- Causality *56*
    Errors in Causal Reasoning *58*
- Working as a Team *61*
- Self-Study *61*

3. Research Ethics: People behind the Numbers *65*

- Risk Assessment and the Medical Model *66*
- Selecting the Research Topic *69*

- Protecting Research Subjects and Respondents   *73*
- Ethical Considerations in Research Design   *80*
- Ethical Considerations in Data Analysis   *82*
- Ethics and Collegiality   *83*
- Ethical Considerations in the Publication of Research Findings   *85*
- Conclusions   *87*
- Working as a Team   *88*
- Self-Study   *88*

PART 2   LINKING THEORY TO RESEARCH

4. Observing the Political World: Quantitative Approaches   *92*

- Considering Research Methodologies   *95*
- Experimental Research   *98*
- Survey Research   *103*
- Pilot Studies   *111*
- Secondary Analysis   *112*
- Content Analysis   *112*
- Case Studies   *114*
- Focus Groups   *116*
- Working as a Team   *116*
- Self-Study   *117*

5. Observing the Political World: Qualitative Approaches   *118*

- Combining Qualitative and Quantitative Research Approaches   *119*
- Elite Interviewing   *123*
- Observation Research   *128*
- Comparative Research   *136*
- Interpreting Qualitative Data   *144*
- Working as a Team   *146*
- Self-Study   *146*

6. Defining the Political World: Concepts *148*

- Conceptual Definitions *152*
  - Example: The Impact of Education on Voting *153*
  - Example: Party Identification *158*
- Sources of Conceptual Definitions *164*
  - Inductive Reasoning *165*
  - Extrapolation *165*
  - Intuition *167*
- Working as a Team *168*
- Self-Study *168*

7. Defining the Political World: Measures *170*

- Concepts, Variables, and Indicators *172*
- Precision in Measurement *182*
- Accuracy in Measurement *189*
- Designing Survey Questions *196*
- Creating Indices *201*
- Working as a Team *203*
- Self-Study *203*

PART 3   STATISTICAL TOPICS

8. Sampling the Political World *206*

- Populations and Samples *207*
- Probability Sampling *213*
  - Introduction to Probability Theory *213*
  - Probability Theory and Sampling *216*
- Sample Size *218*
- Conducting Probability Samples *223*
- Nonprobability Sampling *226*
- Working as a Team *230*
- Self-Study *230*

9. Describing the Political World: Univariate Statistics *232*

- Measures of Central Tendency *233*
- Measures of Variation *243*
- Normal Curve *250*
- Comparing Univariate Statistics between Two Subgroups *253*
- Looking for Bivariate Relationships in Percentage Distributions *256*
- Working as a Team *261*
- Self-Study *261*

10. Assessing the Political World: Inferential Statistics *264*

- Selecting Confidence Levels *267*
- Data Distributions *272*
- Selecting Inferential Statistics *275*
- Chi-Square *275*
- *T*-Tests for Differences between Means *284*
- Mann-Whitney *U*-Test *288*
- *T*-Tests and *F*-Ratios for Interval-Level Relationships *292*
- Working as a Team *294*
- Self-Study *295*

11. Explaining the Political World: Nominal and Ordinal Data *297*

- Measuring the Strength of Relationships *298*
- Measures for Nominal-Level Data *304*
- Measures for Ordinal-Level Data *309*
- Adding a Third Variable to the Bivariate Relationship *318*
  - Spurious Relationships *318*
  - Intervening Variable *319*
  - Reinforcing Variable *321*
  - Multiple Independent Variables *322*
- Contingency Tables with Control Variables *324*
  - The Effect of Age on Political Interest, Controlling for Education *324*
- Self-Study *329*

12. Multivariate Analysis: An Introduction to the Deep End of the Pool *331*

- Measures for Interval-Level Data *331*
- The Standard Error of the Estimate *338*
- Multiple Regression Analysis *344*
- Predicting Attitudes toward Party Leaders: Assessments of Brian Mulroney *347*
- Dummy Variable Regression Analysis *351*
- Predicting Party Leader Ratings in Alberta *352*
- Self-Study *357*

13. Writing the Report *359*

- The Audience *360*
- Constructing an Argument *361*
- Components of the Research Report *363*
    - The Abstract or Executive Summary *363*
    - Introduction *364*
    - Literature Review *365*
    - Research Design *366*
    - Presentation of Findings *367*
    - Discussion *368*
    - Conclusions *369*
    - References *369*
- The Final Polish *370*
- Working as a Team *370*
- Self-Study *371*

References *372*

Index *379*

Introduction

Many students in political science, and indeed in the social sciences more broadly defined, try to avoid research methods courses because they dislike or even fear math. Some resent being confronted with the very numbers and math which they had designed their undergraduate program to avoid. Others are simply anxious about their ability: "Will this be the course that kills my GPA?"

Let's begin, then, with some basic reassurance. To paraphrase former American president F.D. Roosevelt, you have nothing to fear but fear itself. If you passed math in grade 10, you have more than enough mathematical skill to handle the material in this text. If you can add, subtract, multiply, divide, and plug numbers into simple equations, you are as ready as you need to be. The content of this text is primarily *conceptual*. Our goal is to give you the necessary tools to think clearly about research issues in political science, to understand both the power and limitations of quantitative data. True, the math is there, but it is there as a form of conceptual understanding more than as a form of calculation.

Some contemporary research methods books shy away from mathematical computations altogether, recognizing that most students will be working with computer-based statistical packages that will effortlessly do the calculations for them. However, it is our belief that some hands-on familiarity is essential if students are to acquire a sufficient degree of conceptual confidence. Statistical tests and measures can be difficult to understand in the abstract; thus, we will provide simple illustrations to give you the opportunity to work through the basic formulas. It is not our expectation that you will abandon the computer-based programs in favour of pencil and paper, but rather that you will have some firsthand experience with the statistical terminology you will encounter in your own reading and research. You will be more comfortable with that terminology if you have had this opportunity.

In the chapters to come we will take you through the steps entailed in empirical research. How should you conceptualize a research problem? What evidence, or data, should you bring to bear on the problem? How do you measure the concepts you wish to address? How do you describe the research findings? What statistical tests might be used? Under what ethical guidelines should you operate? Throughout the chapters we will try to engage you actively in the text material by providing opportunities for you to test your own thinking and comprehension. These opportunities, identified as *Checking Your Bearings*, are not meant to be formal exercises for which there are right and wrong answers. Rather, they provide the chance to think about the material and to apply it in situations familiar to most readers. The same objectives guide the group discussion topics raised at the end of each chapter.

Throughout the text we will constantly be bringing real data into play through sections that we have identified as *Maps and Illustrations*. These are not literally maps and illustrations; they are real life illustrations frequently drawn from the kinds of surveys and reports that you run across daily in newspapers and on television. Others, and perhaps the most important, will come from the political science and social science literature. Our objective in both cases is the same: to illustrate how quantitative research methods can be used to enrich and expand our understanding of the political world and, in some cases, to illustrate how mistakes can be made.

There is, then, an *applied* character to the text. But this should not imply an avoidance of normative issues. We recognize that an interest in normative issues—the shoulds and oughts of politics—is what draws many students into political science. We also recognize that normative questions cannot be reduced to empirical questions; knowing how the world *is* does not tell us how it *should be*. At the same time, a great deal of normative debate in politics and political science draws upon empirical evidence and understanding. Should there be seat-belt laws? Prohibition of smoking in public places? Controls on violence in television programming? Limitations on campaign spending in federal or provincial elections? Our answers to such questions depend *in part* upon assumptions about empirical effects. Thus, a nuanced empirical understanding of the political world is a means to a richer normative debate and not a way of avoiding such debate. To a large extent, that understanding can come through quantitative methods, although we will also introduce readers to the growing use of qualitative research methods in political science.

While this text emphasizes the benefits of using the scientific method in understanding and evaluating the empirical—or observable—world, it is also important to remain mindful of the limitations of the scientific method, particularly as they relate to the social sciences. Although the scientific method purports to be a way of understanding the world on the basis of observable facts, we will show that at times these facts themselves are a matter of dispute. There are many possible reasons to explain different perceptions of reality, and these will be introduced and explored throughout the text.

Underlying this assumption about the importance of empirical understanding is the reality that research skills are essential in the contemporary labour market. An ability to design, conduct, and, more commonly, *assess* empirical research is no longer a frill; it is rapidly becoming a necessity. Numerical literacy is as essential to today's job market as literacy itself was to the job market of earlier generations. We are convinced that of all the courses you take, research methods courses are the most immediately relevant to getting and keeping a job.

Finally, we would like to emphasize the thematic intent of the book's title, *Explorations*. It is not our intent to give the last word on empirical research methodology, for the field is rich, vast, and complex. Rather, we hope to open some doors, to provide you with a rough understanding of empirical, quantitative research in political science. Our goal is to equip you with both the basic skills you need to handle quantitative research material and an appreciation of the strengths and weaknesses of empirical research. The text, then, is no more than a preliminary exploration. The destinations identified for each chapter are not final destinations but rather way stations on what, for many readers, will undoubtedly turn out to be a much longer journey. For those readers for whom the way stations turn out to be the final destination, we trust that you will find the exploration to have been interesting and helpful as you continue to run up against political issues and debates throughout your life.

We would like to thank the reviewers who took time to comment on the manuscript of this text: Grant Amyot, Queen's University; Gerald Bierling, McMaster University; and David Docherty, Wilfrid Laurier University.

*   *   *   *   *

Statistics Canada information is used with the permission of the Minister of Industry, as Minister responsible for Statistics Canada. Information on the availability of the wide range of data from Statistics Canada can be obtained from Statistics Canada's Regional Offices, its World Wide Web site, at http://www.statcan.ca, and its toll-free access number, 1-800-263-1136.

PART 1

OVERVIEW TOPICS

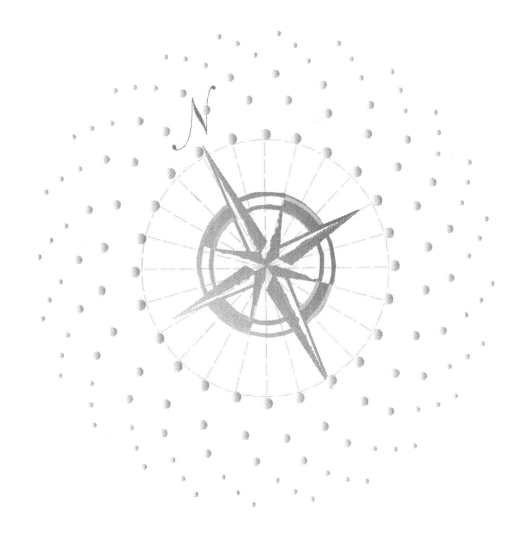

CHAPTER 1

The Scientific Approach to Politics

DESTINATION

By the end of this chapter the reader should

- understand the idea of *science* in political science;
- know the basic postulates of science;
- understand the general methodology of science as applied to the more specific study of politics;
- know the distinction between normative and empirical studies;
- appreciate some of the limitations of the scientific method and some of the critiques of the scientific methodology that have emerged.

One of the goals of an undergraduate education, and in particular one of the goals of a course in research methods in the social sciences, is to help students think critically. By this we mean that propositions or arguments are not accepted unless they are accompanied by sufficiently compelling evidence. Critical thought therefore involves weighing and evaluating the merits of evidence marshalled in support of an argument. Researchers ask whether they understand the evidence in the same way that others do and whether they interpret the implications of the evidence in the same way as others. If the evidence is found wanting because it fails to provide sufficiently strong support or because it does not bear directly on the argument, then the argument can be rejected. Thus, the ways in which we *perceive* and *interpret* evidence are two key aspects of critical thought.

One of the goals of the **scientific approach to politics** is to use critical thought as a guide to our perceptions of the political world. Boldly stated, the scientific study of politics attempts to provide a method whereby observations of the political world can be relatively independent of the observer. Stated more cautiously, it can help in determining not only when political perceptions differ, but why they differ.

Not surprisingly, this book takes the view that it is useful and worthwhile to pursue the goals of scientific analysis. However, we also accept the premise that most political research falls well short of the goal of providing similar observations and interpretations of political reality. Thus, a good deal of our attention will be focused on understanding why political scientists are so often in disagreement about so many of the most fundamental questions of politics. This is not meant to suggest that little progress has been made over time in our understanding of politics. On the contrary, much knowledge has been gained. In some areas of political science, including the study of voting, elections, and political belief systems, the scientific approach has so transformed both political practice and research that they are unrecognizable from early generations. Nonetheless, the scientific approach to politics is not a simple template or cookie cutter that can be applied holus-bolus to any political problem or research question. Its application requires detailed and careful attention from students and researchers alike.

An example of an issue over which there is considerable disagreement may help illustrate the role of the scientific approach. One of the most common features of political life in advanced industrial democracies is the persistence of female underrepresentation in legislative assemblies. Every national legislature in the Organisation for Economic Co-operation and Development (OECD) has fewer women, and usually a lot fewer women, than men. In the 1997 Canadian general election, for example, only 64 of the 301 MPs elected to the House of Commons (21.3%) were women, up from 18.0% in 1993. Hence the *fact* that women are underrepresented in legislatures can scarcely be disputed. Far more controversial, however, are the *explanations* that account for this finding. Some would argue that women are underrepresented out of choice, that women are less inclined than men to seek elective public office. This explanation can be further broken down into the propositions (1) that women and men are socialized to have different preferences and (2) that women and men have different responsibilities throughout the life cycle which, for instance, place a greater onus on women for child-rearing, thus freeing men to engage in other activities, including participating in parties and seeking election. Yet another explanation for differential rates of seeking election is the systematic bias against strong women candidates that may exist in political parties. That is to say, the parties themselves may present barriers to otherwise willing female candidates, making it difficult for them to win nomination for office, particularly in highly competitive ridings.

Which of these three explanations for the underrepresentation of women in legislatures is the most accurate and informative?[1] The answer is important because it can have profound implications for public policy. If female underrepresentation is caused mainly by the parties systematically excluding women, then the solution (assuming, as we do, that this is a problem) may be quite different than if it stems largely from gender-specific differences in the life cycle or gender differences in socialization. (Of course, each of these explanations may contain a partial truth about the causes of differences in political representation.) The key feature of the scientific approach to politics is that it requires the formulation of testable hypotheses and the marshalling of empirical data that can either confirm or fail to confirm the hypotheses. It provides a way of applying empirical data to normative questions and public policy debates.

A POINT ON THE COMPASS

Women's Representation in the Canadian House of Commons

The issue of gender representation in legislative assemblies has been the subject of a considerable body of empirical research. In an article published in 1994, Donley Studlar and Richard Matland addressed the 1984 surge in women elected to the Canadian House of Commons, a surge that increased the number of elected women MPs from 10 in 1979 (3.5%) and 14 in 1980 (5.0%) to 27 in 1984 (9.6%). The empirical question they asked was whether the 1984 increase was a fluke stemming from the unexpectedly large number of Progressive Conservative MPs elected from Quebec. This question stemmed from the assumption that the Conservatives had nominated female candidates in Quebec ridings they expected to lose, but then won. After a sophisticated statistical analysis, the authors concluded that "it becomes difficult to credit the conventional wisdom that the rise of women in the Canadian House of Commons in 1984 was the product of an accident, a fluke in which intended Conservative sacrificial lambs were surprisingly elevated because of a massive swing of the Quebec electorate toward the Progressive Conservative party. Such an explanation ignores the broader patterns of candidacy underlying the rise of women in 1984" (77).

By submitting the 1984 election results to an empirical test, the authors were able to show that what might have been considered an idiosyncratic event in Canadian politics could better be seen as confirmation of much broader currents of change common to most Western democratic states.

EMPIRICAL AND NORMATIVE ANALYSIS

The goal of *all* political analysis is to advance our knowledge and understanding of the political world. There are two dominant forms of political analysis: normative and empirical. **Normative** analysis is prescriptive in nature and addresses how society and political life *should be*. This is the realm of political theory and philosophy. Because it entails the discussion of ideals, normative political analysis is inundated with value judgments and preferences. Normative discussions invoke convictions and feelings, things that are terribly important but are also difficult to measure and observe empirically in day-to-day life. In addition, people often disagree about the "truth" of normative statements, for they bring different values, priorities, and moral perspectives into play. For example, consider the debate on capital punishment. Both sides of the debate are presented as fact, in statements such as "It is wrong to kill anyone, even murderers" and "It is wrong to allow those who take life to continue life." Yet which position one sees as true depends upon one's own values and beliefs; the distinction is normative, not factual. We can identify normative analysis by the use of value-laden terms such as "good," "bad," "right," "wrong," "should," "must," and "ought." Many political debates concern normative issues, since people often disagree about what ends should be sought and the best means for reaching such ends.

A POINT ON THE COMPASS ──────────────

Normative and Empirical Approaches to Democracy: Robert Dahl

An interesting example of the difference between the normative and empirical approaches to political analysis is seen in the work of Robert Dahl, who devoted much of his long academic career to the study of democracy. Initially, he worked as an empiricist, seeking to explain *how* democracy works. In *Who Governs?* (1961), Dahl explored the distribution of power in New Haven, Connecticut. He found that although power appears to be concentrated in political elites, interest groups have great influence on the decisions elites make, leaving government acting more as a referee between conflicting interests than as a powerful decision-maker with interests of its own. Dahl assumed that all relevant social interests could form groups to lobby the government and that all groups have political weight, and from these assumptions he concluded that democratic politics is not elite dominated. The school of thought that asserts that democracy is a contest between numerous groups and "potential" groups is known as the **pluralist school**, which has been challenged empirically on many fronts. Critics include public choice theorists, who argue that not all interests are equally likely to form lobby groups, and neo-Marxists, who argue that powerful corporate interests have greater status than noneconomic elites in the battle between interests.

Two decades later, the normative component of Dahl's writing emerged more clearly. In *Democracy and Its Critics* (1989), Dahl distinguishes between the ideal and practice of democracy. Political orders based on democratic practices—such as free elections, inclusive suffrage, freedom of expression, and representative government—are defined as "polyarchies," rather than democracies. Polyarchy can be empirically observed: does a country have democratic institutions? If yes, it is a polyarchy. Dahl reserves the word "democracy" for the ideal toward which all polyarchies strive; it is the system under which liberty and self-development flourish. Dahl writes (1989, 322): "In my view, neither political equality nor the democratic process is justified as intrinsically good. Rather, they are justified as the most reliable means for protecting and advancing the good and interests of all persons subject to collective decisions.... [Political equality is] an essential means to a just distribution of freedom and to fair opportunities for self-development." Thus, Dahl's later work clearly makes normative judgments: liberty is *good,* and given that democracy is the best means to liberty, democracy *should* be pursued.

The second branch of political analysis is **empirical** research. Empirical political analysis is descriptive in nature; the goal is to describe and to explain the political world *as it is*, rather than as it should be. Whereas normative analysis is self-consciously "value" based, empirical research purports to be more "fact" based. Factual evidence is gathered from the physical and social worlds; unless a phenomenon can be observed (experienced through the senses), it cannot be considered admissible evidence (Singleton et al. 1988, 31). Knowledge obtained from methods other than observation—such as faith, intuition, or common sense—is not considered empirical knowledge. This is not meant to discredit other ways of knowing, but rather to emphasize the distinction between empirical and nonempirical knowledge. Empiricism requires observation and therefore measurement. In addition, empirical facts must be independently observed and agreed upon by many people. This quality is known as *intersubjectivity.* How one observes an event or a phenomenon is ultimately subjective; as those who have witnessed a car accident can attest, there are often two, three, or even six sides to every story. By requiring that more than one person observe and give a similar account of the event, we are able to increase objectivity. Intersubjectivity also requires that more than one observation occur; in the scientific process this is known as *replication.* Researchers seek out evidence that confirms the findings of other researchers, thus "double-checking" the observations of others. The more people who observe a phenomenon and the more times it is observed, the more willing we are to accept it as fact. An empirical statement does not indicate preferences or values, but rather presents observable facts.

A key issue for empirically based research is the degree to which facts exist independently of the observer. We made reference a moment ago to the fact that witnesses to an accident often report different versions of the "facts" of the case. Quite literally, they have perceived the same events very differently. On a matter such as a traffic accident with the attendant legal and financial implications, it may very well be in the interest of those concerned to perceive things differently: neither driver wishes to be charged with a traffic offence nor to have his or her insurance premiums rise. Thus, there may be an incentive for their perception of reality to be distorted, either consciously or unconsciously.

The view of some researchers is that this particular example of the filtering of "facts" among motorists in a traffic accident is generalizable in perceptions of the social and political world. In this view, "facts" are not completely objective, but instead perceptions of fact are influenced or mediated by the social and political context of the observer. To the extent that this is true, it may be difficult to fully separate facts and values, or the empirical and normative aspects of the study of politics.

There are other ways in which normative and empirical analysis overlap in the study of politics. Empirical research is used to question the conclusions of normative analysis, and normative analysis often employs empirical facts in its arguments. Consider, for example, environmental debates. Environmentalists state empirical facts—endangered species, decreasing ozone levels—before stating normative positions: we *should* clean up the oceans, the air, and so on. Opposition to the environmental movement's normative positions also contains appeals to empirical fact. As Julian Simon (1995, 11) writes, for example, "Every measure of material and environmental welfare in the United States and

CHECKING YOUR BEARINGS

NORMATIVE AND EMPIRICAL STATEMENTS

Identify the following statements as either normative statements or empirical statements:

1. Seat-belt usage decreases automobile-related fatalities.
2. Seat-belt usage ought to be mandatory.
3. Democracy is the best system of government available.
4. Democratic systems, on average, have better human rights records.
5. In terms of demographic weight, women are severely under-represented in legislatures.
6. The electoral system should be changed to ensure a more representative legislature.

   In assessing these statements, note the impact that specific words can make. In the fifth statement, for example, does the addition of the adverb "severely" affect your categorization of the statement as normative or empirical? Can "better" in statement 4 be assessed in empirical terms, or is it inherently normative?

in the world has improved rather than deteriorated ... there is every scientific reason to be joyful about the trends in the conditions of the Earth...." Some of the most contentious environmental debates occur when there is no concrete, agreed-upon empirical evidence; for example, do harp seals really deplete cod stocks? Is the global temperature increasing, or are we just witnessing short-term fluctuations around a constant norm? While this text will be concerned primarily with empirical research, the reader should note how frequently empiricism is used in normative debates.

A POINT ON THE COMPASS

The Interplay of Normative Issues and Empirical Research

It is increasingly rare to encounter normative debates in the public policy arena that are not anchored to empirical evidence. Note, for example, a 1996 column by James Carroll in *The Boston Globe,* which attacked cutbacks to the American foreign aid budget. The column was emphatically normative in tone: the United States *should* do more, indeed much more, than it is doing to provide development assistance to poor nations. However, the normative argument was built on a foundation of empirical evidence relating not only to the amount of aid provided by other countries, but also to American public opinion:

> *The irony is that this new stinginess has been embraced in the name of the American people who are often character-ized as opposed to foreign aid. But that is just not true. Public perceptions may be clouded, but popular attitudes remain large-hearted. For example, a recent University of Maryland survey found that Americans commonly believe that the United States spends far more than it does on for-eign aid—the median assumption was 15 percent of the fed-eral budget. When poll-takers asked what a more appropriate figure would be, Americans responded over-whelmingly that about 5 percent of federal spending should go to help poorer nations.... In fact, the share of the budget devoted to humanitarian foreign aid is less than half of 1 percent. (Carroll 1996)*

Here, the column's author is using public opinion data in an interesting way: what appears to be a public desire for a reduction in foreign aid, from the perception of 15% to 5%, is presented as a willingness to accept an increase from 0.5% to 5%. However, whether the public would be prepared to endorse a tenfold increase if they had better factual information to begin with is not clear.

A second illustration comes from the contentious issue of employment equity legislation, where a rich body of empirical evi-dence has been assembled both to support the need for such leg-islation and to monitor its effect. For example, D.M. Shapiro and M. Stelcner (1987) concluded that there had been only a modest reduction in the male–female earning gap from 1970 to 1980, the impact of pay equity legislation had been minimal during that period, and that "the elimination of these disparities, therefore, requires a broader range of policy initiatives." Thus, empirical evi-dence is used to buttress a normative argument about the way the world should be.

WHAT IS SCIENCE?

At its root, science is a set of rules that help us understand the world around us. The rules describe *how* we know, not *what* we know. Science, therefore, is a method for acquiring knowledge rather than the knowledge itself. We would call something science not because of the subject that was being studied, but because of the *way* in which it was being studied. If a study is done according to the rules of science, then it is science. The scientific method consists of formulating hypotheses about the causal relationship between variables and empirically testing the hypotheses. The goal is to ensure that many observers, acting independently, will make similar observations, and draw similar conclusions, about the cause-and-effect relationship.

HARD AND SOFT SCIENCES

By understanding science as a method of gaining knowledge, it is possible to extend the application of the scientific method beyond the "hard" sciences of physics, chemistry, and the like to include the "softer" areas of human interactions in social relations. This has given rise to the development of social scientific research in the areas of anthropology, archaeology, economics, history, political science, sociology, and others. (Whether psychology is a hard or soft science depends upon the branch of the discipline.) As we shall see, applying the scientific method to social relations brings with it a number of attendant problems, some related to science generally and others more specific to studying people. While researchers need to be aware of these limitations, they usually find that the advantages of the scientific approach far outweigh its disadvantages.

One significant difference between much of the research that takes place in the hard versus soft sciences is the amount of control that the researcher has over the research setting. The laboratory, a site for highly controlled experiments, remains a mainstay of much research in the hard sciences. As a result, researchers have a high degree of success in isolating the few variables selected for study. In the soft sciences, by contrast, the laboratory is replaced for the most part by field research, whether through survey research, participant observation, focus group analysis, or case studies. These methods provide a variety of ways in which researchers attempt to control for extraneous factors, but in general they are less efficient in doing so than are controlled laboratory experiments. The result is that alternative independent variables may confound the analysis.

A second difference between the hard and soft sciences is the level of agreement within the scientific communities about the measuring and measurement of concepts. For example, in physics, researchers share a common understanding of such terms as mass, density, heat, and speed. According to Thomas Kuhn in *The Structure of Scientific Revolutions*, such agreement characterizes mature sciences, enabling the progression from one paradigm (a framework for understanding) to another. By contrast, the soft sciences are characterized by considerable disagreement over the definition and measurement of key terms. For example, disagreement persists—and perhaps always will persist—over the definition of terms such as democracy, effective representation, and social class (a topic explored in more detail in Chapters 6 and 7).

A third difference between the hard and soft sciences is the degree of determinacy of the results. In the hard sciences, the goal is to derive laws of behaviour. In the soft sciences, though, the presence of human agency—free choice—means that outcomes are never completely determined. Thus, instead of deriving laws of behaviour, the social sciences use probability in stating the generalized form of causal relationships. For example, social sciences tend to use probabilistic phrases such as "young people are less likely than the middle-aged to participate in politics" rather than deterministic phrases such as "young people participate less in politics than the middle-aged."

There are a number of features of the scientific method that make it an attractive epistemology, or approach to knowledge. One strength is that it attempts to remove, or at least to minimize, the effect of the observer on the observed. Two people working independently of one another in exploring a given topic, and using the same methodology under similar conditions, should perceive the same result. In this respect, the scientific method begins with the assumption that no single observer is uniquely suited to perceive the real world in ways that are denied to all others. Thus, because of the independence of results from observers, no observer is inherently better able to acquire scientific knowledge. This principle points to the central place that replication has in science. If the results of a scientific study cannot be independently verified, they are not accepted as an addition to the body of knowledge in that area of inquiry. Therefore, it is essential that results of scientific research are reported in ways that enable others to verify them through replication, or the repeated testing of the empirical relationships.

A POINT ON THE COMPASS ───────────

Postmodernism

The assertion that the effects of the observer on the observed can be minimized is hotly contested by the proponents of *postmodernism*. The underlying premise of postmodernism is that reality is socially constructed and that the observer cannot be separated from what he or she purports to see. Furthermore, not only will one construction of the world differ from another, but there is no method, and certainly no scientific method, that enables us to determine which perspective is accurate or correct. Indeed, postmodernism calls into question such notions as accurate or correct; the perspective that prevails will be the one backed by those with power. In this sense, power defines the nature of reality.

Postmodernism has had a dramatic impact on the arts, cultural studies, the humanities, and the social sciences. Although the tenets of postmodernism are themselves hotly contested, they should be taken into account by anyone hoping to be conversant with contemporary political and cultural dialogue. For an excellent conceptual introduction, see Pauline Marie Rosenau, *Post-Modernism and the Social Sciences: Insights, Inroads, and Intrusions* (Princeton: Princeton University Press, 1992).

A second strength of the scientific approach results from its orientation toward cause and effect. In all scientific research, there is some outcome, or set of outcomes, that one wishes to explain. This outcome, or effect, must be clearly stated and defined. There must also be at least a minimal amount of **variance** to be explained. This means that there must be some change over time or across space or differences in outcome patterns across cases in the sample. Thus, for example, one could not explain why people voted in an election if everyone voted; there is no variance in electoral participation to explain. The causes of voting (or nonvoting) could be examined only if a comparative referent was introduced by including a set of nonvoters in the database.

The task of the research then becomes one of finding which characteristics cause people (or cases) to vary in outcome. Research will usually involve testing the strength of alternative causes of an outcome. Continuing with the example of the likelihood of voting, one could speculate that education may be a factor that affects turnout: people with a higher level of education are more likely to vote than those with lower education. This is called a research **hypothesis**. We are proposing (hypothesizing) that increased education leads to an increased tendency to vote. At the outset of the research we do not know whether or not this hypothesis is true. But for a variety of reasons (other research that we have read, our personal experience, our intuition) we believe this may be true. However, there will be other probable or at least possible causes of voting turnout that we wish to examine. For example, an alternative hypothesis is that people with higher incomes are more likely to vote. Still another is that people who are more interested in politics are more likely to vote.

Each of these hypothesized causes of voting focuses on the characteristics of individuals. If, however, one was using cross-national data, then different characteristics of the political system could also be used to explain differences in turnout. For example, one might hypothesize that voting is more likely in those systems that minimize the costs of voting, such as those that register voters automatically. In addition, the perceived closeness of the race, the frequency of elections, the differences between political parties or between governing coalitions also could lead to differences in rates of turnout. By highlighting the importance of the cause-and-effect structure of research hypotheses, the scientific approach ensures that research remains targeted at evaluating alternative causes of phenomena and rejecting those that are less powerful.

A third strength of the scientific approach is that it can be used not only to explain but also to *predict* events or outcomes. The approach assumes that there is an order and structure to the real world and that through a careful application of the methods of science the order can be known and understood. This assumption of patterned behaviour, based on relationships of cause and effect, implies that we can gain knowledge of the present and, through that knowledge, predict future behaviours or events. And, of course, both the explanations of present events and predictions about the future are themselves subject to further empirical verification.

Fourth, the scientific approach tries to draw lawlike generalizations about the real world. Our understanding of specific events or outcomes, although useful in its own right, is of greater value to the extent that it reveals a more enduring quality about relationships among phenomena. Thus, for example, although it may be highly useful to know what effect, if any, the federal government's expenditures had on spiralling inflation and unemployment during the 1970s, it is even more useful to know the general effect that government spending has on inflation and unemployment. Does the effect of the 1970s hold across time? Across countries and different economic systems? This impulse to generalization is a core feature of the scientific project. The lawlike generalizations are formulated as **theories**; we will explore theory development in Chapter 2.

The scientific method is often referred to as **positivism**. The principles underlying the positivist approach in social science can be traced back to 18th-century sociologist Auguste Comte (Neuman 1994, 58). Positivism is based on empiricism and determinism: it is believed that almost everything can be objectively measured (empiricism) and that every event has an explanation or cause (determinism). The postulates of science are extrapolations of these positivist principles.

SUMMARY

Strengths of the Scientific Method

1. It attempts to minimize the effect of the observer on the observed.

2. It directs our attention to the dynamics of cause and effect.

3. It can be used not only to explain but also to predict.

4. It seeks lawlike generalizations that can be applied to the political world across time and space.

POSTULATES OF SCIENCE

The scientific method asserts that knowledge can best be acquired by following certain rules or sets of rules that can lead to the formulation of lawlike generalizations about the social and political world. This methodology is predicated on certain beliefs about nature and about how nature can be known. If we do not accept these beliefs, then the scientific method itself becomes less compelling. Furthermore, in an ironic twist on the usefulness of the scientific method, these **postulates** themselves are not testable through the scientific method. Although this foundational paradox has led some to reject the validity of the scientific method, others are prepared to accept, or at least to turn a blind eye to, this incongruity while judging the usefulness of scientific research by its output.

We find that all empirical research is premised on the following six postulates (see Nachmias and Nachmias 1987, 6–9):

1. *Nature Is Orderly.* Earlier we discussed the characteristic feature of scientific research as centring around cause-and-effect relationships. Such an orientation has meaning only when one accepts the belief that natural phenomena are ordered in causal sequences. The belief that everything has a cause, that nothing is random, is known as **determinism**. In some aspects of our lives, a belief in the ordered sequencing of events is noncontroversial. For example, in baseball we know that a home run ball results from the force of its impact with a baseball bat, which causes the ball to travel over the fence. The scientific method can be used when nature is ordered in such a way, and applying the scientific method to social and political reality implies a belief in a similar type of ordering. It implies, for example, that people do not protest at random or that revolutions do not occur by chance alone. In short, political attitudes, beliefs, and behaviours are not random occurrences. This does not imply, of course, that all people respond identically when faced with similar situations, for we know this is not the case. (One of the reasons for variation may be that people experience similar situations in dissimilar ways; thus, one could say that the situations differ.) Nonetheless, use of the scientific method in political science implies a belief in the causal ordering of social and political reality, even if our understanding of that ordering is very limited at this time.

2. *We Can Know Nature.* The belief that nature is orderly is devoid of empirical implications if the order cannot be revealed to us. Consequently, science postulates that through a rigorous application of the scientific method, the pattern of natural phenomena can be revealed. This belief also implies that no one has a privileged position in the search for knowledge. An awareness of the pattern assumed by a causal relationship does not spring from one's special gifts of perception, nor is the structure of reality divinely revealed. Instead, knowledge about nature is available in equal measure to anyone and everyone. Furthermore, such knowledge results from an application of the scientific method, not from the personal characteristics of the observer. Some may use that method with greater precision, insight, or creativity than others, but it is ultimately the method itself that reveals the patterned structures of natural and social phenomena.

3. *Knowledge Is Superior to Ignorance.* The third postulate of science, that knowledge is superior to ignorance, is based on the assumption that our awareness of the world around us can be one

of two types: we can be ignorant about that reality or about the underlying causes of that reality, or we can understand them correctly and have knowledge of them. Ignorance of reality is a recipe for superstition about cause and effect and an invitation to paralysis in the face of social problems. The position of science is that it is always preferable to have a correct understanding of nature than to misunderstand it. Part of the reason for this is that if one wishes to alter the present or future reality, one must at a minimum understand how that might be achieved. For example, a strategist for one of the political parties could increase her party's standing in the electorate only if she correctly understands why people support one party over another. A further reason for the superiority of knowledge to ignorance is the belief that knowledge and understanding can be ends in themselves. Knowledge is important not only because it is instrumental in helping us solve problems; we believe that knowledge is desirable in and of itself. A greater understanding of our world and environment, be it social, political, physical, intellectual, or otherwise, is believed to be part of the task of being human.

4. *Natural Phenomena Have Natural Causes.* The fourth postulate of science is that natural phenomena have natural causes. Another way of describing this is to say that those aspects of social and political reality that we can perceive can be explained by other things that we can perceive. The postulate holds that attitudes and behaviour in the natural world are not produced by supernatural, or spiritual, forces. Thus, once again, all observers can equally observe the natural world as well as the causal influences within the natural world. As Agent Scully observed on the *X-Files*, "nothing happens in contradiction to nature, only in contradiction to what we know of it."[2]

If it is true that all natural phenomena have natural causes, then one might ask, "Why have we not been able to isolate these causes more completely and strengthen our lawlike generalizations?" The reasons for this are complex and will be discussed at many places throughout this book. It should only be noted at this point that one of the most important reasons for the limited success of the social sciences to date concerns problems of measurement and measurement error. There are some aspects of the natural world that cannot be measured very accurately or reliably; thus, their linkage to social and political behaviour remains highly underdeveloped. In other cases, our knowledge is simply too incomplete. For example, the importance of DNA in the inheritance of physical characteristics is well known. Yet at this time we do not know the degree to which one's attitudinal and behavioural characteristics are transmitted through DNA. Is there a genetic link in the development of political ideologies? In participatory strategies? In aggressive behaviour? We do not know the answer because essential research has not yet been completed.

A second question that arises from the postulate of natural phenomena having natural causes is the role of spirituality in the uncovering of nature. Does one have to be an atheist to use the scientific method? The answer is no. Although it is possible to interpret the scientific method, and in particular this fourth postulate of science, as a denial of God, one could also understand the divine presence as providing the limits of the scientific method. This latter view sees divine presence as part of the residual category in scientific research. A **residual** is everything outside the explanatory factors in a model. Thus, spiritual factors are included along with other influences that cannot be identified, isolated, and measured as causal influences. To identify the impact of spiritual or divine phenomena, one would need to use a research method other than the scientific method. At this time, the residual element in our understanding of the social and political worlds is immense and thus provides ample room for spirituality to be brought into play.

5. *Nothing Is Self-Evident.* The postulate that nothing is self-evident is an affirmation that knowledge is not derived *a priori* or by intuition. Everything is subject to empirical testing through the scientific method. This idea that nothing is self-evident was captured eloquently by René Descartes, a 16th-century philosopher and one of the founders of the scientific method. Descartes began his inquiry by denying the existence of everything and then accepting only those propositions that could be *proven* to be true. He went so far as to deny his own existence until it could be proven otherwise. Descartes' proof of his existence was expressed in his famous assertion, "I think, therefore I am." That is to say, because I am doing human things, like thinking, therefore I am human and my existence is confirmed, although others challenged the logic of his demonstration. Another way to think about this postulate is to assume that nothing is beyond scientific investigation. There are no aspects of the natural world, including the social and political world, that are outside the domain of science. Nothing is off-limits.

Whether the area of inquiry relates to the causes of war, the development of political ideologies, the stability of government, the determinants of political participation, or the rise of neocorporatism, the scientific method can be used in uncovering the natural order. Furthermore, science would challenge other ways of knowing, such as knowledge gained through communication with supernatural forces, as invalid. If knowledge is not subject to the rules of science, which in turn make it available to all who apply those rules, then it is rejected.

6. *Knowledge Is Derived from the Acquisition of Experience.* The last postulate of science is that knowledge is acquired through a continuous application of the scientific method. It stems from repeated observation, careful testing, and a replication of the results under varying conditions. This postulate would also seem to imply that scientific knowledge is cumulative, each step building upon preceding steps. However, there are several alternative views about the advancement of knowledge. One is that the development of scientific thought is paradigmatic, that it comes by leaps and bounds rather than by gradual, incremental change. A **paradigm** is a body of knowledge within which investigators agree on the general ordering of nature. Some suggest that advances in science come about as monumental shifts in paradigms; one world view is replaced by another when incremental gains in new knowledge gradually erode existing paradigms to the point of collapse. Paradigm shifts often entail a considerable amount of struggle against an established orthodoxy until a new view ultimately prevails.[3] This suggests that there is always a prevailing view within the scientific community, and individuals either subscribe to that view and conduct "normal science" or fight to replace that view, while struggling against the institutional strength of the orthodox paradigm. (Radical feminists and postmodernists more broadly defined, for example, would see themselves as struggling against the positivist paradigm embedded in this text.) A second argument is that scientific advances themselves tend to be random occurrences and that science is more often characterized by disorder than by order. Nonetheless, whether scientific advances occur through cumulative incremental change, paradigm shifts, or at random, there is a general agreement that the critical factor is the accumulated experience that accompanies the continual application of the scientific method.

SUMMARY

Basic Postulates of Science

1. Nature is orderly.

2. We can know nature.

3. Knowledge is superior to ignorance.

4. Natural phenomena have natural causes.

5. Nothing is self-evident.

6. Knowledge is derived from the acquisition of experience.

A POINT ON THE COMPASS

Thomas Kuhn and *The Structure of Scientific Revolutions*

Thomas Kuhn's publication *The Structure of Scientific Revolutions,* first published in 1960 and then republished in 1970, had a profound and far-reaching impact on our understanding of the social dynamics of knowledge in both the hard and soft sciences. Kuhn argued that while science routinely progressed through incremental, piecemeal increases in knowledge—what he calls normal science—incrementalism does not account for major paradigm shifts such as that from an Earth-centred to a Sun-centred solar system and from Newtonian physics to quantum mechanics. These paradigm shifts, which were indeed revolutionary, could only be understood by looking at the sociology of knowledge. Knowledge, in other words, is socially constructed; we see the world not only through our instruments but also through paradigms that are the products of complex social, cultural, and political interactions. Paradigm shifts do not emerge effortlessly from incremental change, but rather are the consequence of power struggles between competing paradigms and the proponents of such paradigms:

> *... a new theory, however special its range of application, is seldom or never just an increment to what is already known. Its assimilation requires the reconstruction of prior theory and the re-evaluation of prior fact, an intrinsically revolutionary process that is seldom completed by a single man and never overnight. (1970, 7)*

> Kuhn's work changed the way in which we see science and thus in itself constitutes a paradigm shift of far-reaching proportions.

THE METHODOLOGY OF SCIENCE

Thus far in our discussion we have insisted on the need to use the scientific method to acquire knowledge about nature, including knowledge about the nature of social and political life. This empirical approach can be used to gain knowledge about things as they are, which is to say, knowledge of social and political reality. Such empirical knowledge can be contrasted with normative knowledge, or knowledge about things as they ought to be or as we would wish them to be. This contrast in the study of politics is usually reflected in the differences between political philosophy and empirical political science. Political philosophy typically focuses on normative questions: What is the good life? What is the meaning of justice? What is the most desirable social order? It often focuses on questions of what is right and wrong, good and bad. Empirical political science, in contrast, is generally more concerned with discovering why things are as they are. Why are some countries more stable than others? More successful at managing their national economy? Why do people vote as they do? Although values may underlie some questions of empirical research (for instance, the researcher might prefer political stability to instability, or he may prefer lower unemployment to lower inflation), the research itself cannot and does not claim to provide insight into normative issues. Empirical research cannot be used to conclude that increased inflation is superior to increased unemployment, although it could draw out some of the implications of either event or reveal who has the power to impose their preferred policy options. One can use the results of empirical research to pursue preferred policy outcomes, but the preferences for outcomes are themselves not empirically derived.

The methodology of science is a set of sequential steps that guide the research enterprise. Because all scientific research uses these essential steps, any particular research project is linked by the scientific method to the larger research enterprise. In beginning a project, therefore, it is useful to think of oneself as part of a broader research community, with your research building on previous research in a particular area and representing a continuation of investigations into that topic. Likewise, the research that you produce is also subject to further replication, and subsequent research may either reject or accept the conclusions drawn in your study. Note, however, that your conclusions cannot be *proven* by subsequent research.

Steps in the Scientific Method

1. *Identify the Problem.* All scientific research begins with a problem, which involves variation on some outcome or event. Why do some people support separatism in Quebec while others are opposed? Why do people support some parties rather than others? Why do some people calculate their income tax honestly and others cheat? Why are some countries more stable than others? When does conflict escalate into war? The "problem," or the outcome, in social scientific research is called the **dependent event** and is measured by the **dependent variable**. It is the thing we are trying to explain.

A POINT ON THE COMPASS

Block Voting in Quebec

It has often been observed, and frequently in a critical manner, that the Quebec electorate tends to vote as a block in federal elections. This behaviour, it is assumed, gives Quebec disproportionate influence on national election outcomes, the formation of national governments, and the shape of the national political agenda. But is this observation, and the conclusions that stem from it, supported by the facts of the case? Is there a theory or problem here that can be subjected to empirical testing?

In 1995, Herman Bakvis and Laura Macpherson published a detailed empirical investigation of block voting in Quebec. The cohesion of the Quebec electorate was compared to that of other provinces, and the dynamics of electoral swings within Quebec were explored. Their analysis, which reached from 1878 to 1993, concluded that block voting in Quebec was a "social fact" that set Quebec apart from other provinces. It was also shown that "Quebec results in seats are much more likely to determine which political party forms the [federal] government than those of Ontario, despite Ontario's greater size and number of seats" (691). However, the analysis also demonstrated that block voting was not confined to the francophone electorate in Quebec, that it cut across linguistic communities. Finally, the authors suggested that their investigation shows that regionally concentrated minorities, such as Quebec francophones, are well served by Canada's single-member, first-past-the-post electoral system.

This article provides an excellent illustration of how empirical research can expand and qualify our understanding of political life. An informal, seat-of-the-pants understanding takes us only so far. And, at times, it may take us in the wrong direction.

The dependent event has a number of important features. First, it must contain sufficient variation that can be explained. If all people thought alike or behaved alike, or if all countries behaved alike, there would be little for social science to explain. Fortunately, human attitudes and behaviour are full of inconsistencies and variability, thus making social and political relations fertile ground for scientific research. Nonetheless, it is important that in identifying the problem to explore in your research, you cast the problem in such a way that you highlight the variation you wish to explain. Second, the dependent variable must be susceptible to a clear definition, and it must be measurable. These topics and the problems associated with them are discussed in detail in Chapters 6 and 7. For the moment, it should be recognized that empirical research requires that the dependent event be defined with enough precision and specificity that it can be linked to previous research. Likewise, the dependent variable must be measured in such a way that other researchers are able to replicate your study. As we shall see, the issues of concept definition and operational measurement can create serious difficulties in empirical research, making close attention to these issues an essential component of useful and generalizable findings.

2. *Hypothesize the Cause of the Problem.* The goal of empirical research is to explain variation with respect to the dependent event. One can begin to explain the dependent event by proposing, or hypothesizing, causes of the observed variation across cases or across time. Hypothesized causes are called **independent concepts** and are measured by **independent variables**. The word "independent" implies that the variation in this concept is independent of, or not caused by, variation in the dependent event. The relationship between independent and dependent variables is hypothesized to be a causal sequence from the independent to the dependent variable, and not vice versa. A **hypothesis** is an expected or proposed relationship of the type "A causes B."

For example, it has often been observed that older people are more likely than younger people to hold conservative political views. Thus, there is a relationship, or **correlation,** between age and political thinking. Since empirical research is concerned with identifying causal relationships, it is necessary to ask which of these factors is the independent variable and which is dependent. In this case, it seems fairly obvious that political ideology cannot affect chronological age. One does not become older if one becomes more conservative. Therefore, to the extent that there is a causal relationship between age and ideology, age must be the independent variable and ideology the dependent variable. Right? Not necessarily. Social and political phenomena are often bound together in highly complex relationships. To continue with this example, some research has shown that affluence is positively related to mortality rates (more affluent people live longer) and to ideology (they are also more conservative). Thus, it may be that age and ideology are related, but not according to the simple "aging" hypothesis offered above. It may be that mortality rates are different for groups that fall predominantly into left-wing and right-wing camps (affluent versus nonaffluent). Those to the right tend to outlive those to the left, although this does not mean that you can extend your life span by changing your political beliefs. Therefore, there are more conservative old people not because they have changed their ideology, but because of the presence of a third variable, mortality rates.

An important component of proposing a causal hypothesis is to identify the theory that underlies the effect of the independent on the dependent event. When we speak of "theory" in this sense we refer to generalized statements about the causes of attitudes or behaviour. An example may help illustrate the point. Suppose we want to explain why people voted Liberal, Reform, New Democrat, Conservative, or something else (including abstainers) in the last federal election. How do we explain variation on voting preference? One of the first things we must do is decide which theory of political choice will guide our research. One theory is that voting in Canada is determined mostly by short-term factors and is therefore very unstable. An alternative theory is that people hold relatively firm political allegiances, and voting is character- ized more by stability than change. Of course, it is possible to design a research project that tests both of those theories. Nonetheless, it should be obvious that the selection of independent variables will depend heavily upon which theory one is testing.

A POINT ON THE COMPASS ———————————

Federal Theory and Empirical Research

Canadian scholars of federalism, and particularly the country's leading scholar in the field, Alan Cairns, have argued that the passage of the 1982 Charter of Rights and Freedoms has had a pervasive and even profound impact on the Canadian political culture. The effect has been to heighten the political identities and influence of those groups able to claim constitutional status through their recognition within the Charter. These "Charter Canadians" have changed the nature of constitutional discourse, disrupted executive federalism, and enhanced the role of the courts in the definition and application of public policy. This theoretical contribution by Cairns has been accepted as close to dogma by students of Canadian federalism.

Others, however, have argued that while these changes may indeed have occurred, it is a mistake to attribute them to the introduction of the Charter. Instead, and drawing upon the postmaterialism theorizing of Ronald Inglehart, it is suggested that these changes in Canadian politics reflect broad patterns of social and ideological change that have swept across all Western democracies since the end of World War II. Those individuals coming to age in the era of postwar affluence, Inglehart argues, are less concerned about material well-being and success and are more concerned with aesthetic values and self-expression. The idiosyncratic effects of the Charter, therefore, pale beside the impact of these broader currents of postmaterial change. (Note that postmaterialism is not the same as postmodernism.)

This challenge to the Charter thesis was put to an empirical test by Ian Brodie and Neil Nevitte (1993). Employing data from the 1981 and 1990 World Values Surveys, they found that their "new politics theory" outperformed the "citizens' constitution theory" of Cairns when it came to explaining such things as confidence in political and legal institutions. Their article and the rejoinder by Cairns (1993) provide a useful illustration of the dynamic interplay of theory and empirical data.

3. *Provide Clear Definitions of the Concepts.* Concepts are abstractions used to describe the characteristics of a group or individual case according to a given criterion or quality. Empirical research begins and ends at the abstract, conceptual level in which generalizations are made about social and political life. Some of the concepts that traditionally interest political scientists include, among many others, political participation, social class, political stability, ideology, conflict, and political culture. To conduct research on any of these topics, one must be prepared to define with a great deal of precision the characteristics or features of that abstraction. Most readers are probably not surprised to learn that there can be considerable disagreement within the scholarly community about the meaning of many concepts. For example, one study reported that the concept "culture" had been defined in more than 250 different ways (Eulau 1963) and that study itself does not reflect a wealth of conceptual development over the past 35 years.

An example can illustrate the difficulties that arise when trying to get researchers to agree on the meaning of concepts. Consider the concept of political participation. Several questions emerge when we attempt to define this important concept. Is political participation one thing, or is it a bundle of quite different activities? Do participatory activities differ in degree or in kind? That is, should participatory activities be thought of as being more or less participation or as different types or modes of activities? How far does the domain of the term "political" extend? Is political participation limited to electoral participation, or does it include other activities that can influence political decision-making? Does it include volunteer work for a community association or women's shelter? What about strikes and work stoppages? Are activities directed in the first instance at private market-oriented actors included as political participation? What about strikes among public sector workers or among those employed by Crown corporations or mixed enterprises? Is there a difference between legal and illegal forms of political participation? Empirical political scientists, together with Canadians more generally, may disagree in their answers to these questions. For researchers, those differences are likely to be reflected in different definitions of the concepts under study.

The problem for social science research more generally is that it is difficult to advance our knowledge and understanding of a concept when researchers are working with different definitions. At the same time, it is not possible to "require" that researchers agree on common definitions. Part of the research enterprise itself is to provide the intellectual freedom for researchers to pursue research in a manner that they themselves define as suitable and appropriate. The requirement to publicize the results of one's research in independent, peer-reviewed journals and books ensures to a degree that researchers are held accountable for their research decisions. It also emphasizes once again the importance of the idea of a scholarly community conducting a common research enterprise.

4. *Gather Empirical Data.* All empirical research includes a test of a hypothesis. This test requires that data be collected on both the independent and dependent variables, as well as on intervening variables, or those that cause a spurious relationship (the latter two types are discussed more fully in Chapters 2 and 7). There are many different types of data and research design strategies that can be used in the data collection phase. In Chapters 4 and 5 the methodologies of survey research, content analysis, experimental and quasi-experimental design, and qualitative research are all discussed at length. There is no single right or wrong approach to data gathering; each method has its advantages and disadvantages. The key consideration for any researcher is to gather data that best suit the purposes of her specific research questions. For practical reasons of time and money, students often find it expedient to conduct *secondary analysis* on data that have already been gathered by other researchers. In view of the wealth of such data today, as well as their ready accessibility through data libraries and archives, this strategy is also becoming increasingly attractive among faculty and graduate student researchers.

5. *Operationalize the Concepts.* An empirical research project moves from the general or conceptual level to the specific and concrete. This movement from concepts to variables is called **operationalization**. It involves obtaining a specific measurement of the concepts with respect to the data that have been collected. More specifically, it involves assigning a numerical score on a variable to each case in the data set. For some concepts the process is straightforward and noncontroversial. The concept of sex is a good example of a simple concept for most research. Typically, the researcher thinks of sex as being a dichotomous variable, and respondents are scored as male or female. This standard view assumes that people are differentiated into either of two distinct categories. However, this dichotomy may be too simplistic. For

example, it is well known that all humans possess both masculine and feminine hormones. Although, in general, men have more masculine hormones and women have more feminine hormones, some men have more masculine hormones than other men, while some women have more feminine hormones than other women. When one considers sex in these more biological terms, it becomes a continuous variable with everyone having a specific mixture of masculine and feminine aspects. If we turn from sex to *gender*, the measurement situation becomes considerably more complex. Gender is a more socially constructed concept than is sex and, as a consequence, defies simple dichotomization.

Other concepts may be even more intractable in operationalizing because of their multidimensionality. The concept itself may be a combination of attributes on several different criteria. Political participation appears to be a multidimensional concept because of the distinct ways that one can participate in politics. Social class would have a strong claim on multidimensionality because of the different components of the social hierarchy and the variation that may exist across those components, complexities discussed more fully in Chapters 6 and 7. At this stage the key thing to remember is that a variable should reflect as closely as possible the abstract concept that it represents. Recall that research begins and ends at the conceptual level; the conclusions will relate to the abstract concept and not to the particular variable that was used in this single study. To the extent that the variable does not accurately reflect the concept, then the conclusions derived from the research will be distorted.

CHECKING YOUR BEARINGS

YOUTH AND POLITICAL PARTICIPATION

You are a researcher looking at the question, "Do young people participate politically at lower levels than the rest of the population?" What concepts need to be defined before you begin your study? How would you define them? If you do find that young people participate less, what reasons might explain this difference?

6. *Test the Hypothesis or Hypotheses.* One of the defining characteristics of scientific research is that hypotheses are **falsifiable**. It must be possible, through both the logic of analysis and the design of the

research, to demonstrate the absence of a causal relationship between the concepts being examined. If it is not possible to disprove the hypothesized relationship, then the research cannot claim to have been conducted scientifically. Although the emphasis during the research design portion of a research project is on developing and justifying hypotheses about the causal relationship between concepts, the emphasis shifts during the empirical part of the project.

Empirical testing requires that the research hypothesis is inverted, or is replaced by its opposite, called the **null hypothesis.** The null hypothesis states that the two concepts, or variables, are independent of one another and are not causally related. While researchers typically expect the null hypothesis to be false and the research hypothesis to be true, the empirical test is conducted on the null hypothesis for an important reason. The research hypothesis can never be proven to be true; although data can and often do support the research hypothesis, they never prove it unequivocally. This is because another experiment or another empirical test could provide a context in which the hypothesis is disproved. Thus, research hypotheses can be disproved by a single test, whereas they cannot be proven even with a large number of repeated tests. The null hypothesis, on the other hand, is either *accepted* or *rejected.* The null hypothesis that there is no causal relationship between two variables is accepted if an empirical test shows they are independent. Likewise, the null hypothesis is rejected if the empirical test reveals that the variables are related to one another. Therefore, testing hypotheses involves deciding whether to accept or reject the null hypothesis, a matter discussed at greater length in the next chapter.

Recall at this point that the researcher is conducting a single empirical test on a hypothesized relationship between two variables. The research is important not so much for what it reveals about the particular variables in the time and place at which the data were gathered. Instead, it is important to the degree to which the variables represent more general concepts in a more generalized temporal and spatial dimension. We can think about the generalized setting as representing the true relationship between concepts. The empirical test is taken as a measure or proxy of that true relationship.

7. *Reflect Back on Theory.* When drawing conclusions about the research, one moves back once again from the operational level to

the conceptual level. Variables are recast in their generalized form, and conclusions are drawn about the nature of the causal relationships. At this stage, the researcher is able to evaluate the theoretical aspects of the research in light of the empirical evidence. Were the hypotheses confirmed? Which hypotheses and in what ways? What are the implications for the theoretical underpinnings of the study? Does the theory need revision in light of the research? What generalizations can be drawn from the study? Are there policy implications from the results of the research? In what direction should future research in this area be pursued? Remember that one of the chief goals of empirical research is to draw lawlike generalizations about social and political phenomena. These generalized statements find reflection in the theories developed to understand and explain politics. The latter stages of empirical research, therefore, require that one step back from the specific empirical findings and reflect upon the more general patterns of interaction and causality. The continual process of testing, refining, and adjusting theoretical statements of causality forms an essential step in the ongoing research enterprise.

8. *Publicize the Results.* An old saying around universities is that one must either publish or perish. Like many such aphorisms, there is more than a grain of truth to this saying. The weight of one's scholarly publications is the key indicator of academic performance at many universities, and a full curriculum vitae is often richly rewarded. However, although publication certainly fulfils an important institutional function, it serves the more important function of enabling the scholarly community to engage in an ongoing research dialogue. Indeed, one of the responsibilities of researchers is to engage in this dialogue. It is necessary not only to maintain an active research agenda, but also to place the results of those efforts into the public domain for debate, discussion, challenge, and verification.

    All levels of scholarly inquiry have outlets for such dialogue. For undergraduate students the dialogue typically occurs between student and course instructor. Part of the learning process at universities is to accept criticisms of your work, and part of the responsibility of instructors is to provide criticism of students' work in a way that strengthens and improves research. For graduate students, the feedback from course instructors is supplemented with feedback from his or her supervisory committee on independent or quasi-independent research projects in the form of master's theses or doctoral dissertations. For research scholars, including professors, the outlets for publicizing the results of research include scholarly journals, research institute monographs, public lectures or displays, and books. Typically, it is expected that the prepublication stage includes some form of blind peer evaluation process.

9. *Replicate the Results.* The final step in the process of empirical research is to repeat the study using either the same data or data gathered at a different time or in a different setting. This is known as replication. Since the goal of empirical research is to draw law-like generalizations, research results are valuable to the extent that they can be generalized. If similar empirical tests conducted at other times and places fail to produce the same result, one is not able to generalize from the initial test. The importance of replication also reinforces and highlights the need for researchers to systematically and completely describe each stage of the analysis, from the design of the study to defining concepts, gathering data, operationalizing measures, testing the relationships, and drawing conclusions. Only then can the research be replicated and each stage of the research opened to critical examination.

SUMMARY

Steps in the Scientific Method

1. Identify the problem.

2. Hypothesize the cause of the problem.

3. Provide clear definitions of the concepts.

4. Operationalize the concepts.

5. Gather empirical data.

6. Test the hypothesis or hypotheses.

7. Reflect back on theory.

8. Publicize the results.

9. Replicate the results.

CRITICISMS AND LIMITATIONS OF THE SCIENTIFIC APPROACH TO POLITICS

We noted earlier in the chapter that the scientific approach is also known as positivism. It should be mentioned that some people argue that the scientific approach has limited utility for the study of society and politics and recommend alternative approaches to replace positivism. Recall that positivism assumes that reality can be measured empirically, that measurements can be made objectively, and that nature is orderly—every effect has a cause, every event is determined by a prior event. It is these three ideas—empiricism, objectivity, and determinism—that have been subject to criticism. Fortunately, the criticism has been largely constructive; by pointing out the weaknesses of the scientific model, the critics encouraged positivist researchers to refine and adapt their methods.

Many people have difficulty applying the idea of determinism to human behaviour, and for good reason. Determinism suggests that there exists no choice, while most of us know that humans have free will. A pencil has no choice but to submit to the force of gravity; we, on the other hand, have control over our thoughts, feelings, attitudes, and behaviour. Thus, we cannot with certainty predict the actions or reactions of an individual. However, when we look at aggregates of individuals—groups—we can often make generalizations. Social scientists have been able to note *patterns* in human behaviour, patterns that are linked to outside phenomena. For example, we may find that most people whose parents are liberal are also liberal; thus parental ideological views influence those of the child. At the same time, there are always some people who do not fit the pattern: some children of liberals are conservative. Having a liberal parent will increase one's probability of being liberal, but does not determine liberalism.

A second criticism is that not all aspects of reality can be empirically measured. How does one measure beliefs, thoughts, and attitudes? We cannot get inside people's heads and see exactly what is going on; therefore, we must rely on the information they give us, either through their words or their actions. Even when we can access information about beliefs, there are difficulties in quantifying such beliefs and comparing this information across individuals. Did Bob and Sue mean the same thing when they each classified themselves as "highly religious"? Are our subjects being honest with us—and with themselves—when they respond to controversial questions? There are many practical difficulties in measuring reality, and we continually need to ask ourselves if we are in fact measuring what we believe we are measuring. These difficulties, moreover, go well beyond measurement error in survey research; they also include disagreements about the meaning of such terms as full employment, unemployment, pay equity, and democratic government. This issue is known as **validity** and will be explored further in Chapters 4 and 7. The challenge to researchers is to select indicators that most closely tap the concept they wish to measure. In some cases, this can be a difficult task.

The objectivity of the scientific method is also called into question by some critics. It is argued that true neutrality is impossible, that there is no system of study that is value-free. The beliefs and values of the observer will always play a role in the interpretation of the facts, it is argued; thus research always contains a measure of subjectivity. This subjectivity can be positive, since it allows the researcher to be sensitive to the context within which political action (or inaction) occurs, but it can also be the source of inadvertent bias. This criticism is particularly noteworthy for researchers who study a variety of cultures and societies. Political scientists who wish to consider the role of context for their subject often address this criticism by using **qualitative** approaches to their studies. Qualitative research will be explored in depth in Chapter 5.

Other criticisms are more ideological in character. For example, some feminist, postmodern, and class theorists argue that "positivism defends the status quo because it assumes an unchanging order instead of seeing current society as a particular stage in an ongoing process" (Neuman 1994, 66). Attempts to objectively describe and explain the status quo are seen by some as a defence of the status quo, because there is often an implicit assumption that the identified reality is natural and immune to change. Such criticisms vividly demonstrate the fact that political science (and social science in general) lacks a single paradigm to which all can appeal. There is no common overriding view of how the social world is or of how to best measure that world. Even if we can agree on the principle of causality, there is confusion over what are the important social determinants. Some political economists point to the class system or the structure of the international political economy, feminists point to the gendered nature of social and political institutions, and so on. This poses a serious limitation to the advancement of science: if knowledge is to be cumulative, it requires some degree of paradigm agreement (Baxter-Moore et al. 1994, 88). On the other hand, it can be argued that the variety of approaches to the study of politics is an advantage, since it ensures that a diverse set of perspectives and interpretations of the social world is considered.

CHECKING YOUR BEARINGS

SCIENCE AND POLITICS

List the pros and cons of using the scientific method in the study of politics. How do the methods and principles of the scientific method fit with your own conception of politics? Can you think of situations in which the scientific method would be particularly appropriate? Particularly inappropriate? How does the study of political and social life differ from the study of the natural world?

In conclusion, we would argue that despite the criticisms noted, the scientific approach to politics is the best means by which we can work to understand the very complex social world around us. Admittedly, political science has far to go; the discipline is less than 100 years old. Attempts to compare such a "young" science to "older" sciences such as biology and physics are perhaps unfair; think of how little was known about the human body when the study of anatomy was in its infancy stages. The goal of our journey is to advance our comprehension of politics and society. Although the final destination, "truth," may seem far away and beyond our reach, we must keep in mind that we have only really just begun the journey.

WORKING AS A TEAM

1. There are some people who argue that the study of politics, and society in general, can never be considered a "true" science. They suggest, furthermore, that "political studies" is a more appropriate label than "political science." Do you feel the terms "social science" and "political science" are misleading? Can the study of humans in aggregate be a science? What are the pros and cons of "political science" as the name for our discipline? Can you think of a better or more appropriate name?

2. With your discussion group, consider the advantages and disadvantages of applying the scientific method to the volatile public policy question, "Should Canadians support capital punishment?" Are there limits to the application of empirical approaches, or can almost all questions benefit from empirical study? What questions do you see as beyond the reach of the scientific method?

SELF-STUDY

1. How might the concept of "socialism" be approached in normative political analysis? What are the types of questions that might be asked? How might it be approached in empirical political analysis? Again, what questions might be asked? Is either approach superior for increasing our understanding of socialism? What are the strengths and limitations of each? If you were asked to write a term paper on "socialism in the contemporary world," would you adopt a normative approach, an empirical approach, or some blend of the two? How would you justify your choice?

2. What hypotheses would you advance to explain current levels of electoral support for the federal government? Can you offer five or six competing hypotheses? From where do these hypotheses emerge? From your readings? Political science classes? Your political instincts? Editorials in *The Globe and Mail*? If you had to rank your hypotheses in order of plausibility, which would strike you as the most compelling? The least compelling? What evidence would you need in order to test these hypotheses and to choose among them?

NOTES

1. The three explanations discussed do not exhaust the range of possible explanations. Comparative research extending beyond the OECD experience could be particularly helpful in revealing other possibilities.
2. October 4, 1996.
3. In the time of Nicolaus Copernicus (1473–1543), challenging the Earth-centred paradigm of contemporary physics could be quite literally a matter of life and death.

CHAPTER 2

Theory-Oriented Research and the Issue of Causality

DESTINATION

By the end of this chapter the reader should

- have a sound understanding of the role theory plays in empirical political research;
- know the distinctions between quantitative and qualitative research, basic and applied research, and inductive and deductive research;
- appreciate how theories are developed and applied in empirical research and how causal explanations can be both advanced and confused.

When we think of research, most of us picture a laboratory, with men and women in white coats examining test tubes, seeking the cure for cancer, or at least for the common cold. However, as Chapter 1 has argued, the scientific approach can be extended beyond the hard sciences and the laboratory to include the social sciences and the broader social world. In the hard sciences, the scientific approach is used to increase knowledge of the physical world; in the social sciences, it is used to advance knowledge of the social world. This chapter will explore the different research approaches that political scientists use to augment our understanding of politics and society. In particular, the role of theory in political science research will be explored, and within this context we will see why cause-and-effect relationships are difficult to establish in the political realm.

QUANTITATIVE AND QUALITATIVE APPROACHES TO EMPIRICAL RESEARCH

Empirical research is based on observation and interpretation and includes two very different approaches. The first, which typically comes to mind when one thinks of empirical research, is the **quantitative** approach. As the root of the word suggests, this approach seeks to understand political life through the study of a large quantity, or number, of cases. A **case** is a single unit, which could be individuals, legislatures, organizations, or nation-states; in a recent study of the impact of individual judges on Supreme Court of Canada decisions (Heard 1991), the cases were the 121 Supreme Court decisions made under the Charter of Rights. Due to time and financial constraints, one can rarely conduct an in-depth study of large numbers of cases; thus, quantitative research tends to have greater breadth than depth. The research tends to be quite *structured;* for example, a survey researcher will ask the questions listed on her polling sheet and nothing more. Quantitative research designs will be explored in more detail in Chapter 4.

The second approach to empirical analysis is known as **qualitative** research. As its word root suggests, the emphasis here is on quality, or detail. Qualitative researchers attempt to learn about politics through a more thorough study of a small number of cases. In this way, qualitative research can be seen as the polar opposite of quantitative research, emphasizing depth over breadth. Qualitative research is less structured than quantitative research and allows the researcher to explore the subtleties of individual beliefs or group dynamics. For example, an interviewer may be intrigued by something his subject mentions and may choose to follow this point with a spontaneous line of questioning. Qualitative research designs will be explored in detail in Chapter 5.

Each approach has its advantages and limitations. One advantage of the quantitative approach is that the large size of the group studied allows us to make generalizations from the sample to a larger unit, such as society as a whole. The ability to make generalizations is more limited in qualitative research, due to the small size of the group being studied. In addition, quantitative research is often seen as more objective than qualitative research. The research methods employed in qualitative analysis require a greater degree of interpretation on the part of the researcher and are therefore more subjective. However, qualitative research allows for a richer understanding of the political phenomena being studied. Political research often concerns individual beliefs, attitudes, and behaviours, topics that cannot be completely explored by quantitative research. For example, one of the most insightful studies of ideological belief systems in the United States (Lane 1962) was based on in-depth interviews with only 15 male respondents in New Haven, Connecticut. Although the researcher was unable to make empirical generalizations to the American population at large, he was able to provide vivid insights into how "the American Common Man" tries to make sense out of a complex political world.

How one chooses between the two approaches depends upon the research question and objectives of the study. If one wishes to develop generalizations that are broad in scope, the quantitative approach may be more appropriate. If one desires a greater understanding of the phenomena in question, with less concern for generalizability, the qualitative approach is best. Of course, in political science we often wish to achieve both ends. The solution, then, is to combine the two research strategies, allowing the strengths of one to complement the strengths of the other. For example, a researcher might combine a telephone survey (quantitative research) with a series of in-depth interviews (qualitative research) with a small subset of respondents. The survey allows her to ask an identical set of questions to a large sample, while the interviews allow her to explore the issues in depth with a smaller group of individuals.

CHECKING YOUR BEARINGS

QUANTITATIVE AND QUALITATIVE METHODS

Consider the question, "Why do some people abstain from voting?" How would you address this question from a quantitative approach? Whom would you study? What type of questions might you ask? How would your study and questions differ if you were doing qualitative research? What specific advantages and limitations do you see to each approach?

BASIC AND APPLIED RESEARCH

Empirical researchers differ in the reasons they have for conducting studies. Some research is directed at answering specific questions or solving immediate problems. For example, what is the best way to implement a new home-care program? What are the costs and benefits of an employee-training program? How effective has a teenage anti-smoking campaign been? How can a particular party strengthen its appeal among young voters? When research is directed at finding answers to specific problems, with immediate practical usage, it is known as **applied research** (Neuman 1994, 21). Examples of applied research include cost-benefit analyses, social impact assessments, needs assessments, and evaluations of existing programs or policies, all of which provide job opportunities for social science graduates. Applied research is frequently used by governments, businesses, marketing agencies, political campaign organizers, hospitals, and educational facilities to help fine-tune their programs, products, and strategies. Given that such agencies must work with limited resources, it is important that their money and time are put to the most effective and efficient usage. Applied research is used to maximize effectiveness and efficiency, and to do so over the short haul.

A notable form of applied research is *feminist action research* (Reinharz 1992, chap. 10). Indeed, the argument has been made (Lather 1988) that research is feminist *only* if it is linked to action, to attempts to repudiate the status quo. This does not mean that action research is unable to enrich our conceptual or theoretical understanding of the world; it only means that such enrichment cannot be the sole or perhaps even the primary justification for research projects. Research is seen as an essential part of a larger process of social transformation.

Such research, conducted for social purposes defined *a priori*, may fall outside our definitions of scientific research. This so-called *advocacy research* often begins with a premise that one group is socially or economically disadvantaged and proceeds to draw the implications of that disadvantage, or to assume the causes of the disadvantage. For example, for feminist action research, the cause of disadvantage could be the male hegemonic power structure. For aboriginal action research, the cause of disadvantage could be the Eurocentric, materialistic power structure. For labour action research, the cause of disadvantage may be the corporate power structure. But action research need not be based only on the support of the socially disadvantaged; instead, it could be action research conducted in reaction to much support. For example, conservative (re)action research could begin from the premise that the government (through the legislature, the courts, or the administration) acts in support of the disadvantaged. Thus, the governmental/interest group power structure may be the source of the problem. Whether action, or advocacy, research stems from the ideological left or right, it is inconsistent with the scientific method to the extent that it violates the fifth postulate of science discussed in Chapter 1, namely, that nothing is self-evident. If something is taken as an empirical fact, it must be demonstrably true. In other words, a demonstration of the sources of power must be a part of the overall research enterprise.

A limitation of applied research is that it is usually descriptive in nature; it indicates how things are, but does not explain *why* they are that way. Thus, applied research addresses a single question in a very narrow manner and may fail to advance our knowledge of the larger political and social world. **Basic research,** on the other hand, has as its primary goal the broadening of our understanding of political life. Seeking to advance general knowledge, basic researchers (usually academics) examine theories about politics and attempt to formulate explanations and generalizations by empirically testing hypotheses. For example, basic research might address why there are so few women in elected politics and from this research develop a number of explanations and theories. These explanations are not immediately translated into policies to address the problem, but rather add to our foundational understanding of the impact of gender in the political realm. Basic research is *theory-oriented research*, and most academic research falls into this camp.

Thus, in basic research, knowledge is pursued for the sake of knowledge. This is not to say, however, that basic research does not have practical implications. The ideas that emerge from basic research are frequently utilized in applied research, although the importance of basic research may not immediately be seen. We must remember that knowledge is cumulative and continually advancing. W. Lawrence Neuman notes that "Today's computers could not exist without the pure research in mathematics conducted over a century ago, for which there was no known practical application at the time" (1994, 21). Over time, "irrelevant" research findings can have a great impact upon our lives.

Some of the biggest research projects in the history of the Canadian social sciences have combined applied and basic research. In 1989, the Royal Commission on Electoral Reform and Party Financing (the Lortie Commission) launched a sweeping study of campaign-related issues. Twenty-three volumes of research studies, containing over 100 separate reports, were published in the early 1990s, and these volumes will provide much of the core Canadian political science knowledge in this area for years to come. The Royal Commission on Aboriginal Peoples, which reported in late 1996, provides another example. When its research reports are eventually published, they will constitute a massive amount of applied and basic knowledge with respect to Aboriginal peoples. In both cases, the marriage of applied and basic research was complementary and mutually reinforcing.

CHECKING YOUR BEARINGS

BASIC AND APPLIED RESEARCH

You are including a study of "Canada Heritage Minutes" (television commercials that explore Canadian history) in a study of national identity. What type of questions would you seek to answer if you were conducting basic research? Applied research? What kind of study would you use for each—quantitative or qualitative?

Theory: Relationships between Concepts

As academic researchers, our primary goal is to advance theory. Before discussing how we develop a political theory, we should first consider what exactly a theory is and what elements a theory contains. A **theory** is an integrated set of explanations of the political and social worlds. We attempt to understand the complex political world by simplifying reality into theories. A theory identifies a general pattern of behaviour, and from these generalizations we can both make predictions and empirically test hypotheses derived from the theory. For example, we might theorize that support for ideological conservatism varies with social economic status. From this we can make predictions, for instance, expecting two individuals with differing social economic status to show dissimilar support for a conservative party, and we can test the theory with empirical data by seeing if the generalizations fit with our observations. As Jarol B. Manheim and Richard C. Rich note, "[t]heories are simply intellectual tools ... theories are neither true nor false in any absolute sense, but only more or less useful" (1981, 17). Thus, basic research is continually testing hypotheses based on theories to maximize their explanatory power.

Hypotheses are *statements of the relationships between concepts*. A **concept** is a defined term that enables us to organize and classify phenomena. Politician, region, discrimination, power, income, and sexism are all examples of concepts. Obviously, a concept can be either concrete or abstract, which means that some concepts require more elaborate definitions than others if they are to be measured. For example, age is a simple concept; a person's age is equal to the present year less the year they were born. Equality, on the other hand, is a very complex idea, and political scientists differ in how they choose to define this concept. It should also be noted that many concepts have built-in assumptions about how people interact (Neuman 1994, 37). For example, the concept of sexual discrimination assumes (1) that people distinguish between men and women and (2) that these distinctions influence how they behave. If sex is relevant in hiring, and if one sex is preferred over the other, then sexual discrimination occurs. If an assumption is not upheld—if sex is irrelevant in hiring decisions—sexual discrimination does not exist.

In addition to allowing us to classify phenomena, concepts enable us to make comparisons through categorization. Categories designate the *variation* that occurs within a concept. Income can be classified as high, medium, or low; religion can be classified as Protestant, Catholic, Jewish, Muslim, or other. All concepts contain a degree of variation; thus, when we measure concepts empirically, we refer to them as **variables**. We are able to see variation in a concept by identifying the different values, or categories, that exist.

There are a number of ways we can choose to classify concepts, and the choice is often influenced by the type of variation within the concept. Variables may be categorical (or nominal), ordinal, or interval (continuous). The distinction is that categorical differences show qualitative differences between categories. For example, a variable measuring religious denomination could distinguish (1) Catholics, (2) Protestants, and (3) others. The numerical differences between categories (1), (2), and (3) indicate a difference in kind. Other examples of categorical variables include gender (male, female) and vote (Liberal, Reform, Conservative, New Democrat, Bloc Québécois). An ordinal variable ranks the categories such that 1 is less than 2, which is less than 3, etc. An example is religiosity. A variable measuring religiosity, based on frequency of attendance at a religious service, could include the categories (1) never attend; (2) attend once per month or less; (3) attend more than once per month; (4) attend once per week; (5) attend more than once per week. With this ordinal variable, a higher numerical value indicates more frequent attendance at a religious service. The third level of measurement is interval, in which the unit difference between numerical categories is constant. An example is money, measured in dollars. The difference between $5,000 and $6,000 (i.e., $1,000) is twice the difference between $4,500 and $5,000 (i.e., $500). Levels of measurement are discussed in much greater detail in Chapter 7.

The simplest way to classify concepts with discrete values is to identify the dominant categories that exist within the concept, that is, identify the significant points where variation occurs. An example of this treatment is seen in Max Weber's theory of authority. Weber argued that there exist three types of authority: charismatic, traditional, and legal. Charismatic authority is derived from the unique qualities of an individual leader. Traditional authority derives from established patterns:

CHECKING YOUR BEARINGS

CATEGORICAL, ORDINAL, AND INTERVAL VARIABLES

What is the level of measurement of each of the following variables:

- personal income
- social class
- political party affiliation
- partisanship
- type of car owned
- number of children
- sex
- political participation

doing things in a certain way because they have always been done that way. Legal authority derives from the legal specification of the duties (Albrow 1970, 37–40).

When classifying ordinal variables, we often use a **continuum**. We order values of the concept along a dimension, ranging from low to high or from less to more. In his classic work, *An Economic Theory of Democracy* (1957), Anthony Downs arranged political ideologies along a single-dimension continuum. This "left–right spectrum" organizes political ideologies in terms of positions toward the desired role of the state in the economy. Socialism is located to the left on this spectrum, liberalism is positioned in the centre, and conservatism to the right. Downs argued that both political parties and individuals can be located on the spectrum; in fact, a party's location is dependent upon where voters are located. Parties seek to maximize the number of votes they receive and therefore position themselves at the point on the ideological spectrum where the greatest number of voters is located.

There are other means of classifying concepts that should be considered. The **ideal type** is one such means. In this approach a nonexistent ideal is outlined, and observed cases are then compared to this ideal. An example would be Weber's ideal type bureaucracy, organized hierarchically with all rules, procedures, and responsibilities defined impartially (Albrow 1970, 37–40). Although Weber does not suggest that the ideal type bureaucracy exists in reality, it does serve as a model against which to compare existing organizational systems. A final means of classifying concepts is the **typology** (Manheim and Rich 1981, 171), wherein the relationship between two or more concepts is expressed in a way that leads to the creation of new concepts (Neuman 1994, 38). One well-

A POINT ON THE COMPASS

The Conventional Left–Right Spectrum

Left - - - - - - - - - - - - - - - Centre - - - - - - - - - - - - - - - Right

Full government ownership of the means of production	No government ownership of the means of production
Extensive government regulation	No government regulation
Extensive redistribution of income	No redistribution of income

known typology in political science is Aristotle's typology of regimes. Political systems are divided along two dimensions: the number of rulers and the beneficiaries. Note that each of these two concepts has categories of its own: "number of rulers" takes three values (one, few, many), while "beneficiaries" has two values (citizens and rulers). The resultant categories—monarchy, tyranny, aristocracy, oligarchy, polity, and democracy—are the different values of the concept "regime."

We have outlined concepts and the different means for classifying values within a concept. In addition to concepts, a theory requires relationships, or **correlations**, between concepts. Two concepts are correlated if a change in one occurs when there is a change in the other. For example, age and voting are correlated if a change in age is accompanied by a change in voting patterns. Variations occur simultaneously within

A POINT ON THE COMPASS

Aristotle's Typology of Regimes

Number of Rulers	Beneficiary	
	All Citizens	Rulers
One	Monarchy	Tyranny
Few	Aristocracy	Oligarchy
Many	Polity	Democracy

Source: Nicolas Baxter-Moore, Terrance Carroll, and Roderick Church, *Studying Politics: An Introduction to Argument and Analysis* (Toronto: Copp Clark Longman Ltd., 1994).

each concept; thus, the two are said to *covary*. However, a theory does not just state that concepts are correlated, but also indicates the *direction* of the correlation. A **positive correlation** occurs when an increase in value in one concept is accompanied by an increase in the value in the other concept. Similarly, a decrease in the value in one concept is accompanied by a decrease in the value in the other. Thus, the direction of change is the same on each variable. If voter turnout increases when age increases, this is a positive correlation. A **negative correlation** indicates that the direction of change is inverse: an increase on one concept is related to a decrease on the other. A negative correlation does *not* mean that there is no relationship between the two variables; negative refers to the direction rather than the existence of the relationship. To return to the previous example, a negative correlation between voting and age would occur if an increase in age accompanies a decrease in voting. Of course, in order for a relationship to have direction, it must be possible to order the values of the concepts involved. When *either* of the concepts in a relationship cannot be ordered (when either is measured by a categorical variable), the correlation cannot have direction. In such cases, we simply note that the concepts, for example, voter turnout and religious affiliation, are correlated.

Overall, a hypothesis will state the relationships between concepts, and the underlying theory will attempt to explain why these relationships exist. A statement of relationship expressed within a theory is known as a **proposition** (Neuman 1994, 40). Some theories are quite broad in scope, making sweeping generalizations about social and political life. Other theories are less ambitious, seeking, for example, to explain events in a single country rather than all countries.

CHECKING YOUR BEARINGS

EXAMPLES OF THEORY

Consider the two political science theories outlined below. For each, identify the key concepts and the key propositions (relationships between the concepts). Which has a broader scope?

Michels' Iron Law of Oligarchy

Robert Michels, a loyal socialist, studied the inner dynamics of the German Social Democratic Party. Although the party was committed to participatory decision-making, Michels (1962) found that within the party a leadership elite emerged. He reasoned that this was due to the need for organization: in order for a political party to operate efficiently, an elite must emerge to take charge and keep the party on track. Michels also found that the leadership elite often pursued its own interests, rather than those of the party as a whole; in other words, an oligarchy had emerged. Given that a revolutionary democratic party was the last place Michels expected to find self-interested leadership, he concluded that *any* need for organization will be met by the creation of oligarchies, despite contrary claims of democracy: "the government, or ... the state, cannot be anything other than the organization of a minority ... and can never be truly representative of the majority. The majority is thus permanently incapable of self-government" (1962, 351). He summarizes this process in the statement, "Who says organization says oligarchy." This broad assertion is known as the "iron law of oligarchy."

Brodie and Jenson's "Defining the Political" Theory

There are a number of different approaches to the study of political party development. In the mobilization approach, parties "are strategic actors engaged in defining the issues of importance in political conflict and in mobilizing voters behind their issue positions" (Archer et al. 1995, 417). This theory is put forward by Janine Brodie and Jane Jenson (1980), who argue that Canadian political parties have effectively written social class out of the political realm. Political parties are able to control what social cleavages are seen as "important" through the issues they champion. By refusing to focus on issues of social class, the Canadian parties (including the CCF (Co-operative Commonwealth Federation)/NDP) keep class issues from becoming politically relevant. It is in this way that political parties "define the political."

DEVELOPING AND TESTING THEORIES

How does one develop a theory? There are two methods: inductive and deductive. **Inductive** approaches move from data to theory: we begin by observing the world and from our observations develop generalizations and conclusions. For example, if we observe that members of the Canadian Union of Public Employees (CUPE) are more likely than non-members to support the NDP, we might generalize that union membership is correlated with ideological position. (The validity of such generalizations may depend upon the specific union to which members belong; members of the Canadian Auto Workers may be different from CUPE members.) Induction, then, involves the progression from empirical evidence to generalization. Inductive research is often exploratory:

we begin with an open mind and look for patterns in behaviour. An example of inductive theorizing is seen in Alexis de Tocqueville's *Democracy in America* (1863). Tocqueville visited the United States to assess the desirability of the republican system for France. He found that America was characterized by social equality (a lack of aristocracy) and political equality. However, the high levels of equality were correlated with mediocre leadership: the popularly elected representatives were not the best and the brightest men in the country. Tocqueville feared that the love for equality and majority rule would lead to the "tyranny of the majority," in which majority interests are pursued at the expense of minority liberties. Tocqueville concluded by theorizing that increased levels of political equality lead to decreased leadership quality and that democracy threatens the rights and liberties of minorities. Thus, Tocqueville began with an observation and from that observation generalized about the nature of democracy.

Deductive theorizing moves the other way, from the general to the specific. We are engaging in deductive research when we begin with specific assumptions, or hypotheses, and set out to test them in the real world. For example, we may assume that union members will support left-wing parties due to common policy agendas. This proposition leads us to gather data to see if our theory holds: we might survey union members and ask their ideological position or test the degree to which supporters of left-wing parties are sympathetic to concerns of union members, such as the right to collective bargaining. If the evidence confirms our hypothesis, then our theory is supported. Deductive research is often referred to as **hypothesis-testing**, discussed in more detail below. Obviously, deductive research requires that we have a source for our assumptions. Sometimes our source is merely logic: the theory makes sense. Other times, our source is preexisting research or theorizing: the literature suggests that a relationship or pattern exists, and we seek empirical evidence to test it. Take, for example, Tocqueville's theory that democracy is correlated with mediocre leadership. We could test this theory by looking at the quality of leadership in a single country or across countries and time. Is Canada governed by intellectual or economic elites or by "ordinary people"? And, if the latter, is a reduction in the quality of leadership an inevitable result?

It should be noted that inductive and deductive research play off each other. We might notice a pattern in society and from that observation make the broad generalizations necessary to develop a theory (inductive research). Then we might seek to test hypotheses derived from the theory more directly by gathering data from different sources (deductive research). This process of data collection may lead us to note

CHECKING YOUR BEARINGS

INDUCTIVE AND DEDUCTIVE RESEARCH

Consider the relationship between age and political conservatism. How would you examine it *inductively*? What are the observations you have made, and what theories can you develop? How would you examine the relationship *deductively*? What hypotheses could you test? How did you develop these hypotheses? How might you test the hypotheses?

new or different patterns, from which we might generalize into different theories (inductive research). We then would develop hypotheses based on the new theories (deductive research), then test them empirically, and so on. Inductive research tends to be more *exploratory* and broader in scope, whereas deductive research tends to be more directed and narrower in scope.

HYPOTHESIS TESTING

With deductive research we seek to test our hypotheses empirically. Before discussing how we do so, first consider exactly what a hypothesis is. Recall that a proposition states a relationship between two concepts; propositions are combined to create theories. When we empirically test theories, propositions are referred to as hypotheses, and concepts are referred to as variables. Simply stated, then, a hypothesis is a *testable statement of relationship* between two variables. It is a statement, not a question. Usually, a hypothesis will state a *direction* (positive, meaning that variables change in a similar direction, or negative, meaning that variables change inversely) and will contain a *comparison*. Consider the hypothesis, "High-income earners are more likely to support conservatism than low-income earners." A relationship is stated between two variables: income and support for conservatism. The direction of the relationship is positive: as income increases, support for conservatism increases. And the hypothesis includes a comparison: high-income earners are compared to low-income earners. Is the hypothesis empirically testable? Yes, we could measure attitudes toward conservatism among the general population and see if there are differing levels of support among different income groups.

SUMMARY

Characteristics of a Hypothesis

1. It states a relationship between two variables.

2. It states the direction of the relationship if possible.

3. It states a comparison between values of the independent variable.

4. It is empirically testable.

When we formulate hypotheses, we must ensure that they are empirically testable, which means that we do not use normative statements. A hypothesis does not state preferences or judgments. Often, we will have to reformulate our ideas to make them empirically testable. This can be done by making our assumptions more explicit and by ensuring that all the elements of a hypothesis—relationship, comparison, direction, testability—are present. If we start with "democratic regimes are better than authoritarian regimes" (a comparison), we need to consider what we mean by "better." What is regime type being related to? Perhaps we are interested in human rights, and we believe that "democratic regimes have better human rights records than authoritarian regimes." Now we have included a relationship (between human rights and regime type) and a direction (as democracy increases, human rights records improve). This is now a testable hypothesis, rather than a normative statement.

In political analysis our goal is to test our hypotheses or, more specifically, to see if and to what extent those hypotheses are supported by empirical data. We gather empirical data to see if the evidence agrees with or contradicts our hypotheses. As support grows for a particular hypothesis, we gain more confidence in it and are more inclined to see it as "true." However, we never state that we have "proven" a hypothesis.

CHECKING YOUR BEARINGS

DEVELOPING HYPOTHESES

Create hypotheses for relationships between

1. political conservatism and support for deficit reduction;
2. age and political party membership/involvement;
3. regime type and economic system;
4. economic system and distribution of wealth;
5. gender and support for the Charter of Rights and Freedoms.

The reason for this is the importance of skepticism in the scientific method. Recall that science avoids any notions of certainty: if we are certain, we assume perfect knowledge, something scientists are reluctant to claim. There is always the chance that further knowledge will develop, that new information will be discovered, information that may place our "truths" into question. This has happened many times in the history of humankind: it was once believed that the Earth was flat, the Sun revolved around the Earth, heavy objects fell more rapidly than light objects, and atoms were indivisible. Modern scientists and social scientists wish to avoid such errors and therefore refuse to make statements of absolute certain "proof."

Consequently, the process of hypothesis-testing involves examining whether the hypothesis can be shown to be false. In a formal sense, although the development of the hypothesis is based on formulating a "testable statement of relationships" between variables, when testing a hypothesis we focus instead on the *null hypothesis*. The null hypothesis is the negation of the research hypothesis. For example, if the research hypothesis (H_1) states that union members are more likely than nonunion members to support parties of the left, the null hypothesis (H_0) states that union members are not more likely than nonunion members to support parties of the left. The research question then becomes, "Are the data consistent with the hypothesis (H_0) that union members are not more likely to support parties of the left?" If the data are consistent with the null hypothesis, then the research hypothesis has been rejected. If the data are inconsistent with the null hypothesis, then the research hypothesis has been accepted. Although the research hypothesis has not been proven to be true, one would conclude that it has been supported by the data.

Hypothesis-testing can be seen as the gradual elimination of alternative explanations. If we are trying to identify determining factors in party identification, for example, we might consider age, income, religion, region, parents' income, parents' party identification, and gender. Testing might find that age and region do not appear to contribute to party identification. We would then drop hypotheses related to these variables and continue testing the remaining factors. Over time, others would probably drop from contention and new hypotheses emerge; we might, for instance, also choose to test the impact of education and marital status. Some hypotheses would continue to hold up after repeated testing, while others would be eliminated. Those that stay in contention and have the greatest empirical support are considered to be the best explanation *at that point in time* (Neuman 1994, 100). Thus, if after repeated testing, income and parents' party identification remain

A POINT ON THE COMPASS

HYPOTHESIS TESTING

Time 1: Which of the eight potential hypotheses in competition to explain a dependent variable is best?

H1 H2 H2 H4 H5 H6 H7 H8

Time 2: Research tests the hypotheses and shows support for some but rejects others.

Results of Research

Rejected   Still under Consideration

H1 H2 H3   H4 H5 H6 H7 H8

Time 3: Future research tests remaining hypotheses in contention

Results of Research

Rejected   Still under Consideration

H4 H5   H6 H7 H8

New hypotheses developed and added for consideration: H9

Time 4: Future research tests hypotheses still in contention

Results of Research

Rejected   Still under Consideration

H6   H7 H8 H9

New hypotheses developed and added for consideration: H10 H11

Time 5: New hypotheses are developed and enter into the competition. Research now tests the previous as well as the new hypotheses.

Results of Research

Rejected   Still under Consideration

H7 H9   H8 H10 H11

Source: W. Lawrence Neuman, *Social Research Methods: Qualitative and Quantitative Approaches*, 2nd ed. (Boston: Allyn and Bacon, 1994), pp. 101–2.

correlated with party identification, we can say with confidence that the hypotheses are *supported*. We do not, however, state that the hypotheses have been proven.

Before we can conclude that support exists for our hypotheses, we must first reject the **null hypothesis**. As we noted in Chapter 1, the null hypothesis states that *no* relationship exists between two variables. For example, a null hypothesis might state "there is no relationship between age and party identification." Before we can test the hypothesis that "as age increases, support for conservative parties increases," we must first reject the null hypothesis. By rejecting the null hypothesis, we have

CHECKING YOUR BEARINGS

STATING NULL HYPOTHESES

Earlier, you created hypotheses for the relationships listed below. Now restate each in the null form:

1. political conservatism and support for deficit reduction;
2. age and political party membership/involvement;
3. regime type and economic system;
4. economic system and distribution of wealth;
5. gender and support for the Charter of Rights and Freedoms.

established that some sort of relationship exists, and we are free to consider questions of direction.[1] When writing our research hypothesis, we first state a null hypothesis (no relationship exists) and then state an alternative hypothesis (the relationship we think exists). In hypothesis-testing, therefore, we first test the null hypothesis (identified by H_0), and, if it is rejected, we accept our alternative hypothesis (identified by H_a).

To look at a relationship between two variables, we need to arrange them in a way that we can identify patterns. One way to do so is to use **contingency tables** (also referred to as cross-tabulation tables). To create a contingency table, we first need to identify the two variables under question and the number of categories, or values, within each variable. Let's say that our variables are age and support for conservatism. The variable "age" in this example is divided into three categories: young (0–30 years), middle (31–50 years), and old (51+ years). The variable "support for conservatism" is also divided into three categories: low, moderate, and high. To create our table, we place one variable across the top of the table, being certain to place the categories in order (low to high) if the variable is ordinal rather than categorical and to label the variable as well as all categories. We then place the second variable on the left-hand side of the table, again paying attention to ordering and labelling. The result is the table presented in Figure 2.1.

Our next step is to take individual cases and locate them in the **cells** of the table. In a contingency table, the location of a particular case is *contingent* upon its values for each of the two variables. Robert is 20 years old and ranks low on conservatism. To locate Robert on the table in Figure 2.1, we first find his location on the age variable. Because Robert is 20 years old, he will be placed in the "young" category, which is the first *column* of the contingency table. We then need to place Robert according to the second variable. Robert is located in the "low"

FIGURE 2.1

CREATING A CONTINGENCY TABLE

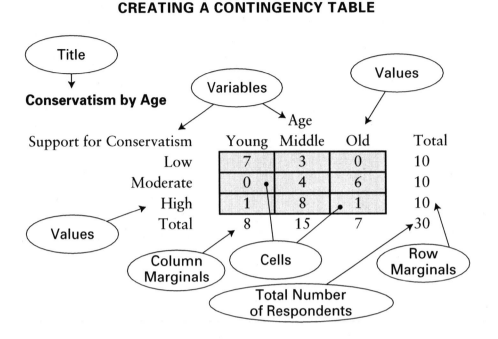

category of conservatism, which is the first *row* of the table. Thus, we place Robert in the cell where "young" intersects with "low conservatism," in this case, in row 1, column 1. Looking at the table, where would you place someone who is 58 years old and moderately conservative? Someone who is 31 years old and highly conservative? To create a contingency table, we must locate each individual case in its appropriate cell. We then total the number of cases in each cell; for example, if the old, moderate conservatism cell (row 2, column 3) has a total of six cases, we place the number 6 in that cell.

Our final step is to total the numbers in each row and column. These totals are known as **marginals**. To find **row marginals**, we add *across* the cells for each row. The two marginals provide the frequency distribution (see Chapter 9) for "support for conservatism." To find **column marginals**, we add *down* the cells for each column. The column marginals provide the frequency distribution for age. The total number of cases in the data set (identified as N) is designated outside the lower right-hand corner of the table. Obviously, the row marginals summed together should be equal to N, as should the column marginals. If they are not, some sort of summation error has occurred. Be sure to double-check your numbers!

When reading a contingency table, we are looking for a patterned relationship or correlation. A **perfect correlation** exists when knowing the value on one variable *always* lets us know the value on the other. In Figure 2.2(a), we see that there is a perfect relationship between age and support for conservatism: *all* young people show low support, *all* middle-aged people show moderate support, and *all* older people show high support. Under these circumstances, if asked to guess the conservatism of a stranger, we would be able to guess correctly 100% of the time as soon as we discovered her age. If she is 22 years old, she will display low support for conservatism. Note, however, that if even one case deviated from this pattern, we would not have a perfect relationship. Figure 2.2(b) represents a **moderate relationship**: *most* young people show low support, *most* middle-aged people show moderate support, and *most* older people show high support. Under these circumstances, if asked to guess the conservatism of a stranger, knowing her age would improve our guessing ability, but we would not have certainty. Thus, if she is 22 years old, there is a good chance that she will display low support (that is our best prediction), but there is also the possibility that she will display moderate or high support. Moderate relationships, of course, will vary in strength; Chapters 10 and 11 provide a number of techniques through which the precise strength of the relationship can be specified. Figure 2.2(c) displays **no relationship**: there is no discernible pattern between age and support for conservatism. Thus, knowing a stranger's age gives us no clue whatsoever as to her conservative views. We will find no relationship if we *failed to reject the null hypothesis.*

If we find a moderate or perfect relationship, we are able to *reject the null hypothesis.* (The statistical tests that provide the decision rules for rejecting or accepting the null hypothesis are discussed in Chapter 10.) Our next question is, "Is the alternative hypothesis supported?" If we have variables that can be ordered, we need to look at the direction of the relationship in the table and see if it corresponds to the relationship direction stated in the alternative hypothesis. If our alternative hypothesis states "as age increases, support for conservatism increases" (a positive relationship), then Figures 2.2(a) and 2.2(b) *support* H_a. However, if our alternative hypothesis states "as age increases, support for conservatism decreases" (a negative relationship), then Figures 2.2(a) and 2.2(b) *do not support* H_a. Some hypotheses do not involve ordered variables and thus cannot involve direction. For example, the hypothesis that "men are more likely to be conservative than women" involves a comparison, rather than a direction. To look for support for the hypothesis, we need to ask if the *pattern observed* matches the *pattern predicted.* If we find that men are indeed more conservative than women,

FIGURE 2.2

LOOKING FOR CORRELATIONS IN CONTINGENCY TABLES

(a) Perfect Correlation

		Age			
		Young	Middle	Old	
	Low	8	0	0	8
Support for Conservatism	Moderate	0	15	0	15
	High	0	0	7	7
	Total	8	15	7	30

(b) Moderate Correlation

		Age			
		Young	Middle	Old	
	Low	5	1	2	8
Support for Conservatism	Moderate	2	12	1	15
	High	1	2	4	7
	Total	8	15	7	30

(c) No Correlation

		Age			
		Young	Middle	Old	
	Low	2	4	2	8
Support for Conservatism	Moderate	4	8	3	15
	High	2	3	2	7
	Total	8	15	7	30

FIGURE 2.3

LOOKING FOR CORRELATIONS IN SCATTER PLOTS

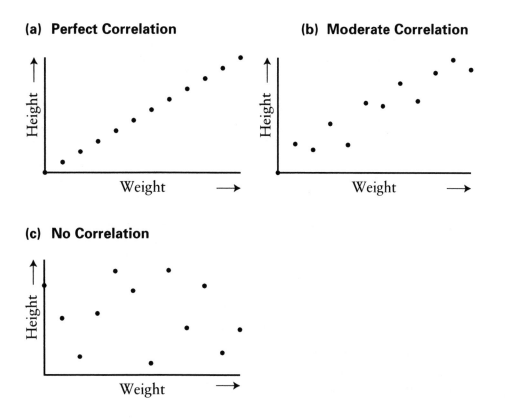

H_a is supported. If, on the other hand, women are found to be more conservative than men, then H_a is not supported.

In some cases correlations can be visually detected in scatter plots or scatter diagrams. Figure 2.3, for example, presents the hypothetical distribution of individuals according to their height (vertical axis) and weight (horizontal axis). Each dot on the diagram represents one individual or case. Figure 2.3(a) shows a perfect correlation; for every increase in height, there is an equivalent increase in weight. (We assume that height drives weight, rather than weight driving height!) Figure 2.3(b) shows a positive but less than perfect correlation; the taller people are, the more they tend to weigh, but a person's height does not allow us to perfectly predict their weight. In Figure 2.3(c), the scatter plot suggests no relationship between height and weight.

CAUSALITY

Until now, we have been looking for relationships between variables: does a relationship exist, and if so, what is the direction of that relationship? However, while recognizing correlations is important in the social sciences, we often wish to go further; more specifically, we want to know *why* two variables, A and B, are related. Does A cause B, or is their covariance accidental? Or is there a third variable, C, that causes both A and B? Recall from Chapter 1 that an important assumption of the scientific approach to politics is determinism: the belief there exist cause-and-effect relationships and that social scientists can, through research, discover the form of these relationships. Of course, few would argue that the underlying causes of human actions are either clear or certain, but the goal in social science is to find *patterns* of behaviour and propose causes to explain those patterns.

Recall also that causal relationships involve cause and effect. Variable X causes variable Y when a "change in X (sooner or later) produces change in Y," "or (because some Xs don't change) Ys tend to line up with fixed values of X" (Davis 1985, 9). How do we determine which variable is the cause and which is the effect? When one event precedes another in time, it is clear which is the cause and which is the effect. We give a plant water and light and it grows. We cast our ballots and a legislature is elected. When one event occurs in reaction to another, we have **temporal order**. The reacting variable (the effect) is dependent upon the preceding event (the cause): the life of the plant depends upon the supply of water and light, and the composition of the legislature is dependent upon the votes cast. As we noted in Chapter 1, the influenced variable is known as the dependent variable. The influencing variable—the cause—is called the independent variable: its values are independent of the dependent variable. The availability of water and light does not depend upon the existence of a single plant; the future composition of the legislature does not determine our individual vote, although our expectations about its composition might do so. Some independent variables are descriptive characteristics of the individual, qualities such as age, sex, race, and religion. These variables are known as **prior conditions** and precede in time such dependent variables as political beliefs and behaviours.

We can graphically represent causal relationships with causal models. Figure 2.4(a) illustrates a simple causal relationship: age (the independent variable) influences income (the dependent variable). The small "+" above the arrow tells us that the relationship is positive; in other words, the two variables change in the same direction. As age

FIGURE 2.4

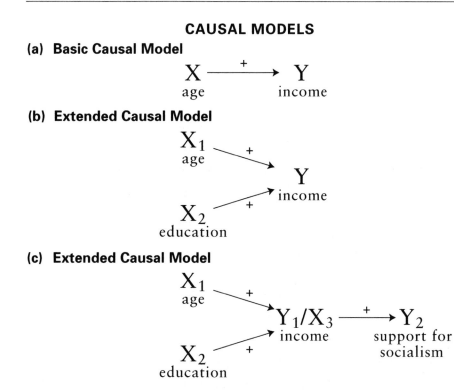

CAUSAL MODELS

(a) Basic Causal Model

$$X \xrightarrow{+} Y$$

age   income

(b) Extended Causal Model

X_1
age

Y
income

X_2
education

(c) Extended Causal Model

X_1
age

$Y_1/X_3 \xrightarrow{+} Y_2$
income   support for socialism

X_2
education

increases, income increases. Relationships between a single independent variable and the dependent variable are **bivariate**; there are only two variables being considered. Some causal relationships involve more than one independent variable; these relationships are **multivariate**. Figure 2.4(b) illustrates a causal relationship between three variables. Both age and education are independent variables, while income is the dependent variable. Note that both relationships are positive.

When there is a chain of influences, with many variables interacting, our causal models become more complex. Figure 2.4(c) illustrates a more elaborate causal model: both education and age are positively related to income, while income is negatively related to support for socialism. As income increases, this model suggests, support for socialism decreases. Note that in this example, income is a dependent variable to age and education, but an independent variable with respect to support for socialism. Causal models help us visualize the relationships between variables; when a large number of variables are involved in a theory, a causal model can often simplify very complex relationships.

Errors in Causal Reasoning

Not all relationships are causal, although unfortunately many people confuse correlation with causation. For example, if there is a rise in crime at the same time as there is a rise in the number of single mothers, some will argue that single motherhood causes crime. However, the world is not that simple. It is entirely possible that a third factor, such as poverty, causes both crime and single motherhood. When a relationship between two variables can be accounted for by a third variable, it is known as a **spurious** relationship. To test for a spurious relationship, we need to examine whether the relationship between variable A and variable B exists without the influence of variable C. If the relationship exists without C, it may be a causal correlation; if **controlling** for C causes the relationship between A and B to disappear, the relationship is spurious. We control for the effects of other variables by holding the values of the third variable constant. Returning to our example, we would need to know whether the relationship between single motherhood and crime can be attributed to a third variable: poverty. Thus, we test if the relationship exists in all socioeconomic groups or if it is isolated to the poor alone. If the relationship between single motherhood and crime disappears when poverty levels are held constant, we have found a spurious relationship; if it exists in all socioeconomic groups, it may be a causal relationship. To be confident that the relationship is causal, we need to be able to eliminate as many alternative explanations of the relationship as possible.

The use of controls to untangle issues of causality is a topic to which we will return in later chapters. At this point, Figure 2.5 provides a simple illustration. In the first table in Figure 2.5, we find the results of a hypothetical investigation of the impact on union membership of voting support for the NDP. Two hundred voters were interviewed, of whom 100 were women and 100 men. Figure 2.5 (a) also shows that 60 of the 200 respondents were NDP voters and that 60 of the 200 were trade union members. Finally, the table shows that individuals who belong to trade unions are more likely to vote for the NDP than are individuals who do not belong to trade unions. Indeed, 62% of union members intend to vote NDP, compared to only 38% of nonmembers. However, when we control for the sex of respondents, we find in Figure 2.5 (b) that the relationship becomes even stronger for men alone, whereas for women alone (Figure 2.5 (c)) the relationship vanishes. We must, then, refine our theoretical explanations to account for the fact that the relationship holds for men, but not for women.

FIGURE 2.5

THE USE OF CONTROLS

(a) Support For the NDP By Union Membership

	Belongs to union		Does not belong		Total	
Votes NDP	$n = 37$	62%	$n = 23$	38%	$n = 60$	100%
Does not vote NDP	$n = 23$	16%	$n = 117$	84%	$n = 140$	100%
Total	$n = 60$	30%	$n = 140$	70%	$n = 200$	100%

(b) Support For the NDP By Union Membership (Men Only)

	Belongs to union		Does not belong		Total	
Votes NDP	$n = 25$	83%	$n = 5$	17%	$n = 30$	100%
Does not vote NDP	$n = 5$	7%	$n = 65$	93%	$n = 70$	100%
Total	$n = 30$	30%	$n = 70$	70%	$n = 100$	100%

(c) Support For the NDP By Union Membership (Women Only)

	Belongs to union		Does not belong		Total	
Votes NDP	$n = 12$	40%	$n = 18$	60%	$n = 30$	100%
Does not vote NDP	$n = 28$	40%	$n = 42$	60%	$n = 70$	100%
Total	$n = 40$	30%	$n = 60$	70%	$n = 100$	100%

Once we know that a causal relationship is possible, we need to consider the order of that relationship. Sometimes social scientists find that it is difficult to ascertain which variable is the cause and which is the effect. When temporal order is not clear—when events appear to occur simultaneously—causality is difficult to establish. We noted that a correlation between single motherhood and crime might be seen as moving from the former to the latter; in other words, it might be posited that single motherhood causes increased crime rates. However, it is possible that the relationship could work in the opposite direction: perhaps crime causes single motherhood. For example, violent crime could lead to fathers being killed or imprisoned, leaving the mother alone to raise the children. Many of the relationships we seek to explore in social science can seem like chicken-and-egg dilemmas. When we cannot clearly determine cause and effect, we have less confidence that a causal relationship exists.

Another common error in causal reasoning is that temporal order necessarily implies causality. This fallacy is similar to assuming that correlation is equated to causation. Just because variable X precedes variable Y is not sufficient grounds to argue that X causes Y; again, we must ensure that some other variable Z does not cause Y. Controlling for other possible causes is the only way we can suggest with confidence that X causes Y. Unfortunately, we can never rule out all possible alternative explanations for social and political behaviour. In addition, temporal order can be difficult to establish in the social sciences. For these reasons, theory is particularly important to political analysis. Many of the gaps in our knowledge are filled by clear reasoning and logic; good data alone are seldom sufficient.

Finally, we should note the **ecological fallacy**. To understand this concept, imagine a study of electoral support for a local referendum on the amalgamation of local governments. In order to test the hypothesis that support for amalgamation will decline as personal income increases, the researchers collect data on average family income and percentage voting no in the referendum for each polling district in the referendum. And, as the hypothesis predicts, polls with relatively high family incomes were more likely to vote no in the referendum than were polls with relatively low family incomes. The researchers then conclude that high-income *voters* are more likely to oppose amalgamation than are low-income *voters*. In coming to this conclusion, the researchers are committing the ecological fallacy. They are assuming that what is true of the polling district—the ecological unit of analysis—is equally true of individuals within the polling districts. They are assuming that because high-income districts are more likely to vote no, so too are high-income individuals. In fact, however, there need not be any relationship between district characteristics and the determinants of individual voting behaviour. There could be no relationship between family income and voting preference for individuals *within* each district, and yet still a relationship between income and vote when the level of analysis shifts from individuals to the polling district. The lesson is that we must be careful in projecting ecological characteristics onto the behaviour of individuals.

This chapter has explored the role of theory in political analysis. Most of the following chapters will explore different ways that we make empirical observations of the social world in our efforts to test our theories and advance our knowledge of the political world. However, before we turn to the application of research methods, we must consider some of the ethical considerations embedded in the research process.

WORKING AS A TEAM

1. With your discussion group, define an "ideal type" political leader. What qualities would he or she possess? How would he or she interact with the public, with political parties, with the media, and with interest groups? Having constructed this ideal, how do you feel existing leaders—federal, provincial, and local—compare to this nonexistent ideal? Who comes closest to this ideal?

SELF-STUDY

1. How many ways can you categorize the following data set (e.g., region, level of unemployment, "have/have-not provinces")? Identify the concepts that you employ. Are these concepts abstract or concrete? Are the variables discrete or continuous? Group each variable (excluding province) into three categories—high, intermediate, and low—and notice how the different provinces are located in the categories of each variable. Do you see any patterns? What relationship does this pattern suggest?

Province	Unemployment	GDP (per capita)	Income > $35,000
Ontario	5.1%	$24,234	14.5%
Alberta	7.2	24,782	15.4
Saskatchewan	7.4	17,052	11.1
Manitoba	7.5	18,581	10.4
British Columbia	9.1	21,065	14.1
Quebec	9.3	19,994	10.6
Nova Scotia	9.9	15,215	9.2
New Brunswick	12.5	14,870	7.7
Prince Edward Island	14.7	12,661	5.7
Newfoundland	15.8	12,567	6.8

Source: Adapted from Statistics Canada, *The Labour Force*, Catalogue No. 71-001, December 1989; *Selected Income Statistics*, Catalogue No. 93-331; and *Provincial Economic Accounts*, Catalogue No. 12-213.

2. For the data set below, create a contingency table with the following categories: region: Western Canada, Central Canada, Atlantic Canada; unemployment rate: low (under 8.0%), moderate (8.1%–10.0%), high (10.1+%).

Province	1989 Unemployment Rate
Ontario	5.1%
Prince Edward Island	14.7
New Brunswick	12.5
Manitoba	7.5
Quebec	9.3
Newfoundland	15.8
Alberta	7.2
Saskatchewan	7.4
Nova Scotia	9.9
British Columbia	9.1

Assume your null hypothesis is "unemployment rates are not correlated with region," and your alternative hypothesis is "unemployment rates are higher in Atlantic Canada than in other regions." Does the table allow you to reject H_0? If so, is there support for H_a?

Source: Adapted from Statistics Canada, *The Labour Force*, Catalogue No. 71-001, December 1989.

3. A common notion in political science is that of the left–right spectrum, with the left representing support for a more interventionist government and the right representing support for minimal government. In surveys, respondents are often asked to locate themselves along this left–right spectrum. You are studying support for the political "right." Your theory is that two factors, family income and age, influence self-placement on the spectrum; more specifically, you believe that as each of these two variables increases, support for the "right" increases. (You also assume that age and family income are not correlated.)

You conduct a survey to test your theory. You ask respondents to locate themselves on a 6-point left–right scale, with 1 representing the extreme left and 6 representing the extreme right. Thus, a respondent who identifies herself as a 5 considers herself to be right-wing, whereas a respondent who identifies himself as a 4 considers himself to be politically moderate, or centre-right in orientation.

Left - - - - - - - - - - - - - Right
1 2 3 4 5 6

Your survey work provides the following data:

Case	Age	Income	Left–Right Placement
1	42	$65,000	5
2	36	$28,000	3
3	55	$58,000	4
4	19	$15,000	2
5	56	$45,000	6
6	25	$29,000	6
7	31	$50,000	2
8	65	$90,000	3
9	23	$31,000	1
10	47	$70,000	5
11	39	$10,000	1
12	50	$35,000	2
13	28	$45,000	4
14	26	$34,000	3
15	49	$58,000	5
16	63	$90,000	5
17	60	$67,000	6
18	38	$39,000	4
19	30	$18,000	1
20	61	$40,000	3

   a. State your null and alternative hypotheses for each possible relationship.

   b. Draw the causal model for your theory. Identify the dependent and independent variables.

   c. Create two bivariate tables (spectrum by age, spectrum by income), classifying the data as follows: age: young = 18–30; middle = 31–49; old = 50+; income: low = $0–$35,000; middle = $36,000–$59,000; high = $60,000+; spectrum: left = 1–2; centre = 3–4; right = 5–6.

   d. Do the tables allow you to reject your null hypothesis? Is there support for your alternative hypothesis? Explain your reasoning.

4. You are conducting an internal review of Acme Inc. The senior officials at Acme are concerned about the low number of women in senior management, despite its policy of promoting managers on the basis of seniority. Your task is to

examine the situation to see if women are being discrimi-
nated against. Acme provides the following data set. Use contingency tables to attempt to resolve the question. If further
data are needed, what are they?

Case	Sex	Rank	Seniority
1	F	Junior	< 5 years
2	F	Junior	< 5
3	F	Junior	< 5
4	F	Junior	5–10
5	F	Middle	5–10
6	F	Middle	5–10
7	F	Senior	> 10
8	M	Junior	< 5
9	M	Junior	< 5
10	M	Middle	< 5
11	M	Middle	5–10
12	M	Middle	5–10
13	M	Senior	5–10
14	M	Senior	>10
15	M	Senior	>10

NOTES

1. As Chapter 10 will discuss, hypotheses sometimes include a specific directionality. Two-tailed tests are used to reject the null hypothesis if no direction is specified, if, for example, the hypothesis is simply that some relationship exists between age and conservatism. One-tailed tests are used when the direction of the relationship is specified by the hypothesis.

CHAPTER 3

Research Ethics: People behind the Numbers

DESTINATION

By the end of this chapter the reader should

- understand the ethical considerations that lie behind the choice of research topics and methodologies;
- appreciate the concerns relating to anonymity, confidentiality, and informed consent;
- be familiar with how ethical considerations are handled in the social sciences.

As readers are drawn into the complexities of statistical analysis in the chapters to come, it will be easy to forget that the numbers encountered in quantitative analysis represent real people. For example, in a table showing that 44.1% of 950 respondents in a survey of the Ontario electorate intend to vote for the Progressive Conservative candidate in the next provincial election, it is easy to forget that this represents 419 discrete individuals who were disrupted from their everyday routine to answer a survey, made assumptions about the survey's legitimacy, and were assured anonymity and confidentiality would be respected. In this chapter, we expose readers to some of the ethical issues and dilemmas that confront political scientists as they engage in a wide variety of research activities relating to the collection, analysis, and publication of data. As you will see, any assumption that quantitative research is immune from ethical considerations because we are dealing with *numbers rather than people* should be quickly discarded.

Ethical considerations emerge from a number of directions. To some degree, they govern the topics we decide to study and, consequently, our choice of research subjects. Ethical considerations may determine the research methodologies we employ. Indeed, the most vigorous ethical standards tend to come into play with respect to data collection: the samples we select, the information provided to subjects or respondents, the precautions taken to ensure confidentiality, and the avoidance of risk. Ethical considerations also come into play in the relationships we have with colleagues, both in specific research projects and within the broader scholarly community. Finally, ethical considerations may determine what we do with research results. Of particular concern is the manner in which research findings can shape the political debate over public policy in democratic states.

The intent of the chapter is to bring this range of ethical considerations into play before readers become entangled in the more technical aspects of political science research. By doing so we also hope to bring the human face of empirical research into sharper focus.

RISK ASSESSMENT AND THE MEDICAL MODEL

Many of the ethical guidelines currently employed in the social sciences find their roots in medical research. When research is being conducted on the introduction of new medications or on the use of alternative treatments or therapies, there can be a significant potential risk to human subjects. For instance, whether an experimental drug has unwanted side effects is not an "academic question" to the subjects in whom those side effects might become manifest. If a new treatment is being tested to see if survival rates following heart surgery can be increased, it is not a matter of indifference to patients whether they are subjected to the new or old treatment. In the early days of medical research, however, research subjects were often recruited without their consent, much less informed consent. Patients who were institutionalized were particularly exposed to research risks. In light of this history, medical researchers have now developed elaborate protocols to ensure that research subjects are fully informed about the nature of the research and the risks to which they may be exposed, and to ensure that participation is voluntary. These protocols have come to provide the model for similar protocols within the social sciences.

Underlying these protocols is the first principle of medical practice: *do no harm*. This is a principle to which social scientists should also adhere. Any potential research gain with respect to description or theory must be carefully weighed against potential risks to research subjects, to the communities from which they are drawn, and, at times, to the researcher himself or herself. As an example of this last risk, Julie Brannen (1988) draws our attention to the psychological costs that may emerge for researchers doing in-depth interviews on sensitive topics.

Unlike professional confidants such as counsellors, psychotherapists, and priests, social science researchers lack their own confessors who can help them come to grips with the troubling information to which they may have been exposed.

But wait, you might say, surely the potential risks in social science research are much less serious than they are in medical research, and thus the ethical considerations less acute. For example, it is hard to argue that a respondent to a national Angus Reid survey is exposed to the same level of risk as the research subject in a new chemotherapy treatment program. Asking someone his or her opinion on issues of the day seems almost risk-free compared to administering new drugs or food additives. However, while most forms of social science research, and particularly most forms of survey research, are *relatively* benign in their potential impact on participants, it would be a mistake to assume that ethical considerations are absent or even that the potential of serious risk to research subjects is absent. The nature of the risk may be quite different from those addressed by the medical model, but risk is not absent. Social science research is with human subjects, and such research cannot escape a concern for the welfare of those subjects. As Bruce Chadwick et al. explain (1984, 15–16), "Whereas the chemist may wish to see which substance or combination of substances will change the composition of the compound under study, the social scientist must make sure that his or her research does not result in any permanent change, damage, or injury to the persons studied."

Risk, it should be stressed, is not always self-evident. Take, for example, the risk associated with self-knowledge. Imagine you have become an unwitting participant in a hypothetical experiment designed to see if people will come to the aid of strangers in real life situations. The researchers have set up a situation in which individuals walking down the street are confronted by strangers apparently experiencing different degrees of distress. In one case it might be someone pretending to be lost, in another case someone who is ill or is being attacked. The researchers want to see if you will come to the stranger's aid and to what extent intervention might be determined by the characteristics of the subject, the "victim," and the event. Let's imagine further that you decide not to intervene and keep walking. At the end of the block a member of the research team stops you, informs you about the experiment, and, in the debriefing, assures you that no one was in fact in distress. Thus, to a degree your mind is set at ease in that you do not have to worry about what might have happened to the individual you ignored. However, you also have to confront what might be some disturbing new knowledge: you have been shown to be the kind of person who ignores strangers in distress. This self-knowledge may be enlightening, but it may be the kind of enlightenment that you would just as soon have done without. In effect, you have been damaged; you have a diminished sense of your own personal worth, the effects of which may be long lasting. The question, then, is whether the researchers had the right to inflict this cost. Was the research ethical?

The message here is self-evident but important. Any proposed research must be assessed not only in terms of the possible advance of descriptive knowledge and/or theoretical insight. It must also be assessed in terms of risk to subjects, communities, and at times to the research team. This assessment is first and foremost an ethical exercise.

CHECKING YOUR BEARINGS

ANIMAL-TESTING

A great deal of medical research entails testing on animal subjects, generally as a prelude to testing on human subjects. Not surprisingly, animal-testing has been the source of much ethical and political debate centring not only on technicalities—are the test animals being treated as humanely as possible, is everything possible being done to minimize pain and discomfort?—but also on whether such testing should be done at all.

Fortunately, perhaps, very little political science research involves animal-testing. Indeed, no cases come to mind. However, the debate on this subject can be a useful way to "prime the pump" for ethical considerations that are relevant for political science research. Consider, then, the following research dilemma. A firm has developed a new food additive that may ameliorate lactose intolerance for hundreds of thousands of people in Canada and millions around the world. To ensure that the additive is safe for human consumption, the firm first intends to feed large amounts of the additive to research rats for four weeks and then to dissect the rats to determine if any abnormalities have shown up in larger than expected numbers. The research program, therefore, will necessitate the death and dissection of literally thousands of rats. Does this strike you as a reasonable price to pay, given the potential of the new additive? Would your opinion change if the research animals were cats? Beagles? Chimpanzees?

SELECTING THE RESEARCH TOPIC

Ethical considerations begin with the selection of the research topic. As Duelli-Klein (1983, 38) points out, our decision about *what* to investigate always precedes the methodological issues of how the research might best proceed. In this context, we must acknowledge the emphasis that universities and colleges place on freedom of intellectual inquiry. If *academic freedom* means anything, it surely means the freedom to pursue research topics that the individual researcher feels are interesting and important. This freedom of inquiry extends beyond academics; it should be a guiding principle for student research. However, this does not exempt researchers from ethical constraints on the conduct of their research, nor does it preclude a concern with the *social relevance* of the research. Furthermore, while researchers may be free to pursue any topic that strikes their fancy, funding agencies are under no compulsion to provide the financial support that may make the research possible. In fact, funds are most likely to be allocated for projects with some social relevance; research driven solely by intellectual curiosity or theoretical concerns faces an uphill, although by no means impossible, battle for funding.

The definition of what is and is not socially relevant takes us quickly into the ethical domain. There are no empirical criteria by which we can determine social relevance; the issue is a normative one. Admittedly, media coverage and the political agenda may send strong cues regarding the relative importance of various issues, and we might use these cues to identify some research topics as having greater social relevance and thus funding appeal than others. However, social relevancy implies something more than salience; it suggests that certain topics *should* be pursued and perhaps that others *should not*.

Much of the discussion in this respect has entailed a variety of problems, both ethical and methodological, that arise when researching *sensitive topics*. But what do we mean by such a term? Broadly defined, socially sensitive research includes studies "in which there are potential consequences or implications, either directly for the participants in the research or for the class of individuals represented by the research" (Sieber and Stanley 1988, 49). This, however, is a very general definition that could embrace virtually the entirety of public policy research. A tighter definition, focused on the presence of risk, is provided by Raymond Lee and Claire Renzetti (1990, 513): "a sensitive topic is one which potentially poses for those involved a substantial threat, the emergence of which renders problematic for the researcher and/or the researched the collection, holding, and/or dissemination of research data." Lee and Renzetti go on to explain that research is more likely to be threatening "(a) where research intrudes into the private sphere or delves into some deeply personal experience; (b) where the study is concerned with deviance and social control; (c) where it impinges on the vested interests of powerful persons or the exercise of coercion or domination; or (d) where it deals with things sacred to those being studied which they do not wish profaned" (1990, 513). There is no suggestion that research *not* be conducted in such areas. Rather, the point is that ethical considerations are likely to be brought into bold relief when research is conducted in the circumstances identified by Lee and Renzetti.

CHECKING YOUR BEARINGS

PUTTING RESEARCH SUBJECTS AT RISK: THE MILGRAM STUDIES OF OBEDIENCE

At times the risk to research subjects can come through increased self-awareness; we may find out that we are not as nice or compassionate as we thought we were. A good example of this risk comes from Stanley Milgram's (1963) famous experimental research on obedience.

Milgram recruited male subjects, aged 20 to 50, from the community to participate in a study of memory and learning, or at least so they were told, at Yale University. Subjects heard that the objective of the study was to determine the impact of punishment on learning and were then "randomly assigned" to be either the "teacher" or "learner" in the experiment. In fact, the subjects were always the teacher, and an accomplice of the experimenter was always the learner. The learner was strapped into an electric chair apparatus in one room, after which the teacher was conducted to an adjoining room where there was an electric shock generator with switches ranging from 15 to 450 V. The switches also had qualitative labels ranging from "slight shock" to "extreme intense shock," "Danger: severe shock," and "XXX." The task of the teacher was to administer electric shocks to the learner whenever a mistake was made. Moreover, the teacher was told to move to a higher level of shock each time a mistake was made. If the teacher resisted an increase in the level of shock, the researcher provided prods such as "it is absolutely essential that you continue." The learner, who could be heard but not seen, and who was not actually being shocked, began to indicate discomfort at the 75 V level. At 120 V he shouted the shocks were painful, at 150 V he asked to be released, at 180 V he screamed he couldn't stand the pain, at 270 V he screamed in agony, and after 330 V made no sound at all (Nachmias and Nachmias 1987, 79).

The experiment was designed to determine at what level of shock obedience would end and the teacher refuse further participation in the experiment. In one of his experiments, 26 of 40 participants administered shocks up to the maximum of 450 V (Nachmias and Nachmias 1987, 79). Milgram's work became so famous because many subjects, when prodded by the researcher, administered very high levels of shock. The "shock" to readers was that American males were obedient to the point of administering severe and dangerous electrical shocks to compatriots in a university-based research experiment.

What do you think about the ethics of this experiment? Was the knowledge gained sufficient to compensate for the risk to subjects? Were the subjects really at risk? How would you feel if you ended up administering severe electric shocks to a fellow student in a study of memory and learning? In the study itself, "subjects were observed to sweat, bite their lips, groan, and dig their fingernails into their flesh" (Milgram 1963, 375); some had uncontrollable seizures. If a similar piece of research was proposed today, do you think it would receive ethical clearance at your own institution? Are there conditions that might be imposed to reduce ethical concerns?

It should also be noted that Lee and Renzetti acknowledge potential risk to the researchers themselves as an ethical consideration. In rare instances this risk may involve the physical safety of the research team. In less extreme circumstances it may entail legal action including the potential of research material being subpoenaed. (Research material is not protected by the conventions of client confidentiality that apply to medical files and legal counsel.) A more general risk is that of "stigma contagion" for those researching unpopular topics. As Lee and Renzetti illustrate (1990, 521), "those involved in the study of sexual deviance have frequently remarked on their stigmatization by colleagues, university administrators, and students." Within political science, such stigmatization could be a concern for researchers studying the extremes of the political left and right, particularly if their research was seen as empathetic rather than critical. It might also be a concern for those investigating public policy in areas of high social sensitivity such as immigration, abortion, or Aboriginal self-government. As a consequence, there is a good chance that researchers will avoid topics that carry the risk of stigmatization. But when this happens, we may all be losers:

> Adverse publicity that could destroy a researcher's career may keep researchers from investigating sensitive topics. Yet, scientific knowledge is especially important precisely because the topics are sensitive ones. Without scientifically based knowledge, fear, prejudice, and ideology dominate public policy and public opinion. (Neuman 1997, 460)

Here it is worth noting that matters of social relevance are of greater importance to some forms of political science research than they are to others. Researchers interested in the complex dynamics of voting behaviour, for example, have not been overly preoccupied with the social relevance of their work; the primary concern is to advance theoretical understanding of voting behaviour and electoral choice in democratic societies. Feminist researchers, on the other hand, place a great deal of emphasis on applied or "action" research. Indeed, Patti Lather (1988) argues that feminist research must be action oriented, that the research and the feminist thought upon which it is based must be directed to social and political change. Feminist researchers also emphasize the importance of involving research subjects in the research enterprise, thereby blurring the distinction between the researcher and the researched. As Shulamit Reinharz (1992, 181) explains:

> In feminist participatory research, the distinction between the researcher(s) and those on whom the research is done disappears. To achieve an egalitarian relation, the researcher abandons control and adopts an approach of openness, reciprocity, mutual disclosure, and shared risk.

As suggested above, part of the hard reality of contemporary social science research is that the availability of research funding may drive the choice of research topics. It is always worth asking, therefore, whether there is an ethical dimension to the proclivities of funding agencies, whether the unavailability of funding squeezes out research which, on ethical grounds, may have some claim to priority. It should be noted, however, that in many cases funding agencies have been instrumental in elevating ethical standards. The primary funding agency for social science research in Canada, the Social Sciences and Humanities Research Council (SSHRC), has been particularly aggressive in requiring that both universities and individual researchers give careful attention to ethical concerns. SSHRC also insists that researchers address the social relevance of proposed research. While grant applications are not assessed exclusively on the basis of social relevance, and funding basic research is part of SSHRC's mandate, social relevance remains an important factor in the funding formulas.

PROTECTING RESEARCH SUBJECTS AND RESPONDENTS

The ethical guidelines governing social science research throw up three interconnected lines of defence around research subjects and respondents: confidentiality, informed consent, and the right to withdraw. We will examine these in turn.

Generally speaking, the assurance of respondent *confidentiality* is a routine aspect of social science research. In survey research, for instance, confidentiality is assured primarily through *anonymity*; respondents' names, addresses, or phone numbers are virtually never part of the data record. Although researchers are interested in the characteristics of their respondents—their age, sex, regional location, income, etc.—they have no interest in their specific identification. It may be very important to know that the research subject is a single white female working at a part-time job and living in metropolitan Toronto, but it is not important to know her name, phone number, address, or SIN. These would only come into play in the initial selection of the sample or if a survey supervisor wanted to telephone respondents to ensure that the interview had actually been conducted and had not been fabricated by a member of the research staff or employee of the data collection firm. We find, then, that names are collected at the time of the interview, if then, only to enable the researcher to ascertain that the interview was, in fact, completed. Names are stripped from the survey as soon as authenticity is confirmed. Only in panel studies will names be kept as part of the record, and even here the information is coded so that specific identifiers can be isolated from the primary data set that will eventually enter the public realm. "John Smith" becomes "case 1383" before any data are released.

In elite interviewing (discussed in Chapter 5), the identity of respondents is a more contentious issue. An interview with a deputy minister in the federal government takes on additional weight because the opinions expressed are expressed by a deputy minister. If anonymity is respected, the interview material becomes less useful. The upshot of this is that the protection of anonymity for individuals holding public office is not required *if* the individual agrees to an on-the-record interview and *if* that agreement is conveyed through signed consent that explicitly waives anonymity. In the event that such consent is not provided, the

A POINT ON THE COMPASS ———————————

Anonymity and Confidentiality

Social science researchers are obligated to protect both anonymity and confidentiality. As Neuman (1997, 452–3) explains, the two are not the same thing:

> *Anonymity* means that subjects remain anonymous or nameless.... *Confidentiality* means that information may have names attached to it, but the researcher holds it in confidence or keeps it secret from the public.... A researcher may provide anonymity without confidentiality, or vice versa, although they usually go together. Anonymity without confidentiality means that all details about a specific individual are made public, but the individual's name is withheld. Confidentiality without anonymity means that information is not made public, but a researcher privately links individual names to specific responses.

researcher has little alternative but to fall back on descriptions like "a senior public servant said . . ." or "an unnamed but senior Liberal party strategist revealed. . . ." Even then, the researcher must be careful that the description provided does not inadvertently reveal the individual's true identity. A published report that described an interviewee as a "greying deputy minister with a decided limp and sinister goatee" would not protect the interviewee's anonymity.

In many cases, research topics will not place subjects at risk and therefore may not bring questions of anonymity and confidentiality into bold relief. For example, imagine a conventional public opinion survey in which 1,000 randomly selected respondents are asked to identify "the most serious issue facing Canada today." If by chance it was disclosed that one of the respondents was Ms. Irene Brown of 115 Bonavista Crescent in Regina and that she had identified unemployment as the most serious problem, it is unlikely that this disclosure would place Ms. Brown at serious risk. Embarrassment, perhaps, but not risk, and even embarrassment would be unlikely unless the survey addressed some aspects of personal behaviour or opinion on sensitive topics. Indeed, it is difficult to imagine to whom such information might be disclosed; there is no ready media or commercial market for the identity of respondents to national surveys. However, if the survey focus was more localized, and if, therefore, there was a chance that the researchers might know the respondents, then breaches of anonymity and confidentiality become more serious. This is particularly so if the research touches on topics with greater sensitivity than "the most serious issue facing Canada today." Imagine, for instance, research in which participants in an AIDS treatment program or a program designed to control spousal abuse were being questioned about their satisfaction with the program. In this case, the inadvertent release of a participant's name could have a serious impact on that individual's employment, community status, and personal relations.

The protection of confidentiality is often woven into broader procedures designed to ensure *informed consent*. Simply put, this means that potential participants (or, in the case of minors, their legal representatives) should be fully informed *in writing* of the nature of the research project, the identity of the researchers, the potential use of the research findings, and any risks to which participants might be exposed. Potential respondents or subjects should also be advised that they are under no obligation to participate in the research project; there must be no "force, fraud, deceit, duress, or other forms of constraint or coercion" (Liemohn 1979, 159; cited in Chadwick et al. 1984, 19). Willingness to participate is conveyed by signing the informed consent form, thus signifying that the participant is proceeding with a full understanding of the research project and any risks that might attend the project. The signed consent form is kept on record as evidence that participants in the research project were, in fact, participating under conditions of informed consent and without coercion.

At times, signed informed consent forms can be problematic. For instance, they are impossible to use in telephone interviews, particularly when respondents are also being assured that their anonymity is being fully protected. Researchers must therefore fall back on an oral statement along the lines described above and upon oral and therefore undocumented consent. It is assumed that the respondent's decision to continue with the interview rather than hanging up is implicit evidence of consent, but not necessarily fully *informed* consent. Many of the same considerations come into play with mailed questionnaires, which are generally returned in a way that does not identify the respondent. Anonymity is thereby protected, but a signed consent form is precluded. Here again, the respondent's willingness to return the completed questionnaire, rather than throwing it away, is taken as evidence of consent. The issue that remains is whether the consent was informed consent.

Informed consent means explaining the nature of the research to potential participants. However, there are limits to that explanation; if

A POINT ON THE COMPASS

Informed Consent and Response Rates

Some researchers may fear that elaborate informed consent procedures will adversely affect response rates in survey research. Potential respondents, it is thought, are more easily retained if the researcher moves quickly to the "meat" of the survey. Conversely, it can be argued that informed consent may positively affect response rates by reassuring potential respondents about confidentiality, anonymity, and the legitimacy of the research project.

The empirical evidence in this regard is at best quizzical. Eleanor Singer (1978) conducted a study of the impact of various informed consent procedures on response rates with an American national probability sample of 2,084 potential respondents. She found that the amount of information provided about the survey to potential respondents had no impact on survey response rates. Variability in the assurance of confidentiality (some respondents were assured of complete confidentiality, while the matter was not even mentioned to others) had no impact on response rates to the survey, although an assurance of confidentiality increased *item response rates* to questions dealing with sensitive issues or personal behaviour. Finally, she found that a request that potential respondents sign an informed consent form reduced the response rate to the survey; 71% of those not asked for a signature completed the survey, compared to 64% who were asked for a signature before the interview and 65% who were told they would be asked for a signature after the interview.

participants are informed about the specific research hypotheses, their behaviour may be affected as a consequence. For example, a research project may be interested in the relationship between partisanship and support for environmental protection and may therefore include questions on both topics in a mailed questionnaire or telephone survey. If respondents know that the relationship between the two is of particular interest to the researcher, they may modify their answers to the environmental questions in order to ensure that their own party is portrayed in the best possible light. As Allan Kimmel (1988, 76) observes:

Few researchers feel that we can do entirely without deception, since the adoption of an overly conservative approach could deem the study of important research areas hardly worthy of the effort. For instance, a study of racial prejudice accurately labeled as such would certainly affect subjects' behavior. Deception studies differ so greatly in the nature and degree of deception that even the harshest critic would be hard pressed to state unequivocally that all deception has potentially harmful effects or is otherwise wrong.

A POINT ON THE COMPASS

Confidentiality and the Internet

Survey work conducted through the Internet confronts conventional ethical considerations and opens up new ethical terrain.

A questionnaire sent out to potential respondents via the Internet faces the same informed consent dilemma that mailed and telephone surveys confront: it is impossible to document consent without forcing the respondent to reveal his or her name, thereby abandoning anonymity. Moreover, one cannot "sign off" over the Internet. Problems of anonymity and confidentiality are further compounded by the nature of e-mail responses. In an Internet survey of western Canadian university students conducted by Carey Hill for her M.A. thesis in political science at the University of Calgary (1998), potential respondents were asked to respond through the conventional reply cues on e-mail systems. However, the electronic replies invariably included an identification tag for the sender, a tag giving the sender's e-mail address and therefore university location. Respondents were assured that the tag would be removed from the questionnaire once it had been downloaded and printed, but respondents had no option but to rely on Ms. Hill's ethical standards. They could not remove the identification tag themselves. It should be noted that Ms. Hill also informed potential respondents of the potential risk. If the risk of breached confidentiality was deemed to be serious, individuals receiving the questionnaire through the Internet could simply not reply.

Informed consent on surveys is often framed in a very bland or abstract fashion: "We are interested in determining public opinion toward a number of current public policy issues, and to that end we would like to ask you a few questions." More specific information about the research hypotheses, information that would distort the data collection exercise, is not included. The rather insipid information provided by such an informed consent statement, which Singer (1983, 185) describes as a "deceit" condition, is justified in part by the rationale that the risks to respondents from a generalized survey instrument are minimal and in part by the assumption that the identification of specific research hypotheses would be of little additional use to potential participants trying to assess the risks of participation.

In this context it is worth mentioning the ethical problems that arise in providing informed consent for *covert participant observation*. This technique, which is discussed in more detail in Chapter 5, entails the researcher working within a group or institution without the members of the group or institution being aware that the researcher is there *as a researcher* and that her observations will be used later in published research findings. In some cases, covert participant observation is the only possible research approach for target populations. As Lee (1993, 143) explains, covert participant observation avoids problems of reactivity: "Because they do not know they are being studied, research participants are not threatened by the research and do not change their behaviour even though to outside eyes it may be considered deviant." However, the ethical problems associated with covert observation are so great that it is seldom used by academic researchers. It is difficult to construct a defensible argument for lying to or misleading people in the interests of social science research. In the context of the present discussion, the point to emphasize is that covert participant observation negates the principle of informed consent (Lee 1993, 143); subjects are not only uninformed about the research, but cannot give their consent. At the same time, it should be recognized that in many cases participant observation only becomes apparent after the fact. A researcher, for instance, may work within a political party or community group *as a citizen* and only later realize that the participation can be blended into subsequent research programs, theoretical explorations, or teaching anecdotes. In such cases, the opportunity for informed consent has passed; the researcher is simply drawing upon life experiences.

The third line of defence for research subjects is the *right to withdraw* from the research exercise at any time. This, of course, is an option that cannot be extended to subjects in covert participant observation,

CHECKING YOUR BEARINGS

DISCUSSION OF SIGNED STUDENT TEACHING EVALUATIONS

Most universities provide a mechanism by which students are able to assess faculty teaching. If student assessments are to be of assistance in improving teaching, it is imperative that they be returned at some point and in some form to faculty members. What is less clear, however, is whether such assessments should be anonymous or signed.

The argument for anonymity hinges on the assumption that students are under some degree of risk, that they might face retaliation by faculty members who were negatively assessed. Such retaliation could be manifest through grading in subsequent courses, negative letters of reference, or rumourmongering. Anonymity reduces the risks to which students are exposed by participating in teaching evaluations. There is a chance, more-over, that in the absence of anonymity students might inflate their assessments of faculty teaching in order to minimize the risk of retaliation.

However, the argument can also be made that anonymity strips students of any responsibility for their actions. Students, in short, could strike out at instructors through the teaching assess-ments and could do so with impunity and for reasons unrelated to teaching performance itself. There would be no check, for instance, on negative assessments driven by personal malice, sexism, or racism. One possible consequence would be that anonymous assessments might be more negative on balance than would be signed assessments.

What do you think? Should the primary concern be to protect the student by using an anonymous instrument? Or should equal concern be placed on protecting instructors by forcing students to take responsibility for their assessments? Is there a middle ground?

which is just one more ethical problem that this research strategy encounters. It should also be noted that the right to withdraw may not be easy to exercise. Note, for example, a 1978 letter to the *American Sociologist* cited by Robert Broadhead (1984, 121). The letter was written by a senior university administrator who had been interviewed by a graduate student:

In spite of the fact that I was very annoyed at being taped without my permission as well as by the questions and felt increasingly defensive and put down, I did not attempt to terminate the interview. Afterwards I realized how difficult it was to cut off an interview while it is in process. It caused me to reflect on the coerciveness of the interview situation. If as an agency administrator I did not feel free to terminate an interview with a graduate student, it must be almost impossible for the typical subject being interviewed by a "social scientist" to do so when the perceived status differences are reversed.

It can be difficult to hang up on someone or to ask an interviewer to leave your house or office. It could be equally difficult for students in a classroom to withdraw from a study being conducted by the course instructor. Thus, although informed consent statements should always include the right to withdraw at any time, this right may not be as effective a means of protection as we often assume. When the right to withdraw is extended, everything must be done to make it possible for participants to exercise that right should they choose to do so.

ETHICAL CONSIDERATIONS IN RESEARCH DESIGN

As we have already discussed, research projects should be designed with a close eye to matters of informed consent, confidentiality, and the protection of anonymity. It is also important that research projects be constrained by the requirements of theory or policy analysis. Even informed consent does not give researchers a blank cheque with respect to the violation of privacy; we should only ask what we need to ask. As Neuman (1997, 445) explains:

Ethical research requires balancing the value of advancing knowledge against the value of noninterference in the lives of others. Giving research subjects absolute rights of noninterference could make empirical research impossible, but giving researchers absolute rights of inquiry could nullify subjects' basic human rights. The moral question becomes: When, if ever, are researchers justified in risking physical harm or injury to those being studied, causing them great embarrassment, or frightening them?

In matters of questionnaire design, this means restricting oneself to questions that can be justified by the theoretical underpinnings of the study. It is important not to ask respondents a barrage of questions just in the hope that something interesting might later emerge from the data analysis. Such fishing expeditions strain the boundaries of ethical behaviour. If, for example, survey respondents are to be asked about their family income or church attendance, there should be a reason for doing so, and a reason that extends beyond "most surveys always ask such questions." In particular, questions that pry into the private lives of respondents, or that may potentially embarrass respondents, must only be asked if there is a compelling research reason to do so. Even then, every effort should be made to avoid embarrassment and to avoid a situation in which the social pressure of the interview situation compels respondents to reveal information or preferences that they would rather not reveal. Here it is not enough to simply assume that respondents are under no compulsion to answer and that if they do so then no harm has been done. There are very real social pressures at work. It should also be noted that interviews that intrude on sensitive matters without a valid justification may generate questionable data. The fact that respondents answer does not mean that they answer truthfully. Therefore, close attention to ethical parameters may yield better research instruments.

Some would argue that survey research itself may be an inappropriate research strategy. Ann Oakley, for example (cited in Finch 1984, 72), criticizes survey research on two grounds: first, for imposing a hierarchical relationship between interviewer and interviewee and second, for objectifying women. Oakley not only maintains that survey research will fail to produce good sociological work on women; she also objects to the technique on the basis of feminist ethics.

Research designs should be respectful of participants' privacy and time. As Allan Kimmel (1988, 139) recommends, "Research subjects should be considered as another 'granting institution,' granting us their valuable time in return for our generation of valuable scientific knowledge." Research that is not designed with adequate attention to ethical considerations may yield poor data, particularly if participants are trapped in an uncomfortable situation. Failure to pay due regard to ethical concerns may also "poison the well" for future researchers, which is why sales promotions beginning with the claim that "we are conducting a survey to determine ..." are so anathema to social scientists. Research participants who are once bitten will be twice shy.

ETHICAL CONSIDERATIONS IN DATA ANALYSIS

In most cases, ethical issues arise before the data analysis begins or after the data analysis has been completed and the researcher is considering how best, or even if, to disseminate the research findings. However, data analysis itself is not totally immune from ethical considerations. In Chapter 10 we will be discussing the choice of *confidence levels* and therefore the risks of making different kinds of errors. As will be seen, our tolerance for different kinds of errors is not without ethical implications if the research is addressing public policy issues. As Kenneth Bailey (1978, 381) notes, researchers can act unethically "by revealing only part of the facts, presenting the facts out of context, falsifying findings, or offering misleading presentations...."

A relatively minor but still interesting issue arises with respect to interview transcripts. When extracts from recorded interviews are used in published research findings, assuming of course that the respondent has given written permission for the taped material to be used in this way, the researcher must decide how faithful she will be to the transcript. The problem is that people's spoken language is quite different from written text. In speech, and thus in transcripts, people often use incomplete sentences, strangely constructed sentences, and odd grammatical configurations, all of which may be perfectly understandable within the context of speech, where the listener has access to visual cues, tone, and emphasis. However, if the spoken words are converted directly to written text, the respondent can appear to be illiterate, bumbling, and incoherent. There is, then, an almost irresistible compulsion to clean up the transcript, to transform the irregularities of the spoken word into more polished written text. But to do so is to alter the data and to change not only the form, but perhaps the nuanced meaning of the spoken word.

There is an established convention of asking respondents to review quotations before publication. This ensures that the quote corresponds with the interviewee's meaning. However, it also opens up the possibility that the interviewee will change his or her mind and, therefore, that the quote eventually used does not correspond with the quote given at the interview itself.

Janet Finch draws our attention to another issue, and that is the possibility that the data analysis may be used against the interests of the group from which respondents were drawn. The concern in her case arises initially from interviews with women and with the "exploitative potential in the easily established trust between women, which makes women especially vulnerable as subjects of research" (1984, 81). Finch then goes on to discuss problems in protecting the *collective* interests of women, protection that cannot be provided by protecting the anonymity or confidentiality of particular women who might participate in a research project. Indeed, Finch raises the possibility of *betrayal*:

> I do not really mean "betrayal" in the individual sense, such as selling the story of someone else's life to a Sunday newspaper. I mean, rather, "betrayal" in an indirect and collective sense, that is, undermining the interests of women in general by my use of the material given to me by my interviewees. It is betrayal none the less, because the basis upon which the information has been given is the trust placed in one woman by another.

Even if the researcher is able to avoid the betrayal that Finch identifies, there is no guarantee that the research material will not be used by others in a way that is contrary to the collective interests of women. The point, then, is that ethical considerations cannot be confined to the mechanics of data collection and analysis and cannot be addressed solely by protecting the interests of research participants.

ETHICS AND COLLEGIALITY

Many of the ethical considerations that are important to the social sciences have less to do with the relationship between researcher and research subject than with relationships *within* the research communities. Ethical considerations extend to how we use the work of others, how we recognize the contributions of others, and how we report research findings.

Students first confront this ethical domain when they learn about the perils of *plagiarism*. It is unethical to take credit for the work, wording, or ideas of others as if they were your own. It is essential, therefore, to acknowledge our sources. If this is not done, then the scientific enterprise is also thrown into risk, for there is no way to trace the evolution of ideas and evidence. Plagiarism is a serious offence within universities and within the broader social science community.

The avoidance of plagiarism is best seen as a minimal condition of ethical behaviour. The respect shown for one's colleagues should go beyond acknowledging the use of their work and ideas. It should extend to fostering a cooperative research environment where ideas and data are shared openly and quickly, where methodologies are fully transparent, and where current research is effectively connected to the work that has gone before.

A POINT ON THE COMPASS ─────────────────

Integrity in Research and Scholarship

The Medical Research Council of Canada (MRC), the Natural Sciences and Engineering Research Council of Canada (NSERC), and the Social Sciences and Humanities Research Council of Canada (SSHRC) have issued a tripartite policy statement on research integrity. The core of this statement addressed the appropriate ethical considerations to be addressed within the research community and among researchers. Five basic principles are identified by the councils:

- "recognizing the substantive contributions of collaborators and students; using unpublished work of other researchers and scholars only with permission and due acknowledgment; and using archival material in accordance with the rules of the archival source;

- "obtaining the permission of the author before using new information, concepts or data originally obtained through access to confidential manuscripts or applications for funds for research or training that may have been seen as a result of processes such as peer review;

- "using scholarly and scientific rigor and intensity in obtaining, recording and analyzing data, and in reporting and publishing results;

- "ensuring that authorship of published work includes all those who have materially contributed to, and share responsibility for, the contents of publications, and only those people; and

- "revealing to sponsors, universities, journals or funding agencies, any material conflict of interest, financial or other, that might influence their decisions on whether the individual should be asked to review manuscripts or applications, test products or be permitted to undertake work sponsored from outside sources."

Source: MRC, NSERC, and SSHRC, *Integrity in Research and Scholarship: A Tri-Council Policy Statement* (January 1994).

ETHICAL CONSIDERATIONS IN THE PUBLICATION OF RESEARCH FINDINGS

Much of the research done in the social sciences is applied research; the intent is not only to map and understand social reality, but also to shape that reality. As Donald Warwick and Thomas Pettigrew (1983, 335) explain:

> Front-page newspaper headlines about economic indicators, voting analyses, national scores on school achievement tests, and a myriad of other topics tell the story. Social science is now taken seriously in public policy. No longer are social science findings and theories of great interest only to those in the discipline. Such work now has *the potential to affect the lives of citizens.* [Emphasis added]

As a consequence, the publication of social science research and the injection of that research into public policy debate bring us face to face with ethical concerns. The argument that empirical research is normatively neutral provides at best a weak defence against ethical considerations, particularly when it is remembered that once the research is in the public domain, it can be used for quite different purposes than originally intended.

The intensity of ethical debate may depend upon the form through which research findings are disseminated. The most common form of dissemination for academic research is through scholarly publications such as the *Canadian Journal of Political Science* or *Canadian Public Policy.* However, dissemination can also take place through the popular press, and indeed the argument can be made that social scientists have an obligation for broad public dissemination. Helen Roberts (1984, 210–11), for example, argues that a strategy of broad dissemination helps fulfil the responsibility to inform respondents about the research findings, increases the general credibility of the social sciences, and increases the impact of research findings on political elites and public policy audiences. At the same time, dissemination through the press often strips away the subtle interpretation that is so important to scholarly inquiry. Issues that are not black-and-white are portrayed that way, because the academic's fascination with endless shades of grey is not shared by journalists and those who write the headlines. There is, then, an unavoidable risk that popular dissemination will distort the research findings. There is also an unavoidable risk that the findings will be used for political and social ends with which the researcher does not approve.

However, lack of dissemination means that the research is not subjected to critical review by other researchers in the field.

One of the more commonplace ethical considerations that arises from the dissemination of survey research findings is their potential impact on social behaviour. Here, the most prominent example comes from preelection surveys, which might credibly be thought to influence voter behaviour. To take a recent illustration, polls conducted prior to the 1997 Alberta election, polls conducted by media outlets, professional polling firms, academic institutions, and individual academics, indicated that the Progressive Conservative government would be reelected, and reelected in a landslide. Now, it is not unreasonable to assume that such poll results might have influenced voter behaviour and perhaps in a way that reinforced the poll results. The question, then, is whether the results should have been released, given the research findings were both describing and shaping electoral realities.

Concern over the impact of surveys on electoral behaviour has led to some legislative constraints. In Canada, for example, it is illegal to publish survey findings within 48 hours of the onset of a federal election. What remains unclear, however, is the *direction* of survey effects. Our ethical concerns may depend upon whether we believe that surveys lead to a *bandwagon* effect, whereby undecided voters opt to support whatever party is placed in the lead by the polls, or an *underdog* effect, whereby voters opt to rally behind the losing side. Somewhat ironically, survey research has failed to provide conclusive evidence of either effect, leading to the comforting belief that maybe the effects cancel out.

It is important that published research provide sufficient methodological information about such things as sampling procedures, the nature and size of the sample, the source of funding, and the wording of specific questions. If this information is not provided, it is difficult to have any confidence in the findings, nor is replication possible. Ideally, the research data themselves—data sets, questionnaires, code books, field notes—will be available to other researchers for secondary analysis. Data that are not released into the public domain within a reasonable period of time can become suspect. It should be noted, however, that the failure to release data can often be traced to a variety of factors that have nothing to do with an attempt to conceal information. The researcher may have been slower with his own analysis than anticipated, may lack the funds to clear up the data for release, or may simply have become overcome with other work.

One of the more difficult problems encountered in the social sciences has to do with the publication of negative findings. It is relatively rare, for example, to see studies of regionalism in Canada that conclude that regionalism has no effect on political values and behaviours, or studies of gender politics that show that gender has no impact. Negative findings lack the appeal of positive findings; they are like a story in the morning paper saying that nothing happened yesterday. It is not the stuff from which headlines are made. Yet as Marie Jahoda points out (1981, 211), if negative findings are not published, we may "accept theories on the strength of one statistically significant divergence from the null hypothesis."

At times the dissemination of research findings may be constrained by prior commitments relating to confidentiality. If, for example, access to particular informants has been secured only through the promise that identities and some forms of information not be revealed, then the researcher may be unable to publish exciting findings.

CHECKING YOUR BEARINGS

DISCLOSURE OF RESEARCH FINDINGS

Imagine you are taking an undergraduate course on sociobiology. Everyone in the class has been asked to undertake a specific research topic and to report back through a class presentation. Your research project involves looking at instances of rape in the animal world. After reviewing a reasonable slice of the published research material, you conclude that rape is a "natural act." (Whether the research in the field supports such a conclusion is not at issue here.) Are there ethical considerations that should be brought into play in presenting this finding to the class? Can a case be made that you should not report the findings? Is there any likelihood that the research findings might affect the behaviour of students in the class? That it might heighten perceptions of risk?

CONCLUSIONS

In bringing this chapter's discussion to a close, it should be stressed that ethical guidelines for social science research are now more than normative, although the normative codes of ethical behaviour that have been adopted by most professional associations are certainly important. Ethical guidelines are generally embodied in specific institutional documents and policed by ethics review committees. It is therefore imperative that researchers of all types, including students building "field work" into term papers and honours theses, know their institution's policies and procedures. "Behaving ethically" is no longer simply a matter of principled behaviour on the part of the researcher, although it is that above all else. It is also a matter of meeting clearly specified institutional requirements that generally entail some form of external review. Given the very serious consequences that can follow from a failure to observe ethical guidelines and the accompanying procedures, it is imperative that researchers familiarize themselves with the institutional environment. When in doubt, ask. If still in doubt, ask again.

This chapter has not identified all of the ethical issues and concerns that political scientists are likely to encounter as they go about their work; we have tried only to highlight a number of particularly important concerns. Our intent throughout has been to bring into focus the people behind the numbers. It should also be noted in conclusion that ethical guidelines are not meant to muzzle the engagement of political scientists in public policy debate. As Warwick and Pettigrew (1983, 356–7) remind us, "policy researchers, like other citizens, have every right to express their policy opinions." At the same time, there is a need to separate the roles of policy advocate and social scientist, to distinguish between empirical research and the normative conclusions one might draw from that research and wish to inject into the political arena.

WORKING AS A TEAM

1. Virtually all universities and colleges have formal ethical guidelines in place for social science research. Find copies of the relevant guidelines for your own institution and discuss their coverage. Do the guidelines seem relevant to political science research? Are there concerns that are not addressed by the guidelines or that are addressed inappropriately in the context of political science research?

SELF-STUDY

1. Imagine that a political debate has erupted within your community over levels of immigration and what contributions immigrants make to Canadian society. A group to which you belong supports increased levels of immigration and is determined to show that opposition to immigration is a minority

opinion within the community. You are commissioned to do a survey of community opinion and find, to your surprise and distress, that the majority of respondents oppose increased levels of immigration. Unfortunately, the press has learned that the survey took place and is pressing you for the results. What are the ethical issues involved in releasing or not releasing the survey findings?

2. Remember the case of Dolly, the lamb, where Scottish researchers were able to clone sheep? What if researchers in the near future develop the technology to clone humans? Should they be allowed to proceed, at least to the point of testing the technology? And who should make this decision? Should it be the scientists themselves? Their employers? The government?

PART 2

LINKING THEORY TO RESEARCH

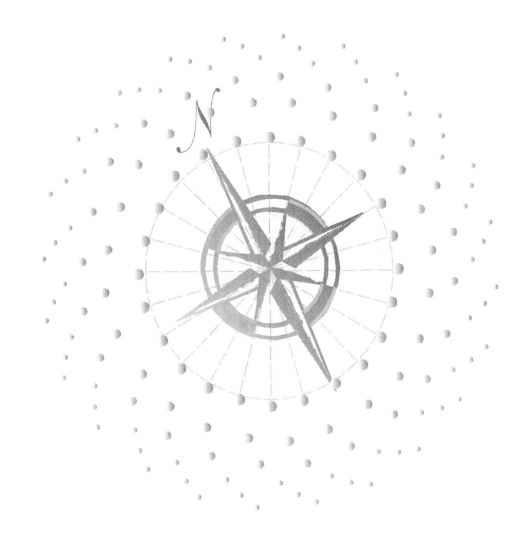

CHAPTER 4

Observing the Political World: Quantitative Approaches

DESTINATION

By the end of this chapter the reader should

- be aware of the variety of quantitative techniques through which social scientists view the political world;
- have an understanding of the basic tools of the craft and an appreciation of how they are used in practice;
- appreciate the parallels between the casual ways in which we all view the political world and the more systematic methods used by social scientists.

We are all observers of the political world. Even if our interest in politics is very limited, if we would rather face a root canal than attend a political meeting or sit through a political speech, the fact remains that things political sweep through our lives. Politicians and events such as elections have a high media profile, and our lives are touched by a multitude of public policies. When we confront growing numbers of students in our classes, pay our income tax or the GST, visit a national park or use public highways, we are rubbing up against the political world. Public policies have an impact on such personal aspects as reproductive technologies, the food we eat, where we smoke, and the medications available to us. And, of course, politics can at times be a matter of life and death. Therefore, we cannot help but be observers of the political world even if our observations are marked by cynicism and suspicion.

Our observations begin as children as we try to make some sense out of the world around us. Initially, we assume that everyone is like us, that we are the prototype from which the social world has been constructed. Others, we anticipate, will share similar emotions, values, and expectations. As we mature, we learn to our delight and sometimes annoyance that this is not the case, that we cannot confidently project our beliefs and preferences onto those around us. We begin to realize that the world is composed of idiosyncratic individuals shaped by backgrounds and circumstances different from our own. However, while we come to appreciate the infinite variety of the human experience, we also come to realize that we cannot afford to treat every individual and every circumstance as unique. To get by, we need a rough-and-ready set of categories, stereotypes, and *generalizations*: "parents exaggerate, teachers do not understand us, politicians lie." When we meet new people and encounter new situations, we tend to slot them into existing categories. As we go along we may change these categories if there are compelling reasons to do so, but as we get older the ways in which we think about the world may become increasingly resistant to change.

In other words, we have no choice but to impose some rough conceptual order on the world around us in order to bring infinite social diversity under some workable control. We hope that the order we impose corresponds to reality, that the way in which we see the world is in fact the way the world is, and thus we search constantly for confirmation. As we talk to others, read, and watch television, we go through an informal reality check. Is the world unfolding as we thought it would, or are some of our operating assumptions flawed? How well do our rough-and-ready generalizations capture the social complexity we confront? If the world is not unfolding as we expect it should, how can we explain the discrepancies?

But what does this have to do with political science and, more specifically, with empirical research methods in political science? Simply put, empirical methodologies allow us to see the political world more clearly and to place our own biases and limitations under some reasonable measure of control. They provide us with means of expanding our field of vision by bringing into play evidence and insights that we might otherwise miss. In this sense, the methods explored in this book are not very different *conceptually* from those we use for more informal observations of the social and political worlds. However, they impose greater order, precision, and reliability and thereby allow us to attach "science" to the study of politics. This chapter is designed, therefore, to introduce some of the quantitative methods political scientists use to explore the political world and to highlight the conceptual and analytical linkages to the ways in which we all try to make sense out of the world around us. The chapter provides a *strategic overview* of the more detailed material covered in later chapters.

Students of politics have a rich and diverse array of research methods at their disposal as they embark upon an exploration of the political world. Many of these are very informal, the kinds of things we all do every day. Much of our political understanding, for example, comes from nothing more than reading the paper, watching the news, and talking to friends. A column in *The Globe and Mail* by Andrew Coyne or Jeffrey Simpson, for instance, or one in *Maclean's* by Barbara Amiel or Diane Francis can provide useful insight for politicians, political scientists, and voters. We rely, in short, on the observations of others who have more direct or immediate access to the political world, people who can give us the "inside scoop," the behind-the-scenes story. However, relying on such informal means has a serious limitation in that our personal vantage points are always limited to a degree. The people with whom we interact are likely to be similar to us in many ways: they will often be of a similar age, occupational profile, social class, and even gender or race. They will generally come from the same region of the country, speak the same language, and come from the same corner of the

CHECKING YOUR BEARINGS

VANTAGE POINTS ON THE POLITICAL WORLD

Stop for a moment and think about where you find most of your political information. Who are the people who are the most important sources of information, and whom do you tend to discount or ignore? What media sources do you pay particular attention to? Are there particular columnists or journalists whom you trust or distrust? Are there some papers or magazines that strike you as more authoritative than others?

Now, do these various sources of information come at the political world from similar or dissimilar perspectives? To what extent are you exposed to a wide diversity of political viewpoints? Or to what extent do the various sources provide only nuanced variations of the same perspective? Do your sources of information provide you with fresh information on the important issues of the day, or do they reiterate the same point of view?

In many cases, we pay particular attention to sources of information that see the world from a similar perspective to our own, and thus we seek or at least find confirmation for our own views, values, and beliefs. It is often difficult and even disquieting to escape the limitations of our own culture, social class, generation, or gender. And yet, if we fail to do so, then our understanding of the political world will be incomplete; it will be hemmed in by the inevitable limits of our own lives.

world, although travel and the Internet allow us to expand the geographical reach of our political observations. In an important sense, we are trapped within our own skin, region, language, and country; thus, our political vantage point is limited.

Research methodologies enable us to reach beyond informal means of political observation. They also enable us to observe the political world in a more systematic way and to convey those observations to others who will accept them as more than personal insights. Empirical methodologies are therefore particularly important for younger scholars who do not have well-established reputations to fall back on, whose word alone is not taken as authoritative. In a similar sense, they are particularly important for new entrants into any aspect of the work world who need to buttress their own interpretations of the world with "hard evidence." Although such evidence does not replace reputation and cannot stand alone without thoughtful argumentation, it has an important role to play in political and social discourse.

If we accept the value of empirical research methodologies, this acceptance does not determine *which* methodologies to employ. Political scientists, and observers of the political world more broadly defined, have a large number of options at their disposal. In the discussion to follow we will highlight some of the available quantitative options and set the stage for the subsequent examination of their more detailed application and statistical properties.

CONSIDERING RESEARCH METHODOLOGIES

When selecting a particular methodology, the researcher has to ask herself a number of questions. What are the goals of the study? How valid is each methodology? And how feasible will the proposed study be? By asking these questions, the researcher can limit the number of (inevitable) research problems that will arise and can ensure a greater degree of confidence in her final conclusions.

Research projects vary in their goals. Some projects attempt to tackle a new subject area in order to promote inductive theory or to provide the descriptive facts necessary for applied research. Others seek to explain why events occurred, what caused their appearance, and so on. There are six basic types of questions we can ask: who, what, where, when, why, and how. "What" questions usually fall into the category of **exploratory research**; the researcher merely wishes to get an idea of what is happening in an unexplored aspect of the political world (Neuman 1994, 18). Exploratory research often benefits from qualitative methodologies, which allow the researcher the greatest insights into group dynamics and individual motivations. **Descriptive research** addresses questions of "where," "how," "when," and "who." We use descriptive research to get an accurate account of a situation; thus, it is often useful for applied research, such as policy studies. Survey research, observation methods, content analysis, and comparative research can all be used effectively for descriptive research projects (Neuman 1994, 19). Exploratory and descriptive research provide the basis for **explanatory research**, which addresses the question "why." Explanatory research focuses on questions of causality, and experiments are the ideal method for this type of research.

After determining the goals of her study, the researcher must then ask, "How valid is my research design?" **Validity**, in this sense, refers to how useful our design is in advancing the knowledge we are trying to obtain. There are two forms of validity that we need to be concerned with when considering research design: internal validity and external validity. **Internal validity** concerns the validity within the study: Are we measuring what we believe we are measuring? Are our conclusions supported by the facts of our study? Have we ruled out alternative explanations and spurious relationships? Internal validity can vary with the degree to which we can control our study. If we are able to hold conditions constant, we can rule out alternative factors, and thus our conclusions are more likely to be supported. In such a case, we have high internal validity. If, on the other hand, there are many factors that we cannot control and therefore many alternative explanations that may compete with our conclusions, we have low internal validity. In a nutshell, low internal validity means that we have less confidence in our conclusions about the study, whereas high internal validity means that we have a strong degree of confidence.

Note that with internal validity, we are concerned with the validity of the study itself. Questions of **external validity** are concerned with the legitimacy of generalizations made from the study. Was the study representative, or was it a "rogue" or "fluke" study, a one-in-a-million occurrence? Can our study allow us to make generalizations about the "real world," or are the conclusions applicable only to the single study? When conducting theory-oriented research, we desire high external validity, since we wish to use the studies to make generalizations about the larger political world. Quite often there are tradeoffs between internal and external validity. The more "realistic" one's study is, the greater the external validity. However, as realism increases, the researcher's level of control over the study decreases, thus reducing internal validity. How the researcher addresses such dilemmas will depend upon her research objectives.

A POINT ON THE COMPASS

The Validity of IQ Tests

IQ (intelligence quotient) tests have long been used to predict not only academic performance but also performance in the broader social and economic worlds. It has been assumed that the tests are independent of academic training, that they measure some innate ability (or lack thereof) rather than the quantity or quality of individuals' formal education. However, research by New Zealand academic James R. Flynn suggests that IQ measures may be far more reflective of environmental circumstance than we have come to believe (Ambrose 1996, D1):

> [The Flynn effect shows] that IQ scores in industrialized nations have shot skyward in recent decades. If intelligence were strictly innate as many psychologists have contended, a rise of this magnitude wouldn't be possible. Geneticists concur on that much, and one conceivable conclusion of this is that people are being made dramatically smarter by environmental factors. That would mean that IQ tests primarily indicate intellectual development at a given moment ... and not a predetermined learning ability. Or possibly people are only getting better at taking the tests and not in the scope and creativity of their intellects, which is a way of saying IQ test results should be viewed as meaningless.

> In short, the *validity* of IQ tests has been cast into doubt.

Source: Jay Ambrose, "We're Smart Enough to Know How Dumb IQ Tests Are," *The Globe and Mail,* 3 August 1996, p. D1.

A final factor to consider is **feasibility**. The fact of the matter is that not all research projects are possible, despite our best intentions or level of interest in the topic. Resources—time, money, personnel, equipment—are always scarce in the researcher's life. Some populations are difficult to access, making research near-impossible and at times dangerous. Some research involves ethical dilemmas that cannot be resolved easily. When selecting a research method, the researcher must be practical; although in theory one approach may be optimal for the study, the reality may be that the research is only feasible if another approach is taken. In research, as in the rest of life, there are often gaps between what we want to do and what we can actually do.

Having outlined these issues for your consideration, we will now explore a variety of quantitative research approaches. In the next chapter we will turn to qualitative approaches, which are less dependent upon the collection of data that is amenable to statistical analysis. The reader should note, however, that many of the specific research approaches discussed in the two chapters can accommodate both quantitative and qualitative methodologies. Case studies and interviews provide only two examples.

EXPERIMENTAL RESEARCH

For most people, the notion of science is associated with **experimental research**. When we think of the ideal for experimental research, it comes from the medical field and the *double-blind experiment*. For example, a researcher may select a set of subjects to participate in a study of a new drug designed to combat hypertension. The drug is the independent variable, and the health of the research subject is the dependent variable. The subjects are randomly divided into two groups: the **treatment group**, which will receive the new drug, and the **control group**, which will receive a placebo that looks like and is administered in exactly the same way as the drug, but which has no medical effect (the proverbial sugar pill). The research is double-blind in that neither the subjects nor the researchers administering and monitoring the experiment know who is receiving the drug and who is receiving the placebo. All subjects participate in a pretest, which notes the pretreatment levels of the dependent variable. Then, once the treatment has run its course, the treatment and control groups are identified, and their conditions are compared through the statistical techniques discussed in later chapters. The double-blind character of the research prevents the researchers from inadvertently, or for that matter intentionally, shading their assessments of the subjects' response to the treatment. If, for instance, the researcher knows that Sonja has received the experimental drug and Jennifer the placebo, and if he has an interest, perhaps even a financial interest, in demonstrating that the treatment works, then he may be more likely to detect positive changes in Sonja's condition. If, however, he does not know who received the drug and who received the placebo, there is no incentive to detect more improvement in one patient than the other. The patients are placed in the same situation; given that they do not know if they received the treatment or the placebo, they are less likely to imagine or exaggerate treatment effects.

The double-blind model is *the* model for experimental research, and it is designed to provide for the sound, scientific measurement of experimental effects. There are three stages to this research: pretest, treatment, and posttest. The treatment is carefully measured and the treatment effects monitored as closely as the subjects will permit. If possible, the experiment is run with subjects who are as similar as possible. Thus, for example, laboratory rats bred to identical specifications might be used. If the rats are identical *except for the treatment*, then the treatment effects are easier to isolate and measure.

It is worth mentioning, incidentally, that for a similar reason a good deal of medical research on human subjects has been restricted to men, partly on the assumption that women would display too much hormonal variation over the course of the treatment. The male body is the "medical norm" (Tavris 1992, 96). The problem, of course, arises when drug therapies tested only on men are then applied to both men and women. It is interesting to note, therefore, that the federal Health Minister recently announced that federal funding for future medical drug trials will be contingent on the inclusion of women as subjects (McIlroy 1996). In the United States, the inclusion of women at all stages of testing is already a condition for federal government funding. It is also worth noting that restricting research to male subjects has not been confined to medical research. A recent Canadian study of the economic benefits of education used only data for males. As Christos Constantatos and Edwin West explain (1991, 128), "it has become almost a tradition in research on returns to educational investment to use only male data. The main reason for this is that *female earning patterns are quite erratic*." [Emphasis added]

SUMMARY
Steps in Experimental Research

1. Randomly assign research subjects to the control and treatment groups.

2. Pretest dependent variable in both groups.

3. Administer treatment condition (independent variable) to treatment group and placebo to control group.

4. Posttest dependent variable for both groups.

5. Compare treatment and control groups.

One reason why experimental research is regarded so positively is that it has high internal validity: by controlling as many factors as possible, the researchers are able to draw causal conclusions. The distinction between the dependent and independent variables is clear, and temporal order can be established. However, most experiments rank low on external validity; it can be difficult to generalize from the study itself to the "real world." In real life situations other factors often influence and/or alter the impact of the independent variable on the dependent variable. The controls used in the laboratory setting do not exist outside the laboratory, and it can therefore be difficult to argue that results from the laboratory setting will occur in the real world.

In political science there are very few opportunities for carefully controlled experimental research. We cannot, for example, study the impact of public policy transformation on political values by dividing a sample of Ontarians into two groups: a treatment group that will live for four years under the Mike Harris Conservative government and a control group that will not. However, the *experimental analogy* can be found in a great deal of political science research. Take, for instance, a comparative survey research study of political beliefs among Ontario and Alberta voters, based on 1,000 respondents divided evenly between the two provinces. Implicitly, the research can be conceptualized in the following way. We draw a sample of 1,000 Canadians and "assign" them to one of two groups: the treatment group, who will live in Alberta, and the control group to whom we will administer the placebo (living in Ontario). We then compare the two groups to see if the treatment effect —living in Alberta—produces different political beliefs from those found in the control group. The same chain of reasoning can be applied to gender differences in political attitudes. We "assign" individuals to one of two conditions: they become male or female. (We leave it to the reader to decide which is the treatment condition and which is the control.) We then allow the subjects to grow up before testing for gender differences in political attitudes and behaviours.

However, the *experimental treatment* in the political world is much less specific, less controlled than in the world of medical research. "Living in Alberta" is a vastly more complex treatment condition than is receiving a precisely measured and carefully administered drug dosage. The Alberta treatment, moreover, could differ dramatically with individual variations in age, education, income, party affiliation, gender, or region of the province. A young woman growing up at the edge of the agricultural zone in the far northwest corner of the province does not have the same "Alberta experience" as the young son of an oil executive living in Calgary; to say they are both Albertans does not take us very far. In a similar fashion, the treatment condition of being male (or female) is extremely complex and multifaceted. We can seldom assume, for example, that two individuals differ *only* in their gender. And even if

A POINT ON THE COMPASS

Mind Experiments in Political Science

Although "real experiments" are extremely rare in political science, *mind experiments* are commonly used, particularly in survey research when respondents are asked to respond to hypothetical events. Even the standard voting preference question used by academic and commercial pollsters is a mind experiment to a degree, for it begins with the hypothetical "If a federal election were held today, for which party would you vote?"

Mind experiments are frequently used when researchers are trying to assess the potential impact of different party leaders. In the run-up to the American presidential nominating conventions, for example, samples of voters are often asked if they would be more or less likely to vote for a particular party if it were led by a number of different candidates. Before the next presidential election in the year 2000, survey respondents are likely to be asked for whom they would vote *if* the election were to be a contest between Democrat Al Gore and Republican Jack Kemp.

In a 1996 poll (Walker 1996) conducted by COMPAS Inc. of Ottawa, a sample of the Canadian electorate was asked how they would vote if the Reform and Progressive Conservative parties were to unite under the leadership of Reform leader Preston Manning, PC leader Jean Charest, or Alberta premier Ralph Klein. The results of this mind experiment suggested that the choice of leader could be a significant consideration for those considering a party merger; 35% of the respondents said they would vote for a Charest-led party, 29% for a Klein-based party, and 26% for a Manning-based party. Of course, none of these combinations was in fact on the table, but the mind experiment conducted in the poll provided useful information for those considering the possibility of merger.

they did, as perhaps in the case of twins raised in the same family setting, the gender treatment remains very complex.

One alternative to experimental research is the **field experiment**. Field experiments attempt to test relationships between variables in the "real world." An example of a field experiment is the *before–after study*. Here, the researcher looks at a group before the independent variable is added and then studies the group again, after the independent variable has been administered. For example, the researcher may study Canada before policy X is implemented and then compare these data to data collected in a post-X policy environment. This approach could be used, for instance, to determine if a ban on smoking in public locations has any net impact on cigarette consumption. A second approach is the *nonequivalent comparison study*. In this approach, the researcher uses two *self-assigned* groups to examine the impact of the independent variable. For example, he might compare British Columbia, where policy X is implemented, with Nova Scotia, where it has not been implemented. Because citizens are not randomly assigned between the two provinces, and because the provinces differ in many ways quite apart from policy X, we cannot argue convincingly that the two groups are equivalent. Thus, we are unable to control for myriad of intervening variables.

An obvious weakness of the field experiment is that there is no researcher-selected control group. Therefore, if changes or differences are seen, we cannot state confidently that they were caused by the independent variable. This weakens the internal validity of the approach. However, field experiments have the advantage of occurring in the "real world." Because of this, external validity is high and generalizations can be made. A second advantage of field experiments is their feasibility: many research questions that do not lend themselves to experiments (e.g., policy studies) can be approached through field experiments.

In either experimental or field experiment designs, we find that subject variation plagues political science research. Two laboratory rats may be all but identical prior to the experimental treatment, but two 25-year-old males will not be identical prior to the experimental treatment of being "assigned" to live in different regions of the country. Nor, for that matter, will the laboratory rats misread questionnaires or shade their responses to appeal to an attractive researcher or interviewer! All of this means that there is a great deal of background noise for empirical research in political science. Regional, class, or gender differences do not leap out of the data because the effects of such influences on political beliefs or behaviours are entangled in and complicated by variance in all of the other attributes that shape political beliefs and behaviours. As a consequence, political scientists often confront much weaker statistical correlations in their empirical studies than do their colleagues in psychology working with more pristine treatment effects. As a further consequence, political scientists are prone to cut themselves a bit more slack in the application of statistical procedures and tests. For example, political scientists often use less rigorous tests of statistical significance (discussed in Chapter 10) than do psychologists and pay less attention to the measurement assumptions underlying particular statistical tests. The argument, albeit one that must be handled with a good deal of caution, is that political reality is too complex, too muddied and muddled, to reveal its secrets to researchers who are overly rigorous in their statistical procedures and tests. There is, then, much greater tolerance for rough-and-ready analysis in explorations of the political world than there is in medical research, a tolerance that stems in part from the often too-quick assumption that mistakes in political research are less likely to cause real harm than are mistakes in medical research.

SURVEY RESEARCH

Much of the material discussed in this text will be drawn from survey research, which, as suggested above, can be seen as a quasi-experimental analogue to medical research. Surveys provide not only a great deal of the empirical database for the social sciences, but also contribute to political and social commentary in the media. Survey research is a ubiquitous feature of modern life, from massive preelection polls to the notice that "4 out of 5 dentists surveyed recommend sugarless gum for their patients who chew gum." It is difficult to read an issue of a major newspaper without running across one or more stories drawing upon survey "evidence" of some sort or another. Public opinion polls are used for insight into everything from voting and consumer behaviour to public policy preferences and sexual behaviour. They offer important glimpses into how the average Canadian or American, the mythical "man in the street," sees the world.[1] In so doing they enable us to compare our own beliefs, values, and preferences to societal norms. Are we typical, different, or even deviant compared to our neighbours, colleagues, and fellow citizens? Polls provide us with a point of comparison, a standard against which we can place our own world views. We can judge whether we sleep more, drink less, exercise more frequently, watch more television, or have fewer pets than others around us. We can also compare the values and beliefs of Canadians to those of other nationalities. We assume, and not always correctly, that polls provide us with a broader, less biased insight into the world than we can get by talking to friends, neighbours, and colleagues.

There is, in this sense, a *voyeur* aspect to survey research. Ideally, and if ethical guidelines were to permit, the researcher would like to peer inside people's heads without disturbing their thoughts by so doing. In practice, however, this is impossible to do. No matter how skillfully designed questions might be, they do disrupt preexisting patterns of

A POINT ON THE COMPASS ————————————

Using Polls to Map the Political Landscape

Public opinion polls enable us to position ourselves on the political landscape, to see how we compare to those around us, and the media presentation of survey information often emphasizes this use. For example, the Canadian Press (1996) coverage of a June 1996 survey of Canadian opinion on pensions began as follows: "If you suspect the Canada Pension Plan will be dry by the time you reach retirement, you're not alone. Six out of 10 Canadians expected the public well will be dry by the time they retire, suggest survey results released Wednesday."

Such stories invite readers to position themselves with respect to the population at large. They allow us to determine to what extent our beliefs are conventional, unusual, or off-the-wall. For example, a 1996 survey conducted by Angus Reid for Southam News reported the following levels of agreement among Canadians at large with a number of statements (Duffy and Evenson, 1996)[2]:

- 87% agreed that "I feel a personal responsibility to make the world a better place";

- 84% agreed that "it's more important for me to understand my inner self than to be rich and successful";

- 42% agreed that "nice guys finish last";

- 54% agreed that "I have too much stress in my everyday life";

- 91% agreed that "people talk too much about rights and not enough about responsibilities";

- 85% agreed that "if you work hard enough you can achieve just about anything in Canada."

It is possible, then, to scan through this information and determine to what extent our own world views correspond to those of other Canadians.

thought, and clumsy questions cause even more disruption. Respondents can be very sensitive to the research environment and may react to the physical characteristics and mannerisms of the interviewer, particularly if the interview touches upon sensitive topics. In such a context respondents may watch the interviewer to see how their answers are received and then tailor later responses to produce a more favourable social response from the interviewers. This general phenomenon is known as the **interviewer effect,** and is more problematic than one might expect. There is also a concern that in some cases survey research may create opinion as much as measure it. In an interview situation, as in other social situations, there is an innate desire to please. Because respondents are unwilling to display a lack of knowledge, or simply because they are trying to be helpful, respondents may make up answers to questions about which they have never thought. For example, an informal survey conducted by one of the authors in an undergraduate political science course at the University of Calgary in the early 1980s asked for the respondents' opinions on a number of issues ranging from capital punishment and the legalization of marijuana to foreign aid for Peru and the advisability of building a bridge linking Prince Edward Island to the mainland. The questionnaire was administered well before any serious discussion of a fixed link to PEI, and Peru, much less Canadian aid to Peru, was not in the news. It could readily be assumed, therefore, that although students might well have had preexisting opinions on capital punishment and marijuana, they would not have preexisting opinions on the fixed link to PEI or foreign aid to Peru. And yet, more than two-thirds of the students provided an opinion when asked.

Even if we are measuring rather than creating, we are often measuring the *potential* profile of opinion should an issue emerge for public debate. Thus, when you read about a survey that concludes that 48% of Canadians believe X or would prefer Y, do not assume that some 14,000,000 individuals are carrying those beliefs or preferences in a conscious, active way. A more appropriate interpretation of the poll would be to conclude that *if* all Canadians were in fact confronted with the question posed to the survey respondents, then close to 14,000,000 would likely believe X and opt for Y. It should be remembered in this context that we should never assume that public opinion is or should be translated in some immediate or automatic fashion into public policy. Public opinion is only one element in a very complex political process; it is sifted and weighed by political actors who must take into account not only the general distribution of opinion but also the intensity with which particular opinions are held, and by whom they are held. Governments, moreover, are not only influenced by public opinion, but seek themselves to shape public opinion as it relates to matters of public policy.[3]

Furthermore, when we encounter polls on voting intentions, we must keep in mind that the popular vote is filtered through an electoral system that does not faithfully translate votes into legislative seats. To know, for example, that the Reform and Progressive Conservative parties each have 15% of the national vote in a recent poll tells us little about how well they might do in terms of seats; it all depends on where the respective party support is concentrated. Surveys, therefore, provide a valuable window on the political process, but they provide far less than the complete picture.

This brings to mind an important limitation on quantitative analysis in Canada. The constraints of party discipline in the House of Commons and provincial legislatures mean there is little to be gained by studying the impact of sociodemographic characteristics or ideological beliefs on the voting behaviour of MPs or provincial legislators. Once you know the partisanship of an elected member, you know how he or she will vote, and there is little if any additional predictive power from knowing more about the individual's personal characteristics. By contrast, a rich roll-call voting literature has been created in the United States, where elected members are less constrained by party discipline and loyalties and, therefore, have greater freedom of action. In short, there is American variance beyond partisanship, but no Canadian variance, to be explained.

A POINT ON THE COMPASS

The Canadian National Election Studies

The primary source of survey data for students of Canadian politics is to be found in the Canadian National Election Studies (CNES). This comprehensive set of cross-sectional studies began with the 1965 federal election and now encompasses the elections of 1968, 1974, 1979, 1980, 1984, 1988, 1993, and 1997, along with the 1992 constitutional referendum. The series tracks many variables over time, although the focus and format of the CNES have changed with changes in the research teams, in our understanding of electoral dynamics, and in the nature of the political landscape. While the CNES surveys concentrate on their respective elections and on explaining the vote, they also pick up a good deal of attitudinal and sociodemographic information, which can be used to address a wide range of other research topics. The data sets are generally available to the political science community at large—including students— within a year or two of the election. Much of the empirical work published in the *Canadian Journal of Political Science* is rooted in CNES data sets. For a historical summary and assessment of the CNES, see Elisabeth Gidengil (1992).

Survey research can take many forms, just as survey samples can be drawn in many different ways. (For a discussion of sampling techniques, see Chapter 8.) The three basic forms are personal interviews, telephone interviews, and mail-back surveys.

Personal, in-home interviews provide the most versatile methodology, because respondents can be presented with a mix of question formats and visual aids. However, they are also very expensive and can be difficult to conduct in a security-conscious environment, where people are uneasy about admitting strangers into their homes. In-home interviews have traditionally enjoyed higher response rates than other survey techniques, but this advantage is now less apparent. Where in-home interviews, or, more likely, "in-office" interviews, have a decided response rate advantage is in elite interviewing. Telephone interviews with elite respondents can be difficult to arrange and conduct, and mail-back questionnaires seldom enjoy a satisfactory response rate.

Telephone interviews are the most common format for contemporary survey research. They are less expensive than in-home interviews and, when coupled with new computer technologies, provide for question versatility, quick data summaries, and speedy analysis. Telephone interviews also avoid some of the security problems confronted by the in-home format, although answering machines and call-screening are causing new and potentially serious problems for locating respondents.

Mailed surveys provide an even less expensive way of conducting survey research. Mailed questionnaires can be longer, more complex, and more interesting in layout and design than in-home or, in particular, telephone questionnaires, but they tend to suffer from relatively low response rates. This is problematic since it cannot be assumed that those who complete the surveys are necessarily similar to those who do not. In fact, we know they are not. It should also be noted, however, that the response rate is in large part a function of the population from which the sample is drawn. General samples, such as the Canadian electorate, tend to have the lowest response rates, whereas samples of highly specific populations often have quite high response rates. (The more specialized and homogeneous the population, the more likely that its members will be interested enough in the topic of the survey to respond.) The Canadian National Election Studies often combine detailed telephone interviews with follow-up, mailed surveys. One advantage of mail-back surveys is that the respondent is more willing to address controversial questions honestly, since there is no interviewer present (in person or in voice) to make judgments. Interviewer effects are therefore eliminated.

A POINT ON THE COMPASS

Innovative Methods to Study Bisexuality

In 1996 the National Health Development and Research Program of the federal Department of Health sponsored a $200,000 telephone survey by a University of Toronto team into the prevalence and character of bisexuality in Canada. Because it is difficult to identify and therefore sample the bisexual community, the research team relied upon a 1-800 phone number through which potential respondents could contact the team and complete the anonymous, 45-minute interview. The survey also employed an unusual form of bilingualism (Strauss 1996, A6):

> The language of the survey is English with a bilingual sexual twist. Those who want to be spoken to in a clinical language will hear that. Those more comfortable with street argot will be spoken to in that. Previous sexual behavioural studies show that while people start out saying they want clinical terms, it is often unsatisfactory when sexual practices are investigated.

These three survey techniques have been adapted to incorporate commercial research opportunities and limited research budgets. *Piggybacking* provides a means by which researchers can add a few questions to a larger survey. Many commercial firms, for example, will conduct regular national surveys with standard demographic questions and some questions of particular interest to the firm. The rest of the questionnaire space is then sold to clients, including private firms, government departments, interest groups, political parties, think tanks, and academics. A single survey may therefore have questions on a wide range of disjointed topics: voting intentions, consumer preferences, reactions to government policy initiatives, lifestyle issues. The disadvantage to the academic researcher is that she does not know the context in which her own questions are being asked; the advantage is a tremendous cost-saving, since the expense of the national survey is spread over a number of clients.

Panel studies provide a valuable means by which to study change over time. Most surveys are *cross-sectional* in that the respondents are interviewed only once and all approximately at the same time. Thus, a detailed snapshot is produced of opinion at that particular point in time, but change over time is difficult to assess. Although one can compare snapshots taken at different points in time, it is difficult to decide if the difference between two snapshots is accounted for by change in the composition of the two groups of respondents or by a real change in social and political attitudes.[4] By contrast, panel studies interview the same respondents at different points in time, thereby facilitating the study of change. For example, the *Bibby Reports* (discussed below) include a group of respondents who participated in the 1975, 1980, 1985, 1990, and 1995 surveys. Panel studies can be expensive to mount in that contact with respondents must be maintained or renewed; the longer the time interval between survey waves, the more complicated the task of tracking respondents becomes. Attrition rates are illustrated by a study of job-related educational training that began with 1985 base line questionnaires completed by 1,000 grade 12 students in six Edmonton high schools and by 600 graduates from the five largest faculties at the University of Alberta. By 1992, 40% of the high school students and 60% of the university graduates remained in the fifth wave of the panel study (Lowe and Krahn 1995, 364). As a consequence of attrition, it is sometimes necessary to replace panel members as the study progresses and early respondents move, die, or lose interest in the project. Recent CNES surveys have included panel components and have used a rolling cross-section ("rolling thunder") strategy in which the close to 3,000 interviews are portioned out over the duration of the campaign. With approximately 80 to 90 interviews being conducted each day, it is possible to track campaign effects and changes in voting intentions over the course of the campaign.

In all forms of survey research there are tradeoffs between complexity, cost, and response rates. As a consequence, there is no *best* way to do a survey; it all depends on the resources you have and the research questions that need to be addressed. The internal validity of survey research depends upon the questions chosen for the study (see Chapter 7), while external validity depends heavily upon the sample chosen (see Chapter 8). If the sample is large and randomly selected, external validity can be high.

As we will see as the text unfolds, conducting survey research can be a very complex undertaking. In essence, however, virtually all survey research follows a similar template. We begin with a *population* in which we have some research interest; the population could be Canadian voters, supporters of a particular party, members of an interest group or religious faith, female MPs, holders of a specific ideological orientation, or whatever. We then devise means by which to draw a *sample* from this larger population; Chapter 8 discusses a variety of ways, some good and some bad, in which this might be done. The next

A POINT ON THE COMPASS ———————————————

The Bibby Reports

One of the most high-profile, mail-based surveys of Canadian public opinion is the *Bibby Report*, published by sociologist Reginald W. Bibby from the University of Lethbridge. Bibby's first study was conducted in 1975 and was based on a mailed survey of 1,917 respondents. The size of the sample, the focus of the study on prominent social issues of the day, and Bibby's energy in publicizing the study's findings quickly established the 1975 Report as a benchmark for Canadian social trends. Bibby repeated the survey in 1980, 1985, 1990, and 1995 and in each survey included a substantial number of respondents from past surveys, thus providing an important panel component. The surveys have continued to rely on mailed surveys, and have averaged 1,643 respondents with a very respectable response rate of nearly 60%. The questionnaires are long, detailed, and cover a wide swath of Canadian social and political life. The accumulated *Bibby Reports* provide a useful series of snapshots of Canadian society and demonstrate how much can be done with relatively modest resources.

step is to come up with a set of questions to *measure* the underlying concepts, values, or beliefs in which we are interested; this step is discussed in Chapters 6 and 7. We may also want to supplement the empirical information with more *qualitative data*; means of doing so are discussed in the next chapter. Once the data are in hand, they must be tabulated and described. Then we find a way of working back from the sample data to the population in which we are interested. Here, the tools of *descriptive and inferential statistics*, to which the second half of this text is devoted, are indispensable.

The details of survey research will be discussed at considerable length in the chapters to follow. The point to stress here is how ubiquitous survey research has become as a research methodology in political science and in the social sciences more generally. This is not to say, however, that it is always done well. Nor is it to deny a large number of complex problems that swirl around virtually all aspects of survey research. Finally, the pervasive nature of survey research should not blind us to the variety of other research methodologies that are available.

PILOT STUDIES

The disciplinary tolerance political scientists show for rough-and-ready analysis is most apparent in *pilot studies* designed to prepare the ground for larger projects. Much of the research done in the social sciences is very expensive; the CNES, for example, have a price tag of close to half a million dollars. As a consequence, researchers often try out their research strategies and questionnaires in smaller, less expensive settings before tackling the main research project. For instance, an Ontario political scientist interested in exploring the empirical relationship between neoconservative beliefs and feminism might begin by running a simple questionnaire in one of her classes, what we call an *accidental,* or *convenience sample.* By analyzing the results and discussing them with her students, she would be able to weed out questions that were too ambiguous, complex, or in other ways problematic. Then she might apply for a small research grant from her university to run a pilot study in the local community; both she and the university would see the pilot project as the foundation for a much larger grant application to an external funding agency such as the Social Sciences and Humanities Research Council. In that grant application she might propose a random sample of the provincial population or perhaps even a national study. As she moves through each stage of this process, the research design becomes more rigorous, and classroom samples of convenience are transformed into systematic random samples of the provincial or national population.

Of course, many pilot studies never spawn larger projects. Subsequent grant applications may be unsuccessful, or perhaps the pilot study yields results that strike the researcher as uninteresting. Sometimes the researcher has moved on to other issues and theoretical concerns. The most problematic case is the one where the researcher wants to do the larger project, but the necessary funding cannot be found. What, then, can be done with the pilot study results themselves? If the pilot study was sloppily designed, in expectation of "doing it right" in the larger study, then the findings may not be publishable in good quality journals. Even if the research was well designed, the site of the pilot study might cause problems. For example, the pilot study might have been done in St. Catharines, Ontario, in the expectation of moving on to a provincial sample. But if the St. Catharines data are all there are, will anyone accept the researcher's argument that St. Catharines is representative of the larger provincial population?

SECONDARY ANALYSIS

Although a good deal of political science research involves the creation of new research materials including surveys, interviews, or content analyses, a good deal also involves the secondary analysis of data collected by others. The reliance on secondary analysis is particularly prevalent with respect to survey analysis, where in many cases the money simply cannot be found to conduct new research. When it cannot be found, existing data sets are brought into play. In many cases, such as the CNES, these data sets provide a rich mine of information that can sustain a wide variety and large number of secondary analyses. Indeed, the CNES are funded with just this purpose in mind; they are conceived as a community resource.

The outstanding advantage of secondary analysis is that it is inexpensive, even cheap. Students, for example, have full access to the CNES without having to contribute in any way to the original data collection costs. Also, when we use other people's data, we can be sure that our own hidden assumptions do not bias question wording, because the questions and measures have been designed by others. The flip side is that the questions available were often designed for other purposes than the researcher doing the secondary analysis has in mind. As a consequence, the available measures may be less than perfect; they are not the way "that I would have asked the question." However, given the tremendous advantage in cost, researchers doing secondary analysis are usually content to make do with what is available.

CONTENT ANALYSIS

At times we are confronted with such a massive amount of information that it is difficult to pick out underlying themes or structures. For example, the media coverage of a federal election campaign is both extensive and complex, and if we are interested in whether that coverage might have been biased in some way, it can be difficult on the basis of casual observation to come to any clear conclusion. **Content analysis** provides a way to break down print or electronic media coverage into bite-sized morsels, which can then be reassembled in such a way that they reveal underlying structures and biases. One might, for example, note the *number* of times different party leaders were mentioned on the national news and, for each mention, note also the setting and *tone* of the coverage. The tone might be documented by recording the adjectives and adverbs that were used and whether these were positive or negative.

A POINT ON THE COMPASS

Content Analysis of Television News

Do Americans and Canadians encounter similar media coverage of international events, or are there pronounced national differences in what we see and hear? Researchers from the University of Windsor (Soderland et al. 1994) examined this question with respect to media coverage of the 1989 American invasion of Panama. They studied 197 news stories carried over a 23-day period by three American (ABC, CBS, and NBC) and two Canadian (CBC and CTV) networks. The study included the prominence of the story, the sources utilized, and the images portrayed of the principal actors. They were able to show, for example, that while President Manuel Noriega was portrayed in a uniformly negative fashion in both countries, President George Bush received more negative coverage in Canada than he did in the United States. However, the more general and perhaps surprising finding was that "with few exceptions, there was a consistency in the news coverage of the Panamanian invasion among the networks and the two countries in which these networks operated" (596).

It would then be possible to compare the party leaders with respect to the amount and kind of media coverage they received.

For example, the European Institute for the Media conducted an extensive content analysis of the media coverage of the two rounds of the 1996 presidential election in Russia (York 1996). The Institute found that Boris Yeltsin received 53% of the media coverage during the first round, compared to only 18% for the Communist presidential candidate, Gennady Zyuganov. Yeltsin's coverage was not only more extensive than Zyuganov's, but was also much more positive. In the first round of the election, Yeltsin enjoyed 492 more positive reports than negative reports, while Zyuganov received 313 more negative than positive media reports. In the second round, Yeltsin's positive reports outnumbered his negative reports by 247, whereas Zyuganov's negative reports outnumbered his positive reports by 241. The Institute, therefore, was able to use content analysis to nail down the particulars of media bias in the Russian election campaign.

Content analysis can be used with written text of any kind, radio and television broadcasts, transcripts of speeches, and Internet communication. Essentially, content analysis is the systematic study of recorded communication. If sophisticated coding schemes are used, it can provide quite penetrating insights. We can use content analysis to study changes in public attitudes over time, for example, by looking at the terms of political discourse in newspapers between 1970 and 1996. Content analysis can also be used to study patterns of communication: do female politicians use less "aggressive" rhetoric than their male counterparts? A disadvantage of content analysis is that it can be very expensive. Transcription and coding are labour-intensive activities; thus, content analysis is often dependent upon substantial grant support. Indeed, the costs have been so daunting that content analyses in political science have been relatively rare. However, the development of powerful new computer software is bringing costs down substantially.

CASE STUDIES

Political scientists are more likely than historians to treat individuals and events as examples of some broader phenomenon, as **case studies**, rather than as something unique. For example, a political scientist doing a study of former prime minister Brian Mulroney would be inclined to treat Mr. Mulroney as a specific case of a more general class or species—perhaps Canadian prime ministers—and thus to use the Mulroney experience to shed light on the broader phenomenon, to *generalize* from the specific case to the larger population of Canadian prime ministers. By contrast, a historian would be more inclined to focus on the details of Mr. Mulroney's own experience and would feel less compelled to speculate on the larger population. This contrast is similar to that between psychiatry and psychology. A psychiatrist is primarily interested in a particular patient (or case) and is prepared to devote months, even years, untangling the idiosyncratic aspects of the patient's life. By contrast, a psychologist is interested in more general patterns of human behaviour. While the treatment of individual patients may still play an important role in the psychologist's career, she is more likely to see many patients facing common problems and is less likely than the psychiatrist to delve at great depth into the case histories of individual patients.

Although these contrasts can be overdrawn, they direct our attention to the fact that most political science research can be seen, implicitly or explicitly, as case study research. There is always a broader phenomenon lying at the back of the researcher's mind. This in turn ties into the theoretical nature of political science research. Describing the case is not enough; something must be done to fit the case into a larger theoretical perspective or framework. Political science, therefore, drives from the specific to the general, from the case or sample to the population within which it is embedded.

When conducting case study research, we focus on a particular individual, political party, government, or organization. The researcher gathers evidence from a variety of sources and combines it to create a picture of the single case. If the researcher does use a variety of sources, and if these sources supply consistent information, the internal validity of the case study can be quite high (White 1994, 130). If there is any interest whatsoever on behalf of the researcher in making generalizations from the case to a broader phenomenon, then the selection of the case study becomes critically important. Is the case representative of the broader phenomenon? Does it shed useful light on the theoretical questions under examination? With case study research, external validity is dependent upon the appropriateness of the case: if the case is representative, external validity is high, but if the case is poorly chosen, external validity can be very low.

A POINT ON THE COMPASS

The Single Case

Although a good deal of political science research rests explicitly or implicitly on a case study format—the use of the particular to explain or shed light on the general—the discipline has also been enriched by biographical and autobiographical treatments of single political leaders. Some have focused on the practice of politics and, while providing an interesting window on such practice and the political personalities of the day, provide less insight into the national fabric and policy issues within which the individual was situated. Autobiographies by Lucien Bouchard (1994) and Jean Chrétien (1994) are recent examples. Others use the subject to provide broader commentary, often quite critical, on the parties or movements with which they were associated; Conrad Black's biography of Maurice Duplessis (1977) provides an excellent example. Still others provide a rich and textured analysis of the policy environment and historical setting in which the individual was situated and helped shape. Examples here would include the two-volume study of Pierre Trudeau by Christina McCall and Stephen Clarkson (1990, 1994) and Denis Smith's biography of John Diefenbaker (1995). In virtually all cases, biographies and autobiographies provide valuable insight into the raw material of political life.

FOCUS GROUPS

A research technique that is analogous in some ways to the pilot study is the **focus group**. Readers may be most familiar with this technique in the context of marketing research: a small group sits in a room and discusses the pros and cons of a product. Is it too harsh? Too bright? Too expensive? Focus groups are not designed to be *representative*; they are simply designed to bring together a group of individuals to discuss a specific product or issue *at length* and *in depth*. For example, prior to its telecast of the 1996 Summer Olympics, NBC Sports conducted focus groups with women across the United States in order to determine what female viewers liked and disliked about conventional sports coverage and how such coverage might be improved to attract a larger female viewing audience for the Olympics (Wente 1996). While a questionnaire in a survey research project may get hundreds and perhaps thousands of individuals to address a topic for a few minutes, a focus group will pull a small handful of people together to discuss the same topic for hours. Focus groups can therefore provide a useful complement to conventional survey research. They allow the researcher to dig beneath the surface opinion captured by the larger survey, to probe for details and nuance. However, running a focus group effectively is not something that just anyone can do. Managing the interpersonal dynamics and drawing out opinions without imposing the researcher's own biases are art forms in themselves.

Focus groups have become particularly important research tools for political parties and campaign organizers. They enable researchers to probe beneath the surface of public opinion, to explore what people *really* like or dislike about political parties, leaders, policies, or advertisements. At the same time, this very depth makes focus groups less amenable to quantitative analysis, and the nonrandom selection of participants makes generalizations to larger populations hazardous at best. As a consequence, focus group research is seldom used by political scientists with a quantitative bent. It is much more attractive as a form of qualitative research, to which we now turn.

WORKING AS A TEAM

1. Have each of your group members collect three to five news clippings about your provincial premier. Try to have a variety of dates and news sources, including Internet and audio transcripts. As a group, do a simple content analysis of the

"clippings." Note the number of positive and negative statements. Are there differences between the news sources or over time? Do group members agree on what constitutes positive and negative descriptions?

SELF-STUDY

1. You are interested in determining whether watching a particular political television commercial alters the level of support for your political party. You have a sample of 100 people with which to work in addressing this question. How would you design the research? What steps would you take? What validity problems would you encounter, and how might these be minimized or addressed?

2. You are curious whether an increase in the number of women elected to legislative assemblies influences the policy outcomes of those assemblies. How would you design a field experiment to address your curiosity? What steps would you take? What validity problems would you encounter, and how might these be minimized or addressed?

3. You are studying the relationship between support for feminism and support for left-wing political issues. How could you use the case study approach to address your research question? What case might you use? What potential sources of information would you consider? How would you increase internal and external validity?

NOTES

1. Of course, their reach goes well beyond the North American and western European settings. For an illustration of the insights that survey research can provide into the dynamics of Chinese politics, see Chan and Nesbitt-Larking (1995), "Critical Citizenship and Civil Society in Contemporary China."

2. The Angus Reid poll was conducted June 4–9, 1996; 1,800 respondents were surveyed, and the margin of error was estimated to be 2.3%, 19 times out of 20.

3. See, for example, the analysis by Roberts and Rose (1995) of the federal government's efforts to shape Canadian public opinion toward the GST.

4. Panel studies eliminate the first possibility and therefore bring the second into bolder relief. However, the comparison of nonpanel snapshots can still be a fruitful line of research. For a comparative look at the 1965, 1968, 1974, 1979, 1980, 1984, and 1988 Canadian National Election Studies, see Clarke and Kornberg (1993).

CHAPTER 5

Observing the Political World: Qualitative Approaches

DESTINATION

By the end of this chapter the reader should

- be familiar with three qualitative research strategies: elite interviewing, observation research, and comparative analysis;
- understand the utility and limitations of each approach and have a basic understanding of how to conduct each form of research;
- appreciate the complementarity of quantitative and qualitative research strategies.

With any research method there are advantages and disadvantages. As Chapter 4 demonstrated, approaches vary in terms of internal and external validity. And, more pragmatically, some approaches require more resources (time, money, personnel) than others. The choice of design will depend primarily upon our research question. In some areas of political science, such as the study of voting and elections, there is a tendency to emphasize quantitative approaches, particularly survey research, over other options. Survey research is efficient in terms of time and resources and can have high validity if the measures and sample chosen are appropriate. The importance of survey research to the advancement of knowledge about the political world cannot be underestimated; indeed, much of this text is devoted to conducting survey research and interpreting survey data. However, survey research specifically, and quantitative research more generally, has its limits. For starters, in order to design an appropriate survey and select a relevant sampling frame, one first needs advanced knowledge of the subject area. In addition, quantitative data can be criticized for lacking depth and context: we read that 58% of the population favours policy

Y, but we can fail to capture the sentiment behind the statistic. Are views held passionately by the respondents, or are people relatively indifferent? Whose opinions are strongly held, and whose are not? Qualitative approaches can be used to address these issues.

Recall from Chapter 2 that qualitative methods emphasize depth of research over scope: researchers are willing to use a smaller sample, but employ techniques that result in a more detailed body of data. As will soon be apparent, the nature of the data also changes. In quantitative research, data are defined by numbers; questions tend to be close-ended, and the interpretations of the responses attempt to be highly objective. In qualitative research, data are more likely to be direct quotations or researcher observations. Questions, when they exist, are open-ended, and the nature of the data—words and phrases—leads to greater researcher subjectivity. It should also be noted, however, that the distinction between quantitative and qualitative research is not always clear. Indeed, the two can best be seen as complementary rather than competing research strategies.

This chapter will explore three qualitative approaches: elite interviewing, observation, and comparative analysis. We will begin by demonstrating how qualitative approaches can be used to enhance quantitative methods, and we will conclude by suggesting methods by which qualitative data can be interpreted. As you will note in working through these approaches, they all raise significant ethical concerns of the type discussed in Chapter 3.

COMBINING QUALITATIVE AND QUANTITATIVE RESEARCH APPROACHES

By selecting a research approach, we are choosing to see the world in a particular way. As Kathleen Driscoll and Joan McFarland (1989, 185–6) write, "Techniques of data collection and analysis are not neutral.... Each technique's usefulness and its limitations are structured by its underlying assumptions. Adopting a research technique means adopting its underlying conceptual framework." Each research design privileges some forms of information over others. Perhaps the best analogy is a line of sight (Berg 1989, 4). If we stand in front of an object, we get one impression of it; standing behind the same object can lead to different observations. Similarly, standing above or below the object gives further nuance to our understanding. To best understand the object, to get the most complete picture, we should take in as many perspectives as possible. The same holds true for understanding political and social phenomena: comprehension grows as we approach data analysis in a variety of ways. The combination of multiple research strategies in social research is known as **triangulation**. As the image of the triangle suggests, triangulation usually refers to the use of *three* different methods of data-gathering, although a researcher may, in fact, choose to use only two or more than three. Research strategies are combined to maximize the variety of data collected. For example, a researcher might combine survey work with interviews and observation research. Focus groups could be followed by a mail-back questionnaire and content analysis. The choice of research methods is determined by the questions one asks and, of course, by the resources available. By selecting different research strategies, we can help address internal and external validity issues. For example, case studies are often weak in external validity but can have strong internal validity. This weakness in external validity might be compensated for by combining the case study with a survey based on appropriate sampling.

The term "triangulation" refers not only to research methods but also to the data themselves and the investigators (Berg 1989, 4–5).[1] For *data triangulation* researchers might choose to vary the temporal dimension by collecting data at different points in time. For example, in the Canadian National Election Studies (CNES) researchers have collected data from a single sample in three waves: before an election, immediately after the election, and then again after a short period of time. It should be noted that the CNES team also vary their methods of data collection; the first two collections are conducted by phone survey, whereas the final collection is a mail-back survey. Data triangulation might also include varying the geographic units from which data are collected, for example, collecting data from three different countries or provinces. *Investigator triangulation* refers to the use of research teams, rather than individuals, to study and interpret events or phenomena. As we all know, three people observing the same event will have differing reports and interpretations of what actually occurred. Increasing the number of observers helps increase our confidence in the interpretations.

The point to be stressed is that the more sources of data available to the researcher, the richer and more comprehensive the analysis will be. More narrowly stated, qualitative research can aid survey research in a number of ways. Qualitative approaches, which tend to be more inductive, give the researcher a greater awareness of his subject matter, which allows for the formulation of the hypotheses and theories necessary for deductive research (Sieber 1973, 1342). Later, when the researcher is designing his survey instrument, qualitative research can aid in the development of survey questions (Sieber 1973, 1348). As we will see, validity and reliability are important issues in the selection of questions: if our measures are invalid or unreliable, our statistical results are rendered meaningless. The data gathered from qualitative methods can act as a check on these validity and reliability issues.

Once survey data are collected, qualitative research can help illuminate the findings. For example, we might find a subgroup in our sample that reports unusual responses. Qualitative study can aid in exploring that subgroup. The subjective meaning of the various responses in survey results can be explored in interviews, and this greater understanding creates a more detailed, nuanced interpretation of the quantitative data (Sieber 1973, 1350). Finally, just as multiple investigators reduce the opportunities for misinterpretation of an event, so too do multiple research strategies reduce the opportunities for analysis based on mismeasurement. If the results from survey research, for example, vary significantly from the results from interviews conducted among the same sample, the researcher needs to question the validity and reliability of one or both of her data sources.

Having spelled out why qualitative research is an important addition to one's study of a phenomenon, we need to consider what characterizes "qualitative" research. One of the defining features is the emphasis placed upon context (Neuman 1994, 319). The qualitative researcher stresses the relevance of time, culture, and circumstance to understanding events and attitudes. Historical context is important to note; for example, many views that were once considered radical are now mainstream, whereas others that were once mainstream are now seen as reactionary. Cultural context is also very relevant, for example, support for women's rights means very different things in Canada and Iran. Issues of historical and cultural context can complicate quantitative analyses since the same survey instrument, used either in different time periods or in different cultural settings, may prove unreliable. Words such as "power" and "authority," for instance, can mean different things to different people and at different times.

Issues of process are also addressed by qualitative methods, where special attention is paid to the sequence of events. Survey research can only really tap correlations; knowledge of which variable came first comes from theory. Qualitative approaches, particularly observation research, allow the researcher to focus on temporal order. Recall from Chapter 2 that temporal order is one of the tests of causation. By allowing us to determine temporal order, qualitative research allows us to look for causal relationships.

Qualitative research is less structured than quantitative research. Questions are more likely to be open-ended, discussions are more free flowing, and observations are less controlled. Many qualitative researchers work with **grounded theory**: they begin with a basic theoretical approach but revise their theory as directed by the data. Therefore, if the data collected contradict their theory, they make the necessary revisions. This is possible because the approach is inductive; the researchers, rather than testing hypotheses, are seeking to make broad generalizations and create theory. Unlike quantitative researchers, who collect all data before beginning analysis, the qualitative researcher begins assessing data as they emerge and revises his theorizing and subsequent research accordingly.

The main advantage of qualitative research is that it allows the researcher to explore more deeply the *meaning* of political phenomena. Whereas quantitative data address questions of "what," with explanations based primarily on previous theorizing, qualitative data directly consider questions of "how" and "why." (These distinctions, however, should not be overdrawn.) Unfortunately, qualitative research can suffer from low reliability (Chadwick et al. 1984, 215), because the subjective interpretation of data can vary among researchers. Interpreting the statistics generated by survey research is relatively straightforward; interpreting statements made by individuals—and considering aspects such as intonation and body language—is more like art than science.

At times, researchers may choose qualitative methods as their primary research approach. This is more common in fields such as anthropology and sociology than it is in political science, but it is increasingly important to political science as the distinctions between the branches of social science continue to blur. Qualitative research sometimes proves to be the most practical research option, particularly when one's research question or population does not allow itself to be subject to nonprobability sampling. For example, a study of food bank users would require purposive sampling, because a good sampling frame on which to base a random sample would be difficult to develop. Some groups are more likely to respond to qualitative approaches such as interviews than to telephone or mail-back surveys. And some populations are just too small to allow for good statistical analyses; the associated margins of error would just be too great. Qualitative methods also allow the researcher to cast a wide subject net, scanning a subject area for issues that he has never considered. Another use of qualitative approaches is to study the problems of implementing public policies (White 1994, 215). A researcher may ask detailed questions of employment insurance recipients, for instance, to determine problems of access or delivery. Recall that inductive research is necessary for deductive research: before testing hypotheses, we must first develop hypotheses. Qualitative methods are a good source of inductive knowledge.

Overall, qualitative research can be seen as more detailed and nuanced than quantitative research. It is worth noting that some scholars have found that female researchers are more likely to use qualitative methods than are males (Neuman 1994, 317). This may reflect a more feminist approach to the social sciences, which stresses the need for a nuanced understanding of each individual's experiences and motivations. Qualitative research methods allow the documentation of individual experience in ways that quantitative research does not. In addition, much of feminist scholarship is characterized by critiques of "objective approaches," whose professed neutrality is considered to be male biased in practice (Grant 1993, 33). Of course, just as survey research benefits from qualitative study, so too do qualitative approaches, feminist or not, benefit from empirical study.

In summary, qualitative analysis is distinguished from quantitative analysis in a number of ways: it places great emphasis on context, it is more open to subjective interpretation, and it is more inductive, all of which make the approach appropriate for descriptive and exploratory research. In practice, the distinction between quantitative and qualitative research approaches is often blurred. The three qualitative approaches we are about to explore—elite interviewing, observation, and comparative research—can be either structured (more quantitative) or unstructured (more qualitative). However, the reader will note that despite possible variations in the level of structure in the approaches, all require attention to context and use nonrandom sampling.

ELITE INTERVIEWING

Political scientists can benefit from the use of **elite interviews** (also known as "intensive interviewing"). Many research questions that we encounter require specialized or "inside" information. For example, to study the dynamics of party caucus, we can interview members of that caucus. To create a leadership profile of a provincial premier, we can discuss his or her style with top aides or with other elected representatives. An elite in this sense is an individual or group with access to the specialized information we need. Thus, the term "elite" is not used in the conventional sense, which suggests privileged political or economic elites (although they may in fact be the group you are studying). For many research questions the size of the elite is very small or is difficult to access. In these cases, random sampling is inappropriate; instead, we do our best to include as many members of the population as possible in the study (Baxter-Moore et al. 1994, 236).

One advantage of elite interviewing is that researchers can access very detailed, directed, and often private, otherwise inaccessible information. Personal information and opinions that a respondent would feel uncomfortable discussing over the phone or writing on a mail-back survey can often be addressed in an intensive interview. The personal contact that occurs during an interview allows for a sense of rapport to develop between the interviewer and the respondent; over the course of the interview trust develops, and the interviewee is more likely to discuss the issues of interest. In addition, the respondent sets aside a greater amount of time for a personal interview than for telephone or mail-back surveys. This allows for more detailed data than can be accessed by telephone and mail-back interviews. It should be noted that certain individuals, including politicians and business elites, are less likely to respond to a telephone or mail-back survey than to an interview. For some, being selected for an interview presents a welcome opportunity to talk at length, explaining personal and political choices.

A second advantage of interview research is that it allows the researcher to "learn from respondents and acquire unexpected information that can lead to truly new ways of understanding the events being studied" (Manheim and Rich 1981, 134). With more structured forms of research (such as survey research), the relevance of particular issues has been predetermined: only issues that are addressed in the questionnaire or poll are included in the study. In an interview, by contrast, the respondent is able to indicate what *he* feels to be important: "At the root of in-depth interviewing is an interest in understanding the experience of the other people and the meaning they make of that experience" (Seidman 1991, 3). By indicating his own priorities and concerns, the respondent may suggest to the researcher a new way of approaching the research question or new avenues to be explored in the research. Clearly, elite interviewing is particularly valuable when little knowledge exists about a subject or when researchers wish to go beyond existing theories and approaches. Recall that, unlike deductive hypothesis-testing, inductive research seeks broad information to aid in the formulation of new theories and hypotheses. Intensive interviewing can be very useful in this process.

Elite interviewing does have its disadvantages. First, and most obviously, the process is very time consuming. In addition to the time spent on the interview itself, the researcher needs to factor in the possibility that respondents will have difficulties fitting the interview into their busy schedules. This can lead to delays in data-gathering. Second, there are the difficulties of processing and comparing data. Unlike standardized telephone polls or mail-back surveys, each elite interview is unique. The researcher usually has a set of central questions to address in the interview, but he may choose to add additional questions in the course of the interview. The conversational style of interviews can lead respondents in different directions, depending upon their personal interests and experiences. Thus, while some "core" data can be compared across respondents, other data may not be amenable to comparisons. This problem is common to most qualitative studies.

A third problem with elite interviewing is that it is *reactive*: the respondents are aware that their answers will be used in a research study, and this may lead them to alter the information given. Thus the survey research problems with interviewer effects and "created opinion" discussed in the previous chapter are by no means absent in elite interviewing. People do not wish to look unknowledgeable and prefer to be seen in the best possible light. The desires for self-promotion and self-protection can lead people to embellish or downplay certain issues; the temptation to act as one's own "spin doctor" is great. In addition, interviewees may present you with information that, although they believe it to be true, is in fact erroneous. (They may also mislead or lie.) Thus, the possibility exists that a researcher will collect data that are either partially or completely false. For this reason, researchers must remember to "never treat what interviewees say as factual data, but rather *treat the fact that they said it as data*" (Manheim and Rich 1981, 134). If, for example, a legislator reports that the popular majority supports capital punishment, we treat the *belief* as data. Beliefs and perceptions strongly influence individual actions and are interesting in their own right. However, if we are interested in a particular "fact" put forth by a respondent, the onus is on the researcher to verify the fact, in this case, by exploring opinion poll data.

Elite interviews take on the tone of a conversation, but some important differences exist. In interviews, one person asks questions and the other answers. In a "normal" conversation, each individual contributes equally, and there is an exchange of ideas. (Of course, we have all had conversations in which the level of contribution is unbalanced; when it is the other person, rather than ourselves, who is dominating the discussion, we often consider the speaker to be a bit of a bore!) In ordinary conversation, if we do not wish to answer a question, we have the option of changing the subject or making a joke. Usually, the other person picks up on such cues and lets the issue pass. In an interview, however, the interviewer is likely to return to these "dismissed" questions in her efforts to obtain the necessary data.

Before conducting the interview, it is important for the researcher to be clear on the data he is seeking. Interview time can pass quickly, and many respondents are fascinating people; it is very possible for the interview time to expire before the researcher has obtained all the necessary information. Note, too, that time is scarce for many people, researcher and respondent alike. For these reasons, it is advisable to have an **interview framework** before entering an interview. The framework is merely a set of questions to be asked of the respondents. Using a framework keeps the researcher on track during the interview and ensures that important, core questions are asked in each interview. This allows the researcher to compare answers provided by different respondents. The researcher still retains flexibility during the interview: inserting questions as they fit naturally into the discussion rather than necessarily sticking to a preset ordering and inserting additional questions when necessary. The framework is only a guide to aid the interview, rather than a strict outline that must be followed absolutely. It also provides a useful cue to the interviewee that her time is not being wasted by inadequate preparation, that the interviewer is not making it up as he goes along.

A POINT ON THE COMPASS ————————————

Quantitative Elite Research

Political elites, including elected representatives, can be studied *en masse* in ways that are analogous to conventional survey techniques. Note, for example, the following illustrations:

- Michael Ornstein and Michael Stevenson (1981) compared elite and public opinion in the run-up to the 1980 Quebec sovereignty-association referendum by drawing upon a national public opinion survey of 3,300 respondents and personal interviews with 602 "elite respondents," including federal and provincial politicians, federal and provincial civil servants, lawyers, academics, and trade union leaders.

- Michael Atkinson and Maureen Mancuso (1985) explored the "elite political culture of corruption" in Canada by drawing a sample of 120 back-bench MPs from the House of Commons. Self-administered interviews were completed with 70% of the sample. The researchers concluded that their respondents did not have views on corruption distinct from those of the general public or independent observers.

How does one create a framework? The researcher starts by asking, "What do I want to know? What topics need to be addressed? What issues are of less importance?" In essence, one must distinguish between what knowledge is wanted and what knowledge is needed, ensuring that the questions tapping "needs" are given higher priority than the questions addressing "wants." As with formulating survey questions, one needs to ensure that the questions are clear and not phrased in ways that "lead" the respondent. In general, questions that can be answered in a "yes–no" manner should be avoided; the goal is to promote discussion. The initial questions should lead into the subject area without threatening the respondent in any way; difficult or highly personal questions should be left for later in the interview, after a sense of rapport and comfort has had a chance to build.

In addition to drawing up an interview framework, the researcher can prepare by investigating the background of the interviewee. The purpose of this is twofold. First, it gives the researcher insights into the personality and style of the interviewee. Rapport is built most easily when we confront people who are similar to us in dress and energy; if you are aware that your interviewee is very formal in speech and dress, for example, matching him on these details can help build the initial comfort level of the interview. Background research also helps prevent the wasting of interview time on information that can be found elsewhere; for example, the interviewee's position in the government and the duties associated with that position might be found in public records. The interviewee has every reason to assume that a researcher has done her homework before conducting the interview; a researcher who devotes considerable interview time to information that can be easily found elsewhere may annoy individuals who see their time as scarce.

Elite interviews should be prescheduled to ensure that the interviewee has sufficient time to spend with the researcher. At the beginning of the interview the researcher should briefly explain the purpose of the meeting, and care must be taken to ensure that the information provided does not reveal your specific hypotheses. Recall that one problem with interviewing (as well as with survey and overt observation techniques) is that the process is subject to reaction: respondents consciously or unconsciously alter their behaviour and responses to fit the researcher's expectations, resulting in biased data. During the interview itself, the researcher should avoid "leading" the interviewee with body language or facial expressions. If, for example, the researcher shows disapproval at certain types of statements, the interviewee may begin to guard her statements.

CONSTRUCTING AN INTERVIEW FRAMEWORK

You are investigating whether Reform Party candidates choose to run for the party because of its populist principles, its economic policies, or its moral agenda. As part of your research design, you have decided that interviews are essential. But whom would you interview and why? Outline the topics you would wish to explore in the interview. What questions could be used to get the information you need? Draft an interview framework.

Meticulous notes should be taken throughout the interview, regardless of whether one uses a tape recorder. Tape recorders may have technical or sound problems (e.g., some statements are inaudible on the tape), and tapes cannot record nonverbal communication such as body language. The body language and voice intonation of the interviewee can prove as interesting as the statements themselves; it is useful to note that the respondent became nervous when a particular topic was broached or scowled when a certain name was mentioned. If a recorder is used, the researcher must first assure the consent of the interviewee. When taking notes, be as clear and thorough as possible; if a statement is particularly important, record it word by word so you can quote verbatim. After the interview, the researcher should write up the notes and transcribe the tapes as quickly as possible. It takes very little time for the memory of the interview to fade, particularly if one is interviewing more than one person.

Jarol Manheim and Richard Rich (1981, 128) write, "The personal interview is simultaneously one of the worst and one of the best data collection tools available to political scientists." Done correctly, the elite interview can lead to new research insights and a richer understanding of the subject area. Done incorrectly, the data risk bias and are difficult to interpret, and the final results are of limited use.

OBSERVATION RESEARCH

One problem with research instruments such as surveys and interviews is that they leave the researcher dependent upon *reported* behaviours. At times, there can be significant disjunctures between reported and actual behaviour, in part because many things have normative social value. Because voting, for example, is seen as a social responsibility, many people claim to have voted when in fact they did not. Often the respondent truly believes he engaged in a particular action—for example, voting for the popular winning party rather than the "losers"—that in fact he did not do. This is particularly true for events that occurred in the past; as the months and years go by, we can forget whom we voted for, how many news programs we watched, and even what organizations we supported financially. Faulty recall, incidentally, can also be a problem in survey research. For example, a study of the impact of the televised debate between party leaders on voting choice in the 1984 federal election relied on interviews conducted as far as five months after the election. As the author (Lanoue 1991, 56) observed, "we are dependent upon the accuracy of respondents' recall of whether they watched the debate, whether or not they voted, and for which party they cast their ballots. As a consequence, it is possible that evaluations of leaders, parties and overall debate performance have been subject to the effects of fading recollection or the contamination of intervening political events." This is an example of the background noise that is common to empirical research in political science and that can lessen the power of statistical analyses.

In addition to problems of reporting false behaviour, there is a tendency to over- and underestimate certain behaviours. For example, let's say you ask Nathan how many hours he studies every day. He reports four hours of concentrated study per day, yet his grades are much lower than classmates who study for the same amount of time. You are wondering what is going on, so you decide to watch Nathan study. Something interesting emerges: although he does indeed spend four hours in the library as he claims, much of that time is spent doing activities other than studying. Nathan spends 10 minutes arranging his papers, goes on three 20-minute coffee breaks, and devotes almost a full hour to rewriting his class notes (a very inefficient study technique). When all these factors are considered, he has actually devoted less than two hours to effective studying and has exaggerated his study time by 100%. When we observe actual behaviour, rather than relying solely on reported behaviour, we are conducting **observation research**.

Observation research (also known as "field research" and "ethnography") has the advantage that events occur in natural circumstances, which means that the external validity of our study can be quite high. We engage in observation research on a casual basis in our everyday lives; "people-watching" can be an enjoyable pastime. Observation allows us to explore interpersonal dynamics, and it is therefore useful for studying group dynamics and political processes. In such research we pay particular attention to context; cultural settings and power relations figure prominently. In fact, ethnography is the process of "describing a culture and understanding another way of life from the native point of view" (Neuman 1994, 333). Observation research can also be used to study populations and events that cannot be studied by methods such as survey research or interviews, for example, studies of the "underworld."

There are two forms of observation research: direct and participant. **Direct observation** involves sitting at the sidelines, watching what is going on. For example, a researcher may sit in on a parliamentary session and watch the dynamics: who speaks and for how long, what are the responses, what is the mood, and so on. Of course, there exists the possibility again for reaction problems: if we know we are being watched, we may begin to alter our behaviour. This phenomenon—altering one's behaviour when under observation—is known as the **Hawthorne effect**.[2] To minimize these reaction effects, the researcher has two options. The first is to conduct research *covertly*, in other words, not telling the subjects that they are being observed. For example, the researcher might sit in Parliament and observe without informing the members. When the forum is public, this can be the best way to conduct observation research. However, in private forums or small group settings where the researcher's presence is sure to be noticed, research must be *overt*: the researcher informs the subjects that they are being observed as part of a research project. As with interview work, the researcher must take care not to reveal his hypotheses. Unlike interviewing, extensive notes are not taken. The goal is for the group or individual to proceed with their activities *as if the researcher were not there*, which requires the researcher to be as inconspicuous as possible. If the researcher is taking detailed notes, his presence is felt more readily. For this reason, the researcher should develop extensive notes immediately after the observations have been completed for the day.

Direct observation can vary in the degree to which it is structured or unstructured. When observation is unstructured, the researcher typically is not looking for any particular patterns; the research is mostly inductive and exploratory. Here, the researcher can consider both the specific behaviours of the subjects and the subjective values attached to those actions (Brown 1981, 169). More structured (and thus more quantitative) research is necessary for hypothesis-testing. In this research, the observer considers only the actions that occur. Prior to the observations, she draws up an **observation schedule**, which is essentially a checklist for recording behaviour (Brown 1981, 178). For example, in our study of parliamentary behaviour, we might create a checklist to tick off who spoke and for how long. Our prior research has suggested to us ways by which to classify behaviours; all we do during the observation research

A POINT ON THE COMPASS

The Hawthorne Effect

Earle Babbie (1989, 215–16) provides us with the following summary of the Hawthorne effect:

> *The need for control groups in social research became clear in connection with a series of studies of employee satisfaction conducted by F.J. Roethlisberger and W.J. Dickson (1939) in the late 1920s and 1930s. These two researchers studied working conditions in the telephone "bank wiring room" [at the Hawthorne plant] of the Western Electric Works in Chicago, attempting to discover what changes in working conditions would improve employee satisfaction and productivity.*

> *To the researchers' great satisfaction, they discovered that making working conditions better consistently increased satisfaction and productivity. As the workroom was brightened up by better lighting, for example, productivity went up. Lighting was further improved, and productivity went up again. To further substantiate their scientific conclusion, the researchers then dimmed the lights:* Productivity again improved!

> *It became evident that the wiring room workers were responding more to the attention given them by researchers than to improved working conditions. As a result of this phenomenon, often called the* **Hawthorne effect**, *social researchers have become more sensitive to and cautious about the possible effects of experiments themselves. The use of a proper control group—studied intensively without any of the working conditions changed otherwise—would have pointed to the existence of this effect in the wiring room study.*

is note frequencies of behaviour. After the session, we examine the data to see if the results fit our hypotheses.

When creating the observation schedule, we must ensure that our indicators are clear; if we leave categories broadly defined, we may have trouble deciding if a given behaviour fits into a particular category. For example, imagine that you are observing a city council session to see if female politicians are more consensual than their male colleagues. How are you going to determine what counts as "consensual" behaviour? Will voice tone be included? Efforts to compromise? An explicit desire to avoid arguments? Clearly, observing "consensual behaviour" can be quite subjective if specific indicators of such behaviour are not included. In addition, if we do not have clearly defined ideas of what a given behaviour is, we may be inconsistent between observations. At one council meeting we may be in a good mood and see everything as efforts to compromise. At a meeting later in the week, after a long day that included a minor car accident and getting yelled at by a co-worker, the world may not seem so rosy, and very little is seen as "consensual." Using specific indicators of behaviour can help overcome such problems. A number of the rules from survey research also apply to the creation of observation indicators: researchers should first operationalize their key concepts to develop valid measures and should ensure that the categories available are mutually exhaustive (that all possible categories are included in the schedule) (Brown 1981, 179).

The second form of observation research is **participant observation**. In this strategy, the researcher becomes part of the community that she is observing. For example, to study the dynamics among political campaign staff, she may volunteer for a campaign. As with direct observation, participant observation can be either overt or covert. One advantage of participant observation is that it allows for greater understanding of context: by becoming a member of the group, one has maximum access to that group's beliefs and world paradigm. An action may

CHECKING YOUR BEARINGS

CONSTRUCTING AN OBSERVATION SCHEDULE

Your task is to explore the interpersonal dynamics of political science professors at the annual faculty retreat. You suspect that as seniority increases, faculty members are more likely to raise "thorny" issues and vigorously defend their positions. In other words, you suspect that a sessional instructor will not raise such issues, while an associate professor will, and that the assistant professor is more likely to back down on her position than is the full professor. Develop your schedule, and identify your key concepts. How will you define "thorny" issues? How will you categorize the faculty? What will constitute "raising" and/or "supporting" an issue?

have significantly different meaning in a particular group context than in the world at large, and in some cases being a member of the group is the only way that a researcher can access this information. Finally, there are some subgroups that can only be accessed through covert participant observation. Consider a sociologist exploring a particular religious cult (or, more positively, "alternative religion") or a police officer investigating drug smuggling. Neither group could be penetrated unless the researcher assumed the identity of a group member.

Participant observation is very context driven and less structured than direct observation, rendering it particularly useful for descriptive and exploratory research (Brown 1981, 173). However, even with unstructured research, the observer should develop a number of issue areas that he wishes to explore which will help direct his study by leading him to pay greater attention to particular issues and dynamics. As with direct observation, note-taking should be kept to a minimum in the presence of the research subjects; in the case of covert observation, note-taking might be restricted to times when the researcher is completely removed from the subjects. The data collected in unstructured observations are collected as **field notes**, detailed descriptions of events and their subjective meanings. The researcher later takes these field notes and looks for emerging groupings, categories, or patterns (Brown 1981, 177).

For participant observation (be it overt or covert) to work effectively, the researcher must be accepted into the group. The process of building trust and rapport can be time-consuming, but is necessary for valid data. W. Lawrence Neuman (1994, 339) notes that "Entry [to a group] is more analogous to peeling the layers of an onion than to opening a door." To access very sensitive information, the researcher must obtain high levels of trust and respect in the group. This can involve adopting the dress, speech patterns, social interests, and personal style of group members; the researcher needs to not only "talk the talk" but also "walk the walk" if he is to be trusted with group secrets and viewpoints. In some cases, assuming the status as a group member can be a difficult task. In the late 1950s, John Griffin sought to study the black community of New Orleans. A white man, he used drugs prescribed by a dermatologist to darken his skin and shaved his head to conceal his straight hair. He then experienced life as a Black man and recounted his experiences in the classic *Black Like Me* (1960).

Although the ethical issues of participant observation have been touched upon in Chapter 3, we also need to consider the risks of the research approach. First, certain forms of participant observation may put the researcher at physical risk should his purposes be discovered.

A POINT ON THE COMPASS ─────────────────

Participant Observation with the Reform Party

It should come as no surprise that many political scientists move back and forth between the study and practice of politics. Indeed, much of the richness and excitement of the social sciences in general comes from this interplay. Political scientists have a wide array of applied skills and knowledge: they have substantive expertise, an ability to write and to think analytically, often a detailed understanding of the public policy process, and, perhaps less frequently, a comprehensive grasp of empirical research methodologies. In this last case, they know how to collect data, orchestrate surveys, design questionnaires, and make complex data stand up and sing for diverse sets of clients.

However, participant observation means more than applying or marketing one's analytical skills. It entails working for governments, parties, interest groups, social movements, or community associations with the objective of improving one's understanding of the political process. Participant observation, therefore, goes well beyond providing a source of anecdotes and illustrations to use in class.

In early 1991, Dr. Tom Flanagan from the Department of Political Science at the University of Calgary was hired as the director of Policy, Strategy, and Communications for the Reform Party of Canada, a position he held until the end of 1992. Flanagan was a member of the party both before and after this appointment, but the appointment provided unprecedented access to the party, its leadership, and its policy and strategic deliberations.

Dr. Flanagan's experiences with Reform were woven into *Waiting for the Wave: The Reform Party and Preston Manning*, published in 1995. While the book is greatly enriched by Flanagan's participant observation, it also goes well beyond his direct experience in providing a detailed historical account of the party and a sophisticated theoretical treatment of Reform's place on the Canadian political landscape. *Waiting for the Wave* illustrates not only how academic work can be enhanced by participant observation, but also how the "kiss-and-tell" aspects of participant observation can be scrupulously avoided.

After the publication of his study, Griffin was hanged in effigy and his family harassed. A second risk comes from the association with the group. Let's imagine that a researcher, studying neo-Nazism in Canada, joins a neo-Nazi group. After the researcher has completed her study, she will always be plagued by that association; taken out of context, she may be seen as a true supporter of the group. Some affiliations can be difficult to shake and may be used to damage the researcher's credibility. For example, in 1963 Gloria Steinem took a job as a Playboy Bunny (a waitress position, not a "Playmate," which is a nude model) to investigate how women were treated in the Playboy clubs. Later, Steinem became a leader in the mainstream feminist movement, and the former Bunny association, taken out of context, proved at times a liability. She reports (1983, 69) "[c]ontinuing publishing by *Playboy* magazine of my employee photograph as a Bunny amid ever more pornographic photos of other Bunnies. The 1983 version [of the Steinem photo] insists in a caption that my article 'boosted Bunny recruiting.'"

A third potential problem with participant observation involves exiting the group. It is possible that one can do such a good job convincing others of group status that disengagement is problematic. Also, the researcher may have developed friendships that are difficult to leave. Finally, the researcher faces the risk of "going native," in other words, becoming so entrenched in a group and so identified with its positions that objectivity is lost (Chadwick et al. 1984, 214). A researcher's sympathy for the group and its causes may lead her to forget why she is there, and rather than providing a balanced analysis of the group, she may turn into an apologist.[3] This problem of bias may lead all of her conclusions to be suspect.

Overall, observation strategies are an important means by which researchers can explore what *really* happens in groups. They give the role of context its due and provide a richer understanding of social

---

CHECKING YOUR BEARINGS

ISSUES IN PARTICIPANT OBSERVATION

"What practical and ethical problems can be anticipated by a researcher planning to use participant observation in order to study a white supremacist organization such as the Ku Klux Klan or the Heritage Front?"

Source: Nicolas Baxter-Moore, Terrance Caroll, and Roderick Church, *Studying Politics: An Introduction to Argument and Analysis* (Toronto: Copp Clark Longman Ltd., 1994). Used with permission of Copp Clark Longman Ltd. © 1994.

dynamics. However, the method requires a great deal of the researcher's time: it is not a method for the uncommitted! Also, in the realm of politics, there are a number of areas that are not open to observation, such as cabinet dynamics. In such cases, researchers must rely on first-hand accounts through elite interviewing or written documentation.

COMPARATIVE RESEARCH

One of the goals of political science is to broaden our understanding of the political world, to be able to make generalizations and increase our predictive accuracy. The challenge is to create generalizations that cut across systems and societies, that are not bound by time and place. Thus, rather than merely describing Canada or the United States or Russia, we seek to understand society and politics *as a whole*, the dynamics of people living in coordinated commonality. However, problems emerge when we try to take the lessons from one country, society, or historical period and generalize to the rest of human civilization. How do we decide which country, which society, should be considered representative of humanity? (The issue of representativeness is taken up in detail in Chapter 8's discussion of sampling.) Many experiences are country-specific. For example, if we were to make generalizations about federalism based solely on the Canadian experience, we might conclude that federalism involves never-ending constitutional struggles over the division of powers. But is this representative of the federal experience in other countries? Only **comparative research** can answer such questions.

There are two chief advantages to comparative research. First, it forces us to realize how many of our conclusions about life and politics are in fact culture-bound (Bahry 1981, 230). Many of our assumptions about politics and society do not hold true in other cultures, and as political scientists we need to distinguish between what is held in common between societies and what is unique to a particular community. Comparative research also allows us to move beyond the study of smaller units to consider *system-level* analysis (Bahry 1981, 231): what do particular systems have in common? Thus, we can look at "democracies" or "federal systems" or "developing countries." From this type of analysis, we can increase our predictive abilities: if we know that qualities A and B usually lead to condition C, and country Z has both A and B, we have a reason to expect C. This can be useful information for the study of subjects such as development, peace efforts, and the global economy.

Comparative research is strongly associated with **historical research**. The distinction between the two is seen in what exactly is being compared. Historical research looks at a single culture over time, whereas comparative research explores the similarities and differences between cultures during a specified period of time (Neuman 1994, 379). One use of historical research is the study of progress, for example, the movement from feudal to industrial to postindustrial society. Social scientists may also choose to combine aspects of the comparative and historical approaches, exploring the history of many cultures. Karl Marx studied the evolution of economic society in a number of cultures before developing his theory of dialectical materialism. He argued that history can be seen as a progression of economic systems, each with an accompanying social superstructure. Humankind moves from primitive community to slavery, then to feudalism, capitalism, and finally socialism. Marx assessed the economic systems of countries in the late 1800s and predicted the emergence of socialism in the developed countries of Europe. Although the emergence of socialism contradicted Marx's theory—Communism developed first in Russia and China, countries that had yet to complete the transition from feudalism to capitalism—his historical-comparative approach has much to recommend it.

The principal issue when beginning comparative research is "which units should be included in the comparison?" What should be compared to what? Random sampling does not provide an answer to such questions for a number of reasons. First, not all political units are suited for all research questions (Bahry 1981, 232). For example, if we were to study the interplay between electoral law and party systems, we would want to include only those countries with true democratic elections, in other words, those with open, competitive elections. States that hold nondemocratic elections, and then use these results to support their authoritarian regimes, must be excluded. Of course, we could always take care of this issue with our sampling frame: we could first begin with a list of only countries we consider democratic and then randomly sample. However, the utility of this is questionable. In Chapter 8 one will see that sampling error increases in random sampling as the sample size decreases; in other words, when sample sizes are very small, the benefits of random sampling are lost, because we are less certain that our selected cases are truly "representative." When comparing political units such as countries rather than individuals within countries, we have a limited number of potential cases; the populations are even smaller when we specify by regime type or legislative systems or some other system-level characteristic. Thus, the second reason that random sampling is not appropriate for comparative research is that the logic behind

A POINT ON THE COMPASS

Using Comparative Research to Study System-Level Traits: Testing Smiley's Theory of Executive Federalism

In *Canada in Question*, Donald Smiley (1980) noted that Canadian decision-making had evolved to a system by which provincial and federal elites negotiated behind closed doors. He termed this elite-dominated decision-making process "executive federalism." Why did executive federalism exist in Canada, when no parallel system emerged in the United States? Smiley argued that the reason lay in the system of government; while federalism alone does not necessarily lead to elite-driven decision-making, the combination of federalism with parliamentary systems of government inevitably creates executive federalism. Parliamentary systems are cabinet- and therefore elite-dominated, allowing executive federalism to emerge, whereas the American federal system is based upon a system of checks and balances, precluding cabinet domination.

In essence, Smiley put forward a rather simple formula: parliamentary systems + federalism = executive federalism. If this formula is valid, then other systems with these two characteristics should also experience executive federalism. Is this the case? Ronald Watts (1989) tested this equation by looking at federal systems in Australia and Germany, and he found that similar elite-dominated politics characterized the two systems. Watts concluded (1989, 455) that "Donald Smiley has been right to emphasize the extent to which 'executive federalism' is a logical dynamic resulting from the combination of federal and parliamentary institutions."

random sampling does not hold for such small populations. *Purposive sampling* best allows the researcher to use her knowledge of the systems to choose political units that allow for the most fruitful comparisons, and in so doing to choose between two main approaches to selecting cases for comparative research.

One approach is to compare very similar systems, seeking to explain differences between them. This **most-similar-systems design** allows researchers to hold constant all shared characteristics between the countries in the attempt to explain variation in the dependent or independent variables. This is perhaps best understood by way of example. Political scientists have noted that the United States is unique from Europe in that it lacks a true socialist ideological voice; although the United States has "left" and "right" parties (the Democrats and the Republicans, respectively), these parties both adhere to the tenets of liberalism, which include the principles of individualism, the free market economy, and meritocracy (the idea that hard work should be rewarded). There does not exist in the United States a viable socialist party that recommends significant levels of state ownership and wealth transfer; such ideas conflict with "the American dream" and are essentially absent from the political psyche. But why does the United States lack a true socialist alternative? In *The Founding of New Societies* (1964), Louis Hartz argues that the American settlement lacked a "tory fragment"; the settlers who arrived did not create a strict class system as existed in Europe. This feudal background was seen by Hartz to be necessary for the development of socialism, and he concluded that the settlement history of the United States can explain the failure of socialism on American soil.

This is all well and good for students of American politics, but should raise some questions in the minds of Canadian students. Canada also has a settlement history and a political culture that is in many ways similar to that of the United States. Yet despite the many similarities between the Canadian and American histories, cultures, and systems (both are democratic federal systems), successful socialist parties have emerged in Canada. Although some may question the true socialist leanings of current New Democratic Parties, the socialist influence on its predecessor, the CCF (Co-operative Commonwealth Federation), is certain. So the question is, given the similarities between Canada and the United States, why has socialism achieved a degree of success in one country and not the other? This question was taken up by Gad Horowitz in his article, "Conservatism, Liberalism and Socialism in Canada: An Interpretation" (1966). Horowitz accepts the thesis that the United States lacked a "tory fragment," but argues that the same was not true for Canada. He asserts that Canada did in fact have a small "feudal fragment." In addition to a degree of feudalism in the French settlements (which Hartz acknowledges), Canada was home to the expelled Loyalists after the American War of Independence. The Loyalists were, in essence, a second Tory fragment, loyal to British traditions and ideas of hierarchy. The Loyalists' Tory influence was felt in Canada due to the small population. Horowitz thus concludes that the Tory fragment provided by the Loyalists allowed Canadian political culture to be more receptive to socialism:

> In Canada, socialism is British, non-Marxist and worldly; in the United States it is German, Marxist and other-worldly....The socialism of the United States ... is predominantly Marxist and doctrinaire, because it is European. The socialism of English Canada ... is predominantly Protestant, labourist and Fabian, because it is British. (1966, 159–60)

By comparing two very similar systems, Horowitz was able to focus all on a single point of variation. All potential explanatory variables, that is, variables that would have been considered in single-state analysis, that the two systems held in common were ruled out, reducing the number of factors that Horowitz needed to explore.

Whereas the most-similar-systems design takes alike systems and seeks to explain variation between them, the second comparative approach works in the opposite manner. The **most-different-systems design** involves taking very dissimilar systems and attempting to explain commonalities between them (Bahry 1981, 236). How could two such very different systems produce the same social outcome? As with the previous approach, the most-different-systems design works by allowing the researcher to eliminate possible sources of explanation: any variable that does not exist in all systems under study is eliminated. For example, Theda Skocpol's *States and Social Revolutions* (1979) explored what the social revolutions in France, China, and Russia held in common. The three revolutions were very different in many respects—in addition to different political cultures, each occurred in a different time period—but important commonalities emerged nonetheless. In the description of her methodology, Skocpol points out that "comparative historical analysis works best when applied to a set of a few cases that share certain basic features" (1979, 40). She then goes on to explain how the three social revolutions in her study do, in fact, share such basic features, even though this similarity may not be immediately apparent:

> All of them, for one thing, happened in countries whose state and class structures had not been recently created or basically altered under colonial domination. This consideration eliminates many complexities that would need to be systematically included in any analysis of revolutions in postcolonial or neocolonial settings.... it is the premise of this work that France, Russia, and China exhibited important similarities in their Old Regimes and revolutionary processes and outcomes—similarities more than sufficient to warrant their treatment together *as one pattern calling for a coherent causal explanation.* (1979, 40–1) [Emphasis added]

Such similarities, however, need not blind the researcher to the unique features of the particular cases. As Skocpol explains (1979, 42):

> For even as we primarily look for and attempt to explain patterns common to France, Russia, and China, we can also attend to the variations that characterize pairs of cases or single cases. These can then be explained as due in part to variations on the shared causal patterns, in part to contrasts among the social structures of France, Russia, and China, and in part to differences in the world-historical timing and succession of the three great Revolutions.

Which comparative research design we choose depends in part upon the theory that underlies our study (Bahry 1981, 236). If our theory is such that we are able to identify ahead of time the variables that may be influential, we can then choose countries that match on these variables, rendering the most-similar-systems design appropriate. However, if we have less knowledge of influential factors, or if we are unable to match countries appropriately on particular variables, the most-different-systems design is preferred. Donna Bahry (1981, 236) writes: "a most-different-systems approach offers us somewhat better control over the factors that might influence or bias what we find, and more assurance that our results are valid."

Researchers will often use case studies or survey research for comparative research. When conducting comparative research, the researcher must be careful about how he operationalizes his variables. A

CHECKING YOUR BEARINGS

CHOOSING A COMPARATIVE APPROACH

Consider the following research questions. Which are better suited for a most-similar-systems design? For which would you use a most-different-systems design? For each, suggest countries that you could use for your study, as well as positing hypotheses.

1. What factors influence voter turnout?
2. What is the relationship between socioeconomic class and partisanship?
3. Is there a relationship between levels of income inequality within a state and that state's behaviour on the international stage?
4. Does state intervention in the delivery of health care result in better overall levels of health within the community?

measure that is appropriate in one culture or society may not measure the same concept in another culture or society. As we noted at the start of this chapter, context is very important. In designing a comparative study, a researcher must be highly cognizant of the social and political context. The goal is to have **equivalent measures** and not necessarily identical measures (Bahry 1982, 233). For example, imagine that you are conducting a study of the role of women in politics in communist and democratic regimes. You decide to compare the number of women holding legislative seats in the national Soviet and American legislatures in the 1980–1987 period. You find that the Soviet legislature has a high proportion of female representatives, while the American legislature has a small proportion of women. From this you conclude that women have greater political roles and power under Communism than under democracy. Would your conclusion be valid? In a word, no. What is missing is attention to context, which results in a variable that measures different things in different countries. In the Soviet system, the legislature had little influence, and the women who sat on its seats held very little power or influence despite their numbers. The assumption that legislative presence has the same meaning in two very different cultures is false. Remember that ultimately our goal is to measure a *concept*; a particular indicator is merely a means by which to measure a concept. As researchers, we must ensure that the indicators we choose are actually measuring our concepts. This may mean using different indicators in different countries or working hard to ensure that the indicators chosen do, in fact, measure the same concept in all countries under study. Obviously, both options require a solid understanding of the societies being considered; the importance of context in comparative research cannot be overemphasized.

A second caution for comparative researchers is known as *Galton's problem*: the researcher must ensure that the units under observation are independent of one another. This can be a problem because societies and cultures do not stay fixed within territorial units. Consider this problem of *diffusion* with respect to Canada and the United States. Although technically distinct states and societies, many American influences are felt north of the Canadian–American border. (The influence of Canada on the United States is less clear.) Most of our television programming is American, as are many of the popular music bands, magazines, books, and so forth. Because of this diffusion of cultural norms and experiences, comparisons of popular culture between Canada and the United States are difficult. Neuman (1994, 391) notes that "cultures rarely have fixed boundaries. It is hard to say where one culture ends and another begins, whether one culture is distinct from another, or whether the features of one culture have diffused to another over time." In the case mentioned above, comparisons of the American and Canadian cultures must also come to grips with the influence of American culture *in Canada*. As barriers to communication steadily decrease, we can expect diffusion problems to become increasingly problematic for social researchers.

A POINT ON THE COMPASS

Comparative Societal Research: The Civic Culture

What is necessary for a democratic regime to survive? Decolonization of African and Latin American states illustrated that democratic institutions are not sufficient; many societies reverted back to nondemocratic practices despite the presence of legislatures and the other paraphernalia of democracy. Some theorists argued that for a democratic regime to survive, the *political culture* must support the principles of democracy; without this societal support, the system is predicted to fail. In their classic *The Civic Culture* (1963), Gabriel Almond and Sidney Verba use comparative analysis of five states (Germany, Italy, Mexico, the United Kingdom, and the United States) to test the relationship between political regime and political culture.

Almond and Verba argued that there are three stages of political culture. The "parochial" stage is characterized by a disinterest in, and almost unawareness of, the government. Citizens live their lives as if the state did not exist. In the "subject" culture the citizen is aware of the state and the impact that it has on her life, but makes little or no effort to influence the workings or outcome of the state. The final stage, the "participant" culture, is defined by both an awareness of the state and a belief that one can and should influence its output and social effect. It is the participant culture that is necessary for a democratic system to survive.

Almond and Verba's analysis has not been free from criticism. Some argue that the measures used to assess public attitudes regarding the system's legitimacy were flawed. Others assert that Almond and Verba failed to note significant variation *within* cultures, for instance, that the working and middle classes exhibit different feelings of "political efficacy" (feeling that one can influence the political system).

Overall, comparative research is useful for ensuring that our theories are not culture-bound and for allowing us to conduct system-level analysis. In comparative research the researcher must pay particular attention to context and must select his cases carefully.

INTERPRETING QUALITATIVE DATA

The very nature of qualitative data—words rather than numbers—makes the process of qualitative data analysis very different from quantitative data analysis. One of the most important differences is *when* data analysis begins. For quantitative research, all the raw data are collected before analysis; the researcher does not begin looking for correlations and patterns until the collection, coding, and data entry stages have been completed. Qualitative analysis, on the other hand, is based on the idea of grounded theory: the researcher begins to look for patterns and relationships early in the process, while data are still being collected, and uses these observations to advance his theory and shape subsequent data collection (Neuman 1994, 405).

A second difference between quantitative and qualitative analysis concerns the goals of the project. In quantitative analysis, the researcher often seeks to test hypotheses; statistics are used to estimate the likelihood that a particular relationship exists in the population. We either "reject" or "fail to reject" the null hypothesis. The ultimate goal is to develop lawlike generalizations and probabilistic statements. In qualitative analysis, the research goals are more modest, and different language is used. Here, the researcher seeks to discover if a given explanation of social behaviour is *plausible*: is it conceivable that A is correlated to B? Is it likely that A caused B? Explanations in qualitative research are divided into two classifications: plausible and unlikely (Neuman 1994, 406).

How does one code data that consist of words and statements? Basically, the researcher orders the raw data around specific themes or concepts. The coding process involves classifying and organizing the raw data. He begins by reading his research notes and coding each important statement or notation according to the dominant theme, for example, "party organization," "attitudes about representation," or "beliefs about the state." These concepts are then subdivided into different values; for example, "attitudes about representation" might be subdivided into "representative should follow own judgment only—trustee," "representative should consult people but make final decision—politico," and "representative should obey majority opinion of constituency—delegate." Of course, the issue of subjectivity comes up with qualitative coding. First, it is ultimately the researcher who decides which concepts are important; previous theories will influence his decisions, but he is also guided by what he subjectively perceives. Second, the researcher decides how to code; one researcher may feel that a particular statement falls into one subcategory of a variable, whereas another might feel that the same statement is evidence of another subcategory. Consider our example of attitudes toward representation: how should a researcher code a statement such as "I do not need to formally consult the constituency because my views are so consistent with the majority"? The speaker admits to never consulting her constituency, which suggests a trustee position on representation. However, her justification for not consulting is that she is already obeying the majority view, a delegate position. How one classifies the statement can vary. Issues of intercoder reliability are not absent from quantitative research, but they are particularly germane to qualitative research.

Once data have been coded, the researcher must then move to analyze the data. Here, the researcher is looking for patterns in the data, relationships between concepts, or sequences of events. One way to do this is to create a **data matrix**, a two-dimensional table that organizes the data relating two variables. This matrix looks similar to a correlation matrix, with one distinction: the data placed in cells are in the form of words, rather than mere numbers. The researcher selects data that illustrate the various themes and relationships; these illustrative statements are often used in the final write-up to substantiate conclusions. If he is studying group interactions or sequence, the researcher may choose to develop diagrams or charts showing linkages. Finally, in an attempt to quantify the data, the researcher may use content analysis to assess the statements recorded and then subject the data to statistical analysis.

Because the researcher is concerned with plausibility, he needs to pay attention not only to the evidence collected, but also to *negative evidence*. Who was not at an event who might have been expected to be there? What predicted statements did a politician not make? What news items failed to gain mention in the news media? The absence of particular phenomena and data can prove very insightful (Neuman 1994, 419–20).

In summary, qualitative analysis can be used in a number of ways to expand our understanding of the political world. When combined with quantitative analysis, qualitative research provides not only a test for our results, but also adds context and colour.

FIGURE 5.1

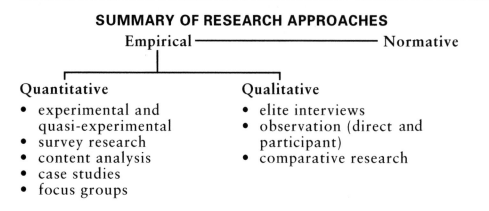

SUMMARY OF RESEARCH APPROACHES

Empirical ——————————— Normative

Quantitative
- experimental and quasi-experimental
- survey research
- content analysis
- case studies
- focus groups

Qualitative
- elite interviews
- observation (direct and participant)
- comparative research

WORKING AS A TEAM

1. Most universities confront an ongoing controversy about how best to assess faculty teaching performance and, more specifically, how best to incorporate student input. Now that you have been exposed to a variety of quantitative and qualitative research approaches, which approach or combination of approaches would be the most appropriate? How would you best assess this class? What, if any, are the ethical issues relating to the assessment of teaching performance, and how might they best be addressed?

SELF-STUDY

1. Your research project is to explore the leadership style of a prominent female legislator with a reputation for her consensual approach to politics.

   a. How could you use elite interviewing to gain insights into her style? Whom would you interview? What questions would you ask?

   b. In addition to the interviewing stage of your research, you are going to use observation techniques. Outline your observation strategies. What type of observations will you use? What data will you be seeking? How will you conduct the research?

   c. Can you use any form of survey research to further your study? Are there other research approaches you could use?

2. Does the electoral system of a country have any impact other than determining how votes are cast and calculated? Maurice Duverger argues in *Political Parties* that a country's electoral system influences the nature of the party system; more specifically, he argues that "the simple-majority single-ballot system favours the two-party system" (1964, 217), and "the simple-majority system with second ballot and proportional representation favour multi-partisanism" (1964, 239).

   a. How could you use comparative analysis to test this thesis? Is a most-similar-systems design or a most-different-systems design appropriate? Explain your reasoning.

   b. What countries would you use?

   c. Considering the need for equivalent measures, what indicators will you use? What is your definition of a "democratic election"? How will you assess the party system: what is required before a party is seen as a legitimate contender?

   d. Canada's party system has been referred to as a "two-plus" system by many writers, due to the presence of third parties that do not present a true governing alternative. Can this experience be fit into the theory?

NOTES

1. The following discussion is sourced to the Denzin quotation in Berg (1989, 5).

2. This effect, named after research conducted in the late 1980s in the Hawthorne Western Electric Plants in Chicago, refers to "any variability in the dependent variable that is not the direct result of variations in the treatment variable" (Jackson 1995, 83).

3. An extreme manifestation of this phenomenon is the Stockholm Syndrome, whereby hostages come to develop strong attachments with their captors.

CHAPTER 6

Defining the Political World: Concepts

DESTINATION

By the end of this chapter the reader should

- appreciate the importance of clear conceptual definitions when conducting empirical research;
- appreciate the difficulties in arriving at clear and consistent conceptual definitions;
- know some rules of thumb that can be applied to the development of conceptual definitions;
- be familiar with issues of measurement with respect to the political world.

The goal of empirical political science is to conduct research in such a way that lawlike generalizations can be made about the political world. Although it is no doubt interesting to know why one voter, say Jack Smith of Richmond, British Columbia, voted for the Reform Party in the 1997 federal election, it is of greater interest to know what are the determinants of voting more generally in Canadian federal elections. The factors that can impinge on voting include many characteristics, such as voters' gender, age, ideology, partisan identifications, attitudes toward party leaders, and the like. But the importance of these factors varies over time and over political space. For example, gender may be more important as a predictor of voting behaviour in the late 1990s than it was in the early 1960s, as women contest more ridings in which their party stands a chance of winning, as policies become more relevant to women, or as women become more likely to lead political parties. Likewise, ideology may be a more important determinant of voting in a province such as Ontario, where the parties themselves appear more ideologically distinct, than in Nova Scotia where the major parties seem to have a higher level of consensus.

To develop lawlike generalizations about the political world, it is necessary to devise models that enable a comparison of alternative possible causes. We began exploring causal models in Chapter 2. The basic structure of such a model is presented in Figure 6.1. In this simple model, there is one hypothesized causal factor and one outcome. The hypothesized causal factor is labelled "A," and the outcome is labelled "B." Following the discussion from the previous paragraph, "B" represents the concept that we wish to explain, namely, voting in Canadian federal elections. A represents the hypothesized cause of that outcome, such as attitudes toward the party leaders. These two concepts are joined by a causal arrow, which runs from A to B. Thus, it is read as attitudes toward party leaders cause Canadians to vote for one party over another in an election. In this model, "attitudes toward party leaders" is the **independent** concept, and voting is the **dependent** concept. Recall that in empirical research a dependent concept is the outcome that we are trying to explain. In brief, we hypothesize that variations in this concept are based on, or depend upon, variations in other elements *inside* the model. Another way of saying this is that the variance is **endogenous** to the model. Thus, in the present example, variation in voting is hypothesized to stem from variation in attitudes toward leaders. The independent concept is the hypothesized cause of the outcome. Variations in the independent concept are hypothesized to depend upon factors *outside* (i.e., **exogenous** to) the model.

Concepts can be independent or dependent depending upon the topic of the research and the way in which the causal structure is specified. Although the dependent concept in the model under consideration is voting, this concept could be independent in a different research program. For example, one might hypothesize that people who voted Liberal in the 1993 federal election were more likely than people who voted for other parties to view Sheila Copps's resignation from

FIGURE 6.1

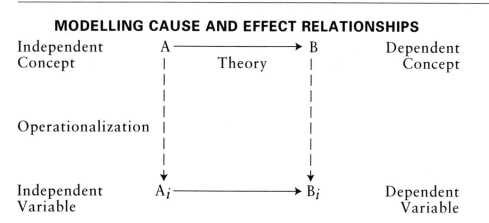

MODELLING CAUSE AND EFFECT RELATIONSHIPS

| Independent Concept | A ⟶ B | Dependent Concept |
| Theory |
| Operationalization |
| Independent Variable | A_i ⟶ B_i | Dependent Variable |

Parliament over the GST as an honourable thing to do. In contrast, those who voted for other parties in 1993 might interpret Copps's actions as cynical and politically manipulative. Thus, voting in the 1993 federal election can be viewed as an independent concept, which causes variation in attitudes toward Sheila Copps's resignation.

Underlying the hypothesized causal connection between attitudes toward party leaders (A) and voting (B) in Figure 6.1 is a **theory** about the causes of voting. A theory can be defined as "a statement of what are held to be the general laws, principles or causes of something known or observed" (*Shorter Oxford English Dictionary,* 2167). Therefore, the theory provides a more generalized statement of the cause of some outcome. We explored the idea of theory in Chapter 2 and found that theories are statements about the relationships between concepts. In the present example, the theory accounting for the relationship between attitudes toward party leaders and voting could be that politics in the electronic age is delivered to people in their living rooms via television. Since television coverage of politics focuses on party leaders and their images (as opposed to a detailed discussion of political issues and policies), we expect attitudes toward leaders to have an important impact on voting preferences. If the results of the research do not support the hypothesized relationship between attitudes toward leaders and voting, then our theory of political behaviour based on media images of party leaders is not supported. Particularly in the social sciences, *statements about causality arise from theorizing.* Thus, our theories, and the concepts embodied in our theories, are extremely important.

The initial stages in developing an empirical research project involve identifying the concepts that will be studied, specifying a hypothesized causal relation, and proposing a theory underlying the relationship. At this stage of the research, these **concepts** are defined as relatively abstract entities. To conduct the empirical research, one needs to move from the level of concepts to the level of **variables** (designated as A_i and B_i in Figure 6.1). Whereas concepts are abstract representations of a phenomenon, variables are the concrete manifestations of that phenomenon in the current research project. Research on the variables will provide the evidence on which to draw conclusions about the hypothesized relationship between concepts. Variables are sufficiently specific that values can be assigned to each person or case in the data set. A variable gets its name by virtue of the fact that these values can vary across the cases.

In effect, much of the statistical component of empirical research involves comparing the variation in one variable with the variation in another. As we will see in subsequent chapters, there are many statistical methods available to test the strength of the relationship between variables. It is important to note, however, that statistical techniques largely are able to assess the strength of association, not the direction of causation. The latter is a matter primarily of research design, in which the researcher hypothesizes a direction of causality and underpins this hypothesis with a more general theory of the causal relationship.

Since empirical analysis is conducted on variables, but we wish to make generalizations about the concepts, it is important that the variables are an accurate reflection of the concepts. We wish to ensure that

CHECKING YOUR BEARINGS

THE DIFFERENCE BETWEEN CONCEPTS AND VARIABLES

Do you understand the difference between concepts and variables? The discussion above suggested that the key difference is that a concept is abstract whereas a variable is concrete. Let's see if we can take this a step further. To say that a concept is abstract does not imply that it is fuzzy or vague. Quite the contrary, we are suggesting that empirical political researchers try to define concepts as precisely as possible. However, even a concept that is defined very precisely can be measured in a variety of ways. A variable is the way in which the concept has been measured in this particular study. When we say a variable is concrete and specific, we mean that the researcher can actually assign a value to every "case" in the study. Any clearer?

Perhaps an exercise will help. Consider the concept "attitudes toward party leaders." What is meant by this concept? Can you provide a specific definition of the concept? You might ask, what kinds of attitudes? In a study of the 1988 Canadian federal election, Richard Johnston and his colleagues suggested that the relevant attitudes toward party leaders concern their "character" and "competence." Do you agree with their definition of this concept? How might assessments of the character and competence of party leaders be measured? Johnston et al. suggest that these dimensions can be measured (i.e., they can be changed into variables) by asking people four questions concerning competence and another four concerning character. The answers to these questions can be combined into "mean" (average) character and competence ratings for each of the party leaders (Johnston et al. 1992, 174–84). Are there other ways of measuring attitudes toward party leaders? (Note: See Chapter 9 for a discussion of "means.")

the relationship between the variables mirrors the relationship between the concepts. This can be accomplished only if the variable is both a precise and an accurate measure of the concept. A discussion of the ways to ensure precision and accuracy in measurement, through the process of operationalization, is taken up in Chapter 7.

CONCEPTUAL DEFINITIONS

In everyday conversation, we often use terms in a way that presupposes that others understand and agree with our conceptualization. Indeed, effective communication requires that a particular word has the same meaning for each person involved in the dialogue. Yet, there is often a certain degree of ambiguity in our conventional use of words. Some of the ambiguity stems from the differences in meaning attached to words when they are used in different contexts. For example, emerging from an 11 a.m. lecture, a student might be overheard saying, "Let's go over to the Student's Union building. I'm starving." In this context, the word "starving" might imply that the student hasn't eaten in the four hours since breakfast, when he had a coffee, some toast, and a piece of fruit. Over lunch, the student might read in the newspaper about a drought in east Africa and learn of the rising death toll of the local population through starvation. Obviously, the comment about his state of hunger upon leaving the classroom was not meant to be equated with the life-threatening condition that starvation presents to many people in the world. In conversation we are often willing to tolerate a certain measure of ambiguity in conceptual definitions while still being able to effectively communicate.

There are other instances in which such ambiguity in everyday language use can lead to ineffective or lack of communication. As a teenager prepares to leave the house on a Saturday night, she might say to her parents: "I'm going out with a group from school. See you later. I'll be home early!" This type of statement is a recipe for miscommunication, since parents and teenagers almost universally have a different understanding of the statement "I'll be home early." Unless the term "early" is defined more precisely, the chances are good that misunderstanding will arise. In fact, in this instance, there may be so much difficulty in coming to a shared understanding of the meaning of the term "early" that communication might be facilitated by doing away with using the terms "early" and "late" in this situation altogether, instead using a term that is defined in such a way that both parties agree. Thus, it may be preferable to say "I'll be home at 11 o'clock," or "I'll be home at midnight." The parents and the teenager would then have a common understanding of the time at which she is expected home. Of course, there may be a downside to using this level of precision, if the intent of the teenager is to come home at 1 o'clock in the morning. From the teenager's perspective there may be advantages to arguing over whether 1 o'clock is "early" or "late" compared to explaining why she is home two hours after the agreed-upon time of 11 o'clock.

The problem of lack of clarity in conceptual definitions plagues those engaged in empirical political research as well. One of the features that continues to differentiate research in the social sciences from that in the natural sciences is the relative lack of agreement in the former around the meaning of concepts. If the goal of research is to test theories of political attitudes and behaviour, and the expectation is that multiple observers will independently arrive at the same observations and conclusions, then it is important to have consistent understandings of the concepts under study. As we shall see, however, such consistency is an elusive goal, as the following examples illustrate.

Example: The Impact of Education on Voting

What impact does education have on voting? To begin exploring this question, we can map a causal relationship as in Figure 6.2. Education is the independent concept (the hypothesized cause) and voting the dependent concept (the hypothesized effect). Notice as well that there is a theory underlying this hypothesized relationship. The theory might be that higher educational achievement leads people to feel themselves a greater part of the political community, and thereby inspires them to higher levels of political activity. Thus, the higher the level of educational achievement, the higher the level of political activity, such as voting. Since this is a positive relationship (an increase in the value of one concept leads to an increase in the value of the other), we include a + over our causal arrow.

To proceed with this research, it is necessary to define the terms "education" and "voting." The theory being tested concerns the impact of education on level of political activity. In this instance, voting is conceptualized as indicative of a certain amount of political involvement or activity. The research is concerned not about whether the person voted for the Liberals, Conservatives, Reform, NDP, or Bloc Québécois, but simply whether or not he or she voted. Thus, we may wish to refer to this concept as "voting turnout" rather than simply voting. Furthermore, voting turnout could be conceptualized either as a **categorical** or a **continuous** concept. Recall that a categorical concept is one

FIGURE 6.2

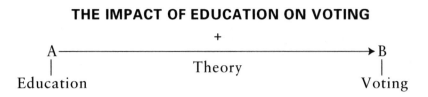

THE IMPACT OF EDUCATION ON VOTING

in which the characteristics of the concept are separate and distinct. A continuous concept is one in which the categories are joined or connected in a sequential manner. For example, examining voting turnout in a single election, we see that the characteristics would be that one voted or that one did not vote. This is indicative of separate or distinct activities, and therefore it is a categorical concept. In contrast, voting turnout could also be conceptualized as being a "disposition to vote," and therefore best measured over time. For example, one could ask in what percentage of federal elections in which the voter was eligible to vote did he or she in fact vote. This conceptualization would result in the creation of a continuous measure of voting, with responses ranging from 0% to 100%. We shall see later that there are important implications in the selection of statistics regarding which approach we follow. At this juncture, the key point to remember is that these different possible conceptualizations of voting turnout could result in researchers lacking consistent definitions of an important concept in their research.

Once we have settled on a definition of voting turnout, we must also define education. On the surface this seems straightforward and uncontroversial: level of education increases with the number of years of formal schooling. Yet slightly below the surface lie a number of questions and concerns that challenge this simple conceptual definition. One of the most obvious concerns is with regard to the change over the past two generations in the meaning of what constitutes a high or a low level of education. Prior to a major expansion in the Canadian postsecondary education system in the 1960s, a university-level education was relatively uncommon. Indeed, even the successful completion of a high school diploma was viewed as a mark of significant educational achievement as recently as the period just prior to World War II. Today, a university-level education has become much more widely available, and it is a much more common achievement. What are the implications of this change for the way in which "level of education" is conceptualized? On one hand, we might agree that people today are simply more highly educated than in the past. From this perspective, level of educational achievement is an absolute quality—what is high for one generation is high for others. On the other hand, the conclusion might be that level of education is a relative quality and that those who achieve high levels of education relative to their age cohort should be considered to have high educational achievement. Such a conclusion would imply that level of educational achievement must be adjusted for the time at which the person was enrolled in the school system.

A second, and possibly more complicating issue, concerns our understanding of how one might achieve a high level of education. At the outset it was suggested that level of education corresponds with the number of years attending an (accredited?) educational institution. But does education always take place within an educational institution? It would seem self-evident that a considerable amount of "learning" takes place both inside and outside the classroom. What role does the classroom experience play in the overall educational process? Such questions are raised not to stretch beyond credulity the meaning of the concept of education, but instead to indicate some of the important debates that are currently taking place at universities across the country. Educators are beginning to ask whether university credits can be given for certain kinds of "life experiences," thereby acknowledging that much learning takes place outside the classroom. If university credit can be obtained for certain life experiences, are these not part of a person's education even if one has not applied for and obtained university credit? If university credit is not viewed as the prime indicator of one's level of educational achievement, then is it possible to arrive at a uniform agreement on the meaning of education? Thus, the issue of whether to include life experiences as a component of educational attainment goes to the very heart of the difficulties often faced in the social sciences of agreeing on the meaning of social concepts.

The third complication that arises in developing a definition of the concept education concerns the connection between years of education and the level of educational achievement. In the secondary education system, there is a difference in courses of study between advanced academic streams (i.e., the International Baccalaureate program), the regular academic stream, and the lower stream. Does the completion of 11 years of schooling in different academic streams equate to the same level of educational achievement? Of course, in the postsecondary education system, such differences in fields of study are even more pronounced. Students might attend a technical training institute (i.e., a business college), a technical college, an arts and sciences community college, or a university, including a university with graduate and professional training. Does enrollment at any of the above for a similar period of time provide the student with a similar level of educational achievement? We might

A POINT ON THE COMPASS ————————————

Changing Definitions of Educational Achievement

In their provocative book, *Transforming Higher Education*, Michael Dolence and Donald Norris (1995, 31–2) contrast postsecondary education using the model inspired by the Industrial Age with that of the Information Age:

> *Under the Industrial Age model, colleges and universities and the training organizations of corporations traditionally created separate, vertically integrated organizations to impart learning. All of the factors of production were included and provided to a largely resident and essentially captive group of learners—geographically isolated learners were served by visiting faculty or remote delivery of instruction. The clustering of the factors of production on the campus was the key competitive advantage. Under this factory/physical campus model of learning, the barriers to entry were huge, and two basic classes of participants existed: providers and learners. During the Industrial Age, higher education has held a virtually exclusive franchise on teaching and certifying mastery in its core areas of interest.*
>
> *In the Information Age, network scholarship will eliminate much of the advantage of vertical integration and the physical concentration of scholarly resources. Not only can learners be anywhere, they can acquire learning and knowledge from sources in any location or mixture of locations. Owning the physical facility where faculty and other expertise reside will not be a critical differentiator in the eyes of many learners. On the other hand, developing the ability to provide expertise, learning, and knowledge to networked learners will be essential. The capacity to measure demonstrated competence and to certify learning in a way that will be accepted by employers will also be a key differentiator. New learning support roles—facilitators, knowledge navigators, and learner/service intermediaries—will become increasingly important.*

anticipate a negative answer to this question—two years as a university student provides a higher level of educational achievement than two years at a technical college. One would need to adjust the definition of educational achievement accordingly. Even within the university, one might ask whether students studying in different areas are obtaining the same level of educational achievement. For example, is two years of study toward an engineering degree similar to two years of study toward a Bachelor of Fine Arts, a Bachelor of Arts, or a Bachelor of Commerce? Furthermore, what impact does different level of performance within the program have on level of educational achievement? Does a student who has completed 15 university courses with an A average have a higher or lower level of educational achievement than a student who has completed 18 courses with a C average?

These might seem like very "technical" issues. Some readers may be thinking that the preceding discussion makes overly complex two relatively simple and straightforward concepts. Everyone knows, you may be thinking, what is meant by the terms "education" and "voting." We will discover, in fact, that what may appear self-evident to you may not be self-evident to others. What is perhaps most important to recognize is the need to be as specific as possible in providing a definition of the

CHECKING YOUR BEARINGS

CONCEPTUAL CLARITY

Is there something unusual about the concepts "voting" and "education" that led to the confusion about their meaning, or is this problem of conceptual ambiguity common in the social sciences and in political science? To answer that question, think of some examples of concepts that could be used in political science research, and ask yourself whether you could provide one and only one definition of the concept.

Try it with the concept of "age." Winston Churchill once said that a person who was a conservative at 20 years old had no heart, whereas a person who was not a conservative at 40 years old had no brain. Thus, he suggests a connection between aging and political belief systems. To examine this hypothesis, one would have to define aging. Can you provide a definition? Do you foresee any problems with this definition? Do you suppose the process of "aging" takes place at the same rate, and in the same way, for all people?

How about the other variable in this model—political belief systems? What do you mean by the term "conservative"? Or "liberal"? Do you think all researchers would agree with your definitions?

key concepts in the research in which you are going to be engaged. Many of the most interesting debates in political science literature are debates over the meaning of concepts. Such debates can only take place, however, if researchers provide clear definitions of the concepts that are included in their analyses.

Example: Party Identification

Party identification was one of the more important concepts to emerge from early studies of voting and elections in the United States. In reporting on some of the first studies undertaken on samples of the American electorate during the 1950s, Angus Campbell and his collaborators at the Center for Political Studies of the University of Michigan developed an attitudinal model of voting. They described the model as consisting of a "funnel of causality." At the wide end of the funnel were the factors that exist in the more distant past or that are further removed (in cognitive space) from the voting decision. As one approaches the narrow end of the funnel, one finds the factors that are most relevant, immediate, and important in the voting decision. These factors invariably are a set of political attitudes and beliefs that impinge directly on the vote. For Campbell et al. the three most relevant such factors were party identifications, attitudes toward party leaders, and attitudes toward political issues. These factors coexist in the sequence outlined in Figure 6.3. This model indicates an important role for party identification in two respects. First, it is one of the three variables that have the most immediate *direct effect* on voting decisions. Second, it is even more important because of the role it plays in influencing the other two prime determinants of voting. In other words, party identification has an important *indirect effect,* through its impact on attitudes toward political issues and on perceptions of the party leaders.

Before turning to a discussion of party identification, it is noteworthy that the dependent concept in Figure 6.3, "vote," differs from the concept "voting" in Figure 6.2. Whereas the previous discussion centred on voting turnout, in the present example vote refers to the direction of voting. That is, the concern is not with whether or not a respondent voted, but for which party he or she voted. In the United States, of course, the main options are to vote for the Democratic or Republican parties, although there is some indication that a broader range of choices may be emerging. In Canada, the options would include Liberal, Reform, Progressive Conservative, New Democrat, and Bloc Québécois among the parties with seats in Parliament, together with a host of other parties that do not control parliamentary seats.

FIGURE 6.3

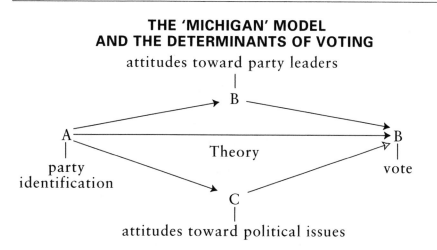

**THE 'MICHIGAN' MODEL
AND THE DETERMINANTS OF VOTING**

The concept of party identification that emerged from the "Michigan" studies derives directly from the empirical findings of the research. In particular, Campbell and his collaborators found that only a very small minority of American voters actually join political parties and pay membership fees. Nonetheless, a large majority of Americans think of themselves as being either a Democrat or a Republican. Furthermore, they found that this psychological attachment tended to develop relatively early in life, was often passed from one generation to the next through the socialization process, and was highly stable for most voters unless there was a particularly tumultuous set of political circumstances. Party identification also tended to exert a strong influence on other political attitudes and beliefs, such as feelings toward the candidates or evaluations of political issues (as outlined in Figure 6.3).

Research on the determinants of voting in other advanced industrial democracies borrowed heavily from the pioneering studies in the United States. This is certainly true of Canadian scholarship.[1] The first book-length treatment of Canadian voting behaviour that used the principles of social psychology as developed by Campbell et al. was Harold Clarke, Jane Jenson, Lawrence LeDuc, and Jon Pammett's *Political Choice in Canada*, published in 1979. Similar to the findings of Campbell et al. in their studies of the American electorate in the 1950s, Clarke et al. found that most Canadians in the 1970s also had a psychological attachment to a political party. However, in contrast to the American findings, which emphasized the stability of party identification and its long-term impact on other political phenomena, Clarke et al. found that party identification in Canada tended to be somewhat more complex. Indeed, they argued that whereas party identification in the United States varied

A POINT ON THE COMPASS ─────────────

American Responses to the 'Michigan' Model of Party Identification

The findings of Campbell and his colleagues regarding the long-term determinants of voting and the stability of party identification generated considerable debate within American political science. Many saw in the Michigan model an argument for irrationality in voting, that voters were guided more by the beliefs of their forebears than by an understanding of the issues at stake in American elections. In one famous response, V.O. Key (1966) declared that "Voters are not fools!"

Others, such as Norman Nie, Sidney Verba, and John Petrocik (1976) argued that the findings of Campbell et al. in *The American Voter* (1960) were accurate for the time at which the study was conducted (the data are mainly from the 1952 and 1956 American National Election Studies), but that the 1950s was a relatively quiet period in American domestic politics, during the presidency of former general and war hero, Dwight Eisenhower. The more turbulent 1960s and 1970s, which saw dramatic increases in the number of protests, demonstrations, sit-ins, and riots in response to the civil rights movement and the Vietnam War, was accompanied by greater instability of party identifications.

The question of the stability of party identification in the United States, and the "rationality" of the electorate, continues to generate interest and research.

along the single dimension of strength of attachment (i.e., the range extended from strong Democrat through weak Democrat, independent, weak Republican, to strong Republican), in Canada the psychological attachment to a political party was **multidimensional**. A multidimensional concept is one in which more than one factor, or dimension, exists within a concept. Clarke et al. suggested that psychological attachments to a political party in Canada consist of three major dimensions: strength, stability, and consistency. Furthermore, they argued that the character of the psychological attachment to a political party in Canada is sufficiently different from that developed by Campbell et al. in the United States to warrant a different name. They used the name "partisanship."

A POINT ON THE COMPASS ————————————————

A Comparison of the Conceptualization of Party Identification and Partisanship

Party Identification (U.S.)	Partisanship (Canada)	
Strong Republican	Strength	Strong identifier
Fairly strong Republican		Weak identifier
Weak Republican		Nonidentifier
Independent		
Weak Democrat	Consistency	Same federally and provincially
Fairly strong Democrat		Different federally and provincially
Strong Democrat		
	Stability	Never changed identification
		Changed identification

The different conceptualization of partisanship stems from the differences that Clarke et al. observed in their study of Canadian voters in the 1970s. They found, for example, that many Canadians hold different partisan attachments at the federal and provincial levels of government. It was not uncommon for a voter to think of herself as a Liberal when asked about federal politics, but to think of herself as a Conservative at the provincial level. Indeed, in many provinces different parties compete at the two levels of government. At the time of their study, the main federal/provincial inconsistency was among the provincial Social Credit and federal Liberals and Conservatives in British Columbia, and among the provincial Parti Québécois and federal Liberals in Quebec. More recently, the federal and provincial distinctiveness between political parties has become even more pronounced, with the emergence of parties such as the Bloc Québécois and Reform, which compete only at the federal level. Supporters of these parties are not able to hold "consistent" identifications at the two levels of government. In contrast, cross-level inconsistency of party identification is much less common in the United States. Since Clarke et al. found that cross-level inconsistency had an important bearing on the character of the psychological attachment to a party, they included this dimension as a component of the conceptualization of partisanship.

A POINT ON THE COMPASS

Consistency in Party Identifications

A debate between David Elkins and Jane Jenson in 1978 regarding the meaning of party identification illustrates the importance of clarity in conceptual definitions:

Elkins (1978, 419–21): "Concepts are like wines; some do not travel well. Thus, a frequent problem concerns whether phenomena with the same label in two societies are really the same. Party identification is a concept which is particularly interesting in this regard ... [E]xhibiting different identifications in different party systems should not be considered evidence of inconsistency ... Jenson et al. do treat contrary federal and provincial party identifications as a form of inconsistency."

Jenson (1978, 437–8): "Concepts do not travel; theories do. The distinction is an important one because the concept party identification and its measurement in different contexts provides students of voting with one of a class of problems in comparative analysis. Comparative analysis implies a search for and the development of general laws about human behaviour, laws which are valid across political systems. The way that this search is carried out is through the development, confirmation and modification of theory.... The more general and abstract the language, the more comparable phenomena that can be found. The more specific and historical the language, the more different things that will be observed."

The other dimension added to partisanship was stability of attachment to a party. Once again, this reconceptualization grew out of empirical research on the character of party attachments. Recall that the "Michigan" formulation of party identification stressed its stability and suggested that it was a long-term attachment to a party passed intergenerationally through the socialization process. In important respects, the transmission of party identification was viewed as similar to the transmission of religious affiliation. Many Americans and Canadians think of themselves as having a religious affiliation, whether or not they formally hold membership in a church congregation. For most, this religious affiliation did not result from a period of detailed and systematic study of the major religious texts—the Koran, the Torah, the Bible, and others. Instead, most people learn about religion from their parents and become adherents of a religious faith through the socialization process. Similarly, the Michigan model of party identification suggested that most voters do not become party identifiers as a result of a long period of detailed and systematic study of the major political ideologies and parties. Party identifications, like religious affiliations, are passed through the socialization process.

Empirical research on voting in Canada suggested that this process of intergenerational transmission of party identification is much less pronounced than it was in the United States in the 1950s. Although many voters did receive political "cues" from their parents as they were socialized into the political system, these political cues seemed far less powerful in influencing attitudes toward other political phenomena such as attitudes toward political leaders or issues. Furthermore, for many Canadians, partisan affiliation seemed to change in response to the parties' changing issue agenda or changing leadership. That is, the causal relationship between partisan attachment and attitudes toward issues and leaders appeared to be in the opposite direction: from perceptions of the leaders to partisan attachment as well as vice versa.

This multidimensional conceptualization of partisanship developed in response to empirical applications of the concept of party identification to a study of Canadian voting behaviour. Partisanship is thus defined as a psychological attachment to a political party, which can vary along the dimensions of strength, stability, and consistency of attachment. Those voters with strong, stable, and consistent attachments to a party are referred to by Clarke et al. as "durable" partisans, whereas those without one or all of these qualities are called "flexible" partisans. Durable partisans resemble in many respects the "party identifiers" discussed by Campbell et al. in their research on public opinion and voting in the United States; these voters have a long-term, stable tie to a party, and this tie colours their perception of the political world, including their attitudes toward the party leaders and their understanding of political issues and events. However, in Canada only about one in three voters is a durable partisan. The rest of the electorate consists of flexible partisans, for whom partisan affiliation is less stable and more likely to change in response to short-term political issues and events. Approximately two in three Canadian voters are flexible partisans, providing Canadian elections with considerable opportunities for change in response to short-term electoral phenomena. The 1993 federal election, which saw the "emerging" success of two parties (Reform and the BQ) and the near-obliteration of two "old" parties (PC and NDP),

CHECKING YOUR BEARINGS

MULTIDIMENSIONAL CONCEPTS

One of the prime goals at the stage of formulating conceptual definitions is to achieve clarity of concepts. This is not to say, however, that the concepts should be simple. As the discussion of party identification and partisanship indicated, concepts in the social sciences may be complex and multidimensional. Consider the following concepts. Devise a definition of each concept that includes only a single dimension. Then offer a multidimensional definition of that concept:

- political participation
- interest in politics
- assessment of party leaders
- neoconservative ideology
- feminism
- environmentalism

How did you do? Were you able to develop both unidimensional and multidimensional definitions? You can check how well your definitions match the definitions of these concepts among social scientists working in the area. One way of doing so would be to search for one of these key terms in the Social Sciences Index. The index will direct you to research published on this topic for the period of the index (you could search an annualized issue). Find the article identified in the index, and look for the author's definition of the concept.

provided a case in point of the dramatic changes that are possible when flexible Canadian partisans go to the polls.

SOURCES OF CONCEPTUAL DEFINITIONS

It is clear that one of the perennial difficulties in the social sciences is defining concepts in such a way that all researchers, and all observers, agree on their meaning. If we wish to conduct research with the goal of formulating lawlike generalizations about the social world, agreement on the meaning of terms would appear to be a basic precondition. Unfortunately, the reality in the social sciences is that agreement on the meaning of terms remains elusive. Furthermore, there is no indisputable guide to which one can turn for the single, authoritative definition of a concept. One can refer to the political science literature, but, as we have seen, that literature is as likely to document disagreement as it is consensus. This does not mean, however, that concepts either have no meaning at all or that they have any meaning one wishes to ascribe, as suggested by the Mock Turtle in *Alice in Wonderland*:

> "Of course not," said the Mock Turtle. "Why, if a fish came to me, and told me he was going on a journey, I should say 'With what porpoise?'" "Don't you mean 'purpose'?" said Alice. "I mean what I say," the Mock Turtle replied, in an offended tone.[2]

Instead, it is to suggest that debate over the meaning of concepts can itself be an important topic of scholarly inquiry. Within the debate, inductive reasoning, extrapolation, and intuition all come into play.

Inductive Reasoning

Although most studies begin with a literature review, an account of the conceptual and empirical terrain mapped out to date, this should not suggest that a researcher can define concepts only in ways in which they have been defined by previous research. Quite the opposite. It is both possible and at times highly desirable to focus a research project on the development of alternative conceptual definitions. Perhaps the most common method of doing so is through the use of **inductive reasoning**. By inductive reasoning we mean using empirical evidence to help form the definition of a concept. An illustration of this can be drawn from the example of party identification given above. When Clarke and his colleagues were examining Canadian voting behaviour in the mid-1970s, they began with the conceptualization of party identification as it was developed in the United States. However, their early studies of this phenomenon in Canada indicated several important differences: they found that many Canadians held different identifications at the federal and provincial levels, and they found that party identifications were not as stable in Canada as they were reported to be in the United States (see Jenson 1975; Jenson 1978; Clarke et al. 1979; LeDuc et al. 1984). Thus, evidence from the application of the concept led to its reconceptualization.

Extrapolation

An alternative method of changing a conceptual definition is to *extrapolate*, even borrow from other fields of study. Political scientists have developed certain conceptual tools for understanding political phenomena, as have economists, sociologists, psychologists, and other

A POINT ON THE COMPASS

Inductive Reasoning and Reconceptualization

The argument above is that evidence from a research project can lead to a new and different definition of a concept. A good illustration of this can be seen in some of the research on political participation. One of the early empirical studies of political participation in the United States was conducted by Lester Milbrath (1965), who argued that there was a hierarchy of participation. The hierarchy, in Milbrath's view, was shaped as a pyramid, with many people near the bottom, exhibiting low levels of participation, and with decreasing numbers of people as one moved up the hierarchy. Milbrath labelled those at the high end of the pyramid "gladiators," those in the middle "participants," and those at the low end "spectators."

In a later study, Sidney Verba and Norman Nie (1972) found that political participation was not arrayed in such a hierarchical fashion. In particular, they found many people involved in protest activities such as marches, demonstrations, sit-ins, including those who were highly involved in such participatory activities, often were not involved in more conventional types of political participation, such as voting, donating money to a political party, or running for elective office. This finding led to the conclusion that there were different types or "modes" of participation and that these modes may be relatively independent of one another. Furthermore, different factors may account for the level of activity in different modes of participation. Thus, the empirical evidence led to a reconceptualization of political participation.

social scientists for their fields of study. At times, the concepts developed for one of the social sciences may have important applicability to others. One well-known example of this type of conceptual borrowing can be seen in Anthony Downs's (1957) adoption of a "rational" approach to voting. (Recall that Downs was introduced in Chapter 2.) An economist, Downs attempted to explain voters' decision-making and the relative ideological positioning of political parties using the **deductive reasoning** that is popular in economic analyses. The deductive method begins by the identification of one or more postulates,[3] followed by the derivation of expectations and conclusions based on the postulates. The postulate often used in economic analysis, and used by Downs in his study, is that voters and the leadership of political parties are rational (i.e., self-interested, utility-maximizing) decision-makers. The justification for this extrapolation from economics to politics is that this method has a number of insights for economic decisions involving the marketplace and therefore could provide insight into political decisions involving power, influence, and authority. Whether it does so is a matter of ongoing empirical investigation.

Intuition

Each of the ways of justifying conceptual definitions discussed thus far relies to a considerable extent on how *other* researchers have operationalized a concept. But what about the ideas that are quite unique and independent to *you* as a researcher? What if you have thought about a concept in a way that no one else has thought about it before? Is it not possible to bring one's own creativity to a research project, to define concepts in new ways that speak more directly to one's experience and imagination? The answer to the latter question is a qualified yes. One certainly should not feel restricted to using concepts whose definitions appear less helpful and informative than others that could be imagined. Concepts should be defined to best capture the essence of the quality that is being examined.

However, our experience is that students often do not fully appreciate the scope of previous research on a topic. A vast and continually growing amount of research has been conducted and published on topics in political science. The chances are reasonably good that the ideas that occur to you regarding the best definition of a concept, or the best explanation for variation in a dependent concept, have been examined by others in a different context. What may appear very new to you as you begin to think of yourself as someone engaged in empirical political science may well have occurred to others as well. Thus, two cautionary flags should be raised. First, it is important to check the literature thoroughly for examples of other research that has used conceptual definitions similar to those used in your study. To acknowledge the work of the previous researchers and to connect your findings to those of the broader research community, it is important to provide citations to the previous research. Second, if you are truly the first researcher ever to define a concept in a particular way, it remains important to thoroughly search the literature and to highlight the differences between the way in which you have defined the concept and the way in which it has been defined in previous studies. It is also important in this context to explain why the conceptual definition you have chosen is superior to that used in the previous studies.

In summary, defining concepts in clear and concise ways is an important part of using the scientific method. It is useful to begin from the premise that other political scientists may think about this concept differently than you. Therefore, to avoid misunderstanding about the topic of the research, it is helpful to provide clear definitions of the concepts that will be used in your study. It is also important to recognize that your study will be part of "the literature" in an area of study, so it is useful to provide cross-references to other studies that are related to yours, and which are used as a point of departure for your work.

WORKING AS A TEAM

1. One of the central elements of democratic theory, and one of the most common elements of contemporary political debate, is the concept of *equality*. Discuss in your group various meanings that might be attached to this concept. Can you produce a conceptualization to which everyone can agree?

SELF-STUDY

1. Think of a concept that may be of interest in political science research (political ideologies, political belief systems, voting, political stability, democracy, etc.). Identify three journal articles in which this concept was examined. Describe the way in which the authors define the concept in the three studies. Provide a critique of the conceptual definitions.

    Concept:

    First article:
                    (author, year, title, journal, volume, issue, page)

    Definition:

    Second article:
                    (author, year, title, journal, volume, issue, page)

    Definition:

    Third article:
                    (author, year, title, journal, volume, issue, page)

Definition:

Critique of the three definitions:

2. Participation in politics is variously called "political participation," "political involvement," or "political activity." It is
sometimes defined as a single, simple concept, as a number
of (possibly unrelated) simple concepts, and as a complex,
multidimensional concept. Find an example of each type of
definition in the literature on political participation. Discuss
the usefulness of each.

   a. Political participation:

      Single, simple concept:

      Multiple, simple concept:

      Multidimensional concept:

   b. Political involvement:

      Single, simple concept:

      Multiple, simple concept:

      Multidimensional concept:

   c. Political activity:

      Single, simple concept:

      Multiple, simple concept:

      Multidimensional concept:

NOTES

1. For a discussion of the more general pattern of the influence of American scholarship on research in Canada, see Cairns (1975).

2. Lewis Carroll, *Alice's Adventures in Wonderland and Through the Looking Glass*,
with notes by Martin Gardner (New York: Random House, 1990), 26.

3. A postulate is a statement or claim that one assumes to be true or takes for granted.
The Shorter Oxford English Dictionary (1965), 1554.

CHAPTER 7

Defining the Political World: Measures

DESTINATION

By the end of this chapter the reader should

- understand the process of operationalization and appreciate the research concerns brought to that process;
- know the distinctions between concepts, variables, and indicators;
- be familiar with nominal-, ordinal-, and interval-level variables and with issues of accuracy in the measurement of political phenomena;
- have some experience with the logic behind and creation of scales and indices.

As political scientists, we often find that questions of interest to us are stated as abstractions, for example, Which political system is better? Which economic system promotes the greatest social equality? What is the best means to provide health care? When we approach these matters from an empirical rather than a normative position, we seek factual evidence that can be applied to these abstract questions. In order to obtain such evidence, we first need to transform the concepts embedded in our questions into a form where they can be tackled empirically. The first step in doing so, as outlined in the previous chapter, is a conceptual definition. With that definition in hand, we can then turn to the matter of measurement.

For example, consider the grading of university students. Universities reserve the grade A for those students whose course performance is "excellent." However, "academic excellence" is an abstract concept; thus, how will a professor know which students have earned an A and which have not? In the interests of fairness, the professor needs to quantify academic performance so that all students are comparable. She may decide that students should be judged on three areas: subject knowledge, research skills, and writing ability. Now she needs some method to measure student performance in these three areas. Examinations, homework assignments, and term papers are all methods that might be used. This process—moving from an abstract concept (academic excellence) to a concrete measure (midterm examination mark)—is known as **operationalization**. As we will see, it is not a simple process and at times can be a very contentious one. Think, for instance, of the potential conflicts and controversies that can swirl around the measurement of academic excellence even in a class such as this one! Seldom can we fall back on widely shared rules to make the decisions that have to be made.

CHECKING YOUR BEARINGS

OPERATIONALIZING UNIVERSITY OBJECTIVES

As you know, universities are coming under a good deal of public scrutiny with respect to the objectives of postsecondary education. In their own defence, universities often argue that the public and, more particularly, politicians fail to understand that the objectives of a university education entail more than the acquisition of marketable skills.

Suppose, then, your own premier says, "Fine, I will accept your university's definition of its own mission [which might be to produce graduates with a capacity for independent and critical thought and with the research and analytical skills necessary for success in the 21st century]. Now, show me the evidence that the university is in fact producing such individuals. Show me proof that universities are not simply taking in bright students, aging them four or five years, and then releasing them back into society with no significant increase in their capacity for independent and critical thought, and without the necessary research and analytical skills. In short, show me that the government and public are getting good value for publicly funded postsecondary education."

Given this challenge, how would you operationalize the university's objectives? How would you measure whether students are, in fact, getting better with respect to their ability to think, and whether they are acquiring the appropriate research and analytical skills? What impact has your own education to date had in these respects, and how would you measure this impact? How might you prove that the government and public are getting good value? Or do we simply ask to be taken on faith? Will such a plea carry much weight in an environment of fiscal constraint?

This chapter explores the use of conceptual definitions to select variables and the use of indicators to locate individual cases among the different values of the variable. In addition, we will explore how to select and create the best possible variables and indicators for our research questions. It is in this process of operationalization that the conceptual rubber hits the empirical road.

CONCEPTS, VARIABLES, AND INDICATORS

It is important at the outset to be clear on the difference between a concept and a variable. Recall that a concept is an idea or term that enables us to classify phenomena; equality, order, social class, political culture, and region are all examples of concepts. Obviously, concepts can be relatively abstract (e.g., liberty) or relatively concrete (e.g., region); the more abstract a concept, the more difficult it is to find a definition that is acceptable to one's peers. When we transform our conceptual definition into a quantifiable, observable phenomenon, we have a **variable.**

The distinction between concepts and variables might best be seen by way of an example. "Education" is a concept; we might, for instance, define education as "formal training to develop mental abilities and skills." "Level of education" is a variable that can empirically distinguish between different levels of training. How is the variable "level of education" different from the concept "education"? The variable, unlike the concept, can take on different **values.** We might choose to divide level of education into categories (e.g., low, middle, and high), or we may look at the actual years of education completed by individuals and compare them on a precise basis. The point to stress is that the variable empirically captures *the variation within the concept*. This is a fine but nonetheless important distinction.

Ultimately, our goal is knowledge about the concepts themselves. As we have seen, concepts are the building blocks of theory, and *theories use propositions to state the relationships between concepts.* Variables are our means of tapping and quantifying these concepts, and *hypotheses state the relationships between variables.* We test hypotheses in an effort to find support for our propositions and, by extension, for our theory. It is important to note, however, that as we move from concepts to variables, some degree of meaning or understanding is invariably lost (Manheim and Rich 1981, 45). This is because we are limited by our variables to those aspects of the concept that can be measured empirically. Often, concepts include intrinsic values or meanings that cannot be captured fully by empirical research. For example, many of the benefits that are thought to spring from postsecondary education are not easily captured by empirical measurement. You may be a more thoughtful individual with your degree in hand, but demonstrating this to others can be a difficult task.

A POINT ON THE COMPASS

Abuse of Women in Canadian University and College Dating Relationships

A widespread public discussion of the distinction between conceptual and operational definitions in the social sciences occurred with the release in 1993 of a study examining the abuse of women in Canadian university and college dating relationships. The conclusions of the study, widely reported in the media at the time, were shocking: 35% of Canadian students reported having been physically abused, 45.1% had been sexually abused, and 86.2% had been psychologically abused in a dating relationship (DeKeseredy and Kelly 1993, 148–53). These results were so inconsistent with the conventional understandings of the prevalence of abuse of women in dating relationships at Canadian universities and colleges that their release was greeted with widespread disbelief in much of the popular commentary. The study's operationalization of the concept "abuse" was also challenged in the scholarly community. The researchers' response to their critics presents a highly revealing portrait of the challenges facing researchers working in highly sensitive areas within the social sciences.

DeKeseredy and Kelly define "abuse" as follows: "Any intentional physical, sexual, or psychological assault on a female by a male dating partner was defined as woman abuse" (1993, 146). Thus, they identify three types of abuse. The authors also distinguish between the "incidence" of abuse (a situation that has occurred in the last 12 months) and the "prevalence" of abuse (has occurred since they left high school) (138). Since "prevalence" covers a longer period of time, the prevalence data invariably are higher than incidence data. The study also compared the responses of male and female respondents, but only regarding the behaviour of men toward women, not vice versa.

Let's illustrate with the data on the prevalence rates of psychological abuse:

Type of abuse	Men (N = 1,307)		Women (N = 1,835)	
	%	N	%	N
Insults or swearing	62.4	747	65.1	1,105
Put her (you) down in front of friends or family	25.9	322	44.2	742
Accused her (you) of having affairs or flirting with other men	40.9	495	52.6	901
Did or said something to spite her (you)	65.2	773	72.2	1,216
Threatened to hit or throw something at her (you)	8.0	97	20.6	346
Threw, smashed, or kicked something	30.6	373	37.3	652

The data under the column for men indicate the percentage of men who said they did one of these behaviours to a woman they were dating in the period since they left high school. The data for women are the percentage of women who had these behaviours done to them by a man they were dating in the period since they left high school. When these six questions were combined, DeKeseredy and Kelly found that 86.2% of women had experienced at least one of these behaviours since high school. Based on their operational definition of abuse, they concluded that 86.2% of women had been psychologically abused, and 80.8% of men had been psychologically abusive with a dating partner in the period since high school (1993, 153).

The reaction to this conclusion from the scholarly community was swift and strong. In the following issue of the *Canadian Journal of Sociology,* commentaries appeared by Gartner (1993) and Fox (1993). Gartner challenged the validity of the term "abuse" as operationalized by DeKeseredy and Kelly (we discuss validity in more detail later in this chapter). She argued that the questions used to measure psychological abuse are derived from a commonly used battery of questions called the Conflict Tactics Scales. These questions are introduced to respondents "by noting both the normality of disagreements and conflicts between partners in a relationship and the range of different ways disagreements are dealt with" (1993, 314). The term "abuse" is not used in the questions themselves. Furthermore, as the name of the scale implies, the questions are designed to measure "conflict tactics," which may go both ways in a relationship, and not abuse. This latter point is important, Gartner argues, because previous research shows that "women and men are about equally likely to use verbal aggression" (1993, 316). Similarly, Fox (1993) argues that the use of "global" measures of abuse combine the least with the worst offences (e.g., an unwanted kiss with rape) (322). Both Gartner and Fox argue that conflating the two risks trivializes the more serious offences (318–19; 322).

In a set of responses to their critics, DeKeseredy (1994) and Kelly (1994) justify their operational decisions. However, in a revealing description of the publication of the findings, Kelly provides an eye-opening account of her experiences with this study: "Once the data were collected, there was immediate pressure to release them. From the onset, I was concerned about the release of the psychological abuse items.... [W]e agreed to initially release only the marginals for the physical and sexual abuse items and not to release the aggregate of all abuse items and the psychological abuse items until the data had been fully analyzed. Unfortunately, the data were released without my consent, against our express agreement, and in a form that, in my view, distorted the value of the research.... [T]he bulk of the media attention was to the combined total abuse figures and the psychological abuse items" (1994, 83).

This saga stands as stark testimony of the importance of having consistency between conceptual and operational definitions in the social sciences. It illustrates the accuracy of the old adage, "The devil is in the details."

When we choose variables, we strive to select those that most accurately capture our concepts and thereby reduce the amount of meaning that is lost. One way to do so is to use *multiple* variables to tap the same concept. Often, many variables can be seen as legitimate measures of a given concept and particularly of more complex concepts. Consider the concept "political participation," which we will define here as "acting with the intent of directly influencing the political system." One variable that might tap political participation is voting: did the individual vote in the last election or not? Voting is empirically measurable and can take on different values (did or did not vote).[1] However, other variables also provide insight into political participation; party membership, political campaign contributions, lobbying, letter writing, and protest activity are all aspects of political participation. As Figure 7.1 shows, each of these variables captures a piece, but only a piece, of the concept. Some, such as community participation, may capture part of the concept, even though the bulk of community participation is nonpolitical in character. In Figure 7.1, therefore, "community participation" falls largely outside the conceptual domain of "political participation." And, even with a number of variables at our disposal, there will still be "spaces left," conceptual aspects of participation that remain untapped. These spaces are represented by the unshaded parts of Figure 7.1. Ideally, only small sections of the conceptual domain will be left uncovered by our selected variables.

FIGURE 7.1

VARIABLES ASSOCIATED WITH POLITICAL PARTICIPATION

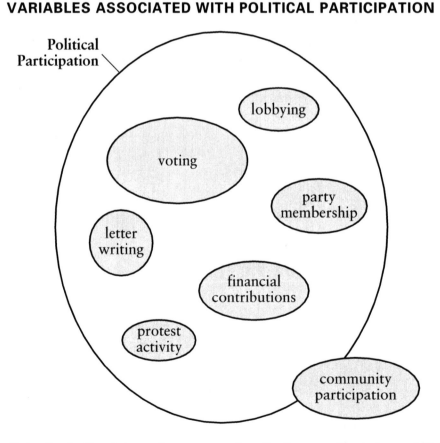

Note: For further information on operationalization, see Manheim and Rich (1981) and Neuman (1994).

Source: Adapted from Lawrence Newman, *Social Research Methods,* 2nd ed. (Boston: Allyn & Bacon, 1994).

Our discussion of grading in the introduction to this chapter provides another example of multiple variables: subject knowledge, research skills, and writing ability are all variables that can be used to quantify the concept "academic excellence." In such cases, when we have multiple variables that appear to measure the same concept, there are likely to be a number of *dimensions* to the concept. The ability to write, for instance, is not the same as knowledge of the subject matter, although we hope there is some relationship (some *positive* relationship!) between the two.[2] We can sometimes combine variables into an index or scale, which will act as a **complex, multiple indicator.** By using multiple variables to quantify the conceptual definition, we are able to capture more fully the meaning of the concept, as Figure 7.1 suggests. This allows us to be more confident when we use the variables to draw conclusions about the concepts. However, as the study of woman abuse in dating relationships illustrates, simply choosing more variables to measure a concept is not necessarily a prescription for better measurement if the variables lack validity (see the discussion of validity below).

Once we have selected the variables to measure a concept, we still need ways to gather information about the variables. The measures are referred to as **operational definitions** or **indicators.** Indicators are the means by which we assign each individual case to the different values of the variable.[3] In the example used in the introduction to this chapter, the grades recorded for examinations, homework assignments, and term papers could be used as indicators for the various dimensions of academic excellence.

CHECKING YOUR BEARINGS

MOVING FROM CONCEPTS TO VARIABLES

For the following concepts, (1) provide a precise conceptual definition, and (2) select three variables to measure each concept. Do you find it easier to select variables for the more abstract concepts, or are the concrete concepts easier to work with? How do your variables differ from the concepts? What is lost by being limited to only three variables? What is lost when you move from concept to variable?

- environmentalism
- political interest
- democracy
- economic growth
- family values

Let's consider the variable "support for feminism." We might understand support for feminism to vary from high through moderate to low support. But what observable facts indicate support for feminism? How do we know whether Jane shows high, moderate, or low support? Possible indicators of support might include stated support in surveys for either feminism or feminist goals, membership in feminist organizations (recorded in membership lists), or financial support for feminist lobby groups (recorded in donation lists). In a recent study of 1,006 Alberta respondents conducted by the authors, feminism was measured in part by responses to the following questions:

- Do you agree or disagree that society would be better off if more women stayed home with their children? (51.5% agreed)

- Do you agree or disagree that we have gone too far in pushing equal rights in this country? (50.6% agreed)

- How important is it to guarantee equality between men and women in all aspects of life? (61.0% thought it was very important, 31.8% somewhat important, and 7.1% not important)

Or consider the variable "economic development." Some commonly used indicators of economic development are GNP (gross national product) and GNP per capita, infant mortality rates, literacy rates, and the proportion of GNP spent on research and development. Information from these indicators can be used to classify countries as "developed" or "developing." There may be multiple indicators of a single variable. For example, in the Alberta survey discussed above, three indicators have been brought into play. Just as multiple variables may allow us to tap more of a concept, multiple indicators may allow us to tap more of a variable. The various indicators, however, will not yield exactly the same results. (If they did, we would only need one.) The United States, for instance, has a poorer record than most Western states with respect to infant mortality, but a better record than most with respect to per capita GNP. Nonetheless, all indicators should point in the same direction; developed countries tend to have higher scores across the board than do developing countries.

To illustrate this point, consider a very simple illustration and then a much more complex illustration. The first comes from a questionnaire administered to grade 10 students who had just completed a summer volleyball camp. The students were asked a very rudimentary question: "Did you enjoy the camp, yes or no?" While the organizers of the camp were pleased that the vast majority of the students said yes, the questionnaire did little to tap the various dimensions of enjoyment. Did students enjoy the coaching? The food? The level of competition? The chance to meet new friends? The social atmosphere? Did they enjoy some elements more than others? What did they like least and most? By asking only one question, and an extremely simple one at that, the organizers missed the opportunity to acquire the type of information that might enable them to plan a better camp the next time around. In short, they needed more than a single indicator of enjoyment.

Next consider social class. As a concept, social class has played an extraordinarily important role in the evolution of social science theory. It is one of the truly "big" concepts, particularly in economics, political science, and sociology. However, it is not easy to capture the theoretical richness of class concepts with empirical indicators. Theoretical nuance is inevitably lost. Certainly one indicator is not sufficient; knowing, for instance, an individual's annual income, education, or occupation alone will not suffice. Class is more than money, more than income, more than occupational location, although all three have a significant role to play. Nor is it easy to pull together multiple indicators, for they do not always move in sync. Education and income are positively correlated, as are education and occupation and occupation and income, but there are many exceptions to the general rule of positive association. It is the relationship between these variables that affects a person's class position.

The multidimensionality of class can be illustrated by a couple of examples. Imagine two individuals who each earn $150,000 per year. If social class were measured solely by *annual income,* they would both be considered as having high class. Now, imagine that one of them earned this income as a physician and the other by selling cocaine. Because these two occupations have such a different *status* in Canadian society, it is no longer apparent that they both have a high social class, even though they have identical incomes. Indeed, the drug dealer has a relatively low social class despite a high income. This type of finding, of course, is not limited to instances in which people are engaged in illegal activities. As a second illustration, assume two respondents who have each graduated from law school, which gives them a high score on a variable measuring education. Imagine that one of them practises corporate law and earns $250,000 annually, while the other works at an inner city legal aid clinic and earns $30,000 annually. Which of these lawyers has the higher social class? In answering this question, be careful to stay within the definition of the concept being measured. Some (idealistic?) students might well prefer to work for a legal aid clinic, and such a position might be viewed as more socially relevant and, for them, more enjoyable. But the question was, which individual has the higher social class? If social class is defined as a multidimensional concept, comprised of levels of education, income, and occupational status, and in which a higher score on each component corresponds with a higher class position, then the answer is simple: the corporate lawyer has the higher social class.

In summary, variables are a means of translating concepts into observable and quantifiable phenomena; indicators are the means or operations used to determine the exact values of our variables. As we move from concept to variable to indicator, we move from broad abstraction to narrow precision. Figure 7.2 presents a fairly simple visual representation of how indicators, variables, and concepts fit together, while a more complex example using multiple indicators and variables is seen in Figure 7.3. (Due to space constraints, the proposition and hypotheses have not been restated in Figure 7.3.) In each figure the objective is to support the *proposition,* that is, the relationship between the two concepts. Hypotheses, variables, and indicators are the tools we use to test the proposition.

Given the importance of selecting proper variables and indicators for our concepts, a justification of their selection should be part of any research report. Choices will always be involved, and you need to be

FIGURE 7.2

A SIMPLE MODEL OF CONCEPTS, VARIABLES, AND INDICATORS

Independent Variable		Dependent Variable
Concept: → Democracy	Proposition: ─────── As democracy increases, human rights increase.	→ Concept: Human Rights
Variable: → Suffrage	Hypothesis: ─────── As suffrage increases, racial minority rights increase.	→ Variable: Racial Minority Rights
Indicator: → % of total pop. eligible to vote	Hypothesis: ─────── As the percentage of the total population eligible to vote increases, minority property rights increase.	→ Indicator: racial minority property rights

Note: For further information on operationalization, see Manheim and Rich (1981) and Neuman (1994).

Source: Adapted from Jarol Manheim and Richard Rich, *Emperical Political Analysis* (New Jersey: Prentice Hall, 1981).

FIGURE 7.3

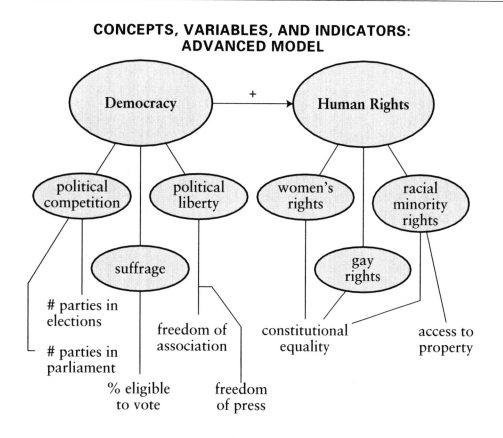

**CONCEPTS, VARIABLES, AND INDICATORS:
ADVANCED MODEL**

able to justify the choices made. By explaining the logic behind our operationalization and demonstrating the linkages between indicators and variables and between variables and concepts, arguments and conclusions are more readily defended. In addition, the need to explain one's choices in operationalization improves the process: when we know we must defend our selections to our peers, we are more likely to take every precaution to avoid criticism.

In this context, it is important to recognize that much of the research done by both students and faculty involves secondary analysis of existing data sets. In such cases, the primary selection of indicators has already been made by others. If, for example, we are using data from the Canadian National Election Studies, we are locked into the measures selected by the CNES research teams. Thus our choices are limited, and we often end up using indicators that are not quite what we would like them to be. This is not to imply that our own design of indicators would necessarily be better, but only that researchers who rely on secondary analysis must use indicators that may have been designed for other research purposes and agendas.

MOVING FROM VARIABLES TO INDICATORS

Using the most recent Canadian National Election Study or a comparable survey, can you find indicators of the following variables?

- support for environmentalism
- level of political interest
- social class
- attitudes toward abortion
- party affiliation

Using the same study, select five additional survey questions. What concepts or variables do you believe these questions were intended to tap? List all possible uses for each of the five questions.

PRECISION IN MEASUREMENT

Our indicators allow us to distinguish between the values of a variable. When indicators are designed, the issue emerges as to how precise the distinctions should be between categories of a variable. There are three basic **levels of measurement** that capture the different levels of precision that variables can take: **nominal, ordinal,** and **interval.** As we will see in future chapters, the level of measurement selected will largely determine the type and power of statistical measures available for analysis: the higher the level of measurement, the more powerful the statistics that are available.

What do we mean by precise? Think about the difference in precision between describing someone as "young" and describing the same person as "21 years of age." Both descriptions can be used for the same individual, but the latter is more precise than the former. The designation "young" omits a great deal of information: we do not know the cutoff point between "young" and "not young," nor do we know where this person sits within the category: is she at the upper limit of the category (as she would be if the category "young" ended at age 22), or does she still have a few years to enjoy being "young" (as she would if the category ended at age 30)? If we were to pursue precision to the extreme, we would have an overabundance of information; age could be specified to the year, date, and even time of birth. Fortunately, such detail is neither required nor desirable for most variables and most research questions. For example, if we are interested in the impact of age on support for neoconservatism, we might expect people in their 20s to differ from those in their 40s or 50s, but we would not expect to find significant differences between those who are 26 and 27. Our goal in research is to form generalizations about groups of people, and that goal by necessity requires that we categorize individuals on the basis of similar and different characteristics. If we pursue such high levels of precision that we end up with an extremely small number of cases in each category, we will be unable to notice patterns or relationships between variables. Overall, we should strive for the highest level of measurement that *is useful for the research question at hand.*

Recall that concepts can be conceptualized as either categorical or continuous. Categorical concepts have characteristics that are distinct and unconnected, while continuous concepts have characteristics that are sequentially connected. Similarly, variables can be distinguished between those that have discrete categories and those whose categories can be placed on a continuum; religious affiliation would be an example of the former, age of the latter. Categorical concepts will result in the selection of nominal-level variables, whereas continuous concepts lend themselves to either ordinal- or interval-level variables. We will outline each level of measurement in turn.

Nominal-level variables are those whose categories cannot be ordered or ranked. Religion, region, and gender are examples of nominal variables, as are "yes–no" distinctions. (For instance, "Do you agree in principle with capital punishment?") Differences exist between the categories of the variable, as, for example, between males and females, and numerical values can be assigned to the categories (e.g., male = 1; female = 2), but there is no mathematical relationship between these values. The values are arbitrary and may be chosen arbitrarily (e.g., male = 2; female = 1). With a nominal-level variable, the numerical values represent differences in kind (e.g., Liberal = 1, Progressive Conservative = 2, Reform = 3, NDP = 4), not in degree. Thus, while the categories of nominal variables are distinct, they cannot logically be ordered. To appreciate how common nominal-level variables and indicators are in political science research, imagine how hamstrung we would be if we could not distinguish survey respondents on the basis of their language, region, sex, religion, or partisan identification.

Ordinal-level variables allow for the ranking of categories. The ranking in an ordinal-level variable is *relative* to the position of the other categories; we do not know the exact distance between the categories, but we can organize the categories along a continuum. "Strongly agree – agree – disagree – strongly disagree," "poor – fair – good – excellent," and the "A – B – C – D – F" grading system are all examples of ordinal rankings.

It is common to encounter rank-ordered data in the social sciences, and most people have an intuitive understanding of data presented in this way. However, there are a number of precautions that must be kept in mind when working with rank-ordered data. The first is that we cannot assume that the distance between ranks is the same. For example, if you were asked to rank-order your first five destinations for a mid-session holiday, there may be a much larger perceptual gap between your first and second choices than between your fourth and fifth choices. You might *really* want to go to your first choice, but be relatively indifferent between choices 4 and 5. Second, and perhaps of greater importance, any rank order always has a bottom, a lowest or a worst, but being ranked last does not necessarily indicate the absence of quality. Let's look briefly at two illustrations.

Many universities use student evaluations of faculty teaching to generate decile ratings; some instructors are ranked in the tenth decile, meaning that their student scores are higher than those received by 90% of their peers, while others are ranked in the first decile, meaning that 90% of their peers had better student perceptions. However, this does not mean that first-decile teachers are necessarily poor teachers; it means only that 90% of the other instructors are viewed by students as *better* teachers. It is possible, therefore, that students in Professor Filibuster's class might describe him as a competent and effective teacher, yet still have their assessments place him in the first decile in comparison with his peers. Ten percent of the professors *have to be* in the first decile. When individuals are rank-ordered, someone must finish last regardless of the quality of their performance. The last place athlete in an Olympic event is still an excellent athlete.

A second illustration comes from a recent decision to rank-order public and Catholic schools in the Calgary system by their pass rates and to release these rankings to the press. Parents, therefore, can see where their children's school, or potential school, is placed. Is it first, second, or last? The problem is that very small differences in the pass rate can have a major impact on rank order. For example, among grade 6 classes in the Catholic system, the difference in pass rates between the number one ranked school and the tenth ranked school was only between 100% and 98.4%. The school that ranked twentieth still had a pass rate of 96.0%, while the pass rate for the school ranked thirtieth had "plummeted" to only 93.2%. Thus relatively minor differences in the measure used to determine rankings can have a substantial impact on the rank ordering. Students, teachers, and parents associated with the school ranked twentieth in the system could well be depressed by their comparative position, even though the substantive difference between their own school and the school ranked first was negligible. In a similar fashion, the first-decile teacher may feel depressed and incompetent, even though most of his students may feel he is doing an effective job.

Interval-level variables can also be placed on a continuum, but unlike ordinal variables, the categories are separated by a standard unit. The distance between 1 and 2, for instance, is the same as the distance between 3 and 4. Thus, with interval data, the value of 4 is twice the size of 2, and 8 is twice the size of 4. Note that this was not the case with ordinal-level data. With ordinal data, 4 is larger than 2, but it is uncertain how much larger it is.

Let's illustrate this difference by comparing an ordinal- and an interval-level measurement of attitudes toward the performance of Jean Chrétien's Liberal government. A five-point Likert scale is a common way of deriving an ordinal-level attitudinal measure in the social sciences. Respondents could be asked the following:

On a scale of 1 to 5, where 1 is "strongly disapprove," 2 is "somewhat disapprove," 3 is "neither approve nor disapprove," 4 is "approve," and 5 is "strongly approve," how would you rate the performance of the Chrétien government?

In response to this question, respondents' scores on the "Chrétien rating" variable would range from 1 to 5. The higher the score, the more positively the respondent feels about the government. But notice that the size of the units on this variable are not constant. That is, the difference between 1 and 2 (strongly disapprove and somewhat disapprove) is not the same as the difference between 2 and 3 (somewhat disapprove and neither approve nor disapprove). By extension, the value of 4 is not twice the value of 2, in the sense that people scoring 4 are not twice as supportive of the government as those who score 2. Because of this, and to anticipate our discussion in Chapter 9, it would not be appropriate to compute an "average," or mean, score based on this question. A mean assumes a constant value between categories.

In addition, the issue of giving "meaning" or "context" to data, an issue that was at the heart of the dispute over the "woman abuse" data discussed above, also adds a measure of subjectivity to social sciences data. For example, some would say that money is an interval-level variable or indicator in the social sciences. A dollar is a dollar, and 10 dollars is half of 20 dollars. But it is also true that money has a different meaning for people, depending upon the context of their social and economic situation. A government policy designed to increase individual

A POINT ON THE COMPASS

Feeling Thermometers

Researchers sometimes try to impose an interval scale by defining a response set in such a way that it appears to have a standard unit between categories. One frequently encountered illustration of such a pseudo interval-level variable is the "feeling thermometer." For example, in Canadian National Election Studies prior to 1988 (when the studies switched from face-to-face interviews to telephone interviews), the feeling thermometer was introduced with the following set of instructions:

> You will see here a drawing of a thermometer. It is called a feeling thermometer because it helps measure people's feelings toward various things. Here is how it works. If you don't have any particular feeling about the things we are asking about, place them at the 50-degree mark. If your feelings are very warm toward a particular thing, you would give a score between 50 and 100—the warmer your feelings, the higher the score. On the other hand, if your feelings are relatively cool toward something, you would place them between 0 and 50. The cooler your feelings, the closer the score will be to zero." (Clarke et al. 1979, 406)

Feeling thermometers can be used to compare politicians, parties, interest groups, countries, or virtually anything.

In a 1995 survey of 1,004 Alberta respondents, the authors asked respondents to locate Premier Ralph Klein, Prime Minister Jean Chrétien, and Reform leader Preston Manning on a feeling thermometer. The average score received by Manning was 47.9, by Klein 53.2, and by Chrétien 57.6. Thus at the time of the survey, the prime minister appeared to be the most popular politician in the province. The thermometer was also used to compare popularity across different subpopulations of the electorate. It was shown, for example, that Premier Klein was more popular among men (average score = 59.2) than he was among women (average score = 48.1).

Feeling thermometers are attractive because respondents are able to use them with respect to a multitude of different objects. However, we cannot assume that the difference between a thermometer rating of 20 and 30, for instance, is the same as that between 70 and 80; the feeling thermometer is not a true interval-level variable. An interval-level scale would presuppose that all respondents internalize feelings of like or dislike using a standard scale, and intuitively this is not to be the case. The trouble is that this differentiation of scales among respondents appears to occur for all attitudinal variables: even if researchers are definitive in the meaning of a response set, it still must be interpreted by the respondents. That process of interpretation, or internalization of the scale, adds a subjective component to its interpretation. It should also be noted in the specific case of the feeling thermometer that most respondents convert the thermometer to a 10-point scale; 40 and 50 are used more frequently than are 43 and 47.

taxes by a flat rate of $1,000 across the board would have a different meaning for people earning $200,000 annually than it would for people earning $25,000 annually. Although the amount is the same, its value varies. Therefore, even "hard" interval-level data in the social sciences can take on ordinal-level characteristics.

Despite these obvious concerns with interval-level data in the social sciences, researchers often assume that their data are interval-level, or sufficiently close to approximate interval-level data. The reason, as we will discuss in much more detail in subsequent chapters, is that interval-level data are amenable to much higher-level statistical techniques and, in particular, provide opportunities for multivariate statistical techniques that offer more analytical insight than do the bivariate techniques common to nominal- and ordinal-level data analysis. The challenge is to understand the assumptions that underlie the data analysis, and to discern to what extent the data analytical techniques violate those assumptions, and with what effect. Understanding that process calls for a combination of both the art and science of data analysis.

Notice the precision differences between the levels of measurement. Nominal-level variables have categories, ordinal-level variables have categories that can be ranked, and interval-level variables have categories that can be ranked with a specified distance (or interval) between the categories. As we stated earlier, there are statistical advantages to using the highest level of measurement available. These incentives can lead some researchers to "artificially" create interval-level variables where nominal- or ordinal-level variables would be more appropriate. For example, instead of using a single nominal-level variable to represent the regions of Canada, one could create a series of "dummy" interval-level variables, such as Atlantic versus non-Atlantic, Quebec versus non-Quebec, etc. Sometimes it is desirable to move *down* in precision, moving, for instance, from interval- to ordinal-level variables. If we do not have enough cases within the categories, we cannot detect patterns, leading us to group interval-level data. In addition, grouped data can be easier to read in a contingency table due to the reduced number of categories. Finally, the calculation of certain measures of strength (addressed in Chapter 11) is easier with grouped data than with interval-level data.

The decision to group data presents the researcher with yet another decision: on what basis should data be grouped? Consider the variable "age." If we have 100 cases, with ages measured in years, how should we construct groups? Should we have three groups—young, middle, old—or perhaps four groups—young, young–middle, middle–old, old? What should be the cut-points between groups? Do we group the data to create equally sized age categories, for example, 0–19, 20–39, 40–59, 60–79, and 80–99, or do we categorize age according to our knowledge about life cycle and cohorts, for example, under 30, 30–65, over 65? Perhaps we should divide the data so that there are roughly the same number of cases in each category, for example, put the first 33 cases in "young," the next 33 in "middle," and the final 34 cases in "old." However you choose to group the data, it is recommended that you have some theoretical justification for your choice.

One question that should always be asked is, "How have other researchers measured this variable?" Is my operational definition consistent with the literature in the area? If so, there usually is no need to

CHECKING YOUR BEARINGS

LEVELS OF MEASUREMENT

What is the most appropriate level of measurement for each of the following variables? Explain why.

- party identification (values = Liberal, Conservative, NDP, Reform, BQ)
- ideological position (values = left, centre, right)
- unemployment rates (values = 0% to 100%)
- development (values = preindustrial, industrial, postindustrial)
- regime type (values = democratic, fascist, communist, authoritarian)
- population (values = 10,000, 20,000 ... 10 billion)

CHECKING YOUR BEARINGS

GROUPING INTERVAL-LEVEL DATA

You are interested in the relationship between age and active involvement in political parties. In order to pursue this interest, you have access to the following data set. How might you group respondents into age categories? What categories, what break points might you use, and how would you justify your choices?

Age	Number of Cases	Age	Number of Cases
18	8	31	2
19	16	32	0
20	4	33	2
21	8	34	3
22	12	35	1
23	7	36	0
24	11	37	2
25	7	38	1
26	10	39	3
27	6	40	4
28	4	41	1
29	1	42	0
30	5	43	3

provide a detailed justification. However, if the operational definition differs from the literature, be sure to highlight this fact and discuss its implications with regard to the comparability of the findings. In short, engage in the scholarly dialogue.

ACCURACY IN MEASUREMENT

As we noted earlier, conclusions about a theoretical proposition are only as good as the variables and the indicators of those variables, upon which the conclusion is based. Do the indicators measure the variables? Do the variables represent the concepts? Are the measures stable, or are different results obtained with repeated use of the measures? To the degree that we have confidence in the measures, we can have confidence in the conclusions. When we are considering the *accuracy* of indicators and variables, we need to look at two issues: *validity* and *reliability*.

We explored the idea of **validity** in Chapter 4 with respect to research design. Something is valid if it does what it was intended to do; thus, an indicator is valid if it measures the variable, and a variable is valid if it represents the concept. Essentially, validity refers to the "degree of fit" between the indicator and the variable or between the variable and the concept (Neuman 1994, 130). Consider, for example, indicators of "support for feminism in Canada." One might use the number of members in NAC (the National Advisory Committee for the Status of Women) as an indicator of support. However, this indicator would be inappropriate: NAC is mostly comprised of member organizations, such as women's shelters and the YWCA, rather than of women who expressly join NAC itself. It is possible, therefore, that many members of NAC are not even aware of their membership. Changing the indicator of support for feminism to the number of member organizations in NAC would produce a more appropriate measure. But would the measure be complete? How would we deal with groups of very different sizes? What about the individual men and women in the population who support feminism and/or feminist principles, but who may not belong to organizations falling under NAC's umbrella? And what about all the members of women's groups not affiliated with NAC? A convincing argument could be made that a study of feminism in Canada would need to look further than NAC alone.

To ensure valid measurements, and thus valid conclusions, we need to select or create measures that are both "*appropriate* and *complete*" (Manheim and Rich 1981, 58). The first step in doing so is acquiring knowledge: the more we know about our subject matter, the more certain we can be that our measures are appropriate and complete. Such knowledge keeps us from making avoidable errors. To continue our example, basic knowledge of Canadian feminism would allow one to know that the antifeminist lobby R.E.A.L. (realistic, equal, active for life) Women would be inappropriate on a list of feminist organizations, despite its funding by the Secretary of State Women's Program. The second step to increasing the completeness and appropriateness of our measures is testing and evaluating the measures. Here there are a number of tests:

- **Face validity:** *on the face of it,* is the measure logical? Does it appear to measure the concept? Can you justify your selection of the measure? Would other people see the logic in the selection? For example, few of us would accept ownership of a pet as a measure of animal rights activism. Face validity tests help address the question of appropriateness.

- **Convergent validity:** this is a comparison of indicators designed to measure the same variable. Logically, if two indicators are measuring the same variable, they should yield similar results for most cases.

Thus, most individuals who score "high" on one measure of conservatism should score "high" on a second measure of conservatism. Since we are using one indicator as a criterion against which the other is measured, it is often preferable that we use a "tried-and-true" measure as the criterion.

- **Discriminant (divergent) validity:** this test is the opposite of convergent validity. If two indicators predict opposing or very dissimilar views, they should yield different results for most cases. For example, imagine an indicator of feminist views—do you agree or disagree that "women and men should have equal access to education and employment opportunities"—and an indicator of antifeminist views—do you agree or disagree that "we would all be better off if women stayed home to raise children." In this case, we would expect a negative correlation between the indicators: most people who agree with one can be expected to disagree with the other. If, on the other hand, we were to find a positive association (those who agree with the former also agree with the latter), we would have reason to question the validity of our measure.

- **Predictive validity:** does use of the measure help us to predict outcomes? To test predictive ability, we need to pilot test the measure in an appropriate population. For example, if we have a measure designed to tap attitudes about gun control, we could pilot test this measure among self-identified NRA (National Rifle Association, a strong antigun control lobby in the United States) supporters. We would predict that strong opponents of gun control by our measure would be more likely than others to belong to the NRA. If they are not, we have reason to believe that the measure may be flawed.

It should be emphasized that indicators and variables are not themselves valid, but rather are valid (or invalid) with respect to the purpose at hand. Validity is a question of "fit"; the same measure may have a poor fit with one concept, yet a good fit with another. Also, it must be noted that perfect validity is an impossible ideal; we cannot find a variable that perfectly represents its concept or an indicator that perfectly measures its variable. This is inevitable given the losses in meaning that occur as we move along the continuum from concept to quantification. The very nature of operationalization requires that concepts and variables be simplified and, in the process, made less valid. Thus, when we discuss validity, we are considering a continuum between "less valid" and "more valid."

One solution to the perpetual existence of validity problems is to use multiple variables and indicators. The goal here is to have the strengths of one compensate for the weaknesses of the other. Louise White (1994, 155–6) writes:

> ... it should be clear that neither variables nor their indicators are totally valid or totally invalid and that most pose some validity problems.... Because it is hard to find measures that are as valid as we would like, it is preferable to rely on two or more variables to measure our concepts, and two or more operational definitions to measure our variables. Usually, no single variable can do justice to a concept or reflect its full meaning, and no single operational definition can do justice to the variables we select.

A POINT ON THE COMPASS

Controversies in the Validity of Measures: Seymour Martin Lipset's *Continental Divide*

In *Continental Divide: The Values and Institutions of the United States and Canada* (1990), Seymour Martin Lipset argues that the differences between Canada and the United States can be attributed to our different histories: [t]he United States is the country of the revolution, Canada of the counterrevolution." Among other things, the historical background of "counterrevolution" has led Canadians to demonstrate greater deference to authority and elites. Canadians, he argues, are a more lawful and peaceful people. Lipset cites differences in rates of violence, crime, and drug abuse, as well as differences in attitudes toward both police authority and gun control as indicators of the Canadian "deference to authority."

But do behavioural indicators such as crime rates provide a valid measure of a predisposition such as deference? Lipset's critics argue that his indicators are often inappropriate and that he fails to take into account important national differences in institutional arrangements. What is at issue, then, is whether Canadians behave differently from Americans (e.g., have a lower crime rate) because of their attitudinal predispositions (e.g., greater deference to authority) or because of the institutional environment in which they behave. This in turn boils down to a debate over the validity of different indicators.

The use of multiple variables and indicators ensures that the least amount of conceptual meaning and nuance is lost.

The second factor to be considered when assessing the accuracy of our measures is **reliability.** A measure is reliable if it is *consistent* regardless of circumstances such as time or subpopulation. Thus, if consecutive weighings on a doctor's scale result in identical or near-identical weights (e.g., 70 kg), the scale is reliable. If you step on the scale and it registers 70 kg on Monday, 95 kg on Tuesday, and 45 kg on Wednesday, the scale is clearly unreliable. Note that reliability does not ensure validity; a scale that is consistently 5 kg low is reliable because it provides the same response with repeated measures (i.e., 70 kg each time). However, it is not valid because it fails to measure what it purports to measure (your weight).

Another way of thinking about the difference between validity and reliability in measures is to consider the distribution of errors. **Random errors** exist when a measure is inaccurate, but the inaccuracy is not systematic. **Nonrandom errors** are systematic errors. For example, consider a 100-point feeling thermometer scale of assessments of the Chrétien government. If asked to rate Chrétien on this scale, a respondent might place the prime minister at 65, which represents a feeling of "warmth" toward Chrétien. But if asked the same question the next day, the same respondent, feeling just as warmly toward the prime minister, might place him at 70. A month later, that same respondent might rate Chrétien at 62, and the next month at 65 again. The respondent, with the same feelings toward the same individual, exhibits slight changes in ratings simply through random error: sometimes the score is a little higher, sometimes a little lower. Now imagine you lived in a country that had an authoritarian regime, and you felt your safety was threatened if you were seen to be critical of the government. If you were surveyed for your feelings toward the political leader, you might choose to inflate your rating (to 100 points on this scale!) for fear that you would be punished if you revealed your true feelings (perhaps you really rate this person at 0). Furthermore, each time you were asked this question, you would respond in the same way. This kind of error is nonrandom, or systematic, error; the error is always in the same direction. A measure is reliable if it is free from random error (i.e., there may be nonrandom error in a reliable measure). A valid measure is free from random and nonrandom error.

How can circumstances such as time and subpopulation affect reliability? An example of an unreliable test over time appears to be the IQ (intelligence quotient) test. Recall from Chapter 4 that IQ tests are designed to measure *innate* intelligence, in other words, raw mental ability. Further, the measurement of IQ is based on the assumption that intelligence is normally distributed in all cultures and all generations: within each population, there is expected to be a small number of low intelligence individuals, a large number of moderately intelligent individuals, and a small number of highly intelligent people. If IQ is a reliable measure of intelligence, the distribution of IQ scores should be similar between cultures and across generations. However, and as noted in Chapter 4, a New Zealand researcher has found that this is not the case: IQ scores are highest in developed countries where educational levels are greater, and within such countries IQ scores have been increasing over generations.[4] This puts the reliability of IQ tests into question. These results also suggest that the IQ tests are not valid; rather than testing raw intelligence, they appear to be testing *educated* intelligence. Obviously, nature and nurture are not easily separated.

For an indicator to be reliable across subpopulations, it must receive similar results across all subgroups. For example, if a measure performs differently for men and women, there is a reliability problem. It is possible that men and women are interpreting the question differently or that different social or cultural factors are interfering with the measure. We often hear that women respond to problems by empathizing, whereas men respond to the same problems by suggesting solutions (one indicator of the popularity of this theory is the success of "self-help" books such as John Gray's *Men Are from Mars, Women Are from Venus*). If such generalizations are true, it is possible that men and women would respond differently to a stated problem. Or consider a survey question concerning body weight. Many young women are socialized to feel they should understate their weight, whereas many young men feel they should overstate their weight. If such a phenomenon occurred, the measure would suffer from reliability problems.

A number of steps can be taken to reduce reliability problems (Neuman 1994, 129). First, as with validity, multiple indicators are useful. Again, the idea is to allow the strengths of one measure to compensate for the weaknesses of the other. Second, our measures will be more reliable if we are clear in our purpose when designing questions or selecting indicators. It is important that indicators are unidimensional. Consider the question, "Are you satisfied with the food and service at this restaurant?" A response of yes may mean that the respondent is happy with both service and food, or it may indicate that he is happy with one but not both. With such "double-barrelled" questions, it is difficult to assess what exactly is being measured. A third suggestion for increasing reliability is to select the most precise measures available.

Unfortunately, there are occasionally tradeoffs between validity and reliability: as we decrease abstraction, we increase reliability, but in doing so, we decrease validity (White 1994, 158). Of course, our goal is to find measures that maximize both validity and reliability. The balance to seek is a measure that is sufficiently exact that it is reliable, yet sufficiently abstract that it captures the meaning of the concept, and therefore is valid.

In all circumstances, indicators can benefit from pilot testing and/or replication (Neuman 1994, 130). As discussed in Chapter 4, pilot tests can be used to pretest a survey instrument within a convenience sample. The purpose of a pilot test is not to tabulate statistics and draw conclusions about population parameters, but to test the validity and reliability of the measures. (In addition, pilot tests can help "troubleshoot" within the research design itself.) Often, if measures are found to be particularly useful and accurate, they are replicated in future studies by other researchers. The reasons for this are threefold: (1) the measures have proven themselves in terms of validity and reliability; (2) replicating measures allows researchers to test the conclusions of others with different samples; and (3) replicating measures allows researchers to detect changes and patterns over time.

CHECKING YOUR BEARINGS

ASSESSING THE ACCURACY OF OUR MEASURES

Suggest three possible survey questions that could act as indicators of the variable "liberalism," indicators that would enable you to distinguish between "liberal" and "illiberal" respondents. How would you assess the validity of each indicator? What steps would you take, and to what conclusions would you come? How would you assess the reliability of the indicators? Would you describe the measures as more valid or more reliable? Formulate three final indicators of liberalism that you feel are accurate measures.

What about survey questions that might serve as indicators for nationalism? Populism? Environmentalism? Neoconservatism? Racism?

DESIGNING SURVEY QUESTIONS

One of the most common research designs in political science is survey research; we use telephone polls, mailed questionnaires, or in-person interviews to gather the information necessary to test hypotheses. In survey research, indicators are the survey questions themselves. Thus, to design accurate indicators, we need to select or design valid and reliable survey questions. Survey research is conducted not only by governments and polling firms, but also by private businesses, nonprofit organizations, educational and health providers, community associations, and campaign management teams. It is quite likely that many of us will have the opportunity to participate in the design of a survey at some point in our lives.

When designing a survey, we need to be mindful that all the information necessary for that study must be captured within the survey instrument. Thus, we will need not only questions addressing attitudes, behaviours, and opinions, but also questions designed to solicit demographic information such as age, income, and education. All variables of interest—be they dependent, independent, or control variables—must be included in one instrument. Ideally, we will begin by making a list of all the relevant variables and all the indicators needed to measure these variables. This helps us ensure that all information is gathered and also prevents us from gathering unnecessary or useless information. There may be a desire when we design surveys to ask questions on every issue from A to Z, but this temptation should be avoided. Time restraints—yours and the participant's—preclude such an approach, as do ethical considerations. We want to keep our survey instruments directed at the question at hand; they should not be seen as "fishing expeditions." If we cannot separate the necessary variables and indicators from those that are superfluous, we need to work on our theory.

The researcher needs to choose a question format. **Closed questions** force the respondent to choose among the presented alternatives, for example, "Which of the following do you prefer: (1) Coca-Cola; (2) Pepsi Cola; (3) another cola brand; or (4) noncola beverages?" **Open questions** allow the respondent to provide her own response, without prompting from categories, for example, "Which cola brand do you prefer? _____ " There are advantages and disadvantages to each format.[5] Closed questions have a number of design advantages: respondents can answer the questions quickly; it is easy to compare the responses of different individuals; and data entry is less complex. In contrast, open questions present a number of data problems: there are many possible answers to any given question, making data entry difficult;

respondents will spend more time on open questions, making the questions less efficient; and comparisons between individuals can be complicated. However, open questions have the advantage of allowing a greater range of answers; the respondent is not limited to or biased by preset response categories and may provide answers that lead the researcher into new theoretical waters. Closed questions often ask the respondent to give a simple response to a very complex issue (Neuman 1994, 233) and, by providing categories for the respondent, may encourage the statement of opinion or knowledge where none exists.

Selection of question format tends to vary with the type of survey instrument. Telephone polls typically rely on closed questions, while in-person questionnaires are more likely to employ a mixture of open and closed questions. Many surveys begin with open-ended questions designed to capture the "top of the head" impressions of respondents before respondents are contaminated by subsequent questions. For example, if the survey is designed to measure public attitudes toward debt and deficit reduction, it would not make sense to ask respondents "What is the most important issue facing Canadians today?" after they had already been exposed to extensive questions about debt and deficit reduction. Front-end, open-ended questions are also used to warm up respondents for the more detailed questions that follow. They try, in short, to establish a conversational format.

When designing questions, there are a number of steps researchers should take to increase indicator accuracy. First, use *neutral language*. It is important that questions are designed in a way that does not bias or "lead" respondents. For example, questions such as "All reasonable people agree that policy A is bad. Do you support policy A?" or "Policy Q will put millions of people out of work. Many children will go hungry as a result of policy Q. Do you support policy Q?" are biased questions. When we use scales (e.g., "strongly agree – agree – disagree – strongly disagree"), it is important that we ensure that the response categories are balanced between positive and negative. For example, a scale with categories "excellent – very good – good – satisfactory – poor" is unbalanced; there are three positive categories, one neutral, and one negative.

Second, be clear. To ensure reliable questions, we must first ensure that all respondents interpret the question in the same way. This necessitates that we are specific regarding the exact information sought. Consider the question, "What is your income?" It is not clear if this means annual income, monthly income, or weekly income. Is the researcher interested in family income, household income, or individual income? Net or gross (pretax) income? In addition to being specific, clarity requires that we keep our questions simple. Avoid double negatives, keep your sentences relatively short, and use common language. It is important not to use jargon or assume detailed knowledge; not everyone knows the definitions of GNP and GDP or the content of policy Q. Finally, clarity demands that each question be limited to only one topic. So-called "double-barrelled" questions such as "How do you feel about the government's policies on military defence and international trade" will lead to reliability problems.

Third, avoid **response sets.** Some respondents tend to be yea-sayers, who agree with virtually any statement placed before them, while others tend to be nay-sayers, who disagree with virtually every statement. It is important in such cases that personality predispositions do not push respondents toward a particular policy position on the questionnaire. For example, if you have five agree–disagree statements designed to test respondents' support for environmentalism, and for each statement "agree" is indicative of a proenvironment position, then yea-sayers will tend to show up as environmentalists and nay-sayers as opponents of environmentalism. It is useful, then, to have batteries of questions where respondents must move back and forth between agreement and disagreement in order to register a consistent position, and where respondents who agree (or disagree) with everything end up in the middle of the scale.

Fourth, keep response categories **mutually exclusive** and **exhaustive.** We need to ensure that all relevant responses (including "no opinion" or "don't know/refused") are provided for by our response categories. In addition, there should be no overlap between categories. Consider, for example, the problems with the following response categories for the question "What is your annual personal net (after tax) income: (1) $10, 000–$25,000; (2) $25,000–$40, 000; or (3) $40,000–$65,000?" Clearly, not all possible responses are included. There is no room for those whose incomes are below $10,000, for those whose incomes are above $65,000, or for those individuals who refuse to answer the question. Thus the categories are not exhaustive. A second problem is that there is overlap between the categories. Should an individual whose income is $40,000 be placed in category (2) or category (3)? The categories are not mutually exclusive; it is possible for an individual to be placed in two categories, rather than just one. A better set of categories for the same question would be: (1) under $10,000; (2) $10,000–$24,999; (3) $25,000–$39,999; (4) $40,000–$65,000; (5) over $65,000; and (6) don't know/refused.

Fifth, select the **highest reliable level of measurement.** When possible, we should select interval-level measures above ordinal-level measures. As we have seen, it is possible after data collection to move from interval- to ordinal-level data through the grouping of data. The reverse, however, is not true: we cannot go from age categories to exact ages. Thus, using higher-level measurements allows us greater flexibility when it comes time to analyze our data. That said, there are some questions, such as income, where we may be inclined to use grouped categories in the question itself, rather than exact numbers. This is because there are some topics about which respondents prefer to be more ambiguous and for which precise answers may be impossible in any event.

Sixth, pay close attention to **question order.** Remember that respondent reactions to a particular question will be shaped by preceding questions, which provide the context for the question. Thus what comes first will contaminate what comes after. For example, imagine a survey measuring both intended vote in the next provincial election and public reaction to health-care spending cuts. If the health-care questions come first, then respondents may be in a different mindset when the voting intention question comes up than they would be if asked at the outset how they would vote "if a provincial election were held today." It is also useful advice to leave intrusive questions to the end of the questionnaire. Some respondents, for instance, may be very touchy when asked about their income or marital status, and may even terminate the interview. If this happens near the end of the interview schedule, most of the information is already in place and therefore the loss is minimized.

Seventh, try to **minimize defensive reactions** by making the respondent as comfortable as possible. Remember that respondents are under considerable social pressure in an interview situation; they want to appear to be knowledgeable and thoughtful. This can create a situation where respondents would rather fabricate a response than not have an opinion or appear not to know the answer. In some cases, therefore, it is important to assure respondents that a socially incorrect response is all right. For example, questions that ask respondents whether they voted in the last election are usually prefaced with a set of acceptable excuses for not voting. It is acknowledged that some people may have been ill, had car or child-care problems, or were called out of town on short notice; the message is that not voting is a perfectly understandable event and that respondents should not be embarrassed by admitting they did not vote. If these steps are not taken, the result is likely to be an inflated estimate of turnout rates. This in turn would make a comparison of voters and nonvoters difficult, since some of the latter, in fact, would be lumped in with the former in the statistical analysis.

Of course, following all of these steps will not guarantee a problem-free research instrument. For one thing, a host of research design and measurement issues will undoubtedly remain. How, for example, should missing data be handled? In measuring political and social attitudes, should we use odd-numbered scales that provide a middle response category for respondents, or should we use even-numbered scales, which force respondents to lean toward one pole or another? For example, scales measuring respondents' self-location on the left–right spectrum could provide either six or seven response categories. In the latter case, a response of 4 provides an option for respondents who do not want to identify themselves with either the left or right. However, if a six-point scale is used, such respondents are forced to choose either 3 (slightly left) or 4 (slightly right).

Finally, we must remember that a fair amount of error and noise is inevitable in survey research. After all, we are dealing with very human subjects who will occasionally fake answers or lie and who will respond to aspects of the interview situation—the sex or age of the interviewer, the artistic quality of the questionnaire, the time of day or night, distractions in the room—as much as they will to the specific questions being posed. The potential sources of error are perhaps best illustrated by questions concerning family income. Some respondents will refuse to disclose their income, while others will inflate it to impress the interviewer. Some people will not know their income; they may, for instance, know their hourly wage but not their after-tax annual income or the precise income of their spouse. As a consequence, there is a good deal of noise associated with survey measures of income, noise which then may make it difficult to measure the impact of income on political attitudes or behaviours.

In any case, researchers should always ensure that their questions are as polite and courteous as possible. Respondents have voluntarily given their time to the research project and should be treated with respect.

SUMMARY

Characteristics of Question Design

1. Use neutral language.

2. Be clear.

3. Avoid response sets.

4. Keep response categories mutually exclusive and exhaustive.

5. Select the highest reliable level of measurement.

6. Pay close attention to question order.

7. Minimize defensive reactions.

CREATING INDICES

We noted earlier in the chapter that social scientists will often use a number of variables to capture one concept and a number of indicators to capture one variable. After the data have been collected, indicators can be combined into an **index,** a single measure of the concept or variable in question.

Index construction generally follows a number of conceptual steps. First, we want indicators that are strongly associated or correlated with one another; this is illustrated by the bold line between indicators 1 and 2 in Figure 7.4. (At the same time, we do not want a degree of association so strong that the indicators are obviously measuring exactly the same portion of the variable.) Second, we want to cover as much of the conceptual terrain as possible and, therefore, the more indicators, the merrier. However, and as indices B and C in Figure 7.4 illustrate, the more indicators we include in the index, the weaker the association is likely to be betweem those indicators. Thus, as our index gets more comprehensive in its conceptual coverage, it also becomes less internally coherent. The trick, then, is to balance the competing needs of broad conceptual coverage and internal coherence. Indices that combine three to six indicators are common in political science research, whereas larger indices are much less common.

In the analysis of a mailed survey of senior university undergraduate students in Australia, Britain, Canada, New Zealand, and the United States, Nevitte and Gibbins (1990) constructed a number of ideological indices. One measured respondent orientations toward feminism and incorporated answers to the following questions:

- Respondents were asked to locate themselves on a seven-point scale between two statements: "women would be better off if they stayed at home and raised families" and "women would be better off if they had careers and jobs just as men do."

- Respondents were asked to locate themselves on a seven-point scale between another pair of statements: "if women tried harder they could get jobs equal to their ability" and "discrimination makes it almost impossible for women to get jobs equal to their ability."

- Respondents were asked if they agreed or disagreed with the following statements:
  - It is the right of a woman to decide whether to have an abortion.
  - If a company has to lay off part of its labour force, the first workers to be laid off should be women whose husbands have jobs.

- Lesbians and homosexuals should not be allowed to teach in schools.
- There should be more laws that aim at eliminating differences in the treatment of men and women.

By combining the responses to these six questions, the researchers were able to create a much more powerful measure of orientations to feminism than would have been provided by any one of the questions alone.

In conceptual terms, the creation of indices is a reasonably straight-forward operation. In practice, however, it brings into play many of the statistical techniques and measures of association addressed in later chapters. It is time, therefore, to turn to those techniques.

FIGURE 7.4

A SCHEMATIC ILLUSTRATION OF INDEX CONSTRUCTION

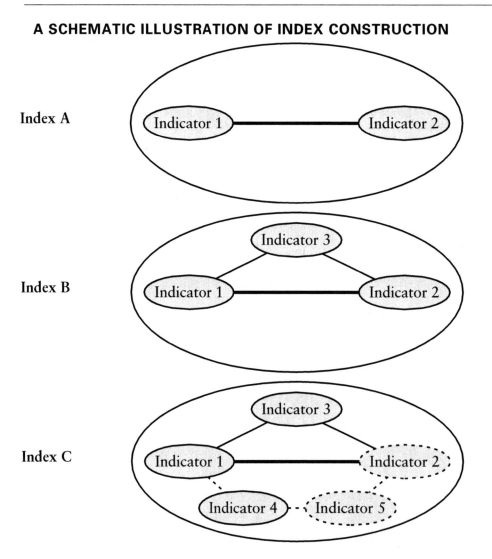

WORKING AS A TEAM

1. With your group, examine the code book for one of the recent Canadian National Election Studies or a similar survey research instrument. Are there questions that appear to be reasonable candidates for an index of liberalism? Feminism? Conservatism? Globalization? What conceptual steps would be involved in the creation of such an index?

2. How would you go about designing a questionnaire to measure teaching effectiveness in a course such as this one? What questions would you ask? Would they be open-ended or closed questions? What would be the advantages and disadvantages of each type? Which strategy would work best: using generic questions that would enable you to compare this course and its instructors to other courses and instructors, or course-specific questions that would enable you to probe the idiosyncratic aspects of this course and its instructor?

SELF-STUDY

1. You have been provided with the research opportunity to explore, through survey research, the relationship between environmentalism and the more general ideological predispositions captured by conventional left–right scales. Your theory is that support for environmentalism is correlated with ideological position; more specifically, you suspect that as support for the "left" increases, support for environmentalism also increases. In preparation for this research, work through the following steps of operationalization:

   a. State your theoretical proposition. What are the main concepts? Provide a conceptual definition for each.

   b. Identify two variables that could be used to quantify each concept. Identify the level of measurement for each variable.

   c. Identify two indicators for each variable. Provide the complete wording for the survey questions, including all response categories.

   d. Select one of the four variables and discuss how you would assess the accuracy of both indicators for that variable.

NOTES

1. Note that surveys that measure voting rates often suffer from "vote inflation": a higher proportion of the sample reports having voted than was the case in the population at large. For example, while the turnout rate in Canadian general elections hovers around 75%, the reported turnout rate in Canadian National Election Studies is often 10% higher. This distortion may be caused by voters being more likely than nonvoters to respond to the survey or by nonvoters in the sample being unwilling to admit that they did not vote.

2. The relationship between independent variables is referred to as multicollinearity. Two independent variables which are themselves related will tend to overlap in their predictive power. For example, we would expect that both knowledge of the subject matter and writing skill will predict academic excellence.

3. You should note, however, that the distinction between variables and indicators is often ignored; literature references to variables are often references to what we have termed indicators.

4. See Jay Ambrose, "We're smart enough to know how dumb IQ tests are," *The Globe and Mail*, 3 August 1996, D8.

5. For a more complete list of the advantages and disadvantages of each format, see Neuman (1994, 233).

PART 3

STATISTICAL
TOPICS

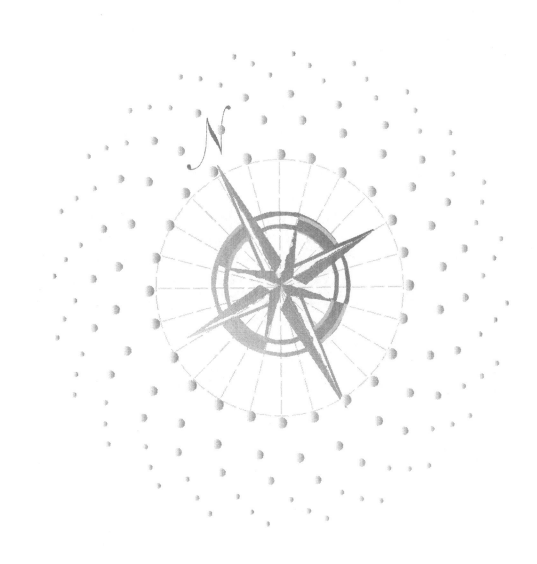

CHAPTER 8

Sampling the Political World

DESTINATION

By the end of this chapter the reader should

- have a thorough grounding in the theory of sampling in the social sciences;
- understand the logic of drawing representative samples from larger populations;
- have been exposed to a number of practical techniques by which samples are drawn;
- understand the basics of probability and know how to apply probability theory in simple situations.

As we move through our personal lives, we continually confront situations in which we attempt to generalize from our own experience, or from the experience of friends and family, to the larger world. We note, for example, that our performance on exams seems to be better if we cram the night before, and wonder if this is true for all students. We feel embarrassed in certain social situations, and wonder if everyone feels the same. We react with anger or dismay to an event, and wonder if others share the same reaction. There is, then, a constant curiosity about generalizing or extrapolating from the particular circumstances of our personal lives to the world around us. To what extent, we ask, are our own experiences, emotions, beliefs, and values typical, or to what extent are they idiosyncratic?

This question is fundamental to social science research, where we are always asking whether our knowledge of a particular event, group, or personality sheds useful light on larger phenomena. Thus, if we are studying a set of elected officials, we are seeking to advance our knowledge of all elected officials; if we are studying a set of nation-states, we aim to increase our understanding of all nation-states with roughly similar characteristics. The group that we wish to generalize about is known as a **population** (another term commonly used is "universe").

Within political science, there are many subjects of interest that involve very large populations. For example, if we wish to discuss the voting behaviour of Canadian females, we are looking at a voting age population of over 10 million individuals. Obviously, we cannot study each member of such a large population, regardless of the research design we select. The solution is to select a **sample** that is *representative* of the population under study, and from the study of this sample to make generalizations about the population as a whole. This chapter will explore the logic of sampling and will outline a number of commonly employed techniques.

POPULATIONS AND SAMPLES

As noted, a population is any group that we wish to study. The first step in commencing a research project is to clearly identify the population to be considered. When doing so, three factors must be considered: the unit of analysis (e.g., individuals, political parties, municipal governments), the geographic location, and the time period to be explored (Neuman 1994, 195). Thus, instead of studying "Members of Parliament," we study "Canadian MPs between 1988 and 1993." If the unit is stated without geographic and temporal qualifications, the population is unclear. Do British MPs count? What about MPs throughout history? By defining our population strictly, it is easy to decide who (or what) should be included in the population and who (or what) should be excluded (Singleton et al. 1988, 134).

When we study a population, the goal is to uncover *characteristics* of the population. How many people vote in municipal elections? What is the preferred taxation policy among Canadian voters? How do feminists feel about neoconservatism? How do neoconservatives feel about feminism? When the responses of *each and every* member (or case) of the population are measured, the resultant characteristic is known as a **population parameter**. For smaller populations, it is possible to obtain information for every unit and tabulate the parameter. For example, if our population is a single section of a political science research methods course, we can tabulate the average height, weight, and grade point for all students with relative ease. However, for larger populations, such as "Canadian citizens in 1996," time and financial constraints as well as practical considerations (it would be impossible to locate *everyone*) make calculation of parameters virtually impossible.[1] The solution to this dilemma is **sampling**: researchers draw information about a characteristic of a sample of the population. This information, known as a **statistic**, is then used to *estimate* the value of the population parameter (Neuman 1994, 196).

Simply put, sampling is the process of drawing a number of cases from a larger population for further study. The advantages of sampling for large populations are many: sampling is efficient and less expensive than a study of the whole population; sampling allows the study to be restricted to a certain time frame; and sampling ensures less data collection and entry needs (Bailey 1978, 72). In addition, when done correctly, sampling can provide accurate estimates of the population parameter. It is important to remember that we are ultimately interested in the

A POINT ON THE COMPASS ─────────

Population Research

Most research in the social sciences relies upon sample data and therefore entails inferences back to population parameters. However, research based on population data is not unknown. Consider the following examples:

- Barry Kay (1981) studied 147 of the 152 federal by-elections held between 1940 and 1980. The excluded cases were noncontested by-elections. Kay, however, was interested in the general phenomenon of by-elections; thus his 1940–80 "population" could still be considered a sample of the larger universe of by-elections held and by-elections to come.

- Kenneth Avio's study (1987) of the exercise of the Royal Prerogative in Canada examined the 440 capital cases considered by the federal cabinet between 1926 and 1957. He found, incidentally, that labourers were more likely to be executed than nonlabourers, and that nonwhite offenders who killed whites were more likely to be executed than were other offenders.

- Doreen Barrie and Roger Gibbins (1989) examined the political careers of all 3,803 individuals who served in the Canadian House of Commons and/or Senate from 1867 to 1984 inclusive.

- Munroe Eagles (1993) looked at all campaign expenditures by federal candidates in Canada during the 1984–88 period. His data, therefore, constitute population data for a particular time period, although his theoretical interests are not bounded by that time period.

population and the population parameters; the sample and the sample statistics are merely a means to these ends.

If we are to use a sample to make generalizations about a population, the sample must be **representative** of the population, "a microcosm, a smaller but accurate model, of the larger population which it is taken to reflect" (Manheim and Rich 1981, 87). Thus, if the population has approximately 30% Asians, 60% Caucasians, and 10% African-Canadians, a representative sample will consist of a similar racial distribution. Keep in mind, however, that we often do not know anything about the population characteristics other than what we can gather from the sample statistics. We would never know, for example, how many Canadians actually support capital punishment or employment equity, for the population will never be asked. As we will see, therefore, population characteristics can be estimated but seldom proved.

Three important factors influence the representativeness of a sample: the accuracy of the sampling frame, the sample size, and the method by which the sample is selected. A **sampling frame** is a list of all the units in the target population. If our target population is students at Canadian universities during the 1996–97 school year, our sampling frame would list all registered students. Ideally, our sampling frame would capture every member of the target population (Singleton et al. 1988, 135), meaning that not a single individual or case would be missing from the list. However, this is rare, particularly for large populations. Records are often incomplete and are subject to change. Consider the sampling frame for our population of university students. We would begin by obtaining student registration lists from all universities, but the lists would not include students who registered late and would include individuals who are no longer members of the target population (due to death or dropout). Another problem is that for many populations, there does not exist any official or even unofficial list that can be used as a sampling frame. For example, what is the sampling frame for a target population of "Canadians" in 1996? Lacking an official list of Canadians, researchers often turn to indirect lists, such as driver's licences and telephone directories. Of course, these lists are also incomplete, failing to capture (in the case of the former) nondrivers and new drivers and (in the case of the latter) those without telephones, new telephone subscribers, and those with unlisted telephone numbers. These incompletions undermine the representativeness of a sample because "the excluded persons usually constitute some distinguishable and homogenous group" (Bailey 1978, 73). Those without telephone service, for instance, are most often poor; the use of a telephone directory as a sampling frame thus leads to the underrepresentation of the poor. In addition to exclusion problems, most lists used as sampling frames fail to account for changes to the population due to birth, death, or migration.[2]

The point to stress is that almost all sampling frames will be to some degree inaccurate. The challenge to researchers is to find a sampling frame that minimizes such inaccuracies. One technique popular among telephone survey researchers is the random generation of a list of tele-

A POINT ON THE COMPASS

The Importance of Sampling Frames: The Case of *Literary Digest*

The most notorious and often-cited example of a poor sampling frame involves a mail-back survey conducted by *Literary Digest* in 1936. Seeking to predict the outcome of the 1936 presidential election, a contest between Democrat Franklin D. Roosevelt and Republican Alf Landon, the *Digest* staff sent surveys to 10 million Americans (Neuman 1994, 196). The sampling frame consisted of a number of lists including automobile registration lists, telephone directories, and the *Digest*'s subscription list (Singleton et al. 1988, 133). From the 2 million responses gathered, the *Digest* predicted a landslide election for Landon, when in fact Roosevelt was elected.

Although many flaws have been noted with the *Literary Digest* survey,[3] one of particular interest here is the mismatch between sampling frame and target population. The target population was all eligible American voters, but the sampling frame failed to cast such a broad net. Recall that the election occurred in 1936, a time when many of the American poor and lower middle class could not afford telephones, automobiles, or subscriptions to magazines such as the *Literary Digest*. Given that support for the Democratic Party in 1936 came largely from the working and lower middle classes, the failure of the *Literary Digest* to include the poor in their sample led to embarrassing results. The moral of the story? Researchers must think carefully when selecting a sampling frame, considering not only who is included but also who is excluded. Efforts must be made to ensure that as much of the target population as possible is included in the sampling frame. If our sampling frame is inappropriate or biased, we cannot make generalizations to the target population with any degree of confidence.

phone numbers. This process involves the computer generation of telephone numbers; therefore, the sampling frame is all active telephone numbers. This method is an improvement on the use of telephone directories as a sampling frame, because it includes newly listed and unlisted telephone numbers and eliminates cancelled numbers. However, persons without telephone service remain excluded.

It should be noted that not all target populations have any listing (be it direct or indirect) to which we can refer. This may be due to an unwillingness on the part of individual members to identify publicly with a given population; homeless persons, drug addicts, and rape victims are all examples of such hard-to-identify populations. In such situations, the researcher has difficulty establishing a truly representative sample. We will return to discuss studying hard-to-access groups later in the chapter.

A POINT ON THE COMPASS

The Hite Reports

A more contemporary example of problematic sampling frames comes from the work of American sociologist Shere Hite on human sexuality. *The Hite Report: A Nationwide Study of Female Sexuality* was first published in 1976, and *The Hite Report on Male Sexuality* was published next, in 1981. Both books, which contain detailed and often vivid accounts of sexual behaviour, were bestsellers and received extensive media coverage. The two books, and subsequent publications by Hite, have helped establish new empirical norms of sexual behaviour in the United States. However, whether the research findings are *representative* of the American public is unclear when one turns to the sampling frames and methodology.

The report on female sexuality was based on slightly over 3,000 replies to more than 100,000 questionnaires which were distributed during the early 1970s. The response rate itself is problematic; are the 3,000 respondents representative of the 100,000 individuals who received copies of the questionnaire? However, what is even more problematic is the sampling frame used for the distribution of the questionnaire. The questionnaire was distributed through the National Organization for Women, abortion rights groups, women's newsletters, and university women's centres (1976, xix). Notices asking readers to write in for copies of the questionnaire were published in *The Village Voice, Mademoiselle, Brides,* and

Ms. magazines. Just under 10% of the completed questionnaires came from women readers of the men's magazine *Oui*. The question, then, is whether this sampling frame, or assortment of sampling frames, could generate a representative sample, particularly given the added problem of low response rates.

The report on male sexuality was based on 7,239 replies to 119,000 questionnaires (1981, xvii–xix). Here, the sampling frames included men's clubs, church organizations, and male readers of the first *Hite Report*, *Sexology* magazine, *Penthouse*, and *Sexual Honesty, By Women for Women*.

To be fair, Hite addresses the matter of representativeness with considerable caution and finesse. Indeed, her methodological discussions are well worth reading in and for themselves. However, her publications still speak to the experiences of men and women, broadly defined. The message, inadvertent though it may be, is that this is how American women and men feel, believe, and behave. And yet, unless we have some confidence in the representativeness of the sample, it is difficult to place ourselves against the norms of the Hite reports. Do her respondents in fact reflect the American norm? The norm for men and women in general? Given that we have no independent measure beyond our own limited personal experience regarding what the population norm might be, the question is extremely difficult to answer.

The second factor that determines the representativeness of a sample is sample size, and we will turn to this matter shortly. The third factor is the method by which the sample is selected. Sampling techniques can be divided into two categories: those that are based on probability theory and those that are not. Probability sampling is the preferred mechanism, since it allows researchers to test the representativeness of their sample, but there are times when nonprobability sampling is unavoidable and/or acceptable. The discussion of these two approaches to sampling provides much of the content of this chapter. At this point, we only want to stress that all three factors are important and that weakness with respect to one cannot be compensated by strength with respect to another. As we saw in the *Literary Digest* example, a sample drawn from a poor sampling frame does not become better or more accurate by becoming bigger.

CHECKING YOUR BEARINGS

SELECTING SAMPLING FRAMES

For each of the following target populations, identify a list that could serve as a sampling frame. What limitations (potential inaccuracies and omissions) can you identify for each list?

- small Toronto businesses, 1995
- admissions, City Hospital, January 1996
- Nova Scotia voters, 1998
- Canadian citizens, 1998
- Vancouver heroin addicts, 1998
- Quebec sovereigntists, 1998

PROBABILITY SAMPLING

Sampling based on probability theory allows us to estimate the likelihood that our sample provides a representative picture of the population. Recall that our goal is to use the sample to calculate estimates, known as statistics, of the population parameters. In order for these estimates to be useful, we need to be confident that our sample is an accurate representation of the population. Probability theory allows us to state with a specified degree of confidence that our sample is, in fact, representative.

Probability sampling can be understood as the **random selection** of a sample; every case in the population has an equal chance of being selected for the sample. This means that the individual characteristics of a case (e.g., race, age, income, sex) have no influence on whether that case is selected for the sample. In addition, the selection of one case is *independent* of all other cases selected: the selection of A for the sample does not influence whether or not B is selected, or, in other words, the probability of B being selected (Singleton et al. 1988, 137–8). To understand probability sampling, we first need a basic understanding of probability theory. After this brief introduction, we will move to discuss the impact of sample size and various techniques of probability sampling.

Introduction to Probability Theory

When we are considering probabilities, we want to estimate the likelihood that a particular outcome will occur. For example, if we roll a die, what is the probability that we will get a 6? If we pull a card from a deck, what is the probability that it will be a diamond? In sampling, we are interested in questions such as, What is the probability that we will select person A for the sample? Or what is the probability that our sample statistic will fall within a given range of values?

Probabilities can range from zero to one. A probability of zero indicates that there is *no* chance of an event occurring. A probability of one indicates that there is a 100% chance of the event occurring; it is certain. To calculate the probability of an event occurring, we divide the number of possible *favourable outcomes* by the total number of *possible outcomes*. For example, if we have 10 students, and 6 are female, our probability of randomly selecting a female student's name from a hat is equal to 6 (number of favourable outcomes) divided by 10 (number of total outcomes), which means that the probability of selecting a female student is 0.6. Another way of expressing this is to state that there is a 60% chance that a female student will be selected. To calculate the probability of a single event, we use the formula $P(A) = r/n$, where $P(A)$ is the probability of event A, r is the number of favourable outcomes, and n is the number of total outcomes.

Often we are interested in the probability of two or more events occurring together. The joint occurrence of two events is calculated by the formula $P(AB) = P(A) P(B|A)$, where $P(AB)$ signifies the probability of the joint occurrence of events A and B, $P(A)$ is the probability of event A, and $P(B|A)$ is the probability of event B *after* event A. When events A and B are *independent*, $P(B|A) = P(B)$. For example, what is the probability of rolling two dice and getting two 6s? Each die is independent of the other, so

$$P(A) = \frac{1}{6} = 0.17;$$

$$P(B|A) = P(B) = \frac{1}{6} = 0.17;$$

$$P(AB) = P(A) P(B|A) = (0.17)(0.17) = 0.029.$$

Therefore, there is a 2.9% chance that rolling two dice will result in two 6s. Note, incidentally, that probability equations use a number of different notations to indicate multiplication: A *times* B may be written as $A \times B$, $(A)(B)$, $A(B)$, or AB.

Events A and B are *dependent* when the outcome of A influences the outcome of B. For example, if we are selecting cards from a deck, what is the probability that we will select two diamonds in a row?[4] Note that after we have selected the first diamond, both the number of diamonds (r = favourable outcomes) and the number of cards (n = total outcomes) have reduced:

CHECKING YOUR BEARINGS

CALCULATING PROBABILITIES

Exercise 8.1

Calculate the probabilities of the following events:

1. selecting a face card from a deck of cards.
2. flipping a coin and getting "heads."
3. rolling a die and getting a 6.
4. buying three home lottery tickets and winning the prize, assuming 200,000 tickets were sold and only one prize is given.

$$P(A) = \frac{13}{52} = 0.250;$$

$$P(B|A) = \frac{12}{51} = 0.235;$$

$$P(AB) = P(A)\,P(B|A) = 0.250(0.235) = 0.059.$$

There is a 5.9% chance that we will select two consecutive diamonds from a full deck.

CHECKING YOUR BEARINGS

Exercise 8.2

Calculate the probabilities of the following events:

1. You have the names of 16 Liberals, 12 Reformers, and 5 New Democrats in a hat. What is the probability that, upon selecting three names, you will select all Liberals? All Reformers? All New Democrats?
2. What are the odds of rolling a single die and getting "6" five times in a row?
3. You have bought one ticket of 10,000 tickets on a home lottery. The lottery procedure is to return tickets to the draw after each prize is awarded, thus ensuring everyone is eligible for every prize. If there are three prizes, what is the probability that you will win one of them? What is the probability that you will win all three?

Probability Theory and Sampling

Knowledge of probability theory is necessary to understand the principles of random sampling, both how it is conducted and why samples based on probability theory produce accurate estimates of population parameters. The principle of random sampling is rather straightforward and resembles a lottery (Manheim and Rich 1981, 89). Each case has an equal probability of being selected: $1/n$. **Simple random sampling** is the process by which every case in the population is listed, and the sample is selected randomly from this list. For large populations, each case is assigned a number, and then a computer randomly selects numbers that will comprise the sample. There are practical limitations to the application of simple random sampling,[5] but the principle underlies all forms of probability sampling.

Probability theory allows us to determine the probability that our calculated sample statistic is a good estimation of the population parameter, for statisticians have found that sample statistics (used to estimate the population parameter) distribute themselves around the population parameter in a normal (bell-shaped) distribution. An example will help clarify this point, which is discussed in more detail in Chapter 10.[6] You are given the following data set:

Name	Number of Pets
Arnie (A)	3
Beth (B)	1
Cathy (C)	2
Derek (D)	0
Ethel (E)	2
Frank (F)	4

The population size in this example is 6; our universe is restricted to the six individuals. The population parameter we are interested in is the **mean** (or arithmetic average, discussed in the next chapter), which is equal to the sum of the individual scores ($3 + 1 + 2 + 0 + 2 + 4 = 12$) divided by the total number of cases (6); thus, in this example, the mean number of pets owned is 2 (12 divided by 6). However, if we take samples from this population, we will find sample means that differ from the population parameter. If our sample size is 2, there are 15 possible samples, each with its own sample mean, as Table 8.1 illustrates.

Taken together, all the possible sample means for a given sample size create a **sampling distribution**. The sampling distribution of means for this two-case sample illustration is presented in Table 8.2 and graphically presented in Figure 8.1. The sampling distribution is created by

TABLE 8.1

ALL POSSIBLE SAMPLES OF SIZE 2, WITH SAMPLE MEANS

Combination*	Mean	Combination	Mean
AB	2	CD	1
AC	2.5	CE	2
AD	1.5	CF	3
AE	2.5	DE	1
AF	3.5	DF	2
BC	1.5	EF	3
BD	0.5		
BE	1.5		
BF	2.5		

* AB = the sample composed of Arnie (A) and Beth (B); AC = the sample composed of Arnie (A) and Cathy (C), etc.

totalling the number of combinations that present the specified sample mean. For example, in the two-case samples there are two combinations (CD and DE) that have a mean of 1.

We can apply probability theory to determine the probability of selecting any particular mean. For example, in our two-case samples the probability of obtaining a sample mean of 2.5 is equal to 0.2 (3/15 = 0.2); there is a 20% chance that we will select a sample mean of 2.5. As Table 8.2 suggests, our probabilities of obtaining a sample mean close to

FIGURE 8.1

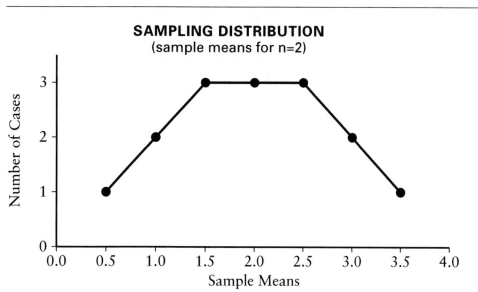

SAMPLING DISTRIBUTION
(sample means for n=2)

TABLE 8.2

SAMPLING DISTRIBUTIONS FROM THE PET ILLUSTRATION

Sample Mean	Number of Samples	Probability
0.5	1	0.07
1.0	2	0.13
1.5	3	0.20
2.0	3	0.20
2.5	3	0.20
3.0	2	0.13
3.5	1	0.07

the population parameter (which, as you will recall, is 2) are higher than our probabilities of obtaining sample means that diverge greatly from the parameter; that is to say, you are more likely to get a sample mean that is close to the parameter than one that is not. In our example, the probability of getting a sample mean that is within 0.5 units of the parameter (between 1.5 and 2.5) is 0.6 (9/15 = 0.6). This range is known as a **confidence interval,** a concept to which we will return in Chapter 10.

The difference between the sample statistic and the population parameter is referred to as **sampling error** (Singleton et al. 1988, 143). Thus, a sample mean of 1.5 has a sampling error of 0.5, since it is 0.5 units off the population mean of 2.0. A large sampling error indicates that the sample statistic deviates greatly from the population parameter, whereas a small sampling error indicates that the sample statistic is close to the population parameter.

SAMPLE SIZE

Statisticians have found that sample statistics are more likely to be closer to the population parameter when the sample size is larger than when the sample is small (Singleton et al. 1988, 143); sampling error is reduced as the sample size increases. Given that our goal is to reduce error, it is not surprising that we prefer large samples over small samples; we desire sample statistics that are as close to the population parameter as possible. However, larger and larger samples are also more and more expensive samples. Since resources are always limited, how large should our sample be? To determine the appropriate sample size, we need to consider a number of factors: the homogeneity of the sample, the number of variables under study, the desired degree of accuracy, and the method of random sampling employed.

CHECKING YOUR BEARINGS

CALCULATING SAMPLING DISTRIBUTIONS

Using the "number of pets" data set from the previous example, calculate a sampling distribution for sample means from samples containing three cases. (There should be a total of 20 combinations.) What is the probability of selecting each of the sample means? What is the probability that a selected sample mean will fall between 1.5 and 2.5? What is the sampling error for the sample ABC? For the sample ABD?

Homogeneity refers to how similar a population is *with respect to the variable of interest* (Manheim and Rich 1981, 96). The goal of our studies is to explain variation. Do people differ in their views, and if so, why? Obviously, if everyone were exactly alike, a sample of one—a single case—would suffice; any extra collection of data would be redundant, since it would prove identical to the information that the single case provided. **Heterogeneity** refers to how *dissimilar* a population is with respect to the variable of interest. If everyone were different, we would need to include everyone in the sample in order for it to be representative. Of course, neither pure homogeneity nor pure heterogeneity occurs in populations of interest. What we as researchers need to estimate is how homogeneous or heterogeneous our population is: a highly homogeneous population allows us to use a smaller sample, whereas a highly heterogeneous population requires a larger sample. The appropriate sample size increases as we move along the continuum from homogeneity to heterogeneity.

The number of variables we wish to explore also influences sample size. The more complex our study becomes, the more variables and relationships that we include, the more cases we need in our sample (Singleton et al. 1988, 161). The need for a larger sample stems from the desire to look at subgroups within the sample and to impose statistical controls. A sample of 500 voters, for example, might have only 10 individuals with postgraduate education. If the education variable is necessary to your study, you will need to greatly increase your sample size to *randomly generate* a large enough subgroup to conduct analysis. (Alternative techniques are discussed below.)

A third factor that influences sample size is the desired degree of accuracy. Recall that sampling error decreases as sample size increases. Before conducting an analysis, researchers can state the **margin of error** they are willing to accept, or tolerate (expressed as a percentage).

FIGURE 8.2

CONTINUUM OF HOMOGENEITY

Pure Homogeneity	- -	Pure Heterogeneity
Sample = one	Sample size increases →	Sample = all

Knowing the margin of error allows researchers to state their sample statistics as a confidence interval. For example, a gay rights group may sponsor a survey to determine the level of public support for same-sex marriages. If the survey finds that 57% of the respondents support same-sex marriages, and the sampling error is ±5%, then the sponsors of the survey can conclude that between 52% and 62% of Canadians support same-sex marriages. Researchers can preset the margin of error they want and then, using the information illustrated in Table 8.3, determine the *minimum* sample size required to yield such a confidence level. Of course, researchers may have reasons to exceed this minimum level. For example, a major television network may commission a poll immediately prior to a federal election. Because they will be making a very high-profile prediction regarding the election outcome, they may want to minimize the sampling error by using a larger than usual sample.

TABLE 8.3

MINIMUM SAMPLE SIZES AT A 95% CONFIDENCE LEVEL

Percentage Sampling Error	Minimum Sample Size
±1%	10,000
±2%	2,500
±3%	1,111
±4%	625
±5%	400
±10%	100

Source: Jarol B. Manheim and Richard C. Rich, *Empirical Political Analysis: Research Methods in Political Science* (New Jersey: Prentice-Hall, Inc., 1981), 98.

A POINT ON THE COMPASS ————————————

Sampling Error in Preelection Polls

Preelection polls are now commonly reported in the media with a specified margin of error. For example, a poll reported in *The Globe and Mail* shortly before the 1996 provincial election in British Columbia was based on 630 interviews, and the margin of error for the total sample was estimated to be 3.9%, with a 95% confidence level. Put somewhat differently, if the survey found that 40% of the sample intended to vote for party X, then we could assume that within the population of all BC voters there was a 95% chance that between 36.1% (40% − 3.9%) and 43.9% (40% + 3.9%) would vote for party X. There is also a 5% chance (100% − 95%) that party X would get either less than 36.1% of the provincial vote or more than 43.9%. The odds would be small, but not negligible.

Now let's apply this logic to the actual results of the survey described above. The survey found that 43.3% of the respondents intended to vote for the NDP and 40.9% for the Liberals. Thus there was a 95% chance that the level of support for the NDP within the electorate at large was between 39.4% and 47.2% (43.3% ± 3.9%), and that the level of support for the Liberals was between 37.0% and 44.8% (40.9% ± 3.9%). These ranges suggest *very* different election outcomes. At one extreme, the NDP could end up with 47.2% of the vote and the Liberals with only 37.0%; this would translate into an NDP landslide and a Liberal rout. At the other extreme, the NDP could end up with only 39.4% and the Liberals with 44.8%; the outcome in this case would likely be a Liberal majority. Thus, once we take sampling error into account, the poll published in *The Globe and Mail* was predicting that the outcome would fall somewhere between an NDP landslide and a Liberal majority! Not a very useful prediction. It is perhaps small wonder that media commentators and political aficionados often ignore sampling error when trying to read the entrails of preelection polls.

In the actual election, the Liberals won 42% of the vote compared to 39.6% for the NDP. However, the NDP won more seats— 52 to the Liberals' 44—and formed a majority government.

It should be clear from Table 8.3 that the law of diminishing returns applies to sample size: at a certain point, dramatically increasing sample size results in only modest improvements in accuracy. For example, with a large population, moving from a sample of 100 to a sample of 625 takes us from 10% error down to 4%; increasing the sample size by over six times results in a substantial reduction in error. However, increasing the sample size from 2,500 to 10,000—an increase of four times— results in a mere 1% improvement in accuracy. Given the significant financial costs in increasing sample size, researchers are willing to tolerate some error. Note as well that, as population size exceeds 100,000, the size of the population itself does not influence sample size (Manheim and Rich 1981, 99). Thus, a sample size of 2,500 used for both a study of Toronto and a study of Canada as a whole would have the same degree of sampling error. This explains why national public opinion polls in the United States are generally of the same size as national polls in Canada, even though the American population is 10 times larger. However, population size is a factor in determining sample size for studies of small populations.

A final consideration influencing sample size is the method of sample selection. Probability sampling can be conducted in a number of ways, as we will discuss in more detail. The most common are the simple random sample, the stratified sample, and the cluster sample. We will examine how each sample is conducted shortly, but first it is worth noting that error varies with the different probability sampling approaches. Stratified sampling, which involves homogeneous samples, is more precise than simple random sampling and thus does not require as large a sample. Cluster sampling, on the other hand, is less precise than simple random sampling and necessitates larger sample sizes.

In summary, when selecting sample sizes, we need to consider the homogeneity of our population, the complexity of our study, the degree of accuracy desired, and the form of probability sampling to be utilized. In general, a larger sample is always preferred to a smaller sample, but obtaining large samples is a costly process in terms of both time and money. Bernard Lazerwitz (1968, 278–9) argues that the ideal sample is representative, obtained by probability sampling, and "as small as precision considerations permit, as economical as possible, and gathered as swiftly as its various measurement techniques permit." We seek samples that are just large enough to ensure the precision necessary; any larger is a waste of resources.

CONDUCTING PROBABILITY SAMPLES

As we have already noted, the basic procedure of probability sampling is known as **simple random sampling**. In this procedure, all the cases are listed and assigned numbers 1 ... *N*. Through computer selection or by use of a table of random numbers, cases are selected until the desired sample size is met. Thus, if we had a population of 10,000 and a desired sample size of 2,000, we would number the cases individually from 1 to 10,000 and then randomly select 2,000 cases to serve as our sample. The simple random sample resembles a lottery.

Occasionally, researchers will use a method known as **systematic selection**, rather than the lottery technique. In systematic selection, a *selection interval* (1/*k*) is calculated based on the sample size needed. If, for example, we want 5% of the population to be included in the sample, we need to select one out of every 20 cases (1/20 = 5%), and our selection interval is therefore 20. If we want 1% of the population included in the sample, we need to select one out of every 100 cases (1/100 = 1%), and our selection interval is 100. Once our selection interval is determined, a random number is selected to serve as a starting point; this number is known as a *random start*. For example, if our selection interval is 20, we begin by selecting a random number between 1 and 20; let's use 6. We then add the selection interval until the sample size is reached: cases numbered 6, 26, 46, 66, 86, 106, and so on are selected. Recall that numbers correspond to individual cases; the numbers selected represent the cases that will be included in the sample. Systematic sampling can be more practical and efficient than simple random sampling, but it is less random and thus less accurate than simple random sampling. In addition, it necessitates a random sampling frame; a list of the population that is ordered (e.g., alphabetically) may lead to biased results. One solution is to randomize the sampling frame before beginning systematic sampling (Bailey 1978, 78).

Stratified sampling involves breaking the population into mutually exclusive subgroups, or strata, and then randomly sampling each group. For example, if we are interested in differences between undergraduate and graduate students, we could break the population into two groups—undergraduates and graduates—each with its own sampling frame. We would then randomly sample from each list and combine the subsamples together to construct our larger sample. An advantage of stratified sampling is that it increases the homogeneity of the samples and reduces sampling error (Singleton et al. 1988, 145). Another benefit is that it allows us to focus on small subgroups within the population. If a particular group of interest is small, we may choose to sample a larger proportion of that subgroup to ensure numbers large enough to produce significant statistics. For example, if the population of subgroup A is 100, and the population of subgroup B is 1,000, we may choose to include 50% of A in the sample (for a total of 50 cases) but only 10% of B (for a total of 100 cases).

This procedure is known as *disproportionate stratified sampling*, and it is routinely used in Canada to deal with variance in provincial populations. Imagine, for example, that you have the money to do a national survey of 1,500 respondents on a matter of public policy interest. It is important, therefore, that you report not only on Canadians at large but also on provincial differences. Now, in a purely random sample, 561 respondents could be expected from Ontario and 53 from Saskatchewan. You would have more than enough respondents to provide a reasonable read on Ontario opinion; you would have "oversampled," but you would not have enough for Saskatchewan. Therefore, disproportionate stratified sampling could be used to increase the number of Saskatchewan respondents and to decrease the number from Ontario. The catch is that your final sample would no longer be representative of the Canadian population, for you would have too few Ontario respondents and too many Saskatchewan respondents. To reconstruct a representative national sample, it is necessary to assign *weights* to respondents. If, for example, we had sampled 200 individuals each from Ontario and Saskatchewan, we would assign a weight of 2.805 to each Ontario respondent (200 *times* 2.805 = 561) and a weight of 0.265 (200 *times* 0.265 = 53) to each Saskatchewan respondent. Although this procedure makes mathematical sense, it can be difficult to explain in public forums.

CHECKING YOUR BEARINGS

PROBABILITY SAMPLING[7]

Using the local telephone book, list the first 50 names on page 200 (exclude business listings).

1. What is your target population? What is your sampling frame? What are the limitations of the sampling frame?
2. Using a selection interval of 5 and a random start of 2, select a systematic sample.
3. Divide the list into two strata: males and females. (Place all initialized listings, e.g., B. Smith, in the female strata.) Using a selection interval of 4 and a random start of 1, select a systematic sample.

Cluster sampling is the process of dividing the population into a number of subgroups, known as clusters, and then randomly selecting clusters within which to randomly sample. This is best understood by considering geographic units. Let's say our population is Canada as a whole, and we are conducting individual interviews that require the researcher to travel to the door of each case. If we were to randomly sample all Canadians, we could end up with cases all over the country, resulting in considerable travel costs. Instead, we could use cluster sampling. First, we need to divide the country into clusters, for example, federal electoral constituencies. There are 295 constituencies, and we could randomly select a number of them, say two. These constituencies are then further broken down into clusters of similar population size, for example, municipalities, and again a number of them are randomly selected, say two. We now have four municipalities within two federal constituencies. We then further subdivide into even smaller areas, such as wards, and then city blocks, and then housing units (houses and apartments), using random selection at each stage (Manheim and Rich 1981, 94). The end result is a list of randomly selected but geographically concentrated housing units that will serve as the sample, as expressed in Figure 8.3.

Cluster sampling allows the researcher to greatly reduce costs while using probability sampling for a large population. However, sampling error increases with every sample taken; therefore, the numerous stages of random sampling within the cluster sampling method results in larger sampling errors. To address this problem, researchers need to increase their sample sizes. In the above example the representative nature of the sample could become suspect in the public's eyes if you had poor luck at the first stage of the sampling procedure. If you drew two constituencies in northern Manitoba, would you have a sample that was representative of the Canadian population? In addition, cluster sampling can appear to produce, indeed can in fact produce, samples that on face value are not representative.

In summary, there are a number of means that researchers can employ to obtain probability samples. The advantage of probability sampling is that it allows us to use sample statistics to estimate population parameters. However, not all research problems allow the use of probability sampling, which requires complete sampling frames. Thus, some researchers employ nonprobability sampling, a method inferior to probability sampling, but superior to no sample at all.

FIGURE 8.3

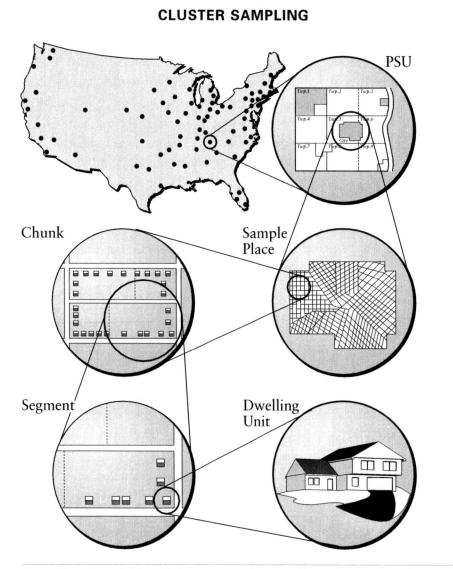

CLUSTER SAMPLING

Source: *Interviewer's Manual: Survey Research Center* (Ann Arbor: Institute for Social Research, University of Michigan, 1969), p. 8-2.

NONPROBABILITY SAMPLING

Nonprobability sampling includes any sampling technique in which each case in the population does *not* have an equal chance of being included in the sample; some cases are more likely than others to be included. This means that we run the risk of **investigator bias**. Because individual cases do not share equal probabilities of inclusion, we are unable to determine the variability in the sample and estimate the sampling error (Singleton et al. 1988, 152). Therefore, we cannot identify margins of error or confidence intervals. These limitations make nonprobability sampling less desirable than probability sampling, because it is more difficult to make generalizations and draw conclusions about the general population.

When is nonprobability sampling appropriate? Singleton et al. (1988, 152) identify four situations in which nonprobability sampling should be used. The first is exploratory research or pilot studies in which the investigator does not seek to make broad generalizations about the population. An exploratory study based on nonprobability sampling might be used to discover trends; the researcher would then follow with a study based on probability sampling to test these trends in the population. Thus, nonprobability sampling can serve as a first research step, followed by probability sampling research. Given that nonprobability sampling can be less expensive and easier to conduct than probability sampling, this process is understandable. In this context, it should also be noted that nonprobability sampling is often used in qualitative research. In elite interviewing, for instance, there may not be a readily identifiable population to which generalizations can be made.

A second use for nonprobability sampling arises when the samples to be drawn are extremely small. This might apply, for example, in a study of MPs who are visible minorities. In such instances, making generalizations from the samples is a matter of judgment on behalf of the researcher. Thus, she may use her advanced knowledge of the subject matter to select the cases in the sample. The third instance in which nonprobability sampling occurs is when sampling frames are unavailable or inadequate; again, the researcher must use judgment in selecting the sample. Finally, nonprobability sampling may be used for studies in which the cases (individuals, organizations, or governments) are likely to refuse to participate. In such instances, the researcher often must make use of the cases available to him or abandon his study.

Nonprobability sampling can take a number of forms. Perhaps the most common is the **accidental sample**, also known as a *sample of convenience* or *haphazard sample*. The researcher gathers data from individuals whom she "accidentally" encounters or are convenient. An example of this is the "man on the street" opinion polling, often done by news programs. Designed to tap the "pulse of the city," such samples are actually quite biased. A poll taken at a weekday noon on a downtown corner is limited to those individuals who tend to be downtown during the week for lunch, typically office workers. Many other individuals in the city, such as students, union workers, homemakers, and the retired, have a very low probability of being included in the sample, and therefore what is stated to be the "common" opinion is actually the

A POINT ON THE COMPASS

University Classes as Samples of Convenience

It is not surprising that many professors turn to their classes as samples of convenience. Students, after all, are close at hand, inexpensive to survey, and generally predisposed or at least resigned to play the respondent role. In some psychology departments there is a formal expectation that students will act as subjects for faculty, graduate, and undergraduate research as long as that research is conducted according to approved ethical guidelines.

Of course, there are also disadvantages to using student respondents or subjects. The primary drawback is that students are not typical or representative of the general population. Seldom are we interested in making generalizations from student samples to the student population; the population that is of interest is the nonstudent population, but generalizations in this respect are suspect. At times, however, research with students can reveal dynamics and relationships that are at least suggestive of broader population dynamics and relationships. For example, a 1994 study of 2,114 students at l'Université de Montréal (Blais et al. 1995) explored the relationship among concerns about the language situation in Quebec, expectations about the short- and long-term economic costs of separatism, and support for sovereigntist and federalist options. The findings that economic expectations had greater weight than linguistic expectations in explaining support for sovereignty and that long-term economic considerations outweighed short-term economic expectations provide useful insights into the broader dynamics of referendum voting in Quebec.

opinion of only a small group. A related, similarly biased form of sampling is any sample that involves **self-selection**, such as call-in programs on the radio or television or mail-in surveys for magazines and newspapers. The sample is limited to those who are exposed to the relevant form of media and who care about the topic enough to participate in the study (Neuman 1994, 197). It is such problems of bias that make the idea of teledemocracy suspect.

Purposive sampling (also known as *judgmental sampling*) involves researcher selection of specific cases; the researcher uses his judgment to select cases that will provide the greatest amount of information. Thus, he may choose cases that appear to be "typical" and use the data gathered to make generalizations, or he may choose cases that appear "extreme" and attempt to understand why they differ from the norm (Singleton et al. 1988, 154). Purposive sampling is particularly useful with specialized populations that are difficult to reach (Neuman 1994, 198) or for populations that lack a sampling frame. For example, a researcher exploring eating disorders might select cases from a hospital outpatient treatment program. A researcher studying the homeless might attempt to discover where the homeless spend their time and attempt to identify a sample. Purposive sampling requires a significant knowledge base of the target population (Singleton et al. 1988, 154).

When purposive or accidental sampling is combined with stratification, the result is known as **quota sampling**. The researcher identifies a number of target groups (strata), for example, men and women, and then sets a quota number that must be met for each group. For instance, the researcher may decide that she needs to sample at least 15 men and 15 women in her study. How the researcher then meets the quota can vary; she may use accidental sampling or use her knowledge to create a purposive sample. It should be stressed that, despite its efforts at greater representativeness, quota sampling has all the bias problems that are present in other forms of nonprobability sampling.

Snowball (or network) **sampling** is often employed to study social networks. Every case in the sample is directly linked to at least one other case in the sample (Neuman 1994, 199). The researcher begins by identifying a few cases and from these cases gets referrals for other cases and continues to branch out. For example, the researcher might interview three self-identified environmentalists, and at the conclusion of the interview ask each respondent to suggest three other environmentalists who could be interviewed. The researcher would then interview the suggested nine environmentalists and again ask for further referrals. This process would continue until sampling is completed. Just as a snowball rolled down a hill picks up snow and grows in size, the sample picks up more cases over time and becomes larger and larger until logistical and financial considerations force the researcher to stop.

This chapter has explored the need for a representative sample in our research. It was noted that representativeness is determined by three factors: sampling frame, sample size, and the method of sampling. As you probably noted, however, the discussion at times became quite technical and began to employ terms with quite specific statistical meanings. It is time, then, to put a more precise statistical vocabulary into place.

CHECKING YOUR BEARINGS

CHOOSING A SAMPLING APPROACH

For each of the following, select a sampling technique. Explain your choice.[8]

1. In-depth interviews with Canadian lawyers, to discuss career satisfaction.
2. Telephone survey of Canadians, to assess voting intentions.
3. Telephone survey of elected officials in your province, to assess the impact of gender on policy preferences.
4. Interviews with members of the gay and lesbian community, to discuss experiences with discrimination.

WORKING AS A TEAM

1. Imagine that your group has been commissioned to conduct a study of drug use among teenagers aged 14 to 18. The agency that commissioned the study is particularly interested in those individuals who in fact use drugs; issues of concern include frequency and type of use, peer pressure, religious beliefs, and degree of social integration. Up to 200 interviews will be funded, and the results of the study will be used to provide policy recommendations to the provincial government.

   Define the population for your study. Is there a sampling frame? What sampling method would you use? What ethical issues might you encounter?

SELF-STUDY

1. You wish to conduct a survey of political science majors on your campus to find out which subject field—Canadian politics, political theory, international relations, or comparative politics—is preferred (adapted from Singleton et al. 1988, 166). The department provides you with a list of all political science majors in the undergraduate and graduate program. This list also differentiates between nonhonours, honours, and graduate students. You will use this list to draw your sample.

a. Identify your target population and sampling frame. What possible problems can you identify with your sampling frame?

b. Explain how you would conduct a simple random sample for this study.

c. Explain how you would conduct a systematic sample for this study.

d. Explain how you would stratify the study on the basis of position (honours, nonhonours, graduate) in the program. What would be the benefit of doing so?

e. Which sampling procedure is best for your research question? (Explain your reasoning.)

2. You now wish to extend your study of political science majors to *all* Canadian universities.

a. Identify your target population and sampling frame. What possible problems can you identify with your sampling frame?

b. How will you obtain a representative sample? Defend your choice of approach, and explain all steps.

NOTES

1. Even the census, which attempts to contact every Canadian household, is unable to reach all citizens. It should also be noted that the Canadian census does not ask respondents if they are in fact Canadian citizens; thus, the census might best be seen as a study of Canadian residents, rather than Canadian citizens.

2. Singleton et al. (1988, 136) note that lists tend to be most accurate at local levels and least accurate at the federal level.

3. One problem is that of nonresponse bias. Mail-back surveys generate a greater response from the middle class and from those with a greater interest in the study. In this case, both the middle class and Landon supporters (who tended to be more passionate about the election than Roosevelt supporters) were more likely to return the surveys than were other groups, thus biasing the survey results toward Landon (Singleton et al. 1988, 133).

4. Example comes from Hayslett (1968, 38–9).

5. Lazerwitz (1968, 279) notes that the limitations are (1) the need for a complete listing and (2) the assumption that cases are statistically independent of one another.

6. The following example is modelled on an example presented in Singleton et al. (1988, 140–4).

7. Adapted from Singleton et al. (1988, 166).

8. Adapted from Singleton et al. (1988, 166).

CHAPTER 9

Describing the Political World: Univariate Statistics

DESTINATION

By the end of this chapter the reader should

- understand and be able to construct frequency distributions;
- understand and be able to compute the descriptive statistics used to measure the *central tendency* of and *variance* within data sets;
- know the properties and characteristics of the *normal curve;*
- appreciate the conceptual underpinnings of the *analysis of variance;*
- be able to use percentage distributions to look for relationships in data sets.

We are all used to describing the world in terms loosely based on statistical concepts. Think, for example, how often you use such phrases as "typical," "representative," or "on average." The goal of this chapter is to sharpen your conceptual language by introducing a number of specific terms used to measure both the average or "central tendency" of data sets and the manner in which individual cases are dispersed around the average. When we calculate measures of central tendency or dispersion, we are looking at just one variable at a time, hence the expression "univariate analysis." As we will see, however, univariate analysis provides the foundation for the more complex forms of statistical analysis to come.

Before the chapter begins to unfold, you should refresh your memory with respect to nominal, ordinal, and interval levels of measurement. Many of the distinctions between the various measures of central tendency will refer to these different levels of measurement. It should also be kept in mind that this chapter is initially concerned with the statistics used to describe sample data. However, as we move through the chapter, the focus will shift toward inferential statistics and the estimation of population parameters. The transition between *descriptive* and *inferential* statistics will come through the discussion of the normal curve. For now, we begin with measures of central tendency, which provide the foundation for descriptive analysis.

MEASURES OF CENTRAL TENDENCY

The description of virtually any data set in the social sciences, and particularly data sets drawn from survey research, begins with the identification of **central tendencies,** or, in more common usage, averages. For example, survey findings in the press frequently start with phrases like "a majority of Canadians believe that ..." or even "Canadians believe that...." There is no assumption that *all* Canadians believe this, and the article will likely go on to point out specific levels of agreement and disagreement. We begin, though, with the *average,* or *typical,* response and then fine-tune the analysis. However, determining this **central value** is not as straightforward as you might expect, for we have three different measures at our disposal. Furthermore, there is no correct measure for all situations, although there are more or less useful measures. Often, our choice depends upon the level of measurement used; interval-level variables provide more options than do nominal-level variables.

Our assessment of the central tendency of variables in a data set usually begins with the visual inspection of **frequency distributions,** which record the possible values of the variable under discussion along with the number of cases associated with each value. Table 9.1 provides an illustration of a frequency distribution. There we find a hypothetical distribution of the number of political science courses taken by graduating majors in political science and the number of graduating students associated with each value. For example, 14 graduating majors had completed 16 courses, and 7 had completed 22 courses. No students completed 26 courses, although it would be possible to do so. Most frequency distributions report not only the number of cases but also the percentage of cases associated with each value of the variable. In Table 9.1, then, we find that 11.3% of the students (13 out of 115) had completed 19 courses. Finally, frequency distributions sometimes report cumulative percentages. In the example provided by Table 9.1, 68.7% of the students (79 out of 115) had completed 20 courses or fewer. Cumulative percentages build from lower variable values to higher

TABLE 9.1

**NUMBER OF POLITICAL SCIENCE COURSES TAKEN BY
GRADUATING POLITICAL SCIENCE MAJORS**

Number of Courses Taken	Number of Students	Percentage of Students	Cumulative Percentage
15	10	8.7	8.7
16	14	12.2	20.9
17	15	13.0	33.9
18	16	13.9	47.8
19	13	11.3	59.1
20	11	9.6	68.7
21	9	7.8	76.5
22	7	6.1	82.6
23	9	7.8	90.4
24	5	4.3	94.8
25	3	2.6	97.4
26	0	0.0	97.4
27	0	0.0	97.4
28	2	1.7	99.1
29	0	0.0	99.1
30	1	0.9	100.0
TOTAL	115	100.0%	100.0%

values; the cumulative percentage for a given score is the proportion of cases with that score *or lower*.

A close visual inspection of a frequency distribution can tell us a good deal. We can see, for example, where the majority of scores fall and whether scores tend to cluster toward high or low variable values. However, it is very difficult to articulate visual impressions for others, or at least to do so with any numerical precision. It is even more difficult to compare such impressions. Hence the need for simple, summary measures of central tendency, and here we have three options.

The **mode** refers to the most frequently occurring value in a distribution of scores. For example, in a 1996 study of the Alberta electorate conducted by the authors, 45.1% of the respondents (454 out of 1,006 respondents) said they would vote Progressive Conservative, 21.0% Liberal, 7.1% Reform (despite the fact that a provincial Reform party did not exist), and 5.2% New Democrat "if a provincial election were held today." (An additional 21.7% did not state a voting intention.) Therefore, the modal value is "Conservative" or, more precisely, the intention to vote Conservative. In Table 9.1, the mode would be 18 courses; more graduating students have taken 18 courses than any other number.

The mode is the least useful of the three available measures of central tendency, in large part because it incorporates only one value—the most frequently occurring value—in a range of values. It therefore fails

A POINT ON THE COMPASS

Practical Usage of the Mode: Anthony Downs and Party Competition

In his 1957 publication, *An Economic Theory of Democracy*, Anthony Downs used unimodal, bimodal, and polymodal images of the electorate to develop some remarkably useful models of party competition. As noted in Chapter 2, Downs's models assumed that all voters could be placed along a single left–right continuum and that their placement would determine the nature of party competition and the number of parties likely to enter the competition.

For example, if the electorate is distributed in a unimodal fashion, as in Figure 9.1(b), then party platforms are likely to converge on the mode as parties compete for the greatest concentration of voters. In this situation party platforms will be similar and only two primary competitors will survive, one placed slightly to the left of the mode and one slightly to the right, with the parties competing for the same modal voters. Minor parties may exist at the tails of the distribution, but there will not be enough voters at the extremes to propel such parties into office.

If the distribution of the electorate is bimodal, as in Figure 9.1(c), then the major parties will locate themselves at the two modes. In this case there will be no convergence in party platforms; parties will appeal to their own constituencies and will not attempt to poach upon the turf of other parties. A polymodal environment (Figure 9.1(d)) will promote a multiparty system, again marked by the absence of convergence among party platforms. Parties will concentrate on mobilizing voters at their own modes and will not venture off in pursuit of the small number of voters to be found in the troughs between modes.

Downs's work shows both the power of economic models and the utility of simple distributional diagrams in illustrating some of the important dynamics of party formation and electoral competition.

FIGURE 9.1

MODAL DISTRIBUTIONS

A) J-Shaped Distribution   B) Unimodal Distribution

C) Bimodal Distributions   D) Polymodal Distribution

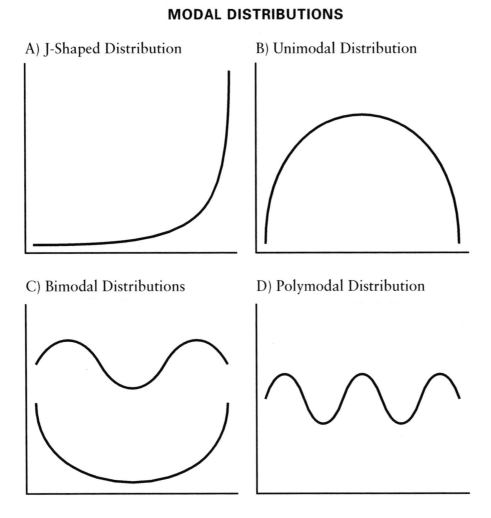

to make use of much of the data. Also, the mode is not a particularly stable measure, since it can change if only a few cases change. In Table 9.1, for instance, the mode would change from 18 to 17 if just one student taking 18 political science courses had dropped a course. Finally, the mode is highly sensitive to how measurement categories are constructed. If, in the Alberta survey described above, we grouped voters into just two categories, those who intended to vote Conservative and those who did not express any such intention, then the mode would no longer be a Conservative voting intention, since 54.9% of the respondents indicated that they would not vote Conservative.

Nevertheless, the mode is not without some utility. First, it is the only measure of central tendency available for nominal data (such as sex, party identification, and religious affiliation), although it can also be used for ordinal and interval data. Second, it is an appropriate measure of central tendency for J-shaped distributions, illustrated in Figure 9.1(a). In such cases, the frequency distribution would be highly *skewed* (discussed below) toward one side of the measure, and the mode would aptly describe where the bulk of cases fell. Third, the mode can be of considerable descriptive utility if we expand the definition from *the* most frequently occurring value to the most frequently occurring values. If we describe a distribution as unimodal, bimodal, or polymodal, as illustrated by Figures 9.1(b) to (d), the description immediately conveys useful images. Finally, it should be noted that finding the mode does not require any calculation; visual inspection of frequency distributions will alone suffice.

The **median**, a measure of central tendency that can be used with both ordinal and interval data, refers to the value above which and below which 50% of the cases fall. It is the midpoint in the *distribution of cases*; it is *not* the midpoint of the *scale* upon which those cases are distributed. To find the median, we order the cases from low to high—hence the need for ordinal or interval data—and then find the middle observation if the number of cases is odd or the midpoint between the two middle observations if the number of cases is even. In Table 9.1, for instance, the median for the distribution of scores is 19. (Note that the midpoint of the *scale* running from 15 to 30 courses would be 22.5.) In a Canadian profile of AIDS victims released in 1996, it was reported that "in the late 1980s and early 1990s, the average age of infection was 23, compared with 32 in the early 1980s" (Gadd 1996). The "average" in this case is the median; half the infections came prior to age 23 and half subsequently.

The precise calculation of the median can be difficult if it falls within an interval. In the Table 9.1 illustration, the median of 19 courses is not an interval because a student cannot take partial credits. The median, therefore, cannot be 19.1 courses. In the AIDS illustration, however, age 23 can be seen as an interval: an individual could be 23 years and one month old, 23 years and two months, and so forth. Formulas do exist for calculating medians for such interval data, but this is unlikely to be something that you would be required to do.

The most common, useful, and stable measure of central tendency is the arithmetic **mean** ($\overline{X}$), which is calculated by adding together all scores in a distribution and dividing by the total number of cases. (*Sample* means are designated by $\overline{X}$; *population* means are designated by σ.) In Table 9.1 this would be done by multiplying each value by the number of cases, summing the scores,[1] and dividing by the total number of cases; the mean works out to be 19.3. (Try the calculations yourself!)

The mean can be thought of as the "centre of gravity" for a distribution of scores (Elifson et al. 1990, 105). Unlike the mode, but like the median, each and every value is included in the calculation of the mean. However, the calculation of the mean uses precise scores, whereas the calculation of the median uses only the order in which scores fall. *When most people talk about averages, they are talking about means.*

$$\text{Mean} = \overline{X} = \frac{\sum Xi}{N}$$

Mean scores should only be calculated if we have interval data. Thus, for example, you can compute your GPA, which is a mean score, because the precise distance between the various grades is known. An A grade is not "somewhat better" than an A– grade; it is exactly 0.3 better on a four-point scale ranging from 0.0 (F) to 4.0 (A). Yet in practice, means are often calculated for ordinal data. This commonly occurs with Likert scales measuring public opinion or political attitudes, scales that may range from strongly agree to agree, disagree, and strongly disagree. It is not unusual to see numerical values attached to these values (strongly agree = 4; agree = 3; disagree = 2; strongly disagree = 1) and then to have mean scores computed. The problem is that we cannot assume that the distance, for instance, between "agree" and "agree strongly" is the same as the distance between "agree" and "disagree." However, and notwithstanding this problem, means are frequently used with ordinal measures such as Likert scales.

A POINT ON THE COMPASS

The Use of Mean Scores with Ordinal Data

Given that the mean score provides a concise summary of central tendency and that the mean corresponds more closely to common understandings of "average" than does the median, it is not surprising that means are often calculated in circumstances where a different measure of central tendency might be technically correct. In a survey of 893 delegates to the Reform Party's 1992 National Assembly, Keith Archer and Faron Ellis (1994, 292) asked respondents the following question:

Some people say that some groups or individuals have more influence over government policy than other groups or individuals. On a scale of 1 (very little influence) to 7 (a great deal of influence) please indicate how much influence you think these groups or individuals have on federal government policy.

We cannot be sure that in respondents' minds the distance from 2 to 3 on this scale was the same as the distance between say 3 and 4 or between 6 and 7, and for this reason the mean is not the most appropriate measure of central tendency. However, the mean scores reported by the authors do make intuitive sense and therefore provide useful insight into the thinking of Reform Party delegates.

Group/Individual	Mean
Federal cabinet	6.0
Quebeckers	5.7
Central Canada	5.4
Media	5.2
Lobby groups	5.0
Banks	4.6
Trade unions	4.0
Feminists	4.0
Environmentalists	3.9
Homosexuals	3.5
Recent immigrants	2.9
First ministers' conferences	3.5
Leader of the opposition	2.3
Senate	2.2
Government backbencher	1.8
Opposition Members of Parliament	1.7
Westerners	2.3
Maritimers	2.2
The average voter	1.5

How do these perceptions of relative political influence square with your own perceptions?

The values of the various measures of central tendency for a given distribution of scores are seldom identical. To illustrate why this is the case, refer again to Table 9.1. Imagine a political science department where students require 15 courses for a degree with a major in political science, but where most students take the minimal number of political science courses needed for their major and degree. In this case, the mode could well be 15 while the mean would be higher, inflated by the smaller number of students who take more than 15 courses *en route* to their degree. The general rule is that the mean, as an arithmetic average, is affected by or is sensitive to extreme scores. Therefore, it is less useful as a measure of central tendency than is the median when distributions are skewed or asymmetrical, with extreme values falling to only one side of the distribution. Measures of average income, for example, can be significantly affected by relatively few individuals with very high incomes; therefore, the mean can give a distorted impression of central tendency. The advantage of the median in such cases is that it is insensitive to extreme scores.

Imagine, for example, a professional basketball team of 10 players whose salaries range from a "meagre" $1 million to a high of $4 mil-

A POINT ON THE COMPASS

Median Measures of Average Income

Because the median is unaffected by extreme scores, it is the preferred measure of central tendency for income distributions. In 1996, for example, Statistics Canada reported (Alberts and Eckler 1996) that the median income for all Canadians, based on tax returns filed in 1995, was $18,500. The median income was defined as "the middle point where half the incomes are above and half are below." The median income for men was $24,900, up 1% from the previous year, while the median income for women was $14,200, up 4%. Median incomes varied not only by gender but also by place of residence:

Yukon	$22,900
Northwest Territories	22,700
Ontario	20,400
British Columbia	19,400
Alberta	19,100
Canada	**18,500**
Quebec	17,000
Manitoba	16,700
Saskatchewan	16,300
Prince Edward Island	16,200
Nova Scotia	16,200
New Brunswick	15,300
Newfoundland	14,000

lion. Imagine further that the mean and median salaries are both $2 million, that the distribution of player salaries is symmetrical about the mean. If the team then releases a $3 million dollar player and hires a superstar with an annual salary of $10 million, the median salary for the team will be unchanged. However, the salary distribution is now skewed toward the high end of the scale, and the mean salary will increase from $2 million to $2.7 million. (Go ahead: work out the math!) If the superstar demanded and received a salary increase to $20 million,[2] the mean salary for the team would increase but the median salary would not. In summary, "when the score distribution is symmetrical, the median has a value equal to the mean. If the distribution is skewed, the median usually lies closer to the bulk of the scores than the mean does" (Wright 1976, 93). In this case, "skewed" refers to the mean being pulled in the direction of extreme scores. Thus, the mean would be greater than the median. The difference between the mean and the median provides a rough measure of how skewed a distribution of scores might be; the greater the difference in the two measures of central tendency, the greater the skew.

Measures of central tendency are used all the time to compare individuals or groups. We talk, for example, about how the average doctor makes more than the average welder or how the average professional basketball player makes *many* times the income of the average political science graduate (assuming, alas, that the two are mutually exclusive categories!).[3] We compare GPAs, batting averages, average heights, average weights, average election turnouts, and average votes received by different political parties. However, comparing groups by looking at

CHECKING YOUR BEARINGS

SELECTING A MEASURE OF CENTRAL TENDENCY

For each of the following, which measure of central tendency would be best for expressing the "average": the mode, median, or mean? Why would you make these choices?

- the average salary paid to all actors in a blockbuster movie
- the average salary of medical doctors
- the average (or typical) supporter of the Liberal Party of Canada
- the average age of undergraduate students in political science
- the average age of first-time voters in federal elections
- your GPA at college or university

FIGURE 9.2

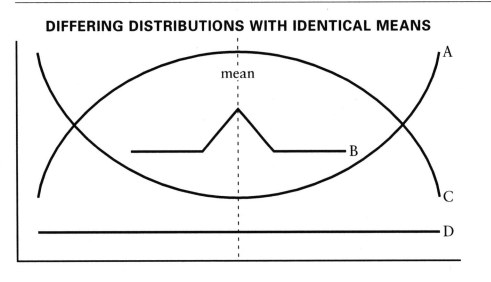

DIFFERING DISTRIBUTIONS WITH IDENTICAL MEANS

differences in central tendencies alone can be a risky endeavour. Figure 9.2, for example, displays a number of possible distributions that all have the same mean score but that differ dramatically in other respects. Thus, for a more useful and meaningful group comparison, we also need to know something about the distribution of scores around the measure of central tendency.

TABLE 9.2

SUMMARY OF THE THREE MEASURES OF CENTRAL TENDENCY

Measure	Level of Data	"How to"	Pros	Cons
Mode	Nominal Ordinal Interval	Use frequency distribution to find most frequent value.	Only measure for nominal data; apt for J-shaped distributions.	Fails to use all information; varies with category construction; unstable.
Median	Ordinal Interval	Place all cases in order, then find middle value.	Stable; not affected by extreme scores; uses all cases.	Does not use precise values.
Mean	Interval	Sum all scores and divide by the total number of scores.	Most reliable; uses all information, including precise values.	Affected by extreme scores.

MEASURES OF VARIATION

Statistical measures for the dispersion of scores around the central tendency are termed **measures of variation**. Just as there are a number of ways in which we can measure central tendency, there are a number of descriptive statistics that can be used to measure the *dispersion* or *variation* within a set of scores. As with measures of central tendency, our choice is determined in large part by the level of measurement. *There are no statistical measures of variation for nominal data*, although this should not prevent the researcher from discussing the dispersion of the data in more qualitative terms. Without such discussion, it is difficult to see how representative the mode is of the data taken as a whole.

The simplest but least useful measure of variation is the **range**, which is the difference between the lowest and highest values in a distribution of scores. If we found, for example, that among the 23,000 medical doctors in Ontario the highest annual income was $1,200,000 and the lowest was $30,000, the income range would be $1,170,000 (the highest value minus the lowest value). However, the range would tell us something about only two of the 23,000 physicians, and we would have no idea if most doctors were near the bottom, top, or middle of the range. The range, which can be used with ordinal or interval measures, ignores all information but the two most extreme scores. Sometimes the range is calculated by taking the difference between the highest and lowest scores and then adding 1. To illustrate why this is the case, imagine a set of scores ranging from 1 to 5. If we subtract the lowest score from the highest score (5 − 1), the range is 4. In fact, five scores are possible: 1, 2, 3, 4, and 5. Therefore, adding 1 gives us a more precise estimate of the range:

$$\text{range} = \text{highest score} - \text{smallest score} + 1.$$

While we can easily calculate how much any particular score deviates from the mean, it is not so easy to put that deviation into perspective. Is the deviation *relatively* small? *Relatively* large? To answer such questions, we need a measure of the *average* deviation from the mean, while at the same time locating individual scores with respect to both the mean and other scores in the data set. The catch, however, is that deviations about the mean will always sum to zero. If we have 10 scores, subtract the mean from each score, and sum the deviations, the total will always be zero. Given, then, that *mean deviation* does not provide a useful measure of variation about the mean, we need to turn to a more complex measure.

The **standard deviation** provides the most common measure of average deviation from the mean. Although the standard deviation may be initially difficult to grasp conceptually, its properties become more readily apparent if we work through the calculations. The standard deviation for a set of scores is calculated by the following steps: (1) find the mean for the set of scores; (2) subtract the mean from each individual score; (3) square each difference, that is to say, each $X_i - \overline{X}$; (4) find the sum of these squared differences; (5) divide that sum by the number of cases; and (6) find the square root for the result of step (5). The fourth step produces the **sum of the squares,** a statistic to which we will return in Chapter 10. If we were to stop at the fifth step, we would have the **variance,** which can be defined as the sum of the squared deviations from the mean, divided by the number of cases. The standard deviation is the square root of the variance:

$$\text{variance} = S^2 = \frac{\sum(X_i - \overline{X})^2}{N};$$

$$\text{standard deviation} = \sqrt{S^2} = S = \sqrt{\frac{\sum(X_i - \overline{X})^2}{N}}.$$

To illustrate the calculation of both the standard deviation and variance—if you can calculate one, then you can do the other—imagine a set of five scores: 4, 4, 4, 4, and 9. The calculations steps are as follows:

1. Find the mean:

$$\text{mean} = \overline{X} = \frac{\sum X}{N} = \frac{25}{5} = 5.$$

2. Subtract the mean from each score: $X - \overline{X}$ in the table below.

3. Square the difference between the mean and each score: $(X - \overline{X})^2$ in the table below.

4. Total the sum of the squared differences (sum of squares): $\sum(X_i - \overline{X})^2 = 20.$

5. Divide the sum of the squares by the number of cases:

$$\frac{20}{N} = \frac{20}{5} = 4 = \text{variance}.$$

CHECKING YOUR BEARINGS

CALCULATING THE VARIANCE AND STANDARD DEVIATION

You have been asked to calculate the "average age" of a group of Progressive Conservative voters. You have also been asked how typical the average is. To this end, calculate the mean age, variance, and standard deviation for the following set of respondents. Round all calculations to the nearest decimal point. If, for example, the mean age is 34.567 years, round to 34.6 years.

A = 21 years	L = 56 years
B = 27 "	M = 62 "
C = 46 "	N = 19 "
D = 65 "	O = 47 "
E = 23 "	P = 58 "
F = 37 "	Q = 51 "
G = 83 "	R = 45 "
H = 22 "	S = 72 "
I = 29 "	T = 18 "
J = 47 "	U = 40 "
K = 41 "	

6. Take the square root of the variance: $\sqrt{4} = 2$.

Score (X)	$X - \overline{X}$	$(X - \overline{X})^2$
4	–1	1
4	–1	1
4	–1	1
4	–1	1
9	4	16

Fortunately, this calculation is routinely done by computer-based statistical packages; therefore, you will seldom need to do it by hand for large data sets.

The larger the standard deviation (or variance), the greater the variability in scores. When variability is low, the mean is more representative of the bulk of the scores than it is when variability is high. Put somewhat differently, the mean is a better predictor of individual scores when the variance is low than when it is high. It should also be noted, however, that the absolute values of the mean and standard deviation are independent of one another. A large mean in absolute terms (say 200 rather than 20) does not necessarily generate a large standard deviation;

the size of the standard deviation depends on how tightly the scores are clustered around the mean rather than on the value of the mean itself. Like the mean, the standard deviation incorporates each and every case in the distribution of scores. Also like the mean, and the variance upon which it is based, the standard deviation is sensitive to extreme scores. Therefore, if outliers exist, the standard deviation will not accurately reflect variability among the bulk of the scores.

A POINT ON THE COMPASS

Means and Standard Deviations

The utility of having measures of both central tendency and variation can be demonstrated by the following table, which compares annual growth rates in provincial economies over the 1962–1991 period. As the mean scores in the table show, the Canadian provinces have differed considerably in their annual growth rates. This, however, is only half the picture. They also differ in variability; Alberta and Saskatchewan, for example, have had much more volatile economies—reflected in the larger standard deviations—than have Ontario or Quebec. If we want to make sense out of the relative economic performance of provincial economies, we need to take both average growth and volatility into account.

	Mean Growth Rate	Standard Deviation of Growth
Yukon and Northwest Territories	6.84	8.14
British Columbia	4.87	3.52
Alberta	5.25	6.39
Saskatchewan	3.37	8.24
Manitoba	3.15	3.16
Ontario	4.09	3.30
Quebec	3.67	2.65
New Brunswick	4.29	4.76
Nova Scotia	4.09	3.41
Prince Edward Island	4.46	4.95
Newfoundland	4.39	3.45
Canada	**4.06**	**2.55**

Source: Michael A. Goldberg and Maurice D. Levi, "Growing Together or Apart: The Risks and Returns of Alternative Constitutions of Canada," *Canadian Public Policy* XX: 4 (December 1994), 343.

To demonstrate this sensitivity to extreme scores, turn again to the simple illustration in the above calculations. Most of the "variance" in that case came from a single score (9). As the calculations show, it is because the deviations from the mean are squared that extreme scores have such a disproportionate effect on the calculation of the variance. That effect is moderated in the calculation of the standard deviation in that by taking the square root, the impact of squaring deviations from the mean is reduced. Note also that the values for the standard deviation (or variance) are always positive; it is impossible to have a negative standard deviation. When you think of it, how could there be less than zero variance? If all scores are identical, then each score would equal the mean, there would be no deviation from the mean, and both the variance and standard deviation would equal zero.

We can use the standard deviation to describe how far an individual case is from the mean. We often hear references to cases being "2 standard deviations from the mean" or "0.5 standard deviation from the mean." Another way to express this is with **standardized scores** (also known as *z-scores*), which are scores expressed in terms of the number of standard deviations they fall from the mean of the total distribution of scores. If, for example, the mean of a distribution was 150 and the standard deviation was 20, then a score of 120 would be –1.5 standard deviations from the mean. Therefore, the score of 120 expressed as a standardized score or z-score would be –1.5. Unlike the standard deviation, standardized scores can be positive or negative. Scores greater than the mean yield positive standardized scores, and scores falling below the mean yield negative standardized scores. In either case they allow us to compare scores in terms of their relative distance from the mean.

Standardized scores enable the comparison of an individual score relative to the scores of a group as a whole. Standardized scores also enable a comparison of scores across different populations. For example, in Canadian National Election Studies, respondents are asked to indicate their feelings toward the party leaders, using a 100-point

TABLE 9.3

SUMMARY OF THE THREE MEASURES OF VARIATION

Measures of Variation	Levels of Measurement		
	Nominal	Ordinal	Interval
Range	X	✔	✔
Standard deviation	X	X	✔
Variance	X	X	✔

feeling thermometer. Let's focus for a moment on assessments of Prime Minister Jean Chrétien and Reform Party leader Preston Manning. Let us assume that the average rating of Chrétien was 55 on the 100-point scale, with a standard deviation of 15, and the mean for Manning was 48, with a standard deviation of 18 units. We could draw two conclusions from these data: Canadians felt more positively toward Chrétien than Manning ($\overline{X}$ = 55 versus 48), and they were somewhat more consensual in their attitudes toward Chrétien than Manning (S = 15 versus 18).

We can extend the analysis from the aggregate data (mean and standard deviation) to the individual level of analysis by comparing raw scores and standardized scores. Assume that one respondent (Jane Porter from Saskatoon) rated both Chrétien and Manning 60 on the 100-point thermometer. By examining the raw score, we might conclude that the party leaders had no effect on her vote, since both were assigned the same score. However, by using standardized scores, a different portrait, and a different conclusion, emerges. Jane's rating of 60 for Chrétien is slightly above the average ($\overline{X}$ = 55) and well within the standard deviation (S = 15). Using the formula for z-scores, we would calculate her z-score for Chrétien as $(60 - 55)/15 = 0.33$. The conclusion would be that Jane's feelings toward Chrétien were 0.33 standard units above the mean. For Manning, however, the calculation is as follows: $(60 - 48)/18 = 0.67$. In this instance, Jane's evaluation of Manning was 0.67 standard units above the mean. Therefore, in comparison with other voters, Jane rated Manning more positively than Chrétien. We could hypothesize that this more positive evaluation had an impact on her voting behaviour.

Let's take another illustration of the use of z-scores, one that is closer to home for many university students, particularly those wishing to be admitted to graduate or professional schools. Let's assume that your major is political science and that your GPA is 3.2 on a 4-point scale. Let's also assume that the GPA of political science majors as a whole is 2.4, and the standard deviation is 0.6. Let's also assume that your friend, and potential competitor for a valued place in the admission to law school, is a psychology major. We'll assume that her GPA is 3.4, and the GPA for psychology majors is 2.8 with a standard deviation of 0.6.

Which of the two should be admitted to law school? Her higher GPA (3.4 versus 3.2) suggests she might be the one most likely admitted. Let's compare performance using z-scores. Your score, which would be called your standardized GPA, is $(3.2 - 2.4)/0.6 = 1.33$. Your friend's standardized GPA is $(3.4 - 2.8)/0.6 = 1.0$. Thus, your standardized score, in relation to all political science majors, is higher than your friend's, in relation to all psychology majors. Leaving aside arguments about the potential superiority of psychology students in relation to political science students overall (i.e., they did attain higher GPAs), the z-scores might lead one to conclude that you should be offered admission to law school ahead of your friend. Thus, the purpose of z-scores is to try to standardize the base of comparison between groups. Standardized scores also provide a conceptual bridge to the discussion of the normal curve.

Computing Standardized Scores

$$\text{Standardized score} = Z = \frac{X_i - \overline{X}}{S}$$

If $Xi = 20$, $\overline{X} = 17$, and $S = 1.4$, then

$$Z = \frac{X_i - \overline{X}}{S}$$

$$= \frac{20 - 17}{1.4}$$

$$= \frac{3}{1.4} = 2.14$$

If $Xi = 50$, $\overline{X} = 55$, and $S = 7$, then

$$Z = \frac{X_i - \overline{X}}{S}$$

$$= \frac{50 - 55}{7}$$

$$= \frac{-5}{7} = -0.71$$

CHECKING YOUR BEARINGS

CALCULATING Z-SCORES

You have been told that the average GPA for political science majors is 2.7. Given this information, convert the following GPAs to z-scores. How would you verbally express such z-scores to someone without a statistics background?

Schulmit:	GPA = 3.41
Andrew:	GPA = 2.76
Christine:	GPA = 3.01
Malinda:	GPA = 3.17
Scott:	GPA = 3.56

NORMAL CURVE

The **normal curve**, or what is often known as the "bell-shaped curve," is a particularly useful statistical concept. Normal curves need not have identical shapes; the example in Figure 9.3 is perhaps the most typical shape, but other normal curves could be more or less peaked than our illustration. However, all normal curves and the **normal distributions** that they contain share a number of characteristics:

- The normal curve is bilaterally symmetrical; its shape is identical to the left and right of the mean.

- As a consequence, the mode = the mean = the median of the normal curve.

- The tails of the normal curve are *asymptotic*; they approach but never quite meet the horizontal axis. As a consequence, *any* value can be placed under a normal curve; the tails stretch to infinity.

- The total area under the normal curve = 1.

- 68.3% of the area under the normal curve falls within ±1 standard deviation of the mean.

- 95.4% of the area under the normal curve falls within ±2 standard deviations of the mean.

- 99.7% of the area under the normal curve falls within ±3 standard deviations of the mean.

The importance of the normal curve does not arise because real data are distributed in a normal fashion; "the normal distribution is a mathematical distribution that is not found in the real world" (Elifson et al. 1990, 149). Real-world distributions, which we often think of as normally distributed, do not actually fit the conditions stated above. For example, we may think of IQ, or weight or height, as being normally distributed. However, if they were normally distributed, *any* score would be possible, no matter how unlikely. We could have, for instance, adults who were 20 metres or 20 centimetres tall. The real world, then, is not normal, *but large parts of the statistical and mathematical worlds are*. This fact is of considerable importance in the chapters to come.

One way to think about how the normal curve is derived, and in particular the importance of the central-limit theorem in survey research, is to consider what happens when we toss coins. Assume that we have an unbiased coin, that is, a coin that is equally likely to land on heads or tails. If we tossed the coin 10 times, we would expect to produce 5 heads

A POINT ON THE COMPASS

The Central-Limit Theorem

Although no real-world data are normally distributed, many statistics are. If we take repeated samples of the same population, a given statistic (e.g., the mean) will follow a normal distribution. Indeed, this is the case even if the data upon which those statistics are based are not themselves normally distributed. As Allen Edwards (1969, 123) points out, "The fact is, that regardless of the shape or form of a population distribution, the distributions of both the sum and the mean of random samples [taken from that population] approach that of a normal distribution as the sample size is increased. This statement is based on an important theorem known as the *central-limit theorem.*" Note the role that sample size plays in this theorem; statistics generated by large samples are more normally distributed than are statistics generated by small samples.

and 5 tails. In doing this, however, we find that we don't always produce 5 heads and 5 tails. Sometimes we get 4 heads and 6 tails or 6 heads and 4 tails. Or we could get 3 heads and 7 tails or 7 heads and 3 tails. There might even be rare occasions when we get 10 heads and no tails. If we did this 100 times, we would find the distribution of samples would approximate a normal curve as shown in Figure 9.3(a).

If the "true" result of tossing coins is an equal number of heads and tails, the samples will be normally distributed around this value. The distribution in Figure 9.3(a) indicates that while not all samples will exactly produce the "true" value, they are likely to approximate it. Furthermore, as is discussed below, we know what proportion of the cases falls within given standard deviations of the mean under the normal curve, a fact that proves to be very useful when testing hypotheses about the statistical significance of findings.

The other significant implication of the central-limit theorem is that as sample size increases, the distribution of cases more closely approximates a normal curve. Let's assume that instead of tossing a coin 10 times over 100 samples, you tossed a coin 100 times over 1,000 samples. (This assumes, of course, that you have a lot of time on your hands!) The larger sample size will ensure that more of the samples will approximate 50 heads and would produce a distribution as shown in Figure 9.3(b).

FIGURE 9.3(a)

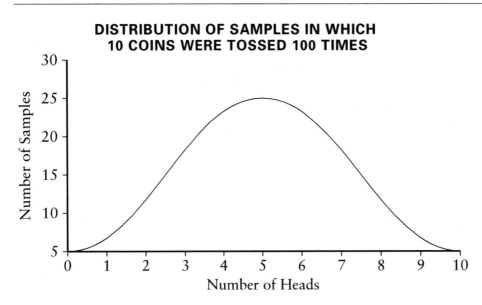

**DISTRIBUTION OF SAMPLES IN WHICH
10 COINS WERE TOSSED 100 TIMES**

As the sample size increases, the distribution of samples collapses more tightly around "true" population value. As a result, with large populations the likelihood of producing results that deviate substantially from the true value is very small.

We can use the idea embodied in the central-limit theorem when we are testing hypotheses. In survey research we draw samples to test hypotheses about the causal relationship between variables. Of course, we're never sure if our particular sample measures the "true" value of a

FIGURE 9.3(b)

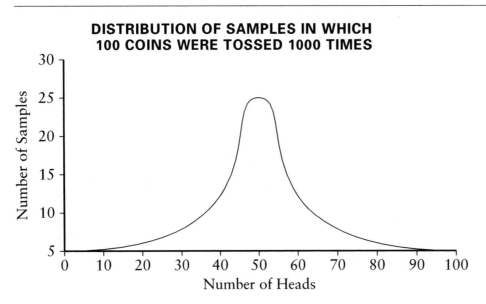

**DISTRIBUTION OF SAMPLES IN WHICH
100 COINS WERE TOSSED 1000 TIMES**

variable and of the relationship between variables. We do know, however, that samples are normally distributed around the true value, and the larger the sample size, the more closely the samples approximate the "true" values.

You will note from Figure 9.4 that 95.4% of the total area of the normal curve falls within ±2 standard deviations of the mean, and 99.7% of the area falls within ±3 standard deviations. You should also note that the area of the normal curve encompassed within ±1.96 standard deviations from the mean includes 95% of the cases, and the area encompassed within ±2.57 standard deviations from the mean includes 99% of the cases. These latter percentage distributions come into play when we take up tests of statistical significance and confidence intervals, which we will explore in the next chapter.

FIGURE 9.4

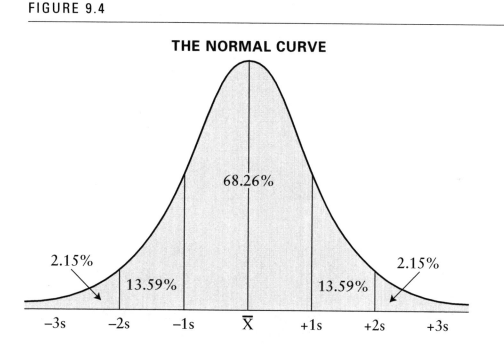

THE NORMAL CURVE

COMPARING UNIVARIATE STATISTICS BETWEEN TWO SUBGROUPS

The discussion to this point has stressed that measures of central tendency and dispersion are closely connected, not only in their calculation (as in the case of the mean and standard deviation), but also in the role they play in interpreting empirical data. To illustrate the interplay between measures of central tendency and measures of dispersion, turn to Figures 9.5(a) and (b), which present two quite different comparisons

STATISTICAL TOPICS

FIGURE 9.5

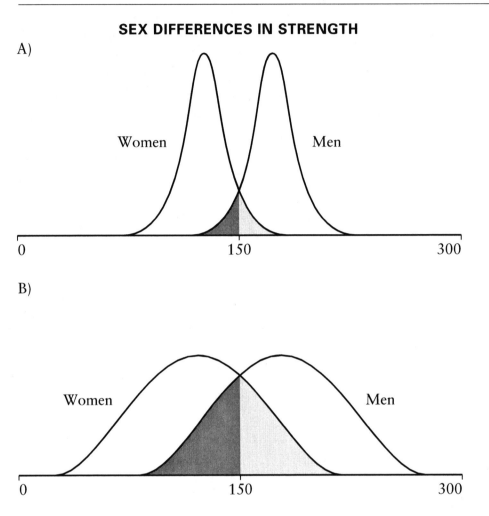

SEX DIFFERENCES IN STRENGTH

A)

Women   Men

0   150   300

B)

Women   Men

0   150   300

of the relative strengths of men and women. The two figures show *hypo-thetical* distributions of two subgroups, men and women, across a scale measuring physical strength; the higher the score on the horizontal axis, the stronger the individual. The means for women are identical in both figures, as are the means for men. In both figures, the mean score for men is higher than the mean score for women; men, on average, are stronger than women. The difference between the two figures comes from the dispersion of scores around the means; in Figure 9.5(a) the scores are tightly bunched around the mean, whereas in Figure 9.5(b) the dispersion is much looser.

Now suppose a fire department is hiring new staff and decides that a minimum strength of 150 is needed to perform satisfactorily as a fire-fighter. Suppose further, and as was often done in the past, that sex is used as a proxy for strength. Instead of actually measuring the physical strength of individual applicants, the fire department decides that any man who applies is strong enough (he is, after all, a man) and that any woman who applies is not (she is, after all, a woman). What errors would be made? In Figure 9.5(a) the shaded section shows the women who might be strong enough to do the job yet who would not be hired, and the cross-hatched section shows the men who might be hired even though they would not have sufficient strength to do the job. In both cases, the errors that would be made by using sex as a proxy measure of strength would be quite small; most men are strong enough to do the job and most women are not. But if we turn to Figure 9.5(b), the potential for error increases dramatically. There are now many more men who might be hired even though they lack sufficient strength, and many more women who would be denied employment even though they have the necessary strength. Sex, therefore, serves as a poor proxy of strength in this case, and a fire department that relied upon it rather than on individual measures of strength would end up with suboptimal firefighters. Figure 9.5(b), we would suggest, illustrates the job discrimination women faced in the past when sex was used indiscriminately as a proxy of strength.[4]

Figures 9.5(a) and (b) can also be used to illustrate some of the complexities in the long-standing debate about sex differences in mathematical ability. Let's suppose hypothetically that *on average* men do have a greater aptitude for math than do women, that men have a higher mean score on some measure of mathematical ability. As we have seen from the firefighter example, the relevance of this difference depends upon the dispersion of male and female scores around their respective means. If the distribution resembles Figure 9.5(a), then we could use sex as a proxy of mathematical ability and assume that, *as a rule*, men are better at math than women. However, if the distribution resembles Figure 9.5(b), then sex cannot be used as a proxy for mathematical ability. In this latter case, *there is no rule*; knowing an individual's sex provides little assistance in predicting his or her ability in math. The sex difference in mean scores is irrelevant. In all likelihood, Figure 9.5(b) more closely approximates social reality in this case than does Figure 9.5(a), if indeed there is *any* sex difference in mathematical ability. Therefore, a female student in a political science research methods course cannot assume that she is labouring under some disadvantage because of her sex!

The point to emphasize is that the contrast between Figures 9.5(a) and (b) stems not from differences in mean scores, but rather from differences in the dispersion of scores around the means. Thus to make sensible intergroup comparisons, and indeed to provide a complete descriptive profile of data sets, we need information on both central tendency and the manner in which scores are distributed about those measures of central tendency. We also need a statistical measure of differences in mean scores to which we can attach levels of confidence. Is the difference in mean scores significant? Or did it occur by chance? We will look at how to assess these questions in the next chapter.

The above discussion of hypothetical sex differences in strength and mathematical ability illustrates the conceptual underpinnings for the **analysis of variance**, or **ANOVA**, one of the most useful statistical techniques in the social sciences. In one form or another, social scientists are often interested in subgroup differences—between men and women, liberals and conservatives, Canadians and Americans, Quebeckers and western Canadians—that are conceptually analogous to the differences in group means discussed above. However, and as we have seen, the difference between groups is only half the story; we also need to know about the dispersion or *variance* of scores within groups. Analysis of variance provides a systematic method for comparing the relative strength of *between-group* and *within-group* differences. Simply put, and as illustrated by the examples discussed above, between-group variance takes on greater importance as within-group variance declines. In other words, small differences between relatively homogeneous groups can be significant, whereas large differences between relatively heterogeneous groups may not be.

LOOKING FOR BIVARIATE RELATIONSHIPS IN PERCENTAGE DISTRIBUTIONS

We began exploring bivariate relationships in Chapter 2, where contingency tables were used to examine the impact of the independent variable upon the dependent variable. In drawing this chapter to a close, we need to return to contingency tables.

At the outset we must stress again that to conduct any form of correlational analysis, tables should be ordered correctly, with the independent and dependent variables in the proper positions (across the top and down the side, respectively) and continuous variables (both dependent and independent) ordered low to high. This is a good practice to engage in with all contingency tables; if you are constructing the table yourself, be certain to organize it properly. If the table is presented to you, be sure to note *how* it is constructed; do not assume that the table is presented in the proper manner. If a contingency table is presented in a different manner, you will need to either make adjustments in how you interpret the table or recreate the table for yourself.

When we read the contingency table, we are looking for patterns. Do the values of the dependent variable line up with values of the independent variable? Is there a clear relationship that supports the research hypothesis? Can the null hypothesis ("no relationship exists") be rejected? Look at Table 9.4, which locates 80 respondents with respect to their income level and ideological self-placement on a left–right scale. Table 9.4 presents the *number* of respondents in each cell, row, and column. Look, now, at the first column, which is comprised of "low-income" respondents. Is there a pattern? Clearly there is. We find most low-income respondents place themselves on the right of the political spectrum. But what happens when income levels are increased? Is support for the ideological right contingent upon income? You will notice a problem when we try to compare *between* columns; because each column has a different number of cases (known as the column marginal), it is difficult to compare across the columns. Is the raw score of 5 in the "middle-income, right" cell equivalent to the raw score of 5 in the "high-income, right" cell? No. In the former, 5 out of 45 middle-income cases (less than 12%) place themselves on the right, while in the latter example, 5 out of 15 cases (over 33%) hold the same ideological position. The need to compare *relative size* when considering bivariate relationships such as that portrayed in Table 9.4 leads to the development of **percentage tables**.

Converting raw scores to percentage scores is easy: we just take the raw score, divide by the marginal, and multiply by 100. Recall that a marginal is the total number of cases in a value of either the independent or the dependent variable. Marginals for values of the independent variable are placed at the bottom of each column and are known as **column marginals**. If we divide the raw cell score by the column marginal and

TABLE 9.4

IDEOLOGICAL SELF-PLACEMENT BY INCOME (NUMBER OF RESPONDENTS)

Ideological Self-placement	Income			
	Low	Middle	High	Row totals
Left	0	10	5	15
Centre	5	30	5	40
Right	15	5	5	25
Column totals	20	45	15	80

multiply by 100, we end up with a **column percentage**. Table 9.5 shows the data from Table 9.4 converted to column percentages. Notice that the column percentage for "low-income, right" is 75%: 15 (raw score) divided by 20 (column marginal), multiplied by 100. Marginals for the values of the dependent variable are located at the end of each row and are referred to as **row marginals**. When we divide the raw cell score by the row marginal and multiply by 100, we end up with a **row percentage**. Table 9.6 presents the raw data from Table 9.4 in row percentages. The row percentage for "low-income, right" is 60%: 15 (raw score) divided by 25 (row marginal), multiplied by 100. Throughout Tables 9.5 and 9.6, the row percentages and column percentages differ. This is because the bases of each—the marginals—are not the same. If a row marginal and a column marginal are equal, then the row and column percentages will be equal.

TABLE 9.5

IDEOLOGICAL SELF-PLACEMENT BY INCOME (COLUMN PERCENTAGES)

Ideological Self-placement	Income			
	Low	Middle	High	Row totals
Left	0%	22%	33%	19%
Centre	25%	67%	33%	50%
Right	75%	11%	33%	31%
Column totals	100%	100%	100%	100%

TABLE 9.6

IDEOLOGICAL SELF-PLACEMENT BY INCOME (ROW PERCENTAGES)

Ideological Self-placement	Income			
	Low	Middle	High	Row totals
Left	0%	67%	33%	100%
Centre	12%	75%	12%	100%
Right	60%	20%	20%	100%
Column totals	25%	56%	19%	100%

Clearly, row and column percentages are not the same thing. Each addresses a different question. The column percentage gives us information about the categories of the independent variable. For our example, the column percentages in Table 9.5 allow us to address the following question: "Among those respondents in each income group, what percentage is right, centre, or left?" Looking at the middle-income column, we see that 22% of those with middle-income levels place themselves to the left of centre, 67% place themselves in the middle of the ideological spectrum, and the remaining 11% place themselves to the right of centre. Turning to the high-income category in Table 9.5, we see that a full third (33.3%) of all respondents are left of centre, a third are centrist in orientation, and the final third are right of centre. Use the same logic to interpret the low-income category on your own.

The row percentage looks within categories of the dependent variable. The question here is, "Among those in each ideological position, what percentage falls in the low-, middle-, or high-income bracket?" We read Table 9.6 as stating that among supporters of the left in our sample, 0% have low incomes, 67% have middle-level incomes, and the remaining 33% have high incomes. In the centrist category, 12.5% are low-income, 75% are middle-income, and 12.5% are high-income. The row percentages for the right supporters can be interpreted similarly. Because the row and column percentages give different types of information, researchers often find it useful in their analyses to create a table that includes not only the raw cell count, but also the row and column percentages. This provides her with a great deal of information in a single table. The primary advantage of percentage distributions is that they provide quick comparative information. However, the raw data are also useful, since they remind the researcher of the original bases upon which the percentages have been constructed. For example, 67% may sound like an important statistic, until the researcher reminds herself that it represents 4 of a total of 6 cases, rather than 670 of 1,000 cases. In other words, while percentage tables allow us to compare relative distributions of subgroups with respect to the independent or dependent variable, the raw data keep us grounded with the data themselves.

When making comparisons with percentages, we always move in the opposite direction of the percentage itself; that is, when using row percentages we compare across columns, and with column percentages, we compare across rows (Neuman 1994, 302). Table 9.5 is a column-percentaged table, so we compare across the rows (categories of the dependent variable). We see that a strong majority of the low-income respondents support the right (75%), while a strong majority of the middle-income respondents support the centre (67%). Among the high-income respondents, support is evenly divided between left, centre, and right. Table 9.6 is a row-percentaged table, so we compare across columns (categories of the independent variable). What do we see when we compare across income groups? In this fictitious sample, the left derives 67% of its support from the middle-income category. Similarly, the centre draws 75% of its support from middle-income respondents. Finally, 60% of the right's support can be credited to the low-income respondents.

Percentage tables are also used to look for relationships. If you find that the cell percentages are very similar, then it is difficult to assert that a relationship exists (Neuman 1994, 302). In order for a relationship to exist, there must be a discernible pattern. One useful way to look for patterned relationships between continuous variables is the "circle-the-largest-cell rule" (Neuman 1994, 302). When using row percentages, we circle the largest percentage in each row, and when comparing using column percentages, we circle the largest percentage in each column. Is there a pattern, or are the highest values scattered? Are the highest values substantially larger than the lower values? If the highest percentages form a diagonal line, there is a **linear** relationship. Some relationships are **curvilinear**; a linear relationship exists for some values, but then "round" off. For example, income might increase with age to the point of retirement and then decline with increases in age from that point on. With time and practice, the researcher can get quite good at "eyeballing" the data (not as painful as it sounds!). You can get to a point where relationships will become more obvious, perhaps even "leaping forth" from the types of tables illustrated above.

One final note: recall from Chapter 2 that, in addition to establishing that a relationship exists, we also need to ensure that the relationship is not **spurious** (that both variables are not influenced by a third outside variable). To do so in correlational analysis, we need to **control** for other possible explanatory variables. Here, we create contingency tables for each value of the control variable and see if the relationship is isolated to only one or a few of the control categories. To continue the example developed above, we could control our analysis of the impact of income on ideological self-position for the effects of gender. To control for gender, we would need to create two separate contingency tables: one that explores ideological self-placement by income among women only and another that looks at ideological self-placement by income among men only. Once these controls have been established, we read the tables in the same manner as any other contingency table.

In summary, contingency tables provide a useful first step in the search for relationships between variables. However, while they illustrate relationships (or the lack thereof) in considerable detail, they do not tell us whether the observed relationship is *significant*, whether the null hypothesis should or should not be rejected. Nor do they tell us the *strength* of the relationship. Contingency tables provide only the foundation upon which tests of significance and measures of strength (correlation coefficients) can be constructed. It is to such tests and measures that we now turn.

WORKING AS A TEAM

1. Return to Figure 9.5(a) and (b). Assume first that your group has conducted a survey of racial differences between two groups in math ability and came up with a pattern similar to Figure 9.5(b): a significant intergroup difference combined with substantial intragroup variability. How would you report these results to the public? How would you counter the likely charge that you were providing empirical support for racism? What would be the ethical considerations with respect to publishing or suppressing the findings?

SELF-STUDY

1. As a class project you have asked 22 of your fellow students to locate themselves on a seven-point left–right scale with values ranging from 1 (far left) to 7 (far right). In order to protect the respondents' anonymity, a letter of the alphabet rather than a name has been assigned to each of the 22 responses. The left–right scale locations were as follows:

A = 6	B = 1	C = 3	D = 7	E = 6
F = 4	G = 4	H = 2	I = 7	J = 5
K = 3	L = 1	M = 6	N = 6	O = 2
P = 1	Q = 3	R = 4	S = 5	T = 2
U = 6	V = 1			

   a. Construct a frequency distribution for the set of scores.

   b. Calculate the cumulative percentages for the frequency distribution.

   c. Find the mode, median, and mean for the distribution of scores.

   d. Calculate the standard deviation and variance for the distribution of scores.

2. For the following data set, create a contingency table including raw data, row percentages, and column percentages. Be certain to order the table properly, identifying the independent and dependent variables. After completing the table, interpret the row and column percentages. Does a relationship appear to exist? If so, what is the nature (direction) of that relationship?

Age Category	Level of Political Interest
Young	Low
Middle	Low
Young	Medium
Old	Medium
Old	High
Middle	High
Young	Low
Middle	Medium
Old	High
Middle	Medium
Young	Low
Middle	Low
Old	Medium
Old	High
Middle	Medium

3. In a 1996 survey of the Alberta electorate conducted by the authors, respondents were asked if they agreed or disagreed with this statement: "Society would be better off if women stayed home when their children are young." The following table presents the numerical distribution of the 435 male respondents and 475 female respondents who either agreed or disagreed with the statement:

	Males	Females	Total
Strongly agree	71	83	154
Agree	140	175	315
Disagree	155	130	285
Strongly disagree	69	87	156
Total	435	475	910

a. Calculate the row and column percentages for this table.

b. Examine the percentage distributions, and determine whether they suggest a relationship between the sex of respondents and their likelihood of agreeing or disagreeing with the statement.

NOTES

1. The symbol for "sum of" is $\sum$.
2. Shortly after this section was written, NBA superstar Shaquille O'Neal signed a contract for more than $23 million Canadian.
3. Note, however, Wright's caution (1976, 97): "the concept of 'average' *is applicable only to scores*, not to the people who provide those scores. Being of average *height* doesn't make you an average *person*."
4. There were, of course, other reasons for discriminating against women, and strength criteria were often used to mask other grounds for employment discrimination.

CHAPTER 10

Assessing the Political World: Inferential Statistics

DESTINATION

By the end of this chapter the reader should

- understand the conceptual nature of tests of significance and the roles that inferential statistics play in hypothesis-testing;
- be familiar with various types of data distributions;
- be able to distinguish between Type I and Type II errors and appreciate the factors to consider in choosing between the two types;
- understand the difference between parametric and non-parametric statistics;
- be able to select and calculate appropriate tests of significance.

We conduct research on *samples* in an effort to gain knowledge about *populations*. The descriptive statistics that we calculate—be they the univariate statistics of Chapter 9, the bivariate statistics of Chapter 11, or the multivariate statistics of Chapter 12—provide us with concrete information about the sample. We can calculate sample means or uncover relationships between two or more variables within the sample, but these are of theoretical interest only to the degree that we can use them to make inferences about the population from which the sample was drawn. This chapter will explore **inferential statistics**, which test the probability that sample statistics are reasonable estimates of population parameters. Inferential statistics provide the bridge between what we know about samples and what we would like to know about populations.

Recall from Chapter 8 that the principles of random sampling are based on probability theory. Inferential statistics address the question,

"What is the probability that the relationship we found occurred by chance in the sample?" Was the sample finding a fluke, or was it reflective of a relationship in the population? Essentially, inferential statistics are used to determine if sample statistics are *representative* of population parameters. If the sample statistic is found to be representative, we say that it is "statistically significant."

Inferential statistics are a crucial step in hypothesis-testing. Hypotheses, which have been discussed in a number of previous chapters, are operationalized statements of propositions; they assert the existence of a relationship between two or more variables. When we gain support for our hypothesis, we gain support for the proposition and the underlying theory. In order to support our hypothesis, we must first reject the null hypothesis, or the supposition that no relationship exists between the variables in the general population. We ask whether there is sufficient evidence to reject the null hypothesis, to conclude that the relationship observed in the data reflects a similar relationship in the larger population. In other words, is the observed relationship *significant*? Or is it *insignificant*; do we conclude that the sample relationship is not sufficiently robust to provide compelling evidence for a similar relationship in the population from which the sample was drawn? It is only once we have rejected the null hypothesis that we can begin to argue in favour of our alternative hypothesis and the theory from which it is drawn. Therefore, a lot is at stake with tests of significance.

The five basic steps of hypothesis-testing[1] are as follows:

1. Formulate the null and alternative hypotheses.

2. Select a confidence level.

3. Calculate the appropriate inferential statistic.

4. Using the table for the test statistic, find the critical value (expected value) at the selected confidence level.

5. If the calculated statistic equals or exceeds the critical value, reject the null hypothesis.[2]

The first of these steps was addressed in Chapter 2; this chapter will explore the remaining steps. Before we begin, however, two important points must be addressed.

First, when we discuss "significance" in this chapter, we are focusing on *statistical significance*, on tests that allow us to assess whether sample statistics are acceptable estimates of population parameters. However, there are some instances where rather weak relationships are found to be statistically significant. Significance tests are affected by sample size;

the larger the sample, the more likely it is that a relationship of a given strength will be significant. Therefore, some trivial relationships from large samples will be "statistically significant," and other potentially interesting relationships from very small samples will be "insignificant." The point to stress is that statistical significance does not always entail *substantive significance*. A relationship or statistic is substantively significant if it is theoretically important, if it plays a role in elaborating, modifying, or rejecting your theory. The need for substantive significance as well as statistical significance requires that the researcher rely not only on inferential statistics, but also on an assessment of the supporting contingency tables and descriptive statistics. We need to look at all parts of the data analysis, rather than relying on summary statistics alone.

Second, inferential statistics are either statistically significant or they are not. Some relationships are not "more significant" than others. The

A POINT ON THE COMPASS

Preelection Surveys and the Margin of Error

In most forms of survey research, and virtually all forms of attitudinal research, we never know what the population parameters are. Surveys provide the best estimate we have of those parameters, but there is nothing against which we can place the survey results to see if they are accurate or correct. We do not know, for example, what proportion of Canadians might support a more liberalized immigration policy; we only know the survey proportions that do so. However, preelection surveys are an important exception to this rule.

It is common for the media to conduct polls shortly before elections are held and use the survey results to predict the election outcome. But in this case, the actual election outcome—the population parameters—will shortly be known, and therefore error on the part of the media outlet will be apparent to all. In short, it is possible to be wrong in this case and, as we saw in some of the Chapter 8 examples, even drastically wrong. Polling organizations and their media clients try to avoid such embarrassment by using unusually large samples in the last preelection poll. This reduces the margin of error and provides greater confidence in the survey results. It is money worth spending if the media outlet wants to protect its credibility.

desire to make such statements arises from a confusion between substantive and statistical significance. If we wish to argue that one relationship is *stronger* than another, and *not more significant*, we need measures of strength (see Chapter 11) rather than inferential statistics. Statistical significance is a statement about the correspondence between the sample and the population and cannot be used to draw conclusions about the relative importance of variables. Students must be clear about this distinction. We advise that when students are exploring for a potential relationship between two or more variables, they look first at the statistical significance of the relationship, which can be assessed by the statistics discussed in this chapter. If the relationship is significant, students can then turn to look at the strength of the relationship and, considering the theoretical context, decide if the relationship is substantively significant.

SELECTING CONFIDENCE LEVELS

Deciding whether or not a relationship exists in the population, whether the covariance found in the data is significant, is by no means a straightforward process. How do we distinguish between random variation in the sample and evidence of a "real" relationship in the population? What standard of proof do we employ? If it were left to each researcher to determine the standards by which the null hypothesis would be rejected, there would be little consistency within or across the social sciences disciplines. When confronted with the same empirical evidence, two researchers could come to very different conclusions. One could decide that the relationship was significant, the other that it was not. What has evolved, therefore, is a set of norms by which null hypotheses are accepted or rejected. These norms are based on probabilities. The question we ask is, "If *no* relationship exists between two variables in the population from which the sample was drawn, what is the probability that by chance alone we would observe a relationship in the sample data?" If the chances are pretty good that the observed relationship could have emerged by chance alone, we tend to discount it and conclude that it is the product of sampling error or random variation. However, if the odds are remote that by chance alone we would have observed a relationship in the sample data, then we tend to reject the null hypothesis, concluding instead that the best explanation for the sample finding is that a relationship indeed exists within the larger population from which the sample was drawn.

But how do we operationalize "pretty good" or "remote"? The scientific norms provide two primary standards, known as **confidence**

levels or **alpha (α) levels.** The first is the 5% ($p < 0.05$) confidence level: we *reject the null hypothesis* if the probability of finding the observed relationship *by chance alone* is less than 5%, or less than five chances in a hundred. The second standard is similar but more rigorous: *we reject the null hypothesis* at the 1% ($p < 0.01$) confidence level if the probability of finding the observed relationship *by chance alone* is less than 1%, or less than one chance in a hundred. Very occasionally you will encounter published research in which a 10% ($p < 0.10$) confidence level is used. Because this is a more lenient test, it tends only to be employed with pretest data or where sample sizes are very small.

Regardless of which standard we use, if we reject the null hypothesis, we conclude that a significant relationship exists. Hence the term "tests" of significance. A significant relationship is one that, within specified limits, we are confident exists in the population from which the sample was randomly drawn. We never reject the null hypothesis with total certainty, for there is always the possibility, no matter how remote, that the observed relationship was the product of chance alone. We can only reject the null hypothesis with varying degrees of confidence; therefore, confidence levels are always specified when tests of significance are reported.

Keep in mind that researchers will use different language to describe the same thing. A 95% confidence level and a 5% confidence level ($p < 0.05$) both mean that the chances of having made an error in rejecting the null hypothesis are less than 5%; a 99% confidence level and a 1% confidence level ($p < 0.01$) both mean that the chances of having made an error in rejecting the null hypothesis are less than 1%. The first approach (95% or 99%) expresses the probability of *not* making an error by incorrectly rejecting the null hypothesis; the second approach (5% or 1%) expresses the probability of making such an error.

The question remains regarding which confidence level to adopt. The answer is by no means clear-cut and depends, in part, on the quality of the data and the consequences of making a mistake. When psychologists work within an experimental setting where measurements of the dependent and independent variables are precise and tightly controlled, they are prone to adopt the more stringent test. They want compelling evidence before rejecting the null hypothesis, and will therefore employ the 0.01 confidence level or even a 0.001 level, refusing in the latter case to reject the null hypothesis unless the chances of being wrong in so doing are less than one in a thousand. Political scientists often work with less robust data and confront greater measurement noise and subject variability, particularly in survey research. As a consequence, they may adopt a less stringent test and reject the null hypothesis at the 0.05 confidence level. As suggested above, sample size also influences the confidence level chosen: researchers with large samples generally employ more stringent significance tests than do researchers with smaller samples. Finally, exploratory studies where the researcher is looking for suggestive findings rather than ironclad results may employ lower levels of confidence, perhaps even the 0.10 confidence level.

No golden rule exists for the choice of confidence levels; therefore, the possibility arises that two researchers could look at the same empirical results with one rejecting the null hypothesis at the 0.05 confidence level and the other failing to do so at the 0.01 confidence level. What is essential is that the researcher make the decision regarding what level of confidence to use *before looking at the empirical results*. This will reduce the temptation of changing confidence levels in midstream in order to convert insignificant relationships ($p > 0.01$) into significant relationships ($p > 0.05$).

You might assume that social scientists would do everything possible to minimize the probability of error by using the most stringent significance tests. However, there are two different types of errors that can be made, and by minimizing the probability of one we increase the probability of the other. A **Type I error**, or "false positive," is made when the null hypothesis is incorrectly rejected; we conclude on the basis of sample results that a relationship exists in the population when in fact it does not. Type I errors are more likely if we adopt a 0.05 confidence level, making it relatively easy to reject the null hypothesis, than if we adopt a 0.01 confidence level. A **Type II error**, or "false negative," is made when we incorrectly fail to reject the null hypothesis; we conclude on the basis of the sample evidence that a relationship does not exist in the population when in fact it does. Type II errors are more likely to be made if we adopt a 0.01 confidence level than if we adopt a 0.05 confidence level. The distinction between Type I and Type II errors is expressed in Figure 10.1.

A POINT ON THE COMPASS

False Positives and False Negatives

The following article, which appeared in a recent issue of *Maclean's* magazine (1997), illustrates some of the practical consequences of false positives and false negatives:

> A small Nova Scotia company ... is marketing what it calls a simple, fast HIV blood-testing kit. The company's owner ...

says the kit shows the presence or absence of HIV—the virus associated with AIDS—in a drop of blood in two minutes, compared with conventional tests that can take up to five days. Preliminary analysis of clinical studies in Calgary, Halifax, St. John's, Nfld., and elsewhere shows the kit produces a false-positive finding in fewer than two percent of the cases—comparable to the performance of other tests— but fails to confirm the presence of HIV [a false negative] in up to five per cent of cases in which the disease was confirmed by other means.

Unfortunately, there is no strategy that minimizes the probability of both Type I and Type II errors. We have to choose, and the choice will hinge upon a number of factors, including the risks associated with either type of error and perhaps even the personality of the researcher (some people are naturally more cautious than others). The best illustration of the stakes involved comes from medical research. Suppose, for instance, that a new drug has been developed which appears to offer a promising treatment for a particular form of cancer. However, before the company that developed the drug can release it for general use, clinical trials must be conducted to see if there are dangerous side effects. The null hypothesis is that there are no side effects. The question is, "What standard should be employed to accept or reject the null hypothesis?" If the researchers conducting the clinical trials make a Type I error, concluding that there are dangerous side effects when in fact there are not, then the opportunity for a promising drug treatment would be missed. If the researchers make a Type II error, concluding that there are no side effects when there are, then a dangerous drug could be unleashed on

FIGURE 10.1

TYPE I AND TYPE II ERRORS

		Reality	
		No relationship	Relationship
Researcher's Conclusion	Relationship	**Type I error**	correct conclusion
	No relationship	correct conclusion	**Type II error**

unsuspecting patients and their physicians. As you can imagine, the company that developed the drug, the researchers conducting the clinical trials, public health officials, insurance firms, patients, and physicians may have quite different views over whether a Type I or Type II error would be more problematic.

In drawing this discussion to a close, we should note that confidence levels can also be established for a range of scores. For example, a polling organization may report that 45% of respondents support the government of the day, and that the poll findings are accurate within ±3%, 19 times out of 20. In effect, the polling organization has established a **confidence interval** and has concluded there is a 95% probability that the percentage of the *population* (in this case, the electorate) supporting the government lies between 42% (45% − 3%) and 48% (45% + 3%). If the polling organization wanted to be even more confident that its poll result fell within population parameters, if it wanted to establish a 99% confidence interval, then the interval would have to be larger. Hence the tradeoff: a small confidence interval provides greater precision but less confidence, while a large confidence interval provides less precision but more confidence. The norm among commercial pollsters is the 95% confidence interval, or "19 times out of 20." This means, incidentally, that one poll in 20 will be a "rogue" poll with results that are not as close to the population mean as the polling organization might suggest. Unfortunately, because population parameters are estimated rather than known, it can never be determined which is the rogue poll and which are the 19 out of 20.

CHECKING YOUR BEARINGS

CHOOSING BETWEEN FALSE POSITIVES AND FALSE NEGATIVES

Imagine you are in a situation where you are trying to decide between two home pregnancy test kits. The box for one promises that the risk of a false positive is only 1 in 100, but the risk of a false negative is 5 in 100. The second kit promises that the risk of a false negative is only 1 in 100, but the risk of a false positive is 5 in 100. Which kit would you choose, and why? If you had to make the same choice with respect to tests for breast cancer or AIDS, would your choice change? If so, why? What factors might lead you to prefer the risk of a false positive to a false negative, or the reverse?

A POINT ON THE COMPASS ────────────

The Substantive Significance of Confidence Intervals

In August 1996, the polling firm Léger & Léger conducted a survey for *The Globe and Mail* and *Le Journal de Montréal* on support for sovereignty in Quebec (Mackie 1996). The survey of 1,001 eligible voters found that 52.5% of decided voters would vote yes in a referendum on sovereignty, and 47.5% would vote no. The margin of error was given as 3.1%, 19 times out of 20.

If we take this margin of error into account, then the 95% confidence interval for a yes vote ranges from 49.4% to 55.6%, and the same interval for a no vote ranges from 44.4% to 50.6%. Thus two very different referendum outcomes fall within the 95% confidence intervals of the Léger & Léger poll. In the first, the sovereigntists would have a commanding majority, winning by a margin of 55.6% to 44.4%. Quebec's departure from Canada would be assured. In the second scenario, the sovereigntists would lose again, although by the narrowest of margins (50.6% no, 49.4% yes, almost exactly the result of the October 1995 sovereignty referendum). Canada would survive to fight another day.

In the final analysis, the poll predicts only that either side could win, although the smart bets would be placed on a yes vote.

Although there is no magic rule for selecting a confidence level, a choice must be made. Once the confidence level has been established, a test statistic must be selected and calculated. To do this, we must first examine the data distributions upon which our inferential statistics are based, and then look more closely at the statistics themselves.

DATA DISTRIBUTIONS

In the previous chapter, we looked in detail at the normal distribution. It was noted that few "real-world phenomena" are normally distributed, although many statistics assume a normal distribution. Because many of our variables of interest do not follow a perfect normal distribution, statisticians have developed different inferential statistics to accommodate the distributions found in real data. These distributions have been used to calculate tables of critical values, which we use in deciding whether or not to reject the null hypothesis.

The sampling distribution of means, known as the *z*-distribution because it is calculated from *z*-scores (standardized scores), is identical in characteristics to the normal distribution. The shape of the normal distribution is fixed, and therefore the critical values for the *z*-distribution are also fixed: at the 95% confidence level the critical value is $z = \pm 1.96$, and at the 99% confidence level the critical value is $z = \pm 2.58$. In this latter case, for instance, we reject the null hypothesis if the *z*-score is greater than 2.58 or less than –2.58. Notice that the critical values are expressed as both positive and negative numbers. This is because the critical regions of the normal curve are found in both the **lower tail** (extreme left region, or negative values) and **upper tail** (extreme right region, or positive values). Thus, researchers must choose between "one-tailed" tests, which consider only one critical region, and "two-tailed" tests, which consider both critical regions.[3] One-tailed tests require a smaller *z*-score for the rejection of the null hypothesis. As a consequence, the adoption of one-tailed tests is contingent upon a clear hypothesis with respect to the direction of the relationship.

One of the most important distributions is **Student's *t*-distribution**, which forms the basis for all *t*-statistics. Student's *t*-distribution assumes a shape similar to that of the normal distribution. However, and unlike the normal distribution, its shape is not fixed. The *t*-distribution for small samples is flatter and wider than the normal distribution; as the sample size increases, the *t*-distribution comes to resemble the normal distribution more and more. We use degrees of freedom to take sample size into account. Once 120 degrees of freedom have been reached, the *t*- and normal distributions are identical. Thus, samples above 120 degrees of freedom have the same two-tailed critical values for *t*-tests as they do for *z*-tests: at the 95% confidence level the critical value is $t = \pm 1.96$, and at the 99% confidence level the critical value is $t = \pm 2.58$. If there are fewer than 120 degrees of freedom, the table in Appendix A must be consulted to find the critical values.

The **chi-square distribution** differs greatly from the normal distribution. As Figure 10.2 shows, it is positively skewed; critical values are found only in the upper tail of the distribution and will always be positive. You will never encounter negative chi-square values. As with the *t*-distribution, the precise shape of the chi-square distribution varies with sample size. Thus, both the *t*- and chi-square statistics require that we calculate the degrees of freedom for the sample. As we will see, the different distributions of *t*- and chi-square lead to different methods for calculating degrees of freedom. For chi-square, degrees of freedom are dependent upon the table dimensions rather than on sample size.

FIGURE 10.2

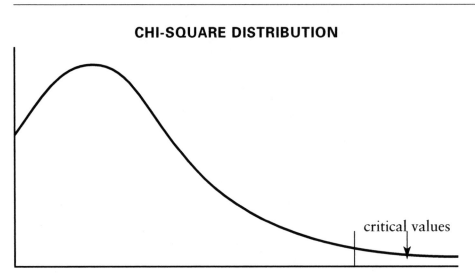

CHI-SQUARE DISTRIBUTION

Similar in appearance to the chi-square distribution is the **F-distribution**, illustrated in Figure 10.3. Notice, however, that the F-distribution, unlike the chi-square distribution, has critical regions in both the lower and upper tails. The F-distribution is used to compare two samples, and its exact shape depends upon the size of both samples. As the sample sizes increase, the F-distribution becomes more symmetrical. Degrees of freedom are determined by sample size.

There are a number of statistical techniques based on these distributions that researchers can use to test hypotheses. We will briefly introduce some guidelines for selecting appropriate inferential statistics, and then we will look more closely at the statistics themselves.

FIGURE 10.3

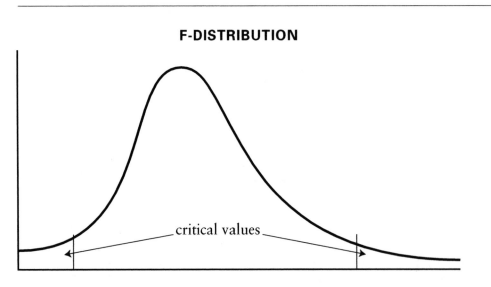

F-DISTRIBUTION

SELECTING INFERENTIAL STATISTICS

How one selects the appropriate inferential statistic depends upon the assumptions underlying the statistic itself. Some statistics, known as **parametric statistics**, have assumptions about the distribution of the data that must be met if they are to be used and interpreted correctly. Less stringent, and thus more widely available, tests are referred to as **nonparametric statistics**. Unlike parametric statistics, nonparametric statistics are not contingent on the parameters of the data distribution (Bailey 1978, 332). It is not assumed, for instance, that the data are normally distributed. Parametric tests are used more often than nonparametric tests in published research and tend to be preferred for a number of reasons: they are more robust (less subject to fluctuations), more powerful, and can at times provide a greater amount of information than nonparametric tests (McCall 1986, 317). At the same time, it is often difficult to meet the many stringent assumptions of parametric tests.

We will explore parametrics and nonparametrics with respect to both inferential statistics and, in Chapter 11, measures of relationship strength. For *inferential statistics*, readers should note that only interval-level variables are able to meet the distribution assumptions of the parametric tests; thus, to use a parametric test, one of the variables must be interval-level. In addition, not even all interval-level variables meet the distribution requirements of the parametric tests.[4] A "rule of thumb" chart for selecting inferential statistics is presented in summary Table 10.8 at the conclusion to this chapter. Please note, however, that there are always exceptions to such guidelines and that due to space limitations, not all possible significance tests have been included in the table or in the chapter.

We will look in turn at the chi-square, the *t*-test for differences between means, the Mann-Whitney *U*-test, and *F*-ratios. In each case we will calculate the test statistic, compare this statistic with the critical value, and, using this comparison, decide whether or not to reject the null hypothesis.

CHI-SQUARE

Chi-square is a test of the independence of two variables. The null hypothesis states that the two variables are independent or unrelated to one another in the population from which the sample was drawn. The chi-square test assesses the likelihood that the relationship observed in the sample is due to chance; in other words, what is the probability that

A POINT ON THE COMPASS ──────

The Debate Over Significance Tests

There is a growing methodological debate in psychology over the use (and misuse) of significance tests. As Christopher Shea (1996) writes, the critics of significance tests "point out that decisions about whether something is due to chance are based on a sliding scale of probability. Therefore, dividing research findings into two categories—significant and not significant—is a gross oversimplification." Not enough attention is paid, critics argue, to the importance of findings and to how much better one treatment might be than another, if both have statistically significant effects.

Part of the reaction to significance tests is manifest in the increased use of *meta-analysis*. This approach pulls together large sets of studies done over the years on particular research questions. Patterns are sought that run through the various studies, patterns that may be statistically significant in some, not in others, but nonetheless are pronounced when the various studies are pooled. In this manner, meta-analysis gets around the problems associated with small samples and is able to bring into play studies that were insignificant in themselves but that give added weight to general patterns of research findings.

As Shea notes (1996, A17), "there are a few reasons why this debate has flared in psychology and not elsewhere. 'Hard scientists' tend to use a wider variety of statistical techniques than social scientists. (For the past five years or so, medical journals have been discouraging over-reliance on the significance test.) Among the social sciences, psychology is the most dependent on experiments using samples, where the significance test is most often used."

Political science may be even more reliant than psychologists on sample data and, therefore, on significance tests. (Political scientists also tend to work with much larger samples than do psychologists, whose experimental research is often based on small samples.) However, the methodological debates that rock and shape psychology often reach political science a generation later.

the relationship does *not* exist in the population? As a nonparametric statistic, chi-square lacks the power of the other significance tests. However, its lack of parameters makes it the only test statistic available when we look at relationships among nominal- and ordinal-level variables. (Nominal variables are nonparametric because the values of the variable—1, 2, 3, 4—refer to differences in kind, not differences in degree; ordinal variables are nonparametric because there is not a standard unit difference between numerical values.) Chi-square has the distinct advantage, as we will see, of being a highly stable measure, one based on a cell-by-cell comparison of the observed relationship and the expected relationship under the null hypothesis.

We can state the null and alternative hypotheses of chi-square as follows:

$$H_0: f_0 = f_e \qquad H_a: f_0 \neq f_e,$$

where f_0 is observed frequencies, and f_e is expected frequencies.

The independence of the two variables is assessed by comparing the *observed frequencies* in a bivariate relationship with the *expected frequencies* that would occur if perfect independence existed. How many cases would we expect in each cell of our contingency table if the variables are independent? We calculate the expected frequencies for each cell of the contingency table and then calculate chi-square by the following formula:

$$\text{chi-square} = \chi^2 = \sum \frac{(O - E)^2}{E},$$

where E is the expected frequency for a given cell, and O is the observed frequency for the same cell.[5]

For each cell in the contingency table we subtract the expected frequency from the observed value to find the difference between the two frequencies. This value must be squared due to the fact that we are summing variation. Recall from Chapter 9 that we need to square the deviations from the mean; if we fail to do so, the deviations total to zero. The same principle applies to the chi-square formula.

Table 10.1 provides an opportunity to work through the chi-square calculations. The table presents the observed values for 100 respondents, categorized by both their sex and support for a hypothetical policy. The question being asked in this analysis is, "Does an individual's sex have an impact on attitudes toward this policy among the population as a whole?" We don't know the answer with certainty, because the population as a whole has not been asked their views on this policy issue. Instead, we have (hypothetical) data from 100 people. Therefore, a more refined question is, "How likely is it that we would find a relationship of the strength observed in Table 10.1 in a sample of this size *if* there was no relationship between these variables in the population?" Thus, we wish to compare the number of respondents in each cell (the observed frequency) with the number of people we would expect to find under the null hypothesis (the expected cell frequency) if the two variables were unrelated.

The data in Table 10.1 present the observed cell frequencies. The upper left cell, for example, shows that 15 of the respondents were women who registered a low level of support for the policy in question. The first step in computing the chi-square is to calculate the expected frequencies for every cell of the contingency table. Thus, for example, we wish to know how many women and how many men would have a low level of support for this policy if sex did not affect support. To answer this question, assume the *marginals* of the table do not change; there are always 55 females and 45 males, and 20 people with low support, 30 with medium support, and 50 with high support. But the numbers *within the cells* can change to reflect the null hypothesis.

One way of thinking about this is to ask what percentage of the total sample population has low support. In this example, it is 20 out of 100 cases, or 20%. If sex does not affect attitudes toward the policy in question, then 20% of women and 20% of men should have low support. How *many* women and men should have low support depends upon the number of men and women in the sample. Since there are 55 women, we can calculate that $55 \times 20\% = 11$, for an expected cell frequency of 11 women. The expected cell frequency for men is $45 \times 20\% = 9$. Notice that to calculate the expected cell frequencies for women we divided the row marginal (20) by the total marginal (100) and multiplied this by the column marginal (55). By changing the order of operations, we derive the following general formula:

$$E = \frac{\text{(row marginal)(column marginal)}}{N}.$$

Thus, for the low-support, female cell, our expected frequencies is 11:

$$E = \frac{\text{(row marginal)(column marginal)}}{N} = \frac{20 \times 55}{100} = 11.$$

If sex and support for policy X are independent, we would expect 11 women to support policy X.

TABLE 10.1

SUPPORT FOR POLICY X BY SEX (OBSERVED VALUES)

	Female	Male	Total
Low support	15	5	20
Medium support	15	15	30
High support	25	25	50
Total	55	45	100

The same calculation is used to determine the expected frequencies for all other cells. Thus, for the low-support, male cell, the expected frequencies is 20 (row marginal) multiplied by 45 (column marginal) divided by 100, which equals 9. The expected frequencies for the medium-support, female cell is 16.5 (30 × 55, divided by 100); the expected frequencies for the medium-support, male cell is 13.5 (30 × 45, divided by 100); and so on. We continue calculating expected frequencies until we have completed the expected frequencies table, shown in Table 10.2. Try calculating the last two expected frequencies on your own.

TABLE 10.2

SUPPORT FOR POLICY X BY SEX (EXPECTED FREQUENCIES)

	Female	Male	Total
Low support	11	9	20
Medium support	16.5	13.5	30
High support	27.5	22.5	50
Total	55	45	100

The next step is to calculate chi-square itself. The chi-square compares the observed frequencies (Table 10.1) with the expected frequencies (Table 10.2). Recall that the formula for chi-square is as follows:

$$\text{chi-square} = \chi^2 = \sum \frac{(O - E)^2}{E}.$$

We need to square the difference between the observed and expected frequencies, and then divide that figure by the expected frequencies. This step must be undertaken for *each cell*. For the low-support, female cell we get the following:

$$\frac{(O-E)^2}{E} = \frac{(15-11)^2}{11} = \frac{16}{11} = 1.45.$$

For the low-support, male cell we have

$$\frac{(O-E)^2}{E} = \frac{(5-9)^2}{9} = \frac{16}{9} = 1.78.$$

This process is repeated for each cell until all values are calculated. Calculate these numbers yourself to ensure that you understand the process. The results are shown in Table 10.3.

TABLE 10.3

OBSERVED AND EXPECTED FREQUENCIES

	Female	**Male**
Low support	cell 1	cell 2
Medium support	cell 3	cell 4
High support	cell 5	cell 6

Cell	**Observed**	**Expected**	$O-E$	$(O-E)^2$	$\dfrac{(O-E)^2}{E}$
1	15	11	4	16	1.45
2	5	9	−4	16	1.78
3	15	16.5	−1.5	2.25	0.14
4	15	13.5	1.5	2.25	0.17
5	25	27.5	−2.5	6.25	0.23
6	25	22.5	2.5	6.25	0.28

We next need to take all of the resultant figures and sum them together:

$$1.45 + 1.78 + 0.14 + 0.17 + 0.23 + 0.28 = 4.05.$$

This final number is chi-square. (We will be calculating chi-square again in Chapter 11, so don't forget the formula!)

We can now use chi-square to determine whether we should accept or reject the null hypothesis. Before doing so, however, we need to calculate the **degrees of freedom** for our table. The degrees of freedom for a table is equal to the minimum number of cells that must be filled before all other cell frequencies are fixed. This concept is best exhibited with an example. Imagine that we have the distribution of cell values displayed in Table 10.4.

TABLE 10.4

CALCULATING DEGREES OF FREEDOM

	A	B	C	Total
Low	3			10
Medium		2		5
High	1		8	15
Total	5	13	12	30

Table 10.4 is not completely filled in; we do not know all of the frequencies for each cell. However, we do have enough information to complete the table on our own. We can begin with the A column. We see from the column marginal that there is a total of 5 cases in the column. Four of the 5 have already been assigned, leaving 1 case for the medium, A cell. We insert this value into the cell. Next, we can turn to the "medium" row. The row marginal is 5; 3 of those cases have now been assigned, leaving 2 cases for the medium, C cell. We write this number into the table and move on. We can continue in this way until the entire table is complete. Why were we able to complete this incomplete table? The answer is that we have just enough information to complete the task; the table has four degrees of freedom, and four cell frequencies were presented. With the four cell frequencies assigned, all other cells became locked into place. However, if only three cell frequencies had been presented, we would not have had sufficient information to complete the table. The table has four degrees of freedom; if only three cells were completed, the other cells could have taken on a number of different values. You should note that the degrees of freedom formula will vary with the test statistic used.

We can calculate the degrees of freedom for chi-square through the following formula:

$$d.f. = (r - 1)(c - 1),$$

where r is the number of rows, and c is the number of columns. In the example just presented, there was a 3×3 table; thus, $d.f. = (3 - 1)(3 - 1) = 2 \times 2 = 4$. Let's return to our earlier chi-square example. There we were using a 3×2 table; thus, $d.f. = (3 - 1)(2 - 1) = 2 \times 1 = 2$. If only two cells in that table had been assigned, all other values would have been fixed. Degrees of freedom are important when we look at the chi-square table.

TABLE 10.5

CRITICAL VALUES FOR CHI-SQUARE

d.f.	p = 0.05	p = 0.01
1	3.841	6.635
2	5.991	9.210
3	7.815	11.341
4	9.488	13.277
5	11.070	15.086

Source: Adapted from Elazar J. Pedhauser, *Multiple Regression in Behavioural Research*, 2nd ed. (USA: Harcourt Brace, 1982), 792.

In the table we find our critical value. A full table is presented in Appendix B, while an excerpt from the table has been presented in Table 10.5. Note that we look down the rows to find the degrees of freedom, and across the columns to find our confidence level. Each cell contains the **critical value** for the given degrees of freedom and confidence level. This is the number that the calculated chi-square must meet or exceed if we are to reject the null hypothesis. Thus, for a 5 *d.f.* table and 99% confidence level, our calculated chi-square would need to meet or exceed the critical value 15.086. For a 1 *d.f.* table and 95% confidence, our critical value is 3.841. Let's return once again to our example. We had a 2 *d.f.* table, and we will assume that we are using a 95% confidence level (used most commonly in political science research). Our critical value is 5.991. How does this compare to our calculated chi-square value? We found chi-square to equal 4.05. Our calculated value does *not* meet or exceed the critical value; therefore, we must conclude that there is a high probability that the sample relationship occurred by chance. The null hypothesis, which stated that the two variables are independent (H_0: f_0 = f_e), cannot be rejected. In other words, we *fail to reject the null hypothesis*. The relationship has been found to be statistically insignificant. If our calculated value had met or exceeded the critical value, we would have concluded that the relationship was, in fact, statistically significant and rejected the null hypothesis. The conclusion, then, is that in the population as a whole, the sex of individuals has no significant impact on attitudes toward this policy question.

SUMMARY

Using the Chi-Square

1. Calculate the expected frequencies table.
2. Calculate chi-square.
3. Determine the degrees of freedom.
4. Find the critical value on the chi-square table.
5. Compare the critical value and the calculated chi-square to draw a conclusion about the null hypothesis.

Chi-square tests are commonly used nonparametric tests for nominal- and ordinal-level relationships. There are, however, a few problems with the chi-square test that should be noted. First, it lacks the power of many of the parametric tests. Second, chi-square values reflect not only independence, but also sample size. As our sample size increases, so too do our calculated chi-square values, making it easy to use chi-square to reject the null hypothesis. Thus, the chi-square test can deem extremely weak and substantively insignificant relationships found in large

CHECKING YOUR BEARINGS

CALCULATING CHI-SQUARE

A researcher is interested in the extent to which Quebec emerges as a "distinct society" on public policy issues having no immediate connection to constitutional policy. To this end he collects survey data on public opinion toward tobacco advertising. Eleven hundred respondents were asked if they favoured a complete ban on tobacco advertising, a partial ban, or no restrictions whatsoever. The pattern of response for Quebec respondents and respondents in the rest of Canada was as follows:

Opinion Toward Tobacco Advertising	Quebec	Rest of Canada	Total
Complete ban	110	450	560
Partial ban	145	280	425
No restrictions	45	70	115
Total	300	800	1,100

Calculate the chi-square for this table. Does the evidence support the conclusion that Quebec is indeed a distinct society?

samples "statistically significant." Researchers should keep this limitation of chi-square in mind when interpreting their data. On the other hand, large samples are often used precisely because we wish to have small margins of error and high levels of statistical significance. The key point to remember, though, is not to confuse statistical significance with a strong relationship (substantive significance).

When we have a nominal- or ordinal-level variable in relationship with a normally distributed interval-level variable, we can use the difference of means t-test, rather than chi-square. It is to this test that we will now turn.

T-TESTS FOR DIFFERENCES BETWEEN MEANS

One way to look for relationships between two variables is to divide the entire sample into subsamples based on the categories of one variable, and then look for differences in univariate statistics (measures of central tendency or variation) between the subsamples. This approach allows us to look at relationships between nominal-/ordinal-level variables and interval-level variables. We use the category of a nominal- or ordinal-level variable to subdivide; for example, we might divide our sample into two subsamples based on sex (men and women) or into three subsamples based on support for policy X (low support, medium support, and high support). This chapter will focus on difference of means tests for two samples. Having subdivided our sample, we then consider the univariate statistics of the *interval-level* variable within each subsample; most commonly, we look to the mean. Are the mean scores for the subsamples similar, or do they differ? This is known as comparing the **difference of means**. If the means are significantly different, this suggests a relationship between the interval-level variable and the nominal-/ordinal-level variable that the subsamples are based on. Thus, our null hypothesis is that the subsamples are the same; there is no difference between the samples and thus no relationship between the two variables. Our alternative hypothesis is that the difference of means is statistically significant, and there is a relationship between the two variables in question. These hypotheses can be stated as follows:

$$H_0: \mu_1 = \mu_2, \quad H_a: \mu_1 \neq \mu_2,$$

where μ_1 designates the *population* mean of sample 1, and μ_2 designates the *population* mean of sample 2.

Recall that we are always interested in parameters, rather than the statistics themselves. Thus, our hypotheses are always statements about the populations, rather than about the samples.

One of the most common significance tests for differences in mean scores is the *t*-test. This is a parametric test; thus, the researcher must ensure that both samples are normally distributed. In order to understand the conceptual architecture of this test, imagine drawing a series of samples from the same population. If you were to calculate the sample means for this series, you would expect the means to be similar but not identical; random variation would preclude identical means. (The larger the samples, the closer the means would be to one another.) Now, suppose you were to draw a sample of men and a sample of women and were to compare the mean mathematical abilities of the two samples. The null hypothesis would be that the two samples were drawn from the same population, which is to assume that there is no difference in math ability between men and women in the population at large. The question, then, is whether the observed difference in math ability between the two sample means is small enough to be attributed to chance alone (the null hypothesis is accepted) or whether it is large enough to suggest that the two samples were drawn from populations that differ in their math ability (the null hypothesis is rejected). To make this choice, we need a measure that takes into account the difference in sample means and the dispersion of scores about the two means.

The *t*-test provides just such a measure. It is based on the null hypothesis that the samples being compared are drawn from the same population and, therefore, that any observed difference in sample means can be attributed to chance alone. In order to apply the *t*-test to a difference in mean scores, we need to know the size, mean, and variance for each of the two samples. The formula for the two-sample *t*-ratio, assuming that the samples are approximately the same size, is

$$t = \frac{\overline{X}_1 - \overline{X}_2}{\sqrt{\dfrac{S_1^2}{N_1} + \dfrac{S_2^2}{N_2}}},$$

where $\overline{X}_1$ is the mean of the first sample, S_1^2 is the variance of the first sample, and N_1 is the size of the first sample; similarly, $\overline{X}_2$ is the mean of the second sample, S_2^2 is the variance of the second sample, and N_2 is the size of the second sample.

We will not review the calculation of means and variance at this time; readers can refer back to Chapter 9 for details on these calculations. We will, however, look at calculating and interpreting the t-test for the difference of means. Imagine two samples, with statistics as follows:

Sample 1: mean = $\overline{X}$ = 8   variance = σ^2 = 1.6   sample size = N = 30
Sample 2: mean = $\overline{X}$ = 5   variance = σ^2 = 2.1   sample size = N = 43

The t-ratio for these samples would be:

$$t = \frac{\overline{X}_1 - \overline{X}_2}{\sqrt{\dfrac{S_1^{\,2}}{N_1} + \dfrac{S_2^{\,2}}{N_2}}}$$

$$= \frac{8 - 5}{\sqrt{\dfrac{(1.6)^2}{30} + \dfrac{(2.1)^2}{43}}}$$

$$= \frac{3}{\sqrt{\dfrac{2.56}{30} + \dfrac{4.41}{43}}}$$

$$= \frac{3}{\sqrt{0.085 + 0.103}} = \frac{3}{\sqrt{0.188}}$$

$$= \frac{3}{0.43} = 6.98.$$

Once the t-ratio has been found, it must be compared to the critical value found in the table of t-values, as presented in Appendix A, and in Table 10.6. Note that for t-tests, degrees of freedom are dependent upon sample size: as sample size increases, so too do degrees of freedom. The formula for calculating the degrees of freedom for difference of means tests is

$$d.f. = N - k,$$

where N is the *total* sample size ($N_1 + N_2 + ...$), and k is the number of samples.

In our example, $d.f.$ equals 71 (73 − 2). In psychology, t-tests are often conducted with quite small samples; therefore, the degrees of freedom play a significant role in interpreting the results of the t-test. In political science, the t-test is generally brought into play with large,

TABLE 10.6

ABBREVIATED DISTRIBUTION OF *t*

d.f.	One-tailed Two-tailed	0.05 0.10	0.025 0.05	0.01 0.02	0.005 0.01
40		1.684	2.021	2.423	2.704
60		1.671	2.000	2.390	2.660
120		1.658	1.980	2.358	2.617

survey-generated samples for which the degrees of freedom play a much less significant role.

You will notice on the *t*-table a distinction between one-tailed and two-tailed tests. If the direction of difference is not important to us, we use a **two-tailed test**. Thus, if we are not interested in whether men or women are better at math, but rather are just concerned whether *any* sex difference exists, we would use the two-tailed test. If the direction of difference does matter to our theory—if, for example, we are testing the hypothesis that men have greater math ability—then we use a **one-tailed test**. Marija J. Norusis (1990, 156) explains the distinction between the two tests: "The procedure [for the one-tailed test] is the same as for the two-tailed test, but the resulting probability value is divided by 2, adjusting for the fact that the equality hypothesis is rejected only when the difference between the two means is sufficiently large and in the direction of interest. In the two-tailed test, the equality hypothesis is rejected for large positive or negative values of the statistic." If we have theoretical justification for using the one-tailed test, it is preferred.

Let's return to our example. We have a *t*-ratio of 6.98 and 71 degrees of freedom. We will use the 95% confidence level and a two-tailed test. Looking at the table, we find that the closest critical value is 2.000. Our calculated value exceeds this critical value, allowing us to *reject the null hypothesis* (H_0: $\mu_1 = \mu_2$) and support the alternative hypothesis (H_a: $\mu_1 \neq \mu_2$). In experimental research, the results suggest that samples were, in fact, drawn from different populations, indicating a statistically significant relationship between the two variables. In survey research, the results suggest a significant difference between categories of the independent variable (e.g., males and females), leading to the conclusion that the relationship did not occur by chance.

An alternative method for looking at the significance of relationships between ordinal- and interval-level variables, or between interval-level variables with non-normal data distributions, is the Mann-Whitney *U* rank-order test.

CHECKING YOUR BEARINGS

USING THE t-TEST

A university decides to generate empirical data showing what a university education pays with respect to personal income. To this end, a survey of 500 respondents from the local community is commissioned, of whom 150 have a university degree and 350 do not. The mean annual income for those respondents with a university degree is $56,000, and the standard deviation is $7,000. The mean annual income for those without a university degree is $51,000, and the standard deviation is $5,000. Calculate a t-test to determine if the survey evidence supports the proposition that "a university education pays."

MANN-WHITNEY U-TEST

The Mann-Whitney U-test is based on the ranking of cases and can therefore be used for relationships where one or both of the variables are ordinal- or interval-level. Like the chi-square test, it is a nonparametric test and is therefore useful when we wish to test relationships in which the interval-level variables do not meet the normal distribution requirements of the parametric tests. Of course, like all other nonparametric tests, the Mann-Whitney U-test does not provide as much information as would a parametric statistic. Thus, if the researcher can use parametric tests, it is usually advised that she do so. The tradeoff, then, is between a less informative, nonparametric statistic that does not introduce important assumptions about the distribution of the data (such as a normal distribution or a linear relationship) versus a parametric statistic that provides more information but that may also have assumptions (normality, linearity) that are not met with the data.

The logic of the Mann-Whitney U-test resembles that of the difference of means test: we compare two subsamples on a particular characteristic and determine if the populations are significantly different. If they are, we conclude that the bivariate relationship is significant. But where the difference of means test compares means, the Mann-Whitney U-test compares rankings. The test works as follows: we combine the two subsamples into a single sample (being certain to remember which case belongs to which sample); we then rank each case, from high to low, according to its score on the variable; and finally, we again subdivide the two samples and total the rankings, comparing the totalled rankings of each subsample. Why would the rankings within the different subsamples matter? Logically, "[i]f the groups have the same distribution, their sample distribution of ranks should be similar. If one of the groups has more than its share of small or large ranks, there is reason to suspect that the two underlying distributions are different" (Norusis 1990, 226). The rankings are summarized into the Mann-Whitney U-statistic, and the significance of the U-statistic is tested with the Z-test statistic. The null hypothesis states that the populations will have equal rankings, whereas the alternative hypothesis states that the rankings will differ. These hypotheses can be stated as follows:

$$H_0: R_1 = R_2, \quad H_a: R_1 \neq R_2,$$

where R_1 is the ranking in population 1, and R_2 is the ranking in population 2.

We will demonstrate the Mann-Whitney U-test with the nominal-interval relationship we considered in the previous section: gender and math performance. We are looking at the final grades of the students in a rather small section of a university math course. Of course, to select the Mann-Whitney U-test over the more powerful differences of means test, we obviously have reason to assume that the math scores in one sample are not normally distributed; in this case, the men's sample has a few "geniuses" who skew the distribution. The samples are as follows:

Men		Women	
Case	Score	Case	Score
1	98	6	82
2	99	7	72
3	56	8	70
4	64	9	90
5	72	10	78

The first step is to look at the two samples as a single sample, and assign ranks. For tied cases, they are "averaged" between the two ranks that they "share." For this sample, case 2 is highest and therefore gets the highest ranking; case 1 is ranked second; case 9 is ranked third; and so on. Note that cases 5 and 7 are tied and are therefore ranked at 6.5 ((6 + 7)/2). The final rankings look as follows:

Men				Women		
Case	Score	Rank		Case	Score	Rank
1	98	2		6	82	4
2	99	1		7	72	6.5
3	56	10		8	70	8
4	64	9		9	90	3
5	72	6.5		10	78	5

The next step is to sum the ranks of each sample. For the men, the rankings sum to 28.5 (2 + 1 + 10 + 9 + 6.5); for women, the rankings sum to 26.5 (4 + 6.5 + 8 + 3 + 5). We then calculate Mann-Whitney U, using the formula

$$U = N_1 N_2 + \frac{N_1(N_1 + 1)}{2} - \sum R_1,$$

where N_1 is the sample size of sample 1, N_2 is the sample size of sample 2, and $\sum R_1$ is the summed rankings of group 1.

Calculating U for this sample, we get

$$U = N_1 N_2 + \frac{N_1(N_1 + 1)}{2} - \sum R_1$$

$$= 5(5) + \frac{5(5 + 1)}{2} - 28.5$$

$$= 25 + 15 - 28.5$$

$$= 11.5.$$

We then need to determine if this U-value is statistically significant. To do so, we calculate a z-value,[6] using the formula

$$Z = \frac{U - \dfrac{N_1 N_2}{2}}{\sqrt{\dfrac{N_1 N_2 (N_1 + N_2 + 1)}{12}}}.$$

For this example,

$$Z = \dfrac{11.5 - \dfrac{5(5)}{2}}{\sqrt{\dfrac{5(5)(5 + 5 + 1)}{12}}}$$

$$= \dfrac{-1}{\sqrt{22.92}} = \dfrac{-1}{4.78} = -0.209.$$

This calculated z-value is compared to the charted critical value. Recall that for z-scores, our critical values are constant: at the 95% confidence level, the critical value is $z = \pm1.96$, and at the 99% confidence level, the critical value is $z = \pm2.58$. As we have learned, if the calculated score meets or exceeds the critical value, we can reject the null hypothesis. Clearly, we fail to reject the null hypothesis in this example: our calculated value of –0.209 falls well short of the 95% confidence critical value of ±1.96.

On the basis of this analysis, we would conclude that sex has no significant impact on math performance. Looking back at the data, we realize that this conclusion could probably also be reached by "eyeballing" the data. For example, although two of the males scored very high on the math test (99 and 98) and were ranked 1 and 2, two other males performed quite poorly (scores of 56 and 64), and ranked 9 and 10 out of 10. In this instance, the wide discrepancy in the performance of the males meant that they performed neither consistently higher nor lower than the women. However, these two groups did have different patterns of performance; the women as a group performed more consistently near the middle of the range; the men were more likely to be high or low. These differences, though, did not register with the Mann-Whitney U-statistic. This serves as an important reminder: whenever possible, look closely at the data as well as at the summary statistic.

Although the Mann-Whitney U-test is useful for all ordinal-level relationships, its use with interval-level variables should be limited to those cases where the interval-level variable fails to meet the normal distribution requirements of the parametric tests. If a normal distribution exists, the researcher should use the difference of means (for relationships with ordinal- and nominal-level variables) or the t-test and F-ratio (for relationships with other normally distributed interval-level variables), which we will now examine.

t-TESTS AND *f*-RATIOS FOR INTERVAL-LEVEL RELATIONSHIPS

In the following chapter we will introduce the basic linear model used to depict relationships between normally distributed interval-level variables. A line is drawn to "best fit" the graphical placement of the data. This regression line has a slope (designated by *b*), which signifies the unit change in one variable for every unit change in the other variable. When the rate of change is more dramatic, the line is relatively steep; when the rate of change is lower, the line is less steep. We can test the "goodness of fit" of the regression line with a statistic known as *R*-square. Inferential statistics are used to assess whether the slope of the regression line is significant and whether the R^2 value is significant. This section will introduce the steps necessary to calculate inferential statistics for linear regression analysis, but will leave all discussion of the linear model for Chapter 12. It should be noted that the *t*-tests and *F*-ratios described in this section are also used to test significance in multiple regression analyses, which will be explored in Chapter 12.

The test of R^2 is a test of the bivariate linear relationship. The null hypothesis states that a relationship does not exist in the population, whereas the alternative hypothesis states that a relationship does exist. Stated in proper form, this is

$$H_0: R^2 = 0 \, ,$$
$$H_a: R^2 \neq 0 \, .$$

To test the R^2 value, we use the *F*-ratio, which is calculated with the formula

$$F = \frac{\dfrac{R^2}{k}}{(1 - R^2)(N - k - 1)} \, ,$$

where *k* is the number of independent variables. For bivariate regression, $k = 1$. Once we calculate the *F*-statistic, we compare this value to the appropriate critical value (derived from a table of critical values of *F*, in Appendix C) to decide whether to accept or reject the null hypothesis.

Imagine that a regression run between two interval-level, normally distributed variables from a sample of 50 cases produces an *R*-square value of 0.30. Is this sample statistic representative of a relationship in the population? To test this, we calculate *F*:

$$F = \cfrac{\cfrac{R^2}{k}}{(1 - R^2)(N - k - 1)}$$

$$= \cfrac{\cfrac{0.30}{1}}{(1 - 0.30)(50 - 1 - 1)}$$

$$= \frac{0.30}{(0.70)(48)} = \frac{0.30}{33.6} = 0.0089$$

We now need to look up the critical value on the F-distribution table, presented in Appendix C and abbreviated in Table 10.7. Notice that the table requires two different degrees of freedom values. The formulas for these are as follows:

$$d.f. \; 1 = k, \quad d.f. \; 2 = N - k - 1.$$

For this example, $d.f.$ 1 equals 1, and $d.f.$ 2 equals 48 ($50 - 1 - 1$). Looking at the table, we can see that the appropriate critical value is 4.04. Our calculated F-value does not meet or exceed the critical value, and we therefore fail to reject the null hypothesis. The relationship has been found to be statistically insignificant.

TABLE 10.7

ABBREVIATED F-TABLE AT THE 95% CONFIDENCE LEVEL

d.f. 1	1	2	3
d.f. 2			
46	4.05	3.20	2.81
48	4.04	3.19	2.80
50	4.03	3.18	2.79

When we test the slope of the regression line, our null hypothesis is that the population slope equals zero; in other words, changes in one variable are not associated with changes in the other. Thus,

$$H_0: \beta = 0 \, ,$$

$$H_a: \beta \neq 0 \, ,$$

where beta is the population slope. To test the significance of our slope, we use a t-test. Here, t is calculated with the formula

$$t = \frac{b}{s_b},$$

where s_b is the standard error of b.[7] (An alternative method of finding t for bivariate relationships is to take the square root of the F-score.) As with the t-test for differences of means, we compare the calculated value to the critical value found in the t-test. Degrees of freedom are equal to $N - k - 1$.

Overall, we have seen that inferential statistics play a central role in hypothesis-testing. But after we have rejected the null hypothesis, we still need to find substantive support for our alternative hypotheses. It is by this means that we are able to advance our theories. This subject will be addressed in Chapters 11 and 12.

TABLE 10.8

SUMMARY SUGGESTIONS FOR SELECTING INFERENTIAL STATISTICS

Variables in Correlation	Suggested Statistic(s)
Nominal-nominal	Chi-square
Ordinal-nominal	Chi-square, Mann-Whitney U
Ordinal-ordinal	Chi-square, Mann-Whitney U
Interval*-nominal	Difference of means
Interval*-ordinal	Difference of means
Interval*-interval*	t-test, F-test
Interval**-nominal	Mann-Whitney U
Interval**-ordinal	Mann-Whitney U
Interval**-interval*/**	Mann-Whitney U

  * Normal distribution of cases.
** Non-normal distribution of cases.

WORKING AS A TEAM

1. Your group has been hired to determine if high school students who have been exposed to educational material on the dangers of smoking are less likely to smoke than students who have not been exposed to such material. By mistake, the data analysis is conducted before a decision has been made on the appropriate level of significance. You now know that there is a difference between the two groups, that students

who have been exposed are less likely to smoke, and that the probability of this difference being attributed to chance alone is 0.02, or 2 chances in 100. You now have to decide whether to employ a 0.01 or 0.05 confidence level for the test of significance. What would you recommend? What are the policy implications of your choice? What are the arguments for erring on the side of Type I or Type II error? What are the ethical issues that come into play?

SELF-STUDY

1. Calculate the chi-square for the following table, which looks at the (hypothetical) relationship between partisanship and support for gun control. Would you accept or reject H_0? What critical value would you use, and why?

	Liberal	PC	Reform	NDP	Total
Support stronger gun control measures	70	15	12	20	117
Oppose stronger gun control measures	50	10	30	20	110
Total	120	25	42	40	227

2. A study has been done to examine whether individuals born in Canada have significantly different annual incomes than individuals born outside the country but now living in Canada. The study included 500 respondents in each category. The mean annual income for those born in Canada was $44,000, with a standard deviation of $6,500. The mean annual income for those born outside the country is $49,000, with a standard deviation of $5,500. Construct a one-tailed and a two-tailed t-test. Which would be the most appropriate? Would you use a 0.01 or 0.05 test of significance? What would you conclude about the difference in annual income between those born inside and outside Canada?

NOTES

1. Adapted from Norusis (1990, 159).

2. Readers with access to data analysis programs such as SPSS should note that the programs will calculate test statistics automatically and compare those statistics to the critical values. Thus, for many, the exercises in this chapter will be more pedagogical than practical.

3. In addition to such inferential statistics purposes, the z-scores table can be used to estimate the percentage of cases between any given standardized score and the mean. This technique will not be explored in this textbook.

4. To test for the normal distributions required for parametric tests, researchers should examine the data with a diagnostics test such as SPSS's EXAMINE or by using histograms and box plots. See Norusis (1990).

5. Some texts use the symbols f_e and f_o to designate "frequencies expected" and "frequencies observed."

6. For small sample sizes of the kind seldom encountered in survey research, z-scores may not be appropriate. For an alternative interpretive table, see Gibbons (1976, 409–16).

7. To calculate the standard error of b, use the formula

$$s_b = \sqrt{\text{variance/sum of squares}}.$$

CHAPTER 11

Explaining the Political World: Nominal and Ordinal Data

DESTINATION

By the end of this chapter the reader should

- understand the use of correlation coefficients to measure the strength of relationships;
- be able to choose from among a variety of correlation coefficients;
- be able to calculate and interpret those coefficients.

Explanatory research is the means by which political scientists explore questions of cause and effect. We know from descriptive research that there is variation within political phenomena of interest, and our goal is to identify the major causes of such variation. For example, people differ in their party support: some people support the Liberal Party, others the Reform, Progressive Conservative, and New Democratic parties. How can we explain these differences? Are there particular factors that predict the party affiliation of given individuals and help explain why others lack any affiliation?

One assumption of the scientific method is that there is order to the universe; people, for instance, do not randomly adopt party affiliations. Rather, it is assumed that specific factors—variables—influence the choice of party affiliation. There is no assumption, however, that any *single* variable determines party affiliation. In social research, we know that there are no perfect correlations in the real world; it is rare that we can explain even most of the variation in the dependent variable by one external cause. For social researchers, this means that in addition to discovering that a relationship exists between the dependent variable and a particular independent variable, we also need to measure and assess the *strength* of that relationship. How much of the variation in the dependent variable is caused by a given independent variable? We can measure the strength of a bivariate relationship with **correlation coefficients**.

When conducting bivariate research, the political scientist needs to address four questions:

1. Is there a relationship?

2. What is the direction of the relationship?

3. Is the relationship significant?

4. What is the strength of the relationship?

We explored the first two questions in Chapters 2 and 9, when we looked for patterns in bivariate contingency tables and percentage tables. The third question was addressed in Chapter 10, where different tests of significance were introduced. This and the following chapter will address the last of these questions by examining measures of strength for bivariate and multivariate relationships.

Once again, the choice among various potential measures of strength will depend upon the level of measurement within the data. When looking at relationships, we are particularly concerned with the level of the dependent variable, whose variance we are trying to explain. Categorical variables (nominal- or ordinal-level of measurement) allow us to use less powerful measures of strength than do continuous variables. This chapter will focus on the first set of (less powerful) measures; Chapter 12 will take up the second set.

MEASURING THE STRENGTH OF RELATIONSHIPS

Most social and political events have multiple causes and influencing factors; indeed, it would be impossible to isolate every single influential factor for such dependent events as "political partisanship," "attitudes toward environmentalism," or "political efficacy." Given that impossibility, the goal of social science research is to identify the most important explanatory variables. What independent events have the most influence on the dependent event? Ultimately, the objective is to increase our *predictive accuracy*; just as the medical researcher wishes to predict the effect of drug A on a patient's health, we wish to predict the impact of independent variable A on a citizen's partisanship or political beliefs. And just as the medical researcher is not dealing with absolutes—there will always be some people for whom drug A has a different effect than clinical trials would suggest—so too must social researchers deal with variations and partial relationships. If we find, for example, that 75% of women vote Liberal, we cannot state with certainty that Tanya will vote Liberal. However, we can state with confidence that, given no information other than gender, Liberal is the *best prediction* for Tanya's vote.

Thus, the overall goal is to identify the independent variable or set of independent variables that allow(s) us to make the best prediction about dependent variables, such as an individual's social and political attitudes. By measuring the strength of a relationship between an independent and dependent variable, we are measuring *the confidence we can place in our predictions*. The strength of the relationship between two variables is measured with **correlation coefficients**, also known as "coefficients of association" or "relationship measures." Correlation coefficients condense the patterns in a contingency table into a single numerical value. When we "eyeball" data, we may fail to notice certain patterns due to inexperience or bias in favour of our hypotheses. Similarly, we sometimes "see" stronger relationships than actually exist. The correlation coefficient minimizes such problems by providing a numerical check on our perceptions. (On the other hand, "eyeballing" the data can provide a useful check of the interpretation of summary statistics!) In addition, correlation coefficients provide a standardized and compact way to convey relationship information to others; they are much easier to report and compare across studies than are complex contingency tables.

A number of correlation coefficients are available, and the appropriate selection depends upon (1) the technical limitations of the coefficients and (2) the level of measurement of the variables. The former issue will be addressed in greater detail when we explore each coefficient. Briefly, however, it is important to recall the distinction between parametric and nonparametric statistics. As Chapter 10 discussed, statistics based on nominal measures are often referred to as **nonparametric statistics** because they are not contingent on particular assumptions about data distribution (Bailey 1978, 332). It should be noted, though, that there are technical limits (such as data distributions) on when we can use a given nonparametric statistic. Ordinal- and interval-level statistics have built-in assumptions about the distribution parameters and are thus called **parametric statistics**. Although parametric tests are used more often than nonparametric tests in published research, and tend to be preferred, it can be difficult to meet the stringent assumptions of the parametric tests. In addition, many of the variables we consider in political science—race, gender, voting choice, religion, party affiliation—are nominal-level measures. For these reasons, political scientists often select nonparametric statistics.

The second factor to be considered when selecting a correlation measure is the level of data measurement. As we have seen, there are three levels of measurement that political scientists are concerned with: nominal, ordinal, and interval. The correlation coefficient one selects depends upon the *lowest level of measurement in the bivariate relationship*, for we always use the correlation coefficient that is most appropriate for the lowest level of measurement. Thus, if we have a bivariate relationship between a nominal-level variable and an ordinal-level variable, we select a correlation coefficient appropriate for nominal-level variables. If we have an ordinal-level and an interval-level variable, we can use ordinal-level measures. And so on. Clearly, to use interval-level measures, we need to have only interval-level variables. (We will explore exceptions to this rule in the next chapter.) When interval-level variables are used with nominal- or ordinal-level variables, the interval-level data are often grouped; for example, age (in years) might be grouped into "young," "middle," and "old." This makes the contingency tables that accompany the correlation coefficient easier to read.

Correlation coefficients at the nominal level typically range from 0 to 1, while at the ordinal level the typical range is from −1 to +1. (Interval-level measures will be addressed in the following chapter.) For both nominal- and ordinal-level measures, 0 signifies no relationship

CHECKING YOUR BEARINGS

SELECTING CORRELATION COEFFICIENTS

For each of the following bivariate relationships, identify (1) the level of measurement of each variable (nominal, ordinal, interval) and (2) the appropriate level of correlation coefficient (assume all distribution assumptions are met):

1. age (in years) and support for environmentalism (ranges from strong support to strong opposition);
2. gender and ideological position (left–centre–right);
3. party affiliation and level of education (number of years completed);
4. union membership and social class (working–lower middle–upper middle–upper);
5. religion and religiosity (church attendance: daily–weekly–monthly– annually–never).

(perfect independence): change in the independent variable is not correlated or associated with change in the dependent variable. The closer the coefficient is to 0, the weaker is the relationship. For nominal-level measures, 1 indicates a perfect relationship: change in the independent variable is always and systematically correlated with change in the dependent variable. The closer the coefficient is to 1, the stronger is the relationship. The same principle holds for ordinal-level measures, with the addition of direction. (Recall that nominal-level variables cannot be ordered and therefore cannot have direction.) For ordinal-level measures, the coefficient can be either positive or negative. A positive coefficient indicates a positive relationship: as the value of the independent variable increases, the value of the dependent variable also increases. A negative coefficient indicates a negative relationship: as values of the independent variable increase, values of the dependent variable decrease, and vice versa. Thus, the ± signification indicates *direction* rather than strength. As with nominal-level measures, we judge strength in ordinal-level relationships according to how close the coefficient is to 0 or ±1. If the coefficient is near 0, the relationship is very weak. If it is near ±1, the relationship is very strong.

For a number of reasons, the strength of a relationship is relative; in other words, coefficients of 0.5 do not always indicate relationships of the same strength. First, and as we will see, some measures of association are relatively more conservative or stringent, while others tend to inflate the strength of the relationship and therefore may be less robust. Second, research design has an impact on the strength of correlation coefficients. Experimental research has the greatest ability to control outside influences and therefore tends to generate relatively strong correlation coefficients. Survey research, on the other hand, is subject to greater amounts of "noise" and measurement error and therefore generates smaller correlation coefficients. Thus, a correlation coefficient of 0.5 might be seen as "moderate" in experimental research, but "strong" in survey research. (It is for this reason that political scientists may be very impressed by correlations that leave their psychology colleagues cold.) Finally, we need to keep in mind the context of our study. The goal is to identify the best predictors of a given dependent event. For some situations, the predictors of a dependent event tend to be so weak that even a rather low coefficient may actually be our best known predictor. For this reason, it is always important to keep the hypotheses in mind. If we expect a strong relationship, we will have higher standards and will read the coefficients with a less generous eye, and vice versa (Baxter-Moore 1994, 323).

We should also call attention to a special class of correlation coefficients, the **proportional reduction in error (PRE)** measures. A PRE measure is basically a ratio of errors (Norusis 1990, 121): we compare the amount of error we have without knowing the independent variable with the amount of remaining error after knowledge about the independent variable is taken into account. In other words, to what degree does knowledge about the independent variable reduce our error in predicting values of the dependent variable? The meaning of a PRE measure is best illustrated with an example.[1] Imagine we have 100 people, whose party affiliations are as follows[2]:

Liberal	60
Reform	30
NDP	10

If one of these individuals were to walk into the room and the above distribution was the only information we had, our best guess about the individual's party affiliation would be Liberal; this would ensure that we were right 60 times out of 100 and wrong 40 times out of 100. Not great odds, but with nominal-level variables such as these, the mode (i.e., the most frequently occurring category) is the best predictive option available.

Now imagine that we find out a second piece of information, the region in which respondents live. Given that regional residence may influence party affiliation, we construct a contingency table—party affiliation by region—and get the distributions in Table 11.1.

How does this affect our guessing abilities? Let's say we need to guess the party affiliation of one of the respondents from the West. What is our best guess? Clearly, the answer is Reform; if we guess Reform, we will be correct 20 times out of 30. What if the individual is from Central Canada? Here, our best guess is Liberal, and we will be correct 25 times

TABLE 11.1

PARTY AFFILIATION BY REGION (PRE EXAMPLE)

Party	Region			
	West	**Central**	**Atlantic**	**Total**
Liberal	10	25	25	60
Reform	20	5	5	30
NDP	0	10	0	10
Total	30	40	30	100

out of 40. Finally, for Atlantic respondents we will guess Liberal, and we will be correct 25 times out of 30. When we combine the results, we find that by using the knowledge provided by the independent variable (region), we are correct a total of 70 times (20 + 25 + 25) and incorrect a total of 30 times (10 + 15 + 5). Thus, our guessing abilities have been improved by adding the knowledge about the independent variable: we have decreased the errors from 40 to 30. What is the *proportionate* reduction of error? To find this, we can use a basic ratio formula:

$$\text{PRE} = \frac{\text{error without IV} - \text{error with IV}}{\text{error without IV}},$$

where IV = independent variable. In this example,

$$\text{PRE} = \frac{40 - 30}{40} = 0.25.$$

The PRE coefficients can be expressed as a percentage; in this case, knowledge about the respondent's region of residence allowed us to improve our guessing by approximately 25%.

This logic is seen in all PRE measures, lambda, gamma, and tau-b being those considered in this chapter, but there are two caveats. First, the formula given above explains the logic of the measures, but is not actually the formula used to calculate lambda, gamma, and tau-b. Thus, the formula is provided for illustrative purposes only. Second, only PRE measures can be expressed as a percentage reduction of error. Other measures—such as Cramer's V—can only be identified in terms of strength and, occasionally, direction. With all correlation coefficients, be they PRE or not, we need to note the strength of the relationship and, for ordinal-level measures, the direction of the relationship.

Having looked at the commonalties between correlation coefficients, we can now turn to the various measures. As we do so, the reader should be aware that some students will find the statistical calculations below to be complex and detailed. Thus, it is recommended that you follow each step carefully, and ensure that each aspect of the calculation is clear before carrying on. It is vital that the steps are individually mastered. You will find that calculating the formulas for yourself on paper or with a calculator will improve understanding. For most of us, merely reading a formula is insufficient and of little use when we attempt to calculate statistics on our own. Also, an understanding of how to calculate statistics enables us to better appreciate and interpret computer-generated statistics. The difference is profound, similar to the distinction between visiting a foreign country with a working knowledge of the language and visiting a foreign country with nothing more than a guidebook of common phrases. It is for this reason that we feel students should be able to calculate statistics by hand.

MEASURES FOR NOMINAL-LEVEL DATA

Nominal-level measures of strength will be used whenever one of the variables in the bivariate relationship is a categorical variable; thus, we may have nominal-nominal, nominal-ordinal, or nominal-interval relationships (interval-level data in such cases are typically grouped). Also, nonparametric nominal-level measures are used when our data fail to meet the requirements of the parametric tests. Recall that nominal-level measures have no direction and vary from 0 (perfect independence) to 1 (perfect correlation). We will look at two measures for nominal-level data: lambda and Cramer's V. Lambda is a PRE measure that is simple to calculate. Cramer's V is a chi-square based measure; thus, the chi-square statistic introduced in Chapter 10 is a step in the calculation of Cramer's V. Although lambda is a more robust measure than Cramer's V and easier to calculate, there are instances in which the use of lambda is not advised. Thus, it is important that students be able to calculate and interpret both measures.

Lambda uses the mode to make predictions. Recall from Chapter 9 that the mode (the most frequently occurring value) is the only measure of central tendency available for nominal-level data. The PRE example presented in the previous section illustrates lambda: both variables (party affiliation and region) were nominal-level, and the mode was used as the best predictor of party affiliation. However, we can calculate lambda in a less involved manner by using the following formula:

$$\lambda = \frac{\sum (f_i) - F_d}{N - F_d},$$

where f_i designates the mode (maximum frequency) in each category of the independent variable, F_d the mode of the marginal totals of the dependent variable (i.e., the largest of the row marginals), and N is the total number of cases.

Return to Table 11.1. To calculate lambda, we need to first find the mode for each category of the independent variable. We find that for the West, the mode value is 20, for Central Canada it is 25, and for the Atlantic region it is 25. Summed together, the modes total 70; thus,

$\sum(f_i) = 70$. The second value we need is the maximum marginal frequency. Quick examination reveals that $F_d = 60$. Finally, we need to know the total number of cases: $N = 100$. Having gathered together the necessary numbers, we are now ready to plug them into the formula:

$$\lambda = \frac{\sum(f_i) - F_d}{N - F_d,}$$

$$= \frac{70 - 60}{100 - 60} = \frac{10}{40} = 0.25$$

Because this is a PRE measure, we can state that knowledge of the respondent's region improved our prediction ability by 25%. The relationship is of moderate strength.

There are two limitations to lambda. First, due to the formulation, the value that lambda takes will vary according to which variable is designated independent. Thus, the researcher must be clear in her theory (and table construction) regarding which variable is dependent. A second limitation is mathematical: if significantly more cases are grouped in one category of the dependent variable (i.e., one row marginal is much larger than the others), lambda will approximate zero. This does not mean that perfect independence exists between the variables.

Table 11.2 presents a relatively modest adjustment to Table 11.1. In particular, it has an additional 10 respondents who are Liberals from the West. All other aspects of the table remain the same.

In looking at the table, we ask whether region affects voting. The data in the table appear to indicate that it does. For example, half the voters in the West supported the Reform Party, whereas only 5 of 40 (12.5%) in central Canada and 5 of 30 (16.7%) in Atlantic Canada supported Reform. If one were a Reform candidate, the chances of success would be much higher in the West than elsewhere in the country. In

TABLE 11.2

PARTY AFFILIATION BY REGION

Party	Region			
	West	**Central**	**Atlantic**	**Total**
Liberal	20	25	25	70
Reform	20	5	5	30
NDP	0	10	0	10
Total	40	40	30	110

addition, New Democrats received 10 of 40 (25%) votes from central respondents, but none from Westerners or those from the Atlantic region in these hypothetical data. Overall, it would appear that regional residence has an impact on voting.

Let's confirm this observation with λ, which as we said is a measure of association for nominal data. The calculations for λ are as follows:

$$\lambda = \frac{\sum (f_i) - F_d}{N - F_d},$$

$$= \frac{70 - 70}{110 - 70}$$

$$= \frac{0}{40} = 0.0$$

In this case, a λ of 0.0 suggests that the errors in predicting the dependent variable have not been reduced at all by adding information about the independent variable. But eyeballing the table clearly shows there is a relationship. What's going on? The answer lies in the distribution of data in the dependent variable. Notice in Table 11.2 that in a total sample size of 110, fully 70 cases (63.6%) are in the Liberal category. Furthermore, as we read across columns of the independent variable, we find the Liberals are the largest group in each category of the independent variable. Therefore, there were 70 correct predictions before knowing the independent variable, and 70 correct predictions after knowing it, for no net improvement. In short, there is a relationship between region and party in Table 11.2, but this relationship is not captured by λ. Furthermore, this is a more general limitation of λ: it often *underestimates* the strength of the relationship between two variables when there is an unequal distribution among categories of the dependent variable. As a consequence, always look at the table when using λ to confirm that it is not underestimating the strength of the relationship. It is also a good idea to run a second measure of association for nominal data, such as Cramer's V, as a check on the robustness of λ.

Cramer's V is based on the test statistic chi-square. (As you will recall from Chapter 10, chi-square compares the observed frequencies in a bivariate relationship with the frequencies that would be expected if perfect independence existed.) The steps for calculating Cramer's V are as follows:

1. Create an expected frequencies table.

2. Using the expected and observed frequencies, calculate chi-square.

3. Using chi-square, calculate Cramer's V.

Let's work through the steps using the data in Table 11.1. How many cases could we expect in the Liberal–West cell if party affiliation and region are independent of each other? How many cases could we expect in the Reform–Atlantic cell? Our first step in calculating Cramer's V is to calculate the expected frequencies for every cell of the contingency table. To do so, we take the row marginal for the cell, multiply it by the column marginal for the cell, and divide by the total number of cases:

$$E = \frac{(\text{row marginal})(\text{column marginal})}{N}.$$

Thus, for the Liberal–West cell, the expected frequency is

$$E = \frac{(\text{row marginal})(\text{column marginal})}{N} = \frac{60 \times 30}{100} = 18.$$

If region and party affiliation are independent, we expect 18 Westerners to be Liberals. We use the same calculation to determine the expected frequencies for all other cells (try the calculations yourself for practice), and thereby produce the expected frequencies in Table 11.3.

TABLE 11.3

PARTY AFFILIATION BY REGION (EXPECTED FREQUENCIES)

	West	Central	Atlantic	Total
Liberal	18	24	18	60
Reform	9	12	9	30
NDP	3	4	3	10
Total	30	40	30	100

Our next step is to calculate chi-square itself. The formula for chi-square, as you will recall, is

$$\chi^2 = \sum \frac{(O - E)^2}{E}.$$

Using this formula, we can calculate χ^2 as follows:

Observed	Expected	$O - E$	$(O - E)^2$	$\dfrac{(O - E)^2}{E}$
10	18	−8	64	3.56
25	24	1	1	0.04
25	18	7	49	2.72
20	9	11	121	13.44
5	12	−7	49	4.08
5	9	−4	16	1.78
0	3	−3	9	3
10	4	6	36	9
0	3	−3	9	3

$$\chi^2 = \sum \frac{(O - E)^2}{E}$$
$$= 40.62$$

For this example, we find that chi-square = 38.84. Having calculated chi-square, we come to our last step: calculate our correlation coefficient, Cramer's V. The formula for Cramer's V is

$$V = \sqrt{\frac{\chi^2}{N(k - 1)}},$$

where k is the minimum number of rows or columns (if the number of rows is smaller, we use rows; if the number of columns is smaller, we use columns).

For a 4 × 3 table, $k = 3$. For a 2 × 3 table, $k = 2$. In this example, we have a 3 × 3 table, so $k = 3$, and $k - 1 = 2$. We know already that $N = 100$ and chi-square = 40.62, so we can put all of these numbers into the formula to get our coefficient:

$$V = \sqrt{\frac{\chi^2}{N(k - 1)}}$$

$$= \sqrt{\frac{40.62}{200}} = \sqrt{0.203} = 0.45$$

We can interpret this coefficient as indicating that there is a moderately strong relationship between party affiliation and region of resi-

CHECKING YOUR BEARINGS

CALCULATING LAMBDA AND CRAMER'S V

For the following table, calculate and interpret both lambda and Cramer's V.

Support For Social Welfare By Gender

	Female	Male	Total
Low support	5	10	15
Moderate support	15	15	30
High support	20	5	25
Total	40	30	70

dence. Cramer's V is *not* a PRE measure, so we cannot make statements about improvements in predictive accuracy.

Now, as the astute reader has probably noted, the Cramer's V coefficient ($V = 0.45$) suggested a much stronger relationship than did the lambda coefficient ($\lambda = 0.25$). It is not uncommon for two summary statistics calculated on the same table to yield different results, although the difference in this case between $V = 0.45$ and $\lambda = 0.25$ seems especially large. In general, because λ is based on a proportional reduction in error interpretation, it is often preferable to V. If the two statistics yielded similar results, then λ would be the reported statistic. When the two statistics diverge, as they do in this instance, we would ask why they diverge. The answer seems to lie in the distribution of the dependent variable. We showed that by adding another 10 cases to the dependent variable, λ was reduced to 0. That suggests that the present distribution probably underestimates the strength of the relationship. And since λ appears to do this, V would be the preferred statistic. But notice that we lose a bit in interpretive power, since V is not based on a proportionate reduction in error. (A V of 0.45 is larger than a V of 0.225, but it is not twice as large.) In conclusion, there is a moderately strong effect of region on voting ($V = 0.45$).

MEASURES FOR ORDINAL-LEVEL DATA

When we have either two ordinal-level variables or an ordinal-level variable and an interval-level variable, we can use ordinal-level correlation coefficients. Recall that ordinal-level tests are parametric tests: before using an ordinal-level measure of strength, we must first ensure that the relationship between the variables is *linear*. Both positive and negative relationships are examples of linear relationships and could be depicted by a straight line (moving up and to the right in the former, down and to the right in the latter). If our relationship is not linear, for example, a curvilinear relationship, we should use the nonparametric, nominal-level measures. To discover if our bivariate relationship fits the parameters for ordinal-level measures, we need to look at our contingency tables carefully. Does the relationship appear positive at some points, then negative (or nonexistent) at others? Pattern inconsistencies in the data suggest a nonlinear relationship. Tables 11.4(a) to 11.4(d) illustrate linear and curvilinear relationships.

TABLE 11.4(a)

CONTINGENCY TABLE SHOWING A POSITIVE RELATIONSHIP

	Low	Medium	High	Total
Low	20	10	0	30
Medium	10	10	10	30
High	0	10	30	40
Total	30	30	40	100

TABLE 11.4(b)

CONTINGENCY TABLE SHOWING NO RELATIONSHIP

	Low	Medium	High	Total
Low	10	10	10	30
Medium	10	10	10	30
High	10	10	20	40
Total	30	30	40	100

TABLE 11.4(c)

CONTINGENCY TABLE SHOWING A NEGATIVE RELATIONSHIP

	Low	Medium	High	Total
Low	0	0	30	30
Medium	10	10	10	30
High	20	20	0	40
Total	30	30	40	100

TABLE 11.4(d)

CONTINGENCY TABLE SHOWING A CURVILINEAR RELATIONSHIP

	Low	Medium	High	Total
Low	0	30	0	30
Medium	10	0	20	30
High	20	0	20	40
Total	30	30	40	100

The two ordinal-level measures of strength considered here are gamma and tau-b. Gamma and tau-b are both PRE measures and can be interpreted in terms of percentage reduction of error. Recall that, when interpreting ordinal-level coefficients, we need to consider not just strength but also direction. A negative number indicates a negative relationship, whereas a positive coefficient indicates a positive relationship. Finally, for both measures, it is extremely important that we ensure that our tables are properly constructed before we begin the calculations. In each description in this section, we will assume that contingency tables are constructed with the independent variable across the top and the dependent variable down the left side; we will also assume that both the independent and dependent variables are ordered from low to high. Thus, before calculating the ordinal-level statistics, our first step is to *check the table construction*. If you are presented with a table that is ordered differently, you will need to reconstruct the table before you can begin your calculations.

Gamma and tau-b are measures that consider ordered pairs of observations. We look at two individual cases, for example, Harry and Sally, and ask how they compare on their rankings for both the independent and dependent variables.[3] Recall that our correlations can be either positive or negative. If we have a positive relationship, an increase in the independent variable will be accompanied by an increase in the dependent variable. When we consider pairs of cases, positive relationships are seen in **concordant pairs**: they exhibit *similar* ordering on the independent and dependent variables. If we have a negative relationship, an increase in the independent variable is accompanied by a decrease in the dependent variable. Negative relationships are seen in **discordant pairs** that exhibit *dissimilar* ordering of the independent and dependent variables.

TABLE 11.5

APPRECIATION BY YEARS OF UNDERGRADUATE STUDY (CONCORDANT AND DISCORDANT PAIRS)

	2 years	3 years	4 years
Low appreciation	Harry		Sue
Medium appreciation		Sally	Mike
High appreciation		Troy	

Consider Table 11.5. Here we are examining the relationship between appreciation for political science and number of years in university. Sally is ranked above Harry on both the independent and the dependent variables. Judging from this pair alone, we would believe that appreciation of political science increases the longer a student is in university. Harry and Sally are an example of a concordant pair. The relationship between time in university and appreciation is positive: as time increases, appreciation increases. Harry and Mike are also an example of a concordant pair: Mike is ranked above Harry on both variables. Similarly, Harry and Troy are a concordant pair. Now consider the pairing of Sally and Sue. Sue ranks above Sally on the independent variable, yet below Sally on the dependent variable. Judging from this pair alone, we would believe that appreciation of political science decreases the longer a student is in university. The pair Sue and Sally is an example of a discordant pair. The relationship between time in university and appreciation is negative: as time increases, appreciation decreases. The pair Troy and Sue and the pair Troy and Mike are further examples of discordant pairs.

If our tables are constructed properly, we can find concordant pairs by looking *down and to the right* of any given cell. The cells in Table 11.6 have been labelled to make this point more clearly. Start in the upper-left-hand corner cell, cell *a*, and look down and to the right. For cell *a*, concordant pairs can be found in cells *e*, *f*, *h*, and *i*. For cell *b*, concordant pairs can be found in cells *f* and *i*. What are the concordant pairs for cell *c*? Clearly, for this cell, we cannot move both down and to the right; therefore, cell *c* does not have any concordant pairs. For cell *d*, the concordant pairs are found in cells *h* and *i*; concordant pairs for cell *e* are limited to cell *i*. For cells *f*, *g*, *h*, and *i*, there are no cells that are both down and to the right, and these cells have no concordant pairs.

TABLE 11.6

FINDING ORDINAL PAIRS

	2 years	3 years	4 years
Low appreciation	a	b	c
Medium appreciation	d	e	f
High appreciation	g	h	i

concordant: discordant: ties dependent   ties independent

We use a similar process to find discordant pairs, moving *up and to the right* of any given cell. Here, we will start in the lower-left-hand corner, cell *g*, and work up. For cell *g*, the discordant pairs will be found in cells *b*, *c*, *e*, and *f*. For cell *h*, discordant pairs are located in cells *c* and *f*. There are no cells up and to the right of cell *i*; thus, cell *i* does not have any discordant pairs. For cell *d*, discordant pairs are found in cells *b* and *c*; for cell *e*, discordant pairs are found in cell *c*. And what of cells *f, a, b,* and *c*? If you said that these cells do not have any discordant pairs due to the absence of cells above and to the right, you are correct.

In summary, concordant pairs are found down and to the right on our tables and reflect positive relationships; discordant pairs are found up and to the right on the same tables and reflect negative relationships. Gamma, the correlation coefficient to which we will turn shortly, looks only at concordant and discordant pairs, comparing the number of concordant pairs with the number of discordant pairs. You will notice, however, that looking at the concordant and discordant pairs does not exhaust all possible pairings. Return to Table 11.5. Notice that there are also a number of **ties**, pairs of cases that differ on one variable but are tied on the other. Sue and Harry differ on the independent variable (Sue has 4 years of university education, while Harry has only 2), yet are tied on the dependent variable (low appreciation of political science). Sally and Mike are also tied on the dependent variable. Notice that we look *across the row* for ties on the dependent variable. Troy and Sally are an example of a tie on the independent variable: both have 3 years of university education, although they differ in their appreciation scores. A second example of a tie on the independent variable is the Sue–Mike pairing. For ties on the independent variable, we look *down the column*. Tau-b considers ties, including both independent variable ties and dependent variable ties. We will now look at how to calculate the coefficients, beginning with gamma.

Gamma is calculated by the following formula:

$$\gamma = \frac{N_s - N_d}{N_s + N_d},$$

where N_s designates the number of similar (concordant) pairs, and N_d designates the number of dissimilar (discordant) pairs. To find N_s, we multiply each cell frequency by the sum of the frequencies of the cells below and to the right, and sum these products. To find N_d, we multiply each cell frequency by the sum of the frequencies of the cells above and to the right, and sum these products.

This is best illustrated by the example in Table 11.7.[4] Notice that the cells have been labelled to make the steps clearer.

TABLE 11.7

IDEOLOGICAL POSITION BY INCOME

Ideology	Income			Total
	Low	**Middle**	**High**	**Total**
Left	0 *a*	10 *b*	5 *c*	15
Centre	5 *d*	30 *e*	5 *f*	40
Right	15 *g*	5 *h*	5 *i*	25
Total	20	45	15	80

To calculate N_s, we multiply down and to the right, and then sum the products:

$$\begin{aligned}
N_s &= a(e + f + h + i) + b(f + i) + d(h + i) + e(i) \\
&= 0(30 + 5 + 5 + 5) + 10(5 + 5) + 5(5 + 5) + 30(5) \\
&= 0(45) + 10(10) + 5(10) + 30(5) \\
&= 0 + 100 + 50 + 150 \\
&= 300.
\end{aligned}$$

To calculate N_d, we multiply up and to the right, and then sum the products:

$$N_d = g(b + c + e + f) + h(c + f) + d(b + c) + e(c)$$
$$= 15(10 + 5 + 30 + 5) + 5(5 + 5) + 5(10 + 5) + 30(5)$$
$$= 15(50) + 5(10) + 5(15) + 30(5)$$
$$= 750 + 50 + 75 + 150$$
$$= 1,025.$$

To calculate gamma, we insert these figures into the following formula:

$$\gamma = \frac{N_s - N_d}{N_s + N_d}$$
$$= \frac{300 - 1,025}{300 + 1,025} = \frac{-725}{1,325} = -0.55.$$

To interpret gamma, we need to keep in mind strength, direction, and the fact that gamma is a PRE measure. Thus, we can interpret this gamma value of –0.55 as indicating a *negative* and strong relationship: as income increases, support for the "right-wing" ideology decreases. Knowledge of the independent variable increased our predictive accuracy by approximately 55%.

Tau-b is also a PRE measure, but unlike gamma it includes ties. It is important to note that tau-b requires *square tables,* that is, 2×2, 3×3, 4×4, and so on. If the independent and dependent variables differ in the number of categories available, tau-b cannot be used. Tau-b is often favoured over gamma because it is a more conservative measure. Gamma can inflate the strength of relationships; tau-b, by including a calculation for ties, is less likely to do so. The formula for tau-b is

$$\text{tau-b} = \frac{N_s - N_d}{\sqrt{(N_s + N_d + T_x)(N_s + N_d + T_y)}},$$

where T_x designates ties on the independent variable, and T_y designates ties on the dependent variable.

To find ties on the independent variable, we remain within the column and move down; to find ties on the dependent variable, we remain within the row and move across. To find T_x, we multiply each cell frequency by the sum of the frequencies of the cells below, and sum these products. To find T_y, we multiply each cell frequency by the sum of the frequencies of the cells to the right, and sum these products. Let's return to the example in Table 11.7.

To calculate T_x, we multiply down in each column, and then sum the products:

$$T_x = a(d + g) + d(g) + b(e + h) + e(h) + c(f + i) + f(i)$$
$$= 0(5 + 15) + 5(15) + 10(30 + 5) + 30(5) + 5(5 + 5) + 5(5)$$
$$= 0(20) + 5(15) + 10(35) + 30(5) + 5(10) + 5(5)$$
$$= 0 + 75 + 350 + 150 + 50 + 25$$
$$= 650.$$

To calculate T_y, we multiply across in each row, and then sum the products:

$$T_y = a(b + c) + b(c) + d(e + f) + e(f) + g(h + i) + h(i)$$
$$= 0(10 + 5) + 10(5) + 5(30 + 5) + 30(5) + 15(5 + 5) + 5(5)$$
$$= 0(15) + 10(5) + 5(35) + 30(5) + 15(10) + 5(5)$$
$$= 0 + 50 + 175 + 150 + 150 + 25$$
$$= 550.$$

To calculate tau-b, we insert these figures into the formula (we already calculated N_s and N_d for Table 11.5 when we calculated gamma):

$$\text{tau-b} = \frac{N_s - N_d}{\sqrt{(N_s + N_d + T_x)(N_s + N_d + T_y)}},$$

$$= \frac{300 - 1{,}025}{\sqrt{(300 + 1{,}025 + 650)(300 + 1{,}025 + 550)}}$$

$$= \frac{-725}{\sqrt{(1{,}975)(1{,}875)}}$$

$$= \frac{-725}{\sqrt{3{,}703{,}125}}$$

$$= \frac{-725}{1{,}924.35}$$

$$= -0.38.$$

We can interpret this tau-b value of –0.38 as indicating a *negative* and moderately strong relationship: as income increases, support for the right moderately decreases. Knowledge of the independent variable increased our predictive accuracy by approximately 38%. Note that the tau-b value suggests a weaker relationship than does the gamma value (–0.55); because tau-b includes information on the number of ties, it tends to be more conservative.

CHECKING YOUR BEARINGS

CALCULATING GAMMA AND TAU-B

For the following table, calculate and interpret gamma and, if possible, tau-b.

Support For Social Welfare By Ideological Position

	Left	Centre	Right	Total
Low support	0	5	20	25
Moderate support	5	15	5	25
High support	15	10	0	25
Total	20	30	25	75

In summary, two measures of strength have been considered for ordinal-level variables. Tau-b is arguably the preferred measure: it includes the greatest amount of information, is least likely to inflate strength, and, as a PRE measure, is easy to interpret. A limitation is that tau-b can only be used for square tables. Gamma is also a PRE measure and therefore has the interpretive advantages of tau-b. However, it fails to include a considerable amount of information and can inflate the strength of the relationship.

CHECKING YOUR BEARINGS

INTERPRETING LAMBDA, CRAMER'S V, GAMMA, AND TAU-B

Interpret the following correlation coefficients in sentence form. Be certain to note strength, direction (where relevant), and PRE (where relevant). Briefly explain why you interpreted strength as you did.

1. gamma = –0.02
2. Cramer's V = 0.4
3. lambda = 0.15
4. tau-b = 0.6

ADDING A THIRD VARIABLE TO THE BIVARIATE RELATIONSHIP

In Chapter 6 we discussed the modelling of a simple bivariate relationship in which a single independent variable is hypothesized to affect a single dependent variable. This takes the form as illustrated in Figure 11.1.

In this type of analysis, we isolate these two variables from the complex interplay of social life and test empirically whether A has a discernible effect on B. Now we'd like to remove the condition of isolation that we imposed and ask whether a true causal relationship exists between these two variables when taking other factors into account. These "other factors" can affect either the independent or dependent variables separately or the relationship between the independent and dependent variables in a variety of ways. It is up to you as a researcher to model the relationship between the variables in your study, and then to conduct an appropriate empirical examination of that model. Let's look at some of the ways in which a "third variable effect" could be added to the simple bivariate relationship.

Spurious Relationships

A relationship is spurious if it exists because of the influence of a third variable. In the example in Figure 11.2, assume that the bivariate analysis showed a relationship between variable A and variable B. Given the way in which the relationship was modelled, the conclusion would be that A causes B. Now, assume that a third variable, C, influences both A and B. In this instance, C causes A to vary and B to vary. Thus, the initial variation that was observed between A and B was not causal, but instead was a byproduct of the effect of C on both A and B. After taking into account the presence of C, we would conclude that the relationship between A and B is spurious.

What should you look for in deciding whether a relationship is spurious? The first question you should ask is whether both the independent and dependent variables covary with a third variable. For many years, data from Canadian National Election Studies showed that Catholics

FIGURE 11.1

A BIVARIATE CAUSAL RELATIONSHIP

Independent   A ———————————→ B   Dependent
                              Theory

FIGURE 11.2

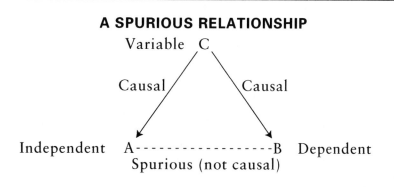

A SPURIOUS RELATIONSHIP

were more likely to vote Liberal, and Protestants were more likely to vote Conservative. Did being a Catholic "cause" people to vote Liberal? This appeared unlikely, because the Liberal Party did not adopt policies that were especially designed to respond to the wants and needs of Catholics; indeed, if anything, the more small "c" conservative policies of the Conservative Party seemed most in line with the preferences of Catholics. So, we would ask whether some other variable relates both to religious denomination and to voting. The answer, of course, is region or province of residence. Residents of Quebec are far more likely than those in other provinces to be Catholic, and for much of this century Quebeckers were likely to vote Liberal. Indeed, once the effect of region was controlled, it was found that within Quebec, Catholics and non-Catholics were equally likely to support the Liberals, whereas in Ontario, for example, Catholics and non-Catholics were equally likely to support the Conservatives. Since there were far more Catholics in Quebec and Protestants in Ontario, it appeared that religion affected voting. However, once region was controlled, the effect of religion disappeared. We would conclude that the effect of religion on voting was spurious. Thus, from an analytical point of view, the thing you should be looking for in testing for a spurious relationship is the strength of the relationship between the initial independent and dependent variables to decrease with the addition of the control variable. Indeed, if the relationship is truly spurious, the strength of the relationship should decrease to 0.

Intervening Variable

An intervening variable is one that comes between an independent and a dependent variable, but the direction of causality flows from the independent variable to the intervening variable to the dependent variable.

The use of intervening variables is one way of providing further elaboration to a theory. For example, assume the initial hypothesis is that education leads to participation in politics: the higher one's level of education, the more likely he or she is to have a high level of participation. But why is this the case? What is it about having a higher level of education that leads one to have a higher level of political participation? A variety of theories could be introduced to explain this relationship, each of which could include specifying an intervening variable. For example, one theory is that people participate in politics when the cost to them of doing so is not too high. Higher levels of education provide people with a greater understanding of politics, which reduces the "cost" of becoming informed about the parties during an election campaign. Therefore, the hypothesis follows that people with higher levels of education will participate in politics because the cost to them of doing so is lower than for people with lower levels of education. Thus, in the model in Figure 11.3, variable C is knowledge about the parties and/or the political process. This model could be extended by including other variables that intervene between level of education and level of political participation. These could include such things as a larger number of social contacts with people actively involved in politics (therefore being more likely to be asked to participate), having a higher income, and therefore taking a greater interest in governmental decisions as they affect the allocation of resources, and other intervening factors.

Note the difference between an intervening variable and a spurious relationship. In the former, the original independent variable is important, because it causes variation in the intervening variable, whereas in a spurious relationship the initial independent variable is not important, because the direction of causality is reversed. In each of the examples of intervening variables, education was hypothesized to affect the intervening variable; that is, higher levels of education led to greater political

FIGURE 11.3

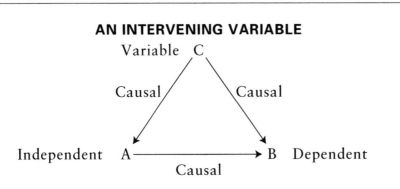

AN INTERVENING VARIABLE

knowledge, more social contacts, or a higher income, which in turn led to higher levels of political participation.

Reinforcing Variable

A reinforcing variable is one that can strengthen and magnify the relationship between an independent and a dependent variable. For example, assume we are examining the effect of gender on attitudes toward abortion. We might find that women are more likely than men to agree that abortion is a matter that should be decided between a pregnant woman and her doctor. A reinforcing variable in this model could be attitudes toward feminism. People who hold views favourable to feminism also are more likely to agree that abortion is a matter that should be decided between a pregnant woman and her doctor. Since women are more likely to be feminists (i.e., to hold views favourable to feminism) than are men, attitudes toward feminism reinforce the relationship between gender and attitudes toward abortion. However, attitudes toward feminism don't replace the effect of gender; instead they complement and reinforce this relationship. This means that the causal connection between gender and attitudes toward abortion persists even after the effect of the reinforcing variable is taken into account. It also suggests that the reinforcing variable does not necessarily have a causal connection with the independent variable. Instead, they may simply covary. When the two variables are reinforcing, however, such as in this example, the impact of the independent variable on the dependent variable is larger among women who hold feminist attitudes than among those who do not.

FIGURE 11.4

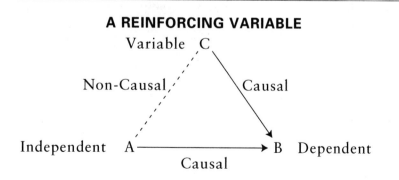

A REINFORCING VARIABLE

Multiple Independent Variables

We also could model a set of causal relationships in which a number of independent variables can have an effect on a dependent variable. This type of modelling is quite common when using multiple regression analysis, because this technique allows us to examine the effect of each of the independent variables under the *ceteris paribus* assumption, that is, assuming all other things are equal. Thus, for example, we could examine the effect of attitudes toward party leaders, attitudes toward political issues, and party identification on voting to see which of these variables is the most important determinant of voting. Such an analysis would try to answer the question 'Are Canadian elections little more than television-oriented popularity contests between the party leaders, or are they the result of policy discussions and debates among the parties and candidates?' To what extent does the government receive a mandate to implement a policy agenda following a Canadian election? Understanding the nature of causality among these competing models provides insight into the character and meaning of Canadian elections, and of course also provides strategic information that can be used by the parties in formulating their election campaigns.

The caution to bear in mind when modelling and empirically testing relationships with multiple independent variables is that the assumption of independence between the causal or independent variables may not reflect the true relationships between these variables in the real world. For example, from the preceding discussion, is it sensible to assume that attitudes toward party leaders, attitudes toward political issues, and party identification are independent of one another? We may believe that Canadian voters' attitudes toward Jean Chrétien are not related to attitudes toward the Liberal Party's position on issues such as government spending, but do we also hold that view about attitudes toward Reform Party leader Preston Manning and the Reform Party's less ambiguous policy of balancing the budget in three years? Likewise, is it sensible to think that in Quebec provincial politics there is no relationship between attitudes toward Quebec sovereignty and attitudes toward

FIGURE 11.5

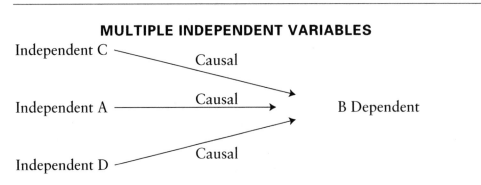

MULTIPLE INDEPENDENT VARIABLES

Parti Québécois leader and Premier Lucien Bouchard? Of course, not all independent variables will be as strongly related to one another as the examples given above. But be aware of the assumptions that accompany the modelling of the relationships in your analysis. If there is reason to think that the independent variables are related to one another, you may wish to reconsider the way in which you have conceptualized the relationship to take into account this interrelationship.

In the remainder of this chapter, we will illustrate the way in which various techniques of data analysis can be used to examine multivariate relationships. As we did in Chapter 10, we will begin with contingency tables and related measures of association. Recall that contingency tables are used both for nominal and ordinal data and are probably the most commonly used techniques for data analysis. The statistical techniques that are used will depend upon the level of measurement of the data; again, generally, we will use measures such as Cramer's V and lambda for nominal data and gamma or tau-b for ordinal data.

CHECKING YOUR BEARINGS

ADDING A THIRD VARIABLE TO YOUR ANALYSIS

We've described various ways in which to add a third variable to the bivariate model. You could check for a spurious relationship by seeing whether a third variable affects both the independent and dependent variables. Alternatively, you could test whether an intervening variable provides a path or channel through which the effect of the independent variable passes *en route* to the dependent variable. We also discussed a reinforcing effect, in which the effect of the independent variable increases with the presence of a third variable. Finally, we discussed a model in which multiple independent variables are hypothesized to affect a common dependent variable. It should be recognized that specifying these alternative models is a task undertaken by the researcher; you determine the structure of the relationships that will be examined in your research project.

A good indication of your understanding of this process is your ability to elaborate a bivariate model in each of the four ways discussed above. Assume the bivariate model examines the impact of education on the level of political cynicism. Develop four alternative models that (1) test for a spurious relationship, (2) specify an intervening variable, (3) identify a reinforcing variable, and (4) postulate a model with multiple independent variables.

However, as the following analysis will demonstrate, measures for nominal data are useful for ordinal data analysis when the relationship is nonlinear.

CONTINGENCY TABLES WITH CONTROL VARIABLES

The Effect of Age on Political Interest, Controlling For Education

When beginning an analysis, it is always useful to map the relationship you wish to examine; this will help you in establishing the direction of causality you are hypothesizing and also will help in identifying the role of each variable: which are the independent and dependent variables, and what is the hypothesized impact of the third variable. For the current example, we will assume that the initial hypothesis is as shown in Figure 11.6.

The initial bivariate relationship is between age and political interest, and the hypothesis is that as age increases, so too does political interest. The multivariate model then suggests that education acts to reinforce the relationship between age and political interest. An analysis of this model includes an examination of the following relationships: (1) age and political interest; (2) education and political interest; (3) age and education; (4) age and political interest, controlling for education.

The data used to test this model are from the 1988 Canadian National Election Study. The age variable was coded into four categories (18–30, 31–45, 46–60, and 61 and over). The education variable has three categories (less than completed high school, completed high school and/or attended technical college, and completed college and/or

FIGURE 11.6

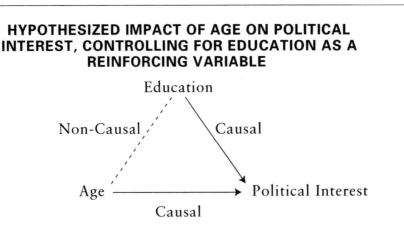

HYPOTHESIZED IMPACT OF AGE ON POLITICAL INTEREST, CONTROLLING FOR EDUCATION AS A REINFORCING VARIABLE

attended or completed university). The measure of political interest is a three-point measure in response to four questions asked regarding respondents' level of interest in politics and the campaign. The data are presented in Tables 11.8 to 11.11(c).

Table 11.8 shows the effect of age on level of political interest. Notice that this relationship is between two ordinal-level variables; therefore, we are anticipating a linear relationship between the variables. The data conform to this expectation and also reveal a moderately strong relationship between the variables. For example, we find that almost one-third (29.4%) of those in the youngest age group have a low level of political interest, compared to only about one-eighth (13.5%) of those in the oldest age group. In addition, the percentage of those with a high level of political interest increases consistently with age, from 34.7% of those aged 18–30, to 46.7% for those 31–45, 55.7% for those 46–60 years of age, and to 62.7% for those over 60 years of age. Since these are ordinal data and the relationship is linear, the gamma and tau-b statistics would be appropriate. A gamma of 0.25 indicates a relationship of moderate strength; therefore, we would conclude that age has a moderate effect on level of political interest.

The effect of education on political interest is shown in Table 11.9. Since education was measured with three categories, we produce a 3 × 3 table. And once again, we find a linear relationship of moderate strength. Almost one-third of those with low education have low interest (31.1%), whereas fewer than one-eighth of those with high education

TABLE 11.8

THE EFFECT OF AGE ON POLITICAL INTEREST

Political Interest	18–30	31–45	46–60	61+	Total
Low	290	303	118	82	793
	29.4%	23.6%	18.1%	13.5%	22.4%
Moderate	355	382	171	144	1,052
	35.9%	29.7%	26.2%	23.8%	29.8%
High	343	601	364	380	1,688
	34.7%	46.7%	55.7%	62.7%	47.8%
Total	988	1,286	653	606	3,533
	100.0%	100.0%	100.0%	100.0%	100.0%

Gamma = 0.25.
Tau-b = 0.17.

TABLE 11.9

THE EFFECT OF EDUCATION ON POLITICAL INTEREST

Political Interest	Education			
	< High School	High School–Technical College	Post-secondary	Total
Low	334	310	144	788
	31.1%	25.8%	11.5%	22.3%
Moderate	334	401	316	1,051
	31.1%	33.4%	25.3%	29.8%
High	406	491	790	1,687
	37.8%	40.8%	63.2%	47.8%
Total	1,074	1,202	1,250	3,526
	100.0%	100.0%	100.0%	100.0%

Gamma = 0.32.
Tau-b = 0.21.

have low interest (11.5%). Conversely, just over one-third of those with low education have high interest (37.8%), whereas almost two-thirds of those with high education have high interest (63.2%). The effect of education on political interest (gamma = 0.32) is even stronger than age on interest (gamma = 0.25).

Table 11.10 shows the effect of age on level of education. Note that these two variables are related, but that the relationship is negative: as age increases, level of education decreases. For example, among those aged 18–30 and 31–45, only 21.2% and 21.6%, respectively, had less than high school education, a figure that increases to 40.5% among those aged 46–60, and to 54.1% for those over 60. On the other hand, of those aged 18–30, 35.5% have a high level of education, a percentage that increases to 44.5% among those aged 31–45, but decreases to 29.9% and 22.0% among those aged 46–60 and those over 60, respectively. In short, the youngest segments of the population have the highest levels of education, a finding that is very consistent with the rapid expansion in the postsecondary education system that occurred in Canada beginning in the early 1960s.

What impact does a negative association between age and education have on the relationship between age and political interest? To obtain an answer, we can rerun the analysis of the effect of age on political interest, controlling for level of education. To control for education means to hold education constant. We do this by running separate analyses, and producing separate contingency tables, for each category

TABLE 11.10

THE EFFECT OF AGE ON EDUCATION

Education	Age				
	18–30	31–45	46–60	61+	Total
< High School	208	277	260	325	1,070
	21.2%	21.6%	40.5%	54.1%	30.5%
High School–Technical College	425	434	190	144	1,193
	43.3%	33.9%	29.6%	24.0%	34.0%
Postsecondary	348	571	192	132	1,243
	35.5%	44.5%	29.9%	22.0%	35.5%
Total	981	1,282	642	601	3,506
	100.0%	100.0%	100.0%	100.0%	100.0%

Gamma = –0.24.

Tau-b = –0.17.

of education. In other words, we ask, What is the impact of age on political interest among those with a low level of education? What is the impact among those with a moderate and a high level of education? Thus, with a three-category control variable, the analysis produces three separate tables, which we label Tables 11.11(a) to 11.11(c).

Table 11.11(a) examines the effect of age on political interest among those with a low level of education. Notice once again that the relationship is linear: as age increases, the likelihood of having a high level of political interest increases as well. Note also that the strength of the relationship has increased, from a gamma for the population as a whole of 0.25 to a gamma of 0.30 among those with a low level of education. It is this latter finding in which we are most interested: a stronger impact of age on political interest among those with a low level of education suggests that education intervened in the relationship between age and interest in a negatively reinforcing manner. A similar finding follows from an analysis of Tables 11.11(b) and 11.11(c). Among those with a moderate level of education, the effect of age on political interest is given by a gamma statistic of 0.36, well above the original gamma of 0.25. Among those with a high level of education, gamma remains strong at 0.32. Thus, among each of the three educational groups, the relationship between age and political interest is higher than among the population as a whole. This indicates that the effect of age on political interest is negatively reinforced by level of education. To put this another way, at present there is a relationship between age and interest that is somewhat offset by the negative effect of age on education. This is due to the significant increase in the availability of postsecondary education during the 1960s, an increase that has led to important differences in educational attainment between younger and older Canadians. Over time, as the level of education among all age groups becomes more common, we would expect the effect of age on political interest to strengthen.

TABLE 11.11(a)

THE EFFECT OF AGE ON POLITICAL INTEREST, CONTROLLING FOR EDUCATION (LOW EDUCATION)

Political Interest	Age				
	18–30	31–45	46–60	61+	Total
Low	83	115	68	64	330
	39.9%	41.5%	26.2%	19.7%	30.8%
Moderate	78	87	75	94	334
	37.5%	31.4%	28.8%	28.9%	31.2%
High	47	75	117	167	406
	22.6%	27.1%	45.0%	51.4%	37.9%
Total	208	277	260	325	1,070
	100.0%	100.0%	100.0%	100.0%	100.0%

Gamma = 0.30.
Tau-b = 0.21.

TABLE 11.11(b)

THE EFFECT OF AGE ON POLITICAL INTEREST, CONTROLLING FOR EDUCATION (MODERATE EDUCATION)

Political Interest	Age				
	18–30	31–45	46–60	61+	Total
Low	147	118	29	15	309
	34.6%	27.2%	15.3%	10.4%	25.9%
Moderate	160	156	54	28	398
	37.6%	35.9%	28.4%	19.4%	33.4%
High	118	160	107	101	486
	27.8%	36.9%	56.3%	70.1%	40.7%
Total	425	434	190	144	1,193
	100.0%	100.0%	100.0%	100.0%	100.0%

Gamma = 0.36.
Tau-b = 0.25.

TABLE 11.11(c)

THE EFFECT OF AGE ON POLITICAL INTEREST, CONTROLLING FOR EDUCATION (HIGH EDUCATION)

Political Interest	Age				
	18–30	31–45	46–60	61+	Total
Low	58	69	16	1	144
	16.7%	12.1%	8.3%	0.8%	11.6%
Moderate	115	139	40	20	314
	33.0%	24.3%	20.8%	15.2%	25.3%
High	175	363	136	111	785
	50.3%	63.6%	70.8%	84.1%	63.2%
Total	348	571	192	132	1,243
	100.0%	100.0%	100.0%	100.0%	100.0%

Gamma = 0.32.
Tau-b = 0.19.

SELF-STUDY

1. For each of the following tables and data sets, calculate and interpret the stated correlation coefficient. Which would you choose to report in your final write-up? For parametric statistics, indicate how you determined linearity.

   a. Opinion on Issue X by Religious Affiliation

	Catholic	Protestant	Jewish	Total
Support X	20	10	0	30
Oppose X	0	10	20	30
Total	20	20	20	60

   Compute lambda and Cramer's V. Use inferential statistics to test statistical significance.

   b. Support for Issue X by Level of Political Activity

	Low Activity	Moderate Activity	High Activity	Total
Low support	5	9	9	23
Moderate support	9	10	9	28
High support	11	6	7	24
Total	25	25	25	75

Compute gamma and tau-b. Use inferential statistics to test statistical significance.

2. For each of the following, interpret in sentence form:

   a. gamma = −0.02.

   b. lambda = 0.7.

   c. Cramer's V = 0.12.

   d. tau-b = 0.3.

NOTES

1. Adapted from Manheim and Rich (1982, 284–86).

2. Other federal parties at the time of writing, in particular, the Progressive Conservatives and the Bloc Québécois, have been excluded from the example in order to keep the explanations as simple as possible. This is not meant to discount the importance or future of any party.

3. Example adapted from White (1994, 318–19).

4. This table is also used as an example in Chapter 9.

CHAPTER 12

Multivariate Analysis: An Introduction to the Deep End of the Pool

DESTINATION

By the end of this chapter the reader should

- understand the use of scatter plots for examining the relationship between interval data;
- be familiar with the assumptions underlying ordinary least squares regression techniques;
- understand the relationship between regression coefficients (the slope) and the standard error;
- be able to interpret a regression analysis table which includes the regression coefficients and standard errors for each of the independent variables, together with the intercept and the value of R^2;
- understand the use of dummy variables in regression analysis.

MEASURES FOR INTERVAL-LEVEL DATA

Recall that interval-level measures of association are parametric tests and as such assume the relationship to be linear; in fact, the most common interval-level statistical technique is known as **basic linear regression**. Almost all advanced statistical techniques follow a logic similar to that of basic linear regression; thus, it is an important technique to understand. Our first step prior to beginning basic linear regression is to test for linearity.[1] Recall that we used a contingency table to look for linearity in ordinal-level variables. However, to do so with interval-level variables would require the creation of an unmanageable table and one that is difficult to interpret. Instead, we use a **scatter plot** to look for linearity in interval-level relationships. A scatter plot is a simple graphic display of our cases. We set up a graph, with the dependent variable along the Y-axis (vertical) and the independent variable along the X-axis (horizontal), and locate each case according to its position on both the X- and Y-axes. We then look at the pattern among the data: does it suggest a linear relationship? A curvilinear relationship? No relationship at all? If we find a pattern that could have a straight line drawn through it, this indicates a linear relationship. Figure 12.1 shows the scatter plot for the very simple data set depicted below:

	X	Y
Case 1	2	8
Case 2	3	5
Case 3	1	4
Case 4	6	9
Case 5	4	7

When using real data in the social sciences, it is rare that we will have a line that perfectly fits, in other words, a line upon which all cases fall exactly. Instead, we seek to find the line that *best fits* the data. This line is known as the **regression line**. The regression line is essentially a line of prediction and is conceptually similar to the PRE (proportional reduction in error) measures. We ask ourselves, without knowledge of the independent variable, what is our best prediction of the value of the dependent variable for any particular case? Given that the dependent variable is measured at the interval level, our best prediction would be

FIGURE 12.1

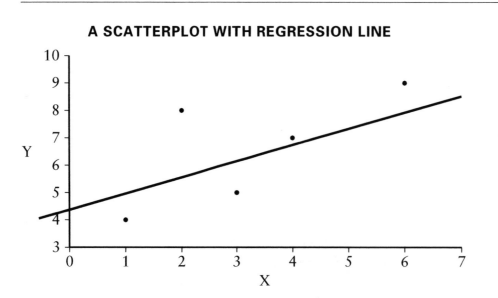

A SCATTERPLOT WITH REGRESSION LINE

the mean. What the regression line provides is a best prediction of dependent variable scores for any given independent variable score. In order to do so, however, the regression line must be calculated according to the **ordinary least squares (OLS)** method.

The OLS method places the regression line in such a way as to minimize the squared deviations between the observed and predicted values. This is analogous to the mean as a predictor of values on a single variable; the mean is the value that minimizes the error in predicting scores on an interval variable. Any other predicted value produces more errors (i.e., larger squared deviations) than the mean. Likewise, the OLS regression line minimizes the errors (squared deviations) in predicting the values on an interval-level dependent variable for any given value on the independent variable.

The OLS formula is used to determine the position of the regression line. It is stated as

$$Y' = a + bX,$$

where Y' is the predicted value of the dependent variable, X is the value of the independent variable, a is the **intercept** and b is the **slope**.

Notice that Y' (the predicted value of the dependent variable) is understood to be a linear function of X (the value of the independent variable); Y' changes only when X changes (see Figure 12.2). The intercept, symbolized by a, is the value of Y' when X is equal to 0. The intercept is a constant and tells us the position of Y' on our graph where the regression line crosses the Y-axis. The slope, symbolized by b, represents

FIGURE 12.2

THE INTERCEPT (A) AND SLOPE (B) OF A REGRESSION LINE

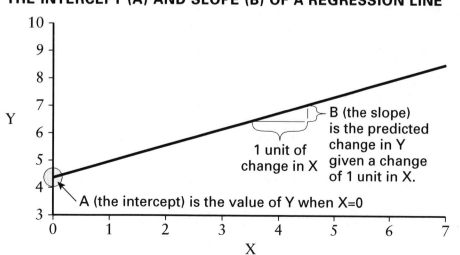

the unit change in Y' for every unit change in X. We have said that the dependent variable varies with the independent variable, but by how much? The slope tells us the unit change, and in doing so indicates the angle that the regression line should take on the graph. The slope also indicates the direction of our relationship: a slope upward and to the right indicates a positive relationship, and a slope downward and to the right a negative relationship.

Let's say that our dependent variable is weekly income (measured in dollars) and our independent variable is university education (measured in years) (Figure 12.3). It is hypothesized that income varies with university education. The data collected and assessed reveal the following regression formula:

$$Y' = 200 + 100X.$$

This formula tells us two things. First, we can see that with no university training ($X = 0$), predicted weekly income (Y') is equal to \$200. We know this because the intercept (a) is equal to \$200. Second, we can see that for every one-year increase in university education (X), we have a \$100 increase in weekly income. We know this because the slope (b)

FIGURE 12.3

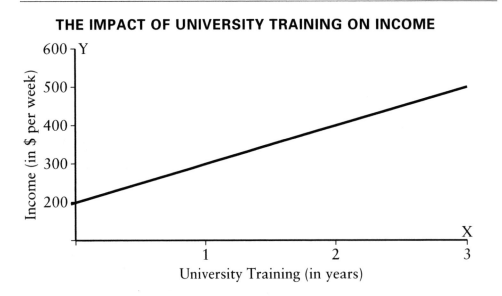

THE IMPACT OF UNIVERSITY TRAINING ON INCOME

is equal to 100. We can see from the slope that the relationship between weekly income and university education is positive: as university education increases, weekly income increases.

Let's try another example (Figure 12.4). Our dependent variable is "total due on speeding ticket" (measured in dollars), and our indepen-

FIGURE 12.4

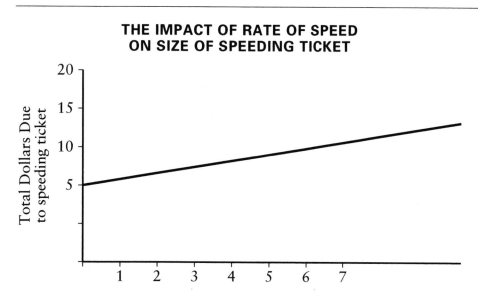

**THE IMPACT OF RATE OF SPEED
ON SIZE OF SPEEDING TICKET**

dent variable is "kilometres over speed limit" (measured in kilometres). Take the time to interpret the following regression formula in writing:

$$Y' = 5 + 0.8X.$$

Hopefully, you came to the following interpretations: (1) with no kilometres over the speed limit, the predicted speeding ticket total is $5; and (2) for every one-kilometre increase in speed above the speed limit, there is an $0.80 increase in the cost of the ticket. Now, you may be saying to yourself, that does not make sense. How can I get a speeding ticket when I have not exceeded the speed limit? Assuming you are living in an area where police are honest, this is clearly not possible. What this illustration shows, therefore, is that the intercept of the regression line can at times be *substantively meaningless*, serving more to help us position the regression line than to accurately predict the values of Y' when X equals zero.

How do we calculate the intercept and the slope? There are specific OLS formulas to determine each. We begin with the slope:

$$b = \frac{\text{sum of products}}{\text{sum of squares}} = \frac{\sum (x_i - \bar{x})(y_i - \bar{y})}{\sum (x_i - \bar{x})^2}.$$

We calculate the slope in a series of steps: (1) find the means of both x and y; (2) from each individual case, subtract the mean; (3) calculate products $(x_i - \bar{x})(y_i - \bar{y})$; (4) calculate the sum of the products; (5) calculate the squares $(x_i - \bar{x})^2$; (6) calculate the sum of the squares; and

(7) calculate the slope. Let's use these steps to calculate the slope for our Figure 12.1 data (the first calculations of each step have been demonstrated for further clarity):

X	Y	$\bar{X}$	$\bar{Y}$	$(y_i - \bar{y})$	$(x_i - \bar{x})$	$(y_i - \bar{y})(x_i - \bar{x})$	$(x_i - \bar{x})^2$
2	8	3.2	6.6	8 − 6.6 = 1.4	2 − 3.2 = −1.2	1.4 × −1.2 = −1.68	$(-1.2)^2 = 1.44$
3	5	3.2	6.6	−1.6	−0.2	0.32	0.04
1	4	3.2	6.6	−2.6	−2.2	5.72	4.84
6	9	3.2	6.6	2.4	2.8	6.72	7.84
4	7	3.2	6.6	0.4	0.8	0.32	0.64
						$\sum = 11.4$	$\sum = 14.8$

$$\bar{y} = \frac{(8 + 5 + 4 + 9 + 7)}{5} = 6.6$$

$$\bar{x} = \frac{(2 + 3 + 1 + 6 + 4)}{5} = 3.2$$

$$b = \frac{\text{sum of products}}{\text{sum of squares}} = \frac{\sum(x_i - \bar{x})(y_i - \bar{y})}{\sum(x_i - \bar{x})^2}$$

$$= \frac{11.4}{14.8} = 0.77$$

Our slope is 0.77; for every one-unit increase in X, there is a 0.77-unit increase in Y.

The calculations for the intercept are much less involved. The OLS formula is

$$a = \bar{y} - b\bar{x}.$$

After calculating the slope, we have all of these numbers available and can quickly calculate:

$$a = 6.6 - 0.77(3.2) = 6.6 - 2.46 = 4.14.$$

Our intercept is 4.14; this tells us that when X is equal to 0, the predicted value of Y is 4.14.

We now know how to calculate the regression line. But how does any of this fit with correlation coefficients? What do regression lines have to do with measures of strength in bivariate relationships? Recall that the regression line is a prediction line: it states what the value of Y is predicted to be at any given value of X. However, the line does not tell us

FIGURE 12.5

WEAK RELATIONSHIP

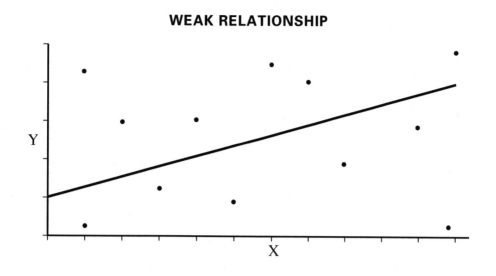

how close the individual cases are to the line, in other words, how good our predictions are. Note that the same OLS equation—identical intercepts and slopes—can represent two very different data sets. Figure 12.5 shows a relatively weak relationship, and Figure 12.6 shows a relatively strong relationship; both have the same slope and Y intercept.

To measure the strength of the linear interval-level relationship, we ask, "How well does the regression line fit the data?" We are assessing "goodness of fit." If there were a perfect bivariate relationship, all of the variation in Y could be explained by X, and all of our cases would line up on the regression line. When we have cases that deviate from the regression line, we have an **unexplained variance**, variation in Y that is

FIGURE 12.6

STRONG RELATIONSHIP

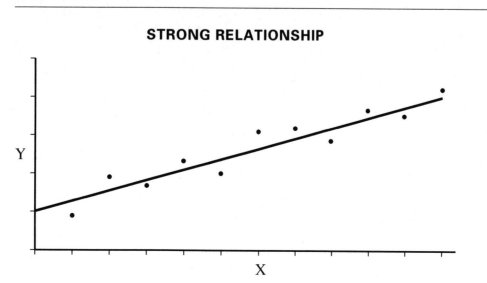

not explained by the value of X. If the total squared deviations from the regression line are relatively large, this means that X does not explain a lot of the variation in Y, and we have a weak relationship. If the total squared deviations from the regression line are relatively small, this means that X captures much of the variation in Y, and we have a strong relationship.

THE STANDARD ERROR OF THE ESTIMATE

Figures 12.5 and 12.6 provide a graphic illustration of the goodness of fit of the regression line for the two sets of data, illustrating a much better fit (and thus a stronger relationship) in Figure 12.6. A statistic used to calculate the goodness of fit of the regression line is the standard error of estimate. As the regression line is analogous to the mean as the "best" prediction of the dependent variable (the mean is the best predictor without the independent variable; the regression line (slope) is the best predictor with the independent variable), the standard error of estimate is analogous to the standard deviation of a mean. That is, the smaller the standard error of estimate, the smaller the error in predicting the dependent variable on the basis of the independent variable.

The identification of the standard error of estimate can be seen in Figure 12.7. The three panels present the same data and illustrate three types of variation. In panel (A), the comparison is between the observed Y values and the mean of Y ($\overline{Y}$). This panel shows the error in predicting the Y value without knowledge of X; we indicated previously that the mean would be the best predictor, since we would minimize the errors of predicting Y via the mean. Panel (B) compares the mean value of Y (i.e., the prediction before knowing the X value) with the predicted value of Y after knowing the X value (i.e., Y'). It is labelled "explained variation" because this is the amount of variation in Y that is accounted for by the X value. Panel (C) compares the observed values of Y with the predicted values of Y, and is labelled the "unexplained variation," or sometimes called the "residual variation." It is the amount of variation in Y that exists after knowing the X values. Notice that the total variation is a sum of the explained and unexplained variations. The unexplained or residual variation is what is used in computing the standard error of estimate. The standard error is given by the following formula:

$$se = \sqrt{\frac{\sum(Y-Y')^2}{N-2}},$$

FIGURE 12.7

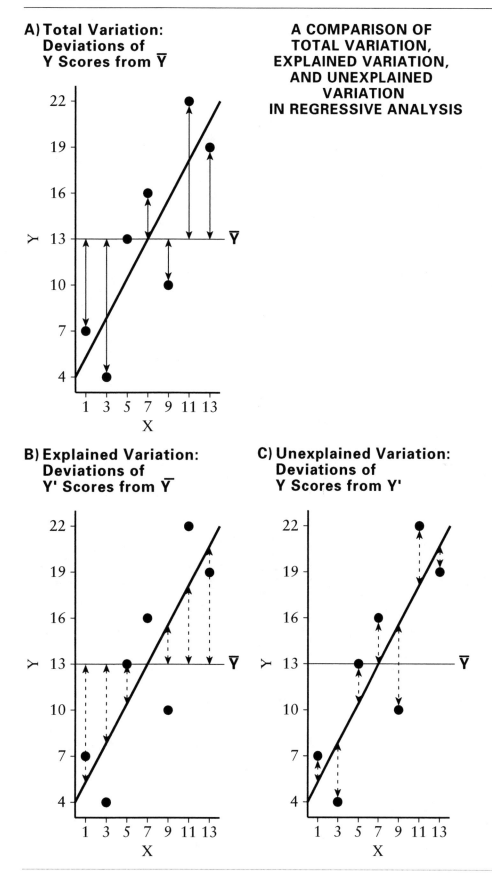

**A) Total Variation:
Deviations of
Y Scores from $\overline{Y}$**

**A COMPARISON OF
TOTAL VARIATION,
EXPLAINED VARIATION,
AND UNEXPLAINED
VARIATION
IN REGRESSIVE ANALYSIS**

**B) Explained Variation:
Deviations of
Y' Scores from $\overline{Y}$**

**C) Unexplained Variation:
Deviations of
Y Scores from Y'**

Source: Adapted from Kirk W. Elifson, Richard P. Runyon, and Audrey Haber, *Fundamentals of Social Statistics*, Second Edition (New York: McGraw-Hill, 1990), 238.

where *se* is the standard error, Y is the observed value of Y, Y' is the pre-dicted value of Y, and N is the number of cases.

Continuing with the example from Figure 12.1, we compute the standard error of estimate by first calculating the predicted value of Y' as follows:

$$Y' = a + bX$$
$$= 4.14 + 0.77X.$$

Using this formula for each value of X, we find Y'.

X	Y	Y' = 4.14 + 0.77X	Y'	(Y – Y')	(Y – Y')²
2	8	Y' = 4.14 + 0.77(2)	5.68	2.32	5.38
3	5	Y' = 4.14 + 0.77(3)	6.45	−1.45	2.10
1	4	Y' = 4.14 + 0.77(1)	4.91	−0.91	0.83
6	9	Y' = 4.14 + 0.77(6)	8.76	0.24	0.06
4	7	Y' = 4.14 + 0.77(4)	7.22	−0.22	0.05
				$\sum$ =	8.42

Using this calculation of the unexplained variation, we can complete the calculation of the standard error of estimate:

$$se = \sqrt{\frac{\sum(Y - Y')^2}{N - 2}}$$
$$= \sqrt{\frac{8.42}{5 - 2}}$$
$$= \sqrt{\frac{8.42}{3}}$$
$$= \sqrt{2.81}$$
$$= 1.68$$

Figures 12.5 and 12.6 above illustrated that a common slope and intercept can represent relationships of very different strength. Thus, it is always useful to evaluate the slope (or the regression coefficient) relative to the standard error. In the present example, the regression coefficient is 0.77 and the standard error is 1.68. This suggests that for each time the value of X increases by one unit, Y increases by 0.77 units. However, on average, we still "misplace" the values of Y by 1.68 units. The obvious question is, "Is the new predicted value of Y a good predictor or a bad predictor?" Or, alternatively, is a standard error of 1.68 large relative to the regression coefficient of 0.77, or is it small?

There are two ways of answering these questions, either by using an inferential statistic and asking how likely this result would occur by chance alone, or by using a summary descriptive statistic, which measures the strength of association. The appropriate statistics—and the ones generated by most of the popular computerized statistics packages—are the t-statistic for statistical inference and r^2 as a measure of the strength of relationship.

Student's t was introduced in Chapter 10 and was given by the formula

$$t = \frac{b}{S_b},$$

where b is the regression coefficient, and S_b is the standard error of estimate.

In the present example, we calculate t as

$$t = \frac{b}{S_b}$$
$$= \frac{0.77}{1.68}$$
$$= 0.46.$$

The degrees of freedom for this example, which has 5 cases and 2 variables, is given by

$$d.f. = N - k - 1$$
$$= 5 - 2 - 1$$
$$= 2.$$

Referring to Appendix A of Chapter 10, which shows the critical values for Student's t, we see that the inclusion of a two-tailed significance test at the 0.05 confidence level, we find the significant value of t is 4.303. The observed value of t in our example is 0.46, which is well short of the critical value required for statistical significance. Therefore, with this very small sample of five cases, we would conclude that the amount of error was such that we have little confidence the relationship did not occur by chance. Therefore, we would not reject the null hypothesis.

To test for strength of relationships in the regression model, we use a correlation coefficient known as **Pearson's r**. In the OLS method, as we have seen, the total squared distances from the regression line should be less than the total squared distances from the mean (also known as the sum of squares, or the **total variance**). Pearson's r asks if this is in fact the case by comparing the **explained variance** in y (i.e., the variance that can be attributed to variation in x) to the total variance:

total variance = explained variance + unexplained variance;

$$\text{Pearson's } r = \frac{\text{explained variance}}{\text{total variance}}.$$

Unfortunately, Pearson's r on its own can be difficult to interpret. However, by squaring Pearson's r, we are able to obtain a better elaboration of its meaning. The result, known as r^2, indicates the proportion of y that can be explained by x and can be read as a percentage. Any value of r^2 tells us the percentage of the variation in y that can be explained by some predictor variable x. Using the regression line, we are able to reduce our prediction errors by the percentage given by the value of r^2. Thus, r^2 is similar (but not identical) in interpretation to PRE measures. We can calculate Pearson's r with the formula

$$r^2 = \frac{\sum(xy)^2}{\sum x^2 \sum y^2}.$$

As with calculating the slope, r^2 requires a series of steps: (1) multiply individual x and y scores; (2) square the products of x and y; (3) sum the squared products; (4) square individual x scores; (5) sum the squared x scores; (6) square the individual y scores; (7) sum the squared y scores; and (8) solve for r^2. Below we have worked through our example data set, showing all calculations for the first case.

x	y	(xy)	$(xy)^2$	x^2	y^2
2	8	$2 \times 8 = 16$	$16 \times 16 = 256$	$2 \times 2 = 4$	$8 \times 8 = 64$
3	5	15	225	9	25
1	4	4	16	1	16
6	9	54	2,916	36	81
4	7	28	784	16	49
			$\sum = 4{,}197$	$\sum = 66$	$\sum = 235$

$$r^2 = \frac{\sum(xy)^2}{\sum x^2 \sum y^2} = \frac{4{,}197}{(66)(235)} = \frac{4{,}197}{15{,}510} = 0.27.$$

In this data set, 27% of the variation in y can be explained by x, and therefore 73% of the variation in y remains unexplained. Note that the r^2 value does not tell you the unit change in y for every unit change in x, nor does it tell you the direction of change. For this information, we need to look at the slope. Also, notice that the r is lowercase. This is used to signify a simple linear regression; only one independent variable is included in the model. When we look at **multiple regression** (multivariate linear models), an uppercase R is used. Multiple regression will be explored in more detail below.

In summary, when using simple linear regression, we take four steps: (1) construct a scatter plot to ensure linearity; (2) calculate the slope and intercept; (3) calculate the standard error of estimate; and (4) calculate r^2 and interpret. Some additional comments should be made about the first step. Readers of academic literature will often find that, after scatter-plotting the variables, the researcher finds that the relationship is not, in fact, linear. However, he or she may wish to use the regression model in the testing due to the power and accuracy advantages of this technique. To overcome this problem of nonlinearity, the researcher will *transform* the variables, for example, using the logarithm of the variable or the cosine and so forth. Various power transformations for variables have been found by statisticians to transform nonlinear relationships into linear relationships. The important thing to remember here is that we are no longer working with the original variables, but rather a transformed variable. For example, we would be looking at the relationship between level of education and the *log* of income. This requires that we

CHECKING YOUR BEARINGS

CALCULATING AND INTERPRETING OLS EQUATIONS AND COEFFICIENTS

For the following data set, (1) test for linearity, (2) calculate and interpret the slope, (3) calculate and interpret the intercept, and (4) calculate and interpret r^2.

Case	Age (years)	Monthly Volunteer Service (hours)
1	18	4
2	63	12
3	47	8
4	56	9
5	36	6
6	42	7

state our interpretations in this form. While this is an advanced technique and therefore beyond the scope of this text, readers can expect to encounter such statistics in the academic literature.

Another technique seen in the literature that is worth noting is the use of **dummy variables**. This technique allows the researcher to use nominal- and ordinal-level variables in the linear model. We use dummy variables in an example below. A second method of exploring the relationships between nominal- or ordinal-level variables and interval-level variables is the **analysis of variance**. A final option, noted earlier in the chapter, is to group the interval-level variable and use nominal- or ordinal-level correlation coefficients.

MULTIPLE REGRESSION ANALYSIS

The simple regression model, using a single independent variable to predict a single dependent variable, can be extended through multiple regression analysis to include additional independent variables. Indeed, one of the most notable advantages of regression analysis is that it enables the simultaneous analysis of multiple predictors in a single equation. This contrasts sharply with the previous discussion of contingency table analysis using nominal or ordinal variables. In the latter instances, the inclusion of additional "control" variables produced a growing number of tables with decreasing cases. For example, we might wish to examine the effect of attitudes of alienation toward the federal government on voting in the 1997 Canadian federal election. The hypothesis may be that those with higher levels of alienation were less likely to vote Liberal than those with lower alienation. Assuming this analysis was conducted on a large sample of 3,000 Canadians, we should be able to examine the impact of alienation with a high level of confidence. Now imagine that we wish to complicate the analysis, by examining whether the relationship varies by province of residence; there is good reason to believe that province may influence the level of alienation and party supported in the election. Using the standard five-region categorization (Atlantic, Quebec, Ontario, Prairies, British Columbia), the inclusion of this single control variable would result in the initial table being broken down into five separate tables, with an average sample size of 600 each (the exact number, of course, would depend upon the number of interviews conducted in each province). We might also expect that voting and level of alienation are influenced by feelings toward the prime minister. If we assume that these feelings are measured on a three-point scale (positive, neutral, negative), the inclusion of the second control variable would produce 3 additional tables for each region, for a total of 15 tables with an average table size of 200 cases. If we assume also that alienation is measured on a three-point scale, and vote has six categories (Liberal, Progressive Conservative, Reform, Bloc Québécois, New Democratic Party, and other), each of the 15 tables would have up to 18 cells. Thus, it can be seen that contingency table analysis, with as few as two control variables, can easily produce a table with too few cases for meaningful analysis.

Yet, the point was made earlier that a characteristic feature of the social sciences, generally, and political science, in particular, is that the world we wish to examine and explain is highly complex, and multiple independent variables may affect any given dependent variable. We often wish to model this complexity into our analysis. Multiple regression analysis is a very useful statistical technique due to its ability to examine simultaneously the effects of multiple independent variables on a dependent variable. The number of independent variables included in multiple regression must be no greater than $N - 1$. When the analysis is based on several thousand cases (Ns), as often is the case with survey research, the number of independent variables that could be included is well beyond the limit of what one might wish to use.

In view of this feature, it is apparent why political scientists may wish to use multiple regression analysis. However, this approach should be used with considerable caution because of the strong assumptions that underlie it. One key assumption is that the independent variables are independent of one another. When this assumption is violated, the analysis suffers from **multicollinearity**, and the coefficients become less robust. A second key assumption is that the regression line exhibits a constant error term across the values of the independent variables. When this assumption holds, the error is referred to as **homoskedastic**, and when the assumption is violated, the error is called **heteroskedastic**. Once again, heteroskedasticity produces less robust regression coefficients. One of the causes of heteroskedasticity is that the relationship between the independent and dependent variables may be nonlinear, as, for example, where Y' may be a logarithmic function of X. In such instances, one may wish to transform the data to more clearly approximate linearity. More generally, though, it is worth noting that the issues of multicollinearity and heteroskedasticity provide significant challenges to the assumptions of multiple regression analysis. Although a more complete discussion of the problems and possible solutions associated with each is beyond the scope of this book, those wishing to apply this statistical technique should consult more advanced materials on the subject.

A third major assumption of multiple regression analysis and, once again, a possible limitation on its use, is the fact that it assumes that the data are measured at the interval level. We suggested in Chapter 2 that few variables in the social sciences meet the rigorous assumption of interval data: the assumption that increases across the values of a variable are characterized by a constant unit. Consider, for example, the 100-point feeling thermometer used in much public opinion and voting research. Respondents are presented with a 100-point thermometer and asked to state their feelings about some political object, for example, Canada or Prime Minister Chrétien. Such measures are often interpreted as interval data. However, if we consider this further, is it reasonable to expect that all voters mean the same thing by the rating of, for example, 65 on such a scale? Does 65 represent considerable "warmth" toward that political object, since it is above the midpoint of 50, or does it suggest considerable dissatisfaction, or "coolness," since it is a full 35 points from 100? Such differences of interpretation speak to the difficulty of assigning an interval category to social data. However, despite such difficulties, many analysts are prepared to accept the conceptual ambiguity in exchange for the more powerful statistical technique available through multiple regression.

With simple regression we examine the effect of a single independent variable on a single dependent variable. We noted that this equation takes the form

$$Y' = a + bX.$$

With multiple regression, we can examine the impact of several independent variables by extending the above equation as

$$Y' = a + b_1X_1 + b_2X_2 + b_3X_3 + \ldots + b_iX_i.$$

The slope (b) of the regression line for each independent variable represents the amount of change in the Y variable for each unit change in X, controlling for (i.e., holding constant) the effects of the other independent variables. It should be borne in mind, though, that the variance within the dependent variable can only be explained once. (Think of the explained variance as a whole pie. Since a part of the pie is eaten by one person, it is no longer available for others to eat. So, too, with explained variance of a dependent variable. Once it has been accounted for by one variable, it is not available for the others.) As additional independent variables are brought into the equation, they can account only for unexplained or residual variance. There are a number of procedures available for specifying the order in which independent variables enter a regression equation, so the effect of this can vary in an equation depending upon which procedure is used. Nonetheless, the general point remains. And it suggests the potential problems that can emerge when independent variables are highly correlated. The effect of two independent variables that have much common explanatory power will show more of the effect attributed to one and less to the other. Thus, it is important to be on the lookout for high levels of correlation among the independent variables.

It should also be noted that the simplified model of the multiple regression equation presented above does not include two different estimates of error. There is error associated with each of the independent variables, and there is error associated with the equation as a whole. Both of these types of error enable us to assess the "goodness of fit" of the model. The error associated with each regression coefficient (i.e., with each b) is called the standard error of estimate (se) and is usually reported along with the regression coefficient. The error associated with the entire equation is referred to as the residual variance. It normally is not reported directly, but can be inferred from its opposite, the explained variance (R^2) of the model, which is normally presented.

When conducting a multiple regression analysis, it is often useful to begin by generating a correlation matrix to examine the relationship between the independent and dependent variables, on the one hand, and among the independent variables. This will enable an initial test of the assumption of independence among the independent variables. Since we discussed previously in the section on simple regression the computation of correlation coefficients, regression coefficients, and standard errors, we will not repeat the computational details for multiple regression. Instead, we will use examples of printed output that one would obtain from a standard statistical package, in this instance, SPSS.

PREDICTING ATTITUDES TOWARD PARTY LEADERS: ASSESSMENTS OF BRIAN MULRONEY

We will use for illustration a model that predicts attitudes toward Brian Mulroney in the 1988 Canadian federal election. You may recall that the 1988 federal election was the second time Canadians went to the polls with Brian Mulroney as Conservative Party leader; the Tories had won a landslide victory under Mulroney in 1984. By 1988, Mulroney's leadership had lost some of its lustre; nonetheless, Mulroney enjoyed leadership ratings as high or higher than the other national party leaders. Because of the assumption that attitudes toward party leaders are important in Canadians' voting decisions (note the use of attitudes toward party leaders as an *independent variable* in the preceding statement), it is useful to try to account for or to explain attitudes toward the leaders (note the switch to viewing this as a *dependent variable*). Based on a reading of previous studies of this topic in the literature in political science, together with extrapolation from some reading you've done in economics and sociology, you might hypothesize the model in Figure 12.8 of the determinants of attitudes toward Mulroney.

Your research design, of course, would provide the rationale for hypothesizing that each of these independent variables affects attitudes toward Mulroney. For example, with the variable "age" you may be testing the theory that voters become more conservative as they age, which leads to the hypothesis that older voters have more positive assessments of Mulroney, the Conservative leader, than do their younger counterparts. Similarly, you might hypothesize that party identification influences attitudes toward party leaders by "colouring" one's view of the political world; Conservatives are more likely than Liberals to view Mulroney through rose-coloured lenses. For the variable examining the impact of the federal government's economic policies, you might be testing the theory that voters are self-interested utility maximizers, and so support the government because they find it in their self-interest to do so. Similarly, you would want to provide a theoretical justification for the inclusion of other independent variables. You are then able to assess the usefulness and accuracy of the competing theories through

FIGURE 12.8

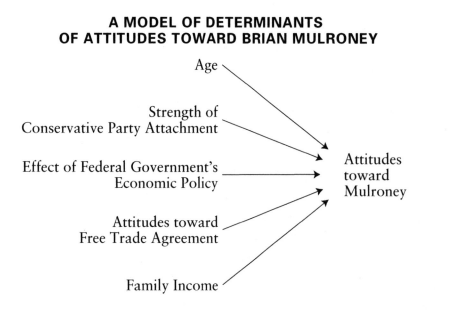

**A MODEL OF DETERMINANTS
OF ATTITUDES TOWARD BRIAN MULRONEY**

the simultaneous inclusion of these variables in the model, which would take the following form:

$$\text{Mulroney} = a + b_1(\text{age}) + b_2(\text{partyid}) + b_3(\text{econpol}) + b_4(\text{freetrad}) + b_5(\text{income}).$$

The correlation matrix for these six variables (i.e., the single dependent variable and five independent variables) is shown in Table 12.1.

The correlation matrix shows that three of the five independent variables are at least moderately related to attitudes toward Mulroney, and two are weakly correlated. It also shows that two of the independent variables—party identification and attitudes toward the Free Trade Agreement—are moderately related ($r = 0.37$). In the context of the 1988 federal election campaign, this latter finding is not surprising, since the Liberal and Conservative parties in particular took such divergent positions on this issue. Although the two independent variables are related, the strength of relationship is not such to suggest that they are measuring the same underlying concept. On the contrary, they clearly seem to be asking quite different things. However, the strength of the correlation is sufficiently large that we need be mindful of possible problems of multicollinearity.

After examining the correlation matrix, we can turn to the multiple regression table. The regression table provides a regression coefficient for each of the independent variables as well as for the constant (i.e., the point of intersection of the Y-axis). In addition, it presents a standard error for each coefficient (printed in parentheses). Normally we are looking for the regression coefficient to be twice the size of the standard error in order that the finding can be said to be "statistically significant." Table 12.2 represents statistical significance with an asterisk (*)

TABLE 12.1

CORRELATION MATRIX OF THE DETERMINANTS OF ATTITUDES TOWARD BRIAN MULRONEY

	Mulroney	Age	Partyid	Econpol	Freetrad	Income
Mulroney	1.000					
Age	0.002	1.000				
Partyid	0.360	0.056	1.000			
Econpol	0.341	−0.001	0.228	1.000		
Freetrad	0.507	0.035	0.372	0.221	1.000	
Income	0.050	−0.098	0.067	0.039	0.172	1.000

TABLE 12.2

THE DETERMINANTS OF ATTITUDES TOWARD BRIAN MULRONEY IN 1988

| | Dependent Variable | |
| | Attitudes toward Mulroney | |
Independent Variables	b	se
Age	−0.04	(0.03)
Partyid	4.99**	(0.61)
Econpol	9.24**	(0.81)
Freetrad	10.32**	(0.51)
Income	−0.45*	(0.20)
Intercept	14.26**	(2.30)

$R^2 = 0.34$.

$*p < 0.05$.

$**p < 0.01$.

at the 0.05 level of significance and two asterisks (**) at the 0.01 level of significance. In addition, a regression table normally presents the R^2 value, indicating the amount of variance in the dependent variable that is accounted for by the dependent variables.

The table shows that three of the five independent variables are very strong and significant predictors of attitudes toward Mulroney, whereas two others are much weaker, and one lacks statistical significance altogether. Regression coefficients should always be interpreted relative to the size of the standard error: the larger the regression coefficient relative to the standard error, the stronger is the effect of the variable. In this example, the strongest predictor of attitudes toward Mulroney is the respondent's position on the Free Trade Agreement issue. The second most important predictor is the perception that the federal government's economic policies have been of benefit to the respondent. Those who felt this way were much more likely to rate Mulroney positively than those who did not. In addition, the strength of Conservative attachment impacted on attitudes toward Mulroney. Each step up the strength of partisanship measure (from non-Conservatives (0) to weak (1), moderate (2), and strong (3) Conservatives) resulted in a 5-point increase in the 100-point feeling thermometer ratings of Mulroney, other things being equal. Income had a weak negative impact on Mulroney ratings; the wealthiest respondents felt less positively toward Mulroney, on average, than their less affluent counterparts. However, the standard error was quite large relative to the regression coefficient, and the relationship barely achieved statistical significance. Finally, the age variable did not achieve statistical significance at all; we would conclude that age does not influence attitudes toward Mulroney, other things being equal.

Thus, the model enabled a fuller comparison of the relative impact of the five independent variables than would have been possible by using a series of contingency tables. It also provides an overall assessment of the importance of these five variables in explaining attitudes toward Mulroney. In this instance, we found that the five independent variables explained 34% of the variance in attitudes toward Mulroney. We might be led to ask what variables could help explain this residual variance. One alternative that has been examined in the political science literature is attitudes toward the personal characteristics of the party leader. Note that in the example just completed, none of the independent variables related to Mulroney's personal characteristics. Instead, we tried to explain attitudes toward Mulroney by reference to respondents' age and income (neither of which was very useful) and by reference to party identifications, perceptions of the government's economic performance, and attitudes toward the Free Trade Agreement, one of the major initiatives of the government. But what about my perceptions of Mulroney's competence or character? Might these also influence my overall assessment of him? The answer, of course, is yes, assessment of Mulroney might very well be influenced by respondents' perception of his personal characteristics. And so, the analysis could continue, with some variables being dropped, such as age and income, and others being added, such as perceptions of Mulroney's character and competence (see Johnston et al. (1992) for a fuller discussion of character and competence as key indicators of leader assessment).

DUMMY VARIABLE REGRESSION ANALYSIS

The preceding example used variables that were assumed to be measured at the interval level to conduct a regression analysis of attitudes toward Mulroney (although in truth several were much closer to ordinal-level variables). But what about those instances in which one or more of the variables of interest are measured at the nominal level. For example, we might be interested in examining the impact of a number of independent variables (such as degree of alienation from the federal government, attitudes toward the party leaders, attitudes toward governmental fiscal restraint) on voting for one of the parties. But the vote variable is nominal level and includes the categories Liberal,

Conservative, Reform, NDP, Bloc Québécois, and other. Since the nominal-level variable is the dependent variable, one would create a series of **dummy variables** and run separate regression equations for each category of the variable (i.e., predict Liberal vote, PC vote, Reform vote, etc.). Each of the parties would be examined through a separate "dummy" variable that measured, for example, Liberals versus non-Liberals, PCs versus non-PCs, and Reform versus non-Reform.

On the other hand, one could also be interested in examining the impact of a nominal-level independent variable. Such variables would be one of two types: dichotomous and multichotomous nominal-level variables. A classic example of a dichotomous nominal-level variable is gender, in which the categories "male" and "female" exhaust the alternatives. One would create a dummy gender variable by labelling one category 1 and the other 0. Thus, one could create a variable called "female" in which female is 1 and male is 0, or a variable called "male" in which male is 1 and female is 0. With a multichotomous nominal variable the situation is only slightly more complicated. Assume we wish to use the variable "region" as an independent variable. In this instance, a series of dummy variables would need to be created, corresponding to the presence and absence of some characteristics. For example, a variable "Atlantic" could be created to signify (1) those who reside in the Atlantic provinces versus (0) those who do not. Similarly, a Quebec variable could be (1) those who reside in Quebec versus (0) those who do not. One could create similar measures for the other regions. However, at this point it is critical to the analysis, when creating a series of dummy variables from a multichotomous nominal-level variable, that one of the categories be suppressed (i.e., not included in the analysis) to prevent the model from being identified and thereby producing meaningless statistics. Instead, the suppressed category becomes the referent with which to conduct analysis on the other variables.

PREDICTING PARTY LEADER RATINGS IN ALBERTA

The following analysis provides an interpretation of a multiple regression analysis that uses a number of dummy variables as independent variables. The analysis that we've chosen for illustrative purposes is an examination of the impact of vote intention and sociodemographic characteristics on ratings of the leaders of the three main parties in Alberta in 1995.

At the time of the 1995 survey, Ralph Klein had been Premier for about two and a half years. He had introduced some of the most substantial budget cuts in Canadian history, a policy that hitherto had been regarded as tantamount to committing political suicide. Yet, public opinion polls were showing that the Conservative Party's support under Klein was, if anything, increasing. Our survey sought to uncover the reasons for the government's growing popularity.

It was our hypothesis that the personal popularity of Ralph Klein had a significant impact on the government's support. Part of the analysis included data in Table 12.3, which brings a wealth of data to bear on the issue of assessments of the party leaders. Let us consider the table in some detail.

The dependent variable is actually three separate dependent variables measuring attitudes toward Ralph Klein, Liberal leader Grant Mitchell, and NDP leader Ross Harvey. Each equation included 22 independent variables, all of which were dummy variables measuring six sociodemographic characteristics (gender, education, age, income, employment status, and area of the province) as well as a vote intention variable (which we conceptualized as a measure of partisanship).

The table includes the regression coefficient *(b)* for each variable and its associated standard error *(se)* in parentheses. It also includes an indication of whether the independent variable has a statistically significant impact on the dependent variable at the 0.05 (*) or 0.01 (**) level of statistical significance. Those entries without an asterisk indicate a relationship that is not statistically significant. The table also includes an entry labelled "constant," which is sometimes called the intercept. This value corresponds to the point at which the regression line crosses the Y-axis. In more substantive terms, it is the predicted value of the attitude toward the party leader without taking account of the independent variables in the table. The final entry in Table 12.3 is the adjusted value of R^2. This value identifies the amount of variation in the dependent variable that is explained by the independent variables.

One of the first things to note about Table 12.3 is that these variables provide quite distinctive explanatory power for the three party leaders: the variance explained for Klein is 47%, compared to only 16% for Mitchell and Harvey. In addition, many of the independent variables have no significant impact on attitudes toward the party leaders. For example, education, age, income, and employment status have no significant effect on ratings of Ralph Klein, other factors being equal. Similarly, these variables tend not to be significantly related to attitudes toward Mitchell or Harvey, with several exceptions. Young respondents (those under the age of 35) evaluated Mitchell and Harvey more posi-

TABLE 12.3

THE EFFECT OF VOTE INTENTION AND SOCIODEMOGRAPHIC CHARACTERISTICS ON PARTY LEADER RATINGS

Criterion Variable	Klein b	Klein (se)	Mitchell b	Mitchell (se)	Harvey b	Harvey (se)
Constant	41.4	(3.8)**	34.6	(3.0)**	31.2	(3.4)**
Vote Intention						
Conservative	29.7	(3.8)**	-3.1	(2.1)	-6.6	(2.4)**
Liberal	-13.1	(3.0)**	9.7	(2.4)**	1.4	(2.7)
NDP	-14.3	(4.0)**	1.2	(3.2)	13.1	(3.6)**
Gender						
Female	-8.3	(2.1)**	4.0	(1.7)*	4.1	(1.9)*
Education						
Less than high school graduation	-3.1	(3.1)	-5.6	(2.4)*	-2.9	(2.8)
University	-3.3	(2.3)	0.5	(1.8)	1.2	(2.0)
Age						
18–24 years	4.2	(3.5)	6.1	(2.8)*	9.3	(3.2)**
25–34 years	4.2	(2.6)	5.9	(2.1)**	7.4	(2.4)**
50–64 years	-0.8	(3.1)	1.2	(2.5)	1.6	(2.9)
65+ years	3.8	(4.5)	-2.4	(3.6)	-4.8	(4.1)
Income						
<$20,000	2.1	(3.6)	0.2	(2.9)	-1.5	(3.3)
$21,000–$40,000	-1.5	(2.7)	1.7	(2.1)	1.4	(2.4)
$61,000–$80,000	-4.9	(3.2)	-1.6	(2.6)	-0.3	(3.0)
$81,000+	-2.0	(3.3)	-1.4	(2.6)	-0.3	(3.0)
Employment Status						
Part-time	-2.8	(3.3)	-2.7	(2.6)	2.1	(3.0)
Retired	2.0	(4.2)	-6.5	(3.4)	-2.0	(3.9)
Unemployed	5.1	(4.8)	-7.0	(3.8)	-1.0	(4.3)
Self-employed	0.3	(3.4)	-4.4	(2.7)	-4.8	(3.1)
Student	0.6	(4.7)	6.3	(3.7)	10.9	(4.3)*
Homemaker	0.0	(4.5)	-5.6	(3.6)	1.9	(4.1)
Area						
Calgary	13.9	(2.8)**	6.8	(2.2)**	1.3	(2.5)
Rural	10.9	(2.5)**	2.6	(2.0)	-1.6	(2.2)
Adjusted R²	0.47**		0.16**		0.16**	

*p < 0.05.
**p < 0.01.

Source: Keith Archer and Roger Gibbins, "What Do Albertans Think? The Klein Agenda on the Public Opinion Landscape," in Christopher J. Bruce et al., eds., *A Government Reinvented* (1997).

tively than did nonstudents, and those with low education had relatively low evaluations of Mitchell.

The three variables with more consistent effects on attitudes toward party leaders were vote intention, gender, and region of the province in which the respondent resides. The most pronounced effects overall are for partisan variables. For example, looking at the predictors of attitudes toward Klein, we find that vote intention, gender, and area of residence are all related at the 0.01 level; this indicates a high level of statistical significance. Next, we compare the size of the regression coefficient in relation to the standard error. In this example, since all the independent variables are dummy variables, ranging from 0 to 1, we can compare the b values, because b is strongly influenced by the measurement of the independent variables. Recall that the regression coefficient indicates the magnitude of increase in the dependent variable for each unit increase in the independent variable. If one of the independent variables has a large range of responses (e.g., a variable measuring age in years, ranging from 18 to 100), it would likely produce a much smaller regression coefficient than, for example, a variable measured from 1 to 3. In the former, each additional year older is likely to produce a small change in the dependent variable, simply because age has over 80 categories.

In the example in Table 12.3, the use of dummy variables for each independent variable enables us to compare across independent variables, since the range of measurement (0–1) is constant. We also will want to compare the relative size of the regression coefficient in relation to the standard error; the greater the distinction between b and se, the stronger the impact of the independent variable.

The strongest determinant of attitudes toward Klein was Conservative vote intention. For example, assessments of Klein on a 100-point scale jumped by almost 30 points among Conservatives, and dropped by 13 or 14 points among Liberals and New Democrats. Note, however, that this trend is much weaker in predicting attitudes toward Mitchell and Harvey. For example, although assessments of Mitchell among Liberal supporters provided an almost 10-point boost for Mitchell, support for the other parties had no significant impact on Mitchell ratings. For Harvey, we see that NDP support has a positive impact and PC support a negative impact. But as with Mitchell, Harvey's "pull" among NDP partisans was considerably less than Klein among Conservatives. Overall, Klein has more appeal among his party's supporters and among nonpartisans or independents in comparison with Mitchell and Harvey.

Gender has an interesting effect in this analysis. The gender variable is measured as 0 equals male and 1 equals female. The coefficient, presented under the heading "female," suggests a higher ranking of the party leaders among women when the coefficient is positive, and a higher ranking of party leaders among men when it is negative. The coefficients in Table 12.3 indicate that Klein's popularity was lower for females than for males, whereas evaluations of Mitchell and Harvey were more positive among women.

The third significant independent variable is area of residence. We find that Klein's support increases among those living in Calgary and among rural residents in comparison with Edmontonians. Similarly, Mitchell was somewhat more popular among those from Calgary than Edmontonians.

On the basis of the data in Table 12.3, we would conclude the following:

- Residents of Alberta have views that were more polarized on Ralph Klein than on the leaders of the other parties. The large number of Conservatives in the province, combined with their strong support of Klein, produced a winning combination.

- A key group in Alberta during the mid-1990s was the group of respondents who were not attached to any party. Klein was rated more highly among this group than were the other party leaders.

- Demographic factors have a mixed effect on attitudes toward the party leaders. Some factors, such as age, education, employment status, and income, have no sustained impact, other things being equal. The lack of a strong impact of social background variables suggests a party system that continues to be characterized by fluid attachments and changeable partisan leanings.

- Gender and region of the province do have an impact on assessments of the party leaders and of Klein in particular. The data provide evidence of a gender gap in leader assessments.

Thus, multiple regression analysis provides considerable analytical advantages. By including a large number of independent variables, we can more accurately map the complex reality of social relations. In addition, the relative impact of variables can be examined directly. It is also worth noting that the logic underlying multiple regression analysis serves in many ways as a gateway to other more complex statistical techniques. Analysis of variance, logistic analysis, path analysis, factor analysis, and LISREL are but a few of the more advanced techniques that are used for quantitative analysis in political science. Once the material from this text has been mastered, you will be prepared to begin exploring these more complex models. In all instances, though, your decision of what statistical technique to employ should be guided by a desire to provide greater insight and understanding of our political world.

SELF-STUDY

1. For the following data set, (1) test for linearity, (2) calculate and interpret the slope, (3) calculate and interpret the intercept, and (4) calculate and interpret r^2.

Case	Age (years)	Job Satisfaction (units)
1	25	8
2	63	2
3	47	4
4	50	3
5	36	5
6	42	4

2. Interpret the following simple regression equations:

   a. political interest (in units) = 18 + 2 age (in years)

   b. final grade (in points) = 5 – 4 skipped lectures

3. Describe and assess the assumptions of regression analysis.

4. Obtain a copy of a machine-readable data set and statistical software such as SPSS. Identify a dependent variable and a set of independent variables. Compute a correlation matrix and discuss. Run a simple regression analysis with one of the independent variables. Now include a second independent variable in the analysis and repeat. Note the differences in the regression coefficient and the standard errors of the variable that initially had been used for the simple regression analysis. Interpret the differences in findings. Now add a third independent variable to the analysis. Repeat the steps from above for both of the first two independent variables.

NOTES

1. There are a number of other assumptions that must be met before using linear regression techniques; see, for example, William D. Berry, *Understanding Regression Assumptions* (Newbury Park, Sage, 1993). This material, however, is beyond the reach of this text.

CHAPTER 13

Writing the Report

DESTINATION

By the end of this chapter the reader should

- have a sound understanding of the strategic considerations in writing a research report;
- understand the components of a research report;
- appreciate the different elements and formats that can be used to convey research findings.

To this point in the book we have discussed a variety of qualitative and quantitative tools for conducting empirical research in political science. In the vast majority of research projects, we are interested in conveying the findings to an external audience; research is seldom done for personal edification alone, although this may be a motivation lying behind the larger research agenda of many scholars. It is through the research report that we convey our findings to an external audience: a course instructor, fellow students, colleagues in a research project, the sponsors of a particular piece of research, the readers of an academic journal, a government department, or members of a community association or interest group. The report, then, is the capstone rather than an incidental stage in the research enterprise. It distils, presents, explains, and defends a complex empirical investigation in a format appropriate to its intended audience.

The research report brings together existing knowledge in the field, new data and information generated by the research project, and the expertise and insights of the author(s). Moreover, it does this in a document designed for a particular audience. In these respects, therefore, the research report is an interactive document. The emphasis is not simply on *presenting* one's research findings; it is on *communicating* those findings to an audience.

In this chapter we will explore the interactive nature of the research report by looking first at audience considerations and then at various components of the report.

FIGURE 13.1

THE RESEARCH REPORT

THE AUDIENCE

A well-written research report is tailored to a specific audience. Because audiences differ in many respects, there is no single, generic format that can be used across all situations. Audiences, for example, will vary in their methodological sophistication. What you might present for the instructor in your course or the assessors for a scholarly journal could be quite different than what you might present in a research report written for a community group. The former will understand quantitative measures of association, such as correlation coefficients, whereas the latter might be best served by a more qualitative discussion of association. It would not be enough, and perhaps would not even be appropriate, to present correlation coefficients; the meaning of covariance must be described in qualitative terms and illustrated. Matters such as tests of significance may be readily understood by one audience, but require detailed explanation for another. Audiences will also differ in the extent to which they are interested in how your research findings fit into the established literature in the field. Your instructor, for example, might be very interested in how you have managed to locate your findings within established disciplinary knowledge, whereas a community group may only want to know the specific results in their case.

All of this means that you must write with a particular audience in mind, remembering their level of sophistication and particular research interests. This does not imply "dumbing down" the analysis for some audiences. It simply means that effective communication entails knowing one's audience and writing to that audience in a way that clearly transmits the material. Of course, this imperative becomes more difficult to handle if you are writing the same research report for more than one audience. In this case, appendices and footnotes can often be used to convey the detail and complexity required by one audience but not another. Keep in mind that statistical or theoretical "jargon" is not necessarily bad; the issue is whether the vocabulary you are using is appropriate for your target audience.

It is useful to remember that research reports will often have secondary audiences which may play an important role in the dissemination of research findings. In this respect, the media is an audience to keep in mind. Research reports are seldom written explicitly for media outlets, and when they are, they convey only a fraction of the information contained in the sample research report to be discussed in this chapter. However, reports written for other audiences often find their way into the media, and through the media into broader dissemination. You would be well advised, therefore, to keep the potential *public use* of research reports in mind. Off-the-cuff comments, or humour directed at a specific audience, may provide unfortunate grist for editorial comment or news coverage. Pleading that you were misquoted or that the comment was taken out of context will not get you off the hook. It makes sense, then, to keep the potential public audience in mind, even if it is not the primary or intended audience. Thus, before finishing the final draft of the research report, give it a last read as if you were encountering your comments in the *Toronto Star* or *Vancouver Sun*. Would you be pleased with the reporting?

CONSTRUCTING AN ARGUMENT

A good research report is more than a collection of findings; it presents a coherent, well-structured, and thoughtful argument. The report is not only addressed to an audience, it tells a story. Thus, like a well-told story, it must set the stage, provide some context, move coherently from step to step, follow a consistent story line or plot, and reach a conclusion. Thinking of the research report in this manner is a good way to keep your specific audience in mind. It also helps you keep to the golden rule of storytelling: don't put your audience to sleep! (Even small children will not be amused if you try to put them to sleep by reading dull political science research reports.) While at times you may find it difficult to write up quantitative research in a lively and engaging fashion, it can be done.

Of course, the analogy between a well-crafted story and the research report should not be overstated, for the two differ in some important respects. The report is theory-driven, or at least reflects theory-driven research, whereas the story sets out to entertain (and perhaps to convey

A POINT ON THE COMPASS ───────────

The Legal Analogue

The components of a good research report are analogous to the components of a good case in a court of law. A lawyer must be aware of legal precedence, just as a scholar must be aware of the existing literature in the field. The lawyer should use her opening statement to capture the interest and attention of the judge and jury. A systematic and solid argument must be developed, one that draws from the facts of the case. While the lawyer is clearly an advocate, it is important not to ignore contrary evidence and soft spots in one's own case. A good argument brings *all* the evidence into play while at the same time emphasizing the most important bits. Ignoring opposing arguments is a poor strategy in court, and ignoring inconvenient or theoretically inconsistent evidence is a poor strategy in the social sciences. A successful lawyer is also attentive to the particular features of the judge and jury, just as the successful research report is crafted with a specific audience in mind. Finally, there must be a strong closing argument; the *facts* cannot be left to speak for themselves. Neither the lawyer nor the social scientist simply reports the facts; it is their expertise that weaves facts into a coherent and compelling argument.

a moral rather than theoretical message). The research report has an explicit thesis statement and employs explicit evidence; the underlying "thesis" of a good story is generally implicit, where it exists at all. The report builds directly and explicitly from the data, and the data analysis is linked back to guiding hypotheses and the literature foundation. Perhaps the most important difference is that the research report is held together by a logical argument, whereas the storyteller can draw from a wider range of integrative techniques including imagery, tone, and metaphor.

It is in the construction of the argument that the expertise of the author comes most clearly into play. The research report should be seen as a creative document, not in the sense of inventing information, but rather in the sense of using language to its fullest extent. It is the creative ability of the author that makes data stand up and jump through hoops.

COMPONENTS OF THE RESEARCH REPORT

As we noted above, there is no generic model of the research report that can be used across all cases and for all audiences. However, there are a number of report *components* that should be addressed in most cases, even though the method by which they are addressed and even the order in which they are addressed will vary according to the report's audience. It is to a discussion of these components that we now turn.

The Abstract or Executive Summary

No matter how brief your report might be, no matter how concise your writing and data presentation, some people will not want to read the entire report, or at least will not want to do so on their first encounter. As a consequence, virtually all publications in scholarly journals include an *abstract* for readers who want to cut to the bottom line, perhaps to determine if the entire report is worth reading in the context of their immediate research interests. Abstracts are particularly useful for readers whose first language is not that in which the report is written; they provide brief overviews that can be digested with minimal effort devoted to translation. For similar reasons of economy, political leaders are notorious for wanting brief *executive summaries*; their days are simply too full to digest more than a page or two. A research study that cannot be summarized on a page, maybe even on a 3×5 card, may never be read, much less digested. Therefore, most reports prepared for public consumption, including those prepared for government departments and interest groups, include executive summaries.

It is excellent practice to prepare an abstract or executive summary for writing projects such as term papers. Think of the exercise as similar to a chance encounter at a party, where someone to whom you are attracted asks you to describe your thesis or current work interests. You have a very limited amount of time in which to make your pitch; if you are too long-winded, too boring, your audience will drift away in pursuit of livelier fare. Thus, you need to present the main findings, and the principal theoretical hooks upon which those findings are hung, in a concise and interesting fashion. A well-written abstract or executive summary does more than describe; it engages and entices the reader. If you find yourself "alone at the party," you know that your executive summary needs more work.

The utility of this writing exercise goes beyond the convenience of busy or lazy readers. It forces you to describe your findings and their significance in a precise, interesting fashion. Writing an abstract or

CHECKING YOUR BEARINGS

WRITING AN ABSTRACT

Find a research report of some reasonable length that does not have an abstract or executive summary attached. You might, for example, use an article in a magazine like *Atlantic Monthly* or *Saturday Night*. Once you have located the article, prepare an abstract of no more than 150 words. Did you find that you were able to capture the major points, findings, and arguments? What kinds of material did you have to set aside? Given your abstract, would there be any need for most readers to read the entire article? What does the article have to offer beyond the information contained in the abstract? Sometimes the answer to this question can be a depressing "very little."

executive summary makes you come to grips with the essential core of your research project. As you will discover, it can often be more difficult to "write short" than to "write long." Preparing the abstract or executive summary could be the most difficult writing assignment in the entire report!

Introduction

The primary objective of the introduction is to capture the reader's interest. The introduction should explain both the research topic and its relevance. It should also present the basic research question or thesis statement, sketch in briefly the line of argument to be pursued, and explain the architecture of the report. A clear and emphatic thesis statement is particularly important. It is not necessary, however, to preview the research findings. The intent is to introduce the reader to the research project, thereby establishing a context for what is to come and an enticement to read the entire report.

Although in many respects the introduction to the research report will resemble the abstract or executive summary, it will generally not provide an overview of the research findings. The similarity between the two will be less disconcerting to you, the author, if you keep in mind that the abstract or executive summary is meant to stand alone; it should be intelligible even if the report itself is never read. The introduction, however, is a part of the research report. It sets the stage for the larger project and is not meant to stand alone.

Literature Review

The importance of this component of the research report will be a function of the report's audience. Reports written as course assignments or submissions to academic journals must include a literature review, although not necessarily labelled as such. The literature review serves a number of important functions. First, readers will expect to see how your research project grew out of the existing literature. What are the holes, lacunae, or contradictions it was designed to address? Are you replicating research done before in a different setting or at a different time? If so, are you incorporating significant innovations in your research design beyond the spatial or temporal change? In short, you must demonstrate how your research fits into the larger body of literature, but is still unique.

Second, the literature review may provide the foundation for many of the empirical measures embedded in your report. For example, if you are exploring the relationship between globalization and support for neoliberalism, you must explain the literature roots of your measures of these terms. As was observed in Chapters 6 and 7, there are many alternative conceptualizations and operationalizations for any given term. If your measure fits with the existing body of literature, its roots within that literature should be acknowledged. If your measure differs from conventional practice, this too should be noted.

Third, readers will want to know how your findings fit into the established knowledge in the field. Have you confirmed, reinforced, challenged, expanded, or contradicted existing knowledge? Have you pushed back the boundaries of knowledge or altered what we thought we knew? All of these questions are important and interesting, and none of them can be addressed unless a literature review has been put into place.

A good literature review is more than a description of what has come before. It should present a *critical* overview of the existing literature, including an identification of problems, omissions, and contradictions. After all, if the existing literature has "said it all," the value of your own report will be thrown into question. Thus, the literature review helps establish the rationale for your research project. It shows how you are improving rather than reinventing the wheel.

Nonetheless, literature reviews tend to be quite abbreviated in reports that are not targeted at an academic or scholarly audience. For example, a report prepared for the Ontario Liberal Party on gender differences in partisan support would be unlikely to include an extensive literature review. The client commissioning the report will be more

A POINT ON THE COMPASS ────────────

Reading Critically

Although students are urged to "read critically," it may not be clear what this exhortation means in practice. By asking the following questions, your skill as a critical reader may be improved:

- Is the methodology adequately explained? Would you be able to replicate the research if you had the resources and inclination to do so?

- Is there a clear thesis statement? Does the author provide a road map for the analysis to come?

- Is there a literature review? Is the research project given a context within social science research on the same or similar topics conducted to date?

- Does the argument proceed logically? Is there a connection between the evidence provided and the conclusions drawn?

- Are the conclusions overstated?

- Is the analysis balanced? Does the author deal with contradictory evidence? With alternative explanations?

interested in the current landscape than in what came before. Even here, however, a brief summary of existing knowledge could be useful to the client. If nothing else, it provides some handle on change over time.

Research Design

In our earlier discussion of the scientific method, we stressed that good science must be capable of replication. If Professor Perrault finds X through method Y, then it should be possible for Professor Santini to come to the same conclusions if she follows the same method. This means that the research method must be clearly identified in the research report. This is done through a detailed explication of the project's *research design*.

But what exactly should be covered in this component of the report? If the research project included the collection of new data, the collection procedures should be described in detail. What ethical issues were encountered, and how were they addressed? Was sampling used? If so, what was the population, the sampling frame, the respondent selection procedures, the possible sources of bias, and the response rate? Were empirical measures constructed for theoretical concepts? If so, how were they constructed? What reliability and validity checks were used? It is not enough, for example, to say that levels of western alienation were higher among native-born British Columbians than they were among recent migrants to the province unless you also indicate how western alienation was measured and how "recent" was defined.

The research design component should cover the study's theoretical points of departure, the hypotheses used to frame the study, and the operationalization of key concepts. It may also provide an explanation for the types of data analysis employed. Perhaps the key thing to remember is that the research design is more than a description of what you did. It is also an *explanation* and a *justification*. If readers are to have confidence in your findings and conclusions, they must first have confidence in your research design.

Presentation of Findings

This is the core of the research report. It is here that your contribution to the existing knowledge in the field is made. Given the importance of this component, there are a number of strategic choices to be made:

- Given that all of the possible findings cannot be presented, which findings should you select and emphasize? Remember, if you try to present everything, the reader may be overwhelmed or lose interest. You must be selective.

- Which findings are important enough to warrant detailed presentation in the form of tables, graphs, and figures? Which findings might be mentioned more in passing?

- What level of methodological sophistication is best for your target audience? Will your audience expect the use of advanced techniques, or would the use of such techniques lose the readers?

Graphical elements can be an important part of a well-designed research report. The old adage that "a picture is worth a thousand words" certainly applies. However, you must remember that figures do not always speak for themselves; they generally require explanatory text. Also remember that graphs and figures can be presented in a variety of ways and that only some ways are appropriate for certain kinds of data. For example, pie charts and bar graphs are appropriate for nominal data, whereas line graphs are not. Complex tables can be difficult for many readers. If they are included, it is essential that you walk the reader through by providing an interpretative guide. Tables are even less likely than charts or graphs to "speak for themselves."

Given that empirical research reports are often "number-rich," you must be careful to use the appropriate numbers. Do not overstate the precision of your data; if the average age of your respondents is 46.253 years, for example, round to 46 years. If a Pearson correlation coefficient is +0.3763, round to +0.38. Be sure to use the appropriate correlation coefficients and to report tests of significance in a consistent manner. Do not, for instance, reject one finding as insignificant at the 0.01 confidence level while accepting another as significant at the 0.05 confidence level.

Also keep in mind the potential importance of negative findings, instances where the null hypothesis was not rejected. Sometimes students and scholars are inclined to stress only positive correlations, the relationships that are found to exist rather than the ones that do not. It may seem uninteresting to report what didn't happen, to note expectations that were not met. However, in many cases negative findings—the absence of a relationship—can be theoretically significant. Imagine, for example, that you were testing for the existence of class differences in partisan support within the Atlantic provinces or for the existence of regional differences in public opinion in the national electorate, and you found there were no statistically significant differences. Such findings could be important in a substantive sense for our understanding of the contemporary political scene. Thus, you should be no quicker to reject negative findings as uninteresting than you should be to accept positive findings as interesting. It may all depend upon your theoretical point of departure and the hypotheses that frame your research.

Discussion

Research reports are often, although not always, constructed so that the data findings are first presented or described and then discussed. In the discussion section the author steps back from the details of the data presentation and tries to explore, usually in more qualitative language, just what the empirical findings might suggest. In many respects, the discussion section involves stepping back from the trees and examining the forest.

It is in the discussion section that you have the opportunity, indeed the obligation, to tie your findings back to the literature review and back to the study's guiding hypotheses. As a general rule, the discussion section should be accessible even to those readers who may not be able to follow the details of your statistical analysis. Many readers will rely upon you to make sense of the data analysis for them; they may read the literature review and research design, and then skip to the discussion.

Conclusions

The conclusions should take the reader back to the report's introduction. Recap the research problem and the thesis statement. Remind the reader what you set out to do, and then discuss to what extent those objectives have been accomplished. Remember, data seldom speak for themselves. You cannot assume that the reader will draw the same conclusions from the data analysis that you yourself have drawn. You need, therefore, to provide some interpretation of the findings.

Some readers will only read your conclusions; they will skip to the bottom line. As a consequence, your conclusions should be strongly and clearly stated. At the same time, you should not ignore nuances that may have emerged in the data analysis or discussion sections. If some readers are to carry away only the concluding paragraph or two of your report, you want to be sure that they do not have a distorted impression of your findings.

The concluding section of the research report often contains recommendations for action, for the next steps that should be taken. If the report is aimed at the scholarly community, such recommendations might be suggestions for future research. If you could do the research again, what might you do differently, and why? Has your research closed off some doors for future research while opening others? If the report is aimed more for a nonacademic audience, the recommendations are more likely to be policy recommendations than suggestions for future research: "In light of the findings of this report, we recommend that your organization take the following steps if it wants to accomplish...." In both instances, the same question applies: "Are your findings actionable?"

References

The list of references at the end of the research report serves two primary functions. First, it provides specific bibliographical details for any theoretical or empirical citations in your report. It therefore allows your reader, should he or she be inclined to do so, to backtrack through the literature foundation for your research. Second, it provides readers with leads they can follow if your findings spark interest. Thus the reference section is an essential complement to the literature review.

Sometimes authors will inflate the reference section by including works that played a peripheral role at best in the research project. While it is essential to include full bibliographic references for any works directly cited in the research report, avoid excess padding. Research reports are seldom judged by the number of references; thoughtful readers expect you to be as selective in your references as you were in the presentation of your findings.

THE FINAL POLISH

We live in a time when personal computers and sophisticated printers mean that even the shoddiest piece of research can be presented in a *very* impressive way. While we would never suggest that style can substitute for content, it is essential to pay close attention to the manner in which research findings are presented. Is the layout of the research report as attractive as possible? Does it have an attractive cover, a useful table of contents? Have you carefully checked for spelling and grammatical mistakes? Remember, if you get the small things wrong, if the report is poorly written or presented, the reader may assume that you have the big picture wrong as well. Packaging is critically important, for it conveys a sense of how careful you have been and how seriously you take the report. Sloppy work is quickly dismissed.

Remember, the report is the capstone. This is where it all comes together. A great deal of painstaking work can be discounted if it is poorly presented. The theoretical import of your work can be lost, along with the implications of your empirical evidence. Thus you owe it to yourself, and to others who may be involved in the research enterprise, to put as much effort into the presentation of your research as you did into gathering the empirical evidence.

WORKING AS A TEAM

1. If you are preparing draft research reports as course assignments, try exchanging drafts and writing up an abstract of no more than 100 words. Read the abstract back to the original author. Does the author accept the abstract as a reasonable distillation? Could you reduce the abstract to 75 words? To 50 words?

2. Have your group pull together a variety of research reports prepared in different formats and for different audiences.

You might, for example, use royal commission reports, stories in news magazines, academic journals, and trade books. How do these different research reports compare with respect to format and components? Do they do the same things in different ways, or do they have little in common?

SELF-STUDY

1. Take one or more of your old term papers, and prepare an abstract of 150 words. Were you successful in capturing the core of the paper? What important elements, if any, were lost? What do you feel needed to be said, but was squeezed out? Now see if you can trim this abstract to only 100 words. Can you trim it to 75 words? How low can you go before the abstract becomes useless?

2. Select two articles from a recent volume of the *Canadian Journal of Political Science* or *Canadian Public Policy*. What similarities and differences exist between the two? Do they present their findings in a similar way? Do they use abstracts in a similar fashion? Do they both include explicit research designs and thesis statements?

References

Akeroyd, Anne V. "Personal Information and Qualitative Research Data: Some Practical and Ethical Problems Arising from Data Protection Legislation." In Nigel G. Fielding and Raymond M. Lee, eds. *Using Computers in Qualitative Research*. London: Sage Publications, 1991: 89–106.

Alberts, Sheldon and Rebecca Eckler. "Income Gap Widening." *Calgary Herald*. 26 July 1996: A1.

Albrow, Martin. *Bureaucracy*. London: Pall Mall Press, 1970.

Almond, Gabriel and Sidney Verba. *The Civic Culture*, abridged ed. Boston: Little Brown, 1965.

Ambrose, Jay. "We're Smart Enough to Know How Dumb IQ Tests Are." *The Globe and Mail*. 3 August 1996: D1.

Archer, Keith and Faron Ellis. "Opinion Structure of Party Activists: The Reform Party of Canada." *Canadian Journal of Political Science* XXVII.2 (June 1994): 277–308.

Archer, Keith and Roger Gibbins. "What Do Albertans Think? The Klein Agenda on the Public Opinion Landscape." In Christopher J. Bruce et al., eds. *A Government Reinvented: A Study of Alberta's Deficit Elimination Program*. Toronto: Oxford University Press, 1997, 462–85.

Archer, Keith, Roger Gibbins, Rainer Knopff, and Les Pal. *Parameters of Power: Canada's Political Institutions*. Toronto: Nelson Canada, 1995.

Archer, Keith and Alan Whitehorn. "Opinion Structure Among New Democratic Party Activists: A Comparison with Liberals and Conservatives." *Canadian Journal of Political Science* XXIII.1 (March 1990): 101–13.

Atkinson, Michael M. and Maureen Mancuso. "Do We Need a Code of Conduct for Politicians? The Search for an Elite Political Culture of Corruption in Canada." *Canadian Journal of Political Science* XVIII.3 (September 1985): 459–80.

Avio, Kenneth L. "The Quality of Mercy: Exercise of the Royal Prerogative in Canada." *Canadian Public Policy* XIII.3 (September 1987): 366–79.

Babbie, Earl. *The Practice of Social Research*, 5th ed. Belmont, CA: Wadsworth, 1989.

Bahry, Donna L. "Crossing Borders: The Practice of Comparative Research." In Jarol B. Manheim and Richard C. Rich. *Empirical Political Analysis: Research Methods in Political Science*. New Jersey: Prentice-Hall, 1981: 230–41.

Bailey, Kenneth D. *Methods of Social Research*. New York: The Free Press, 1978.

Bakvis, Herman and Laura G. Macpherson. "Quebec Block Voting and the Canadian Electoral System." *Canadian Journal of Political Science* XXVIII.4 (December 1995): 659–92.

Banks, Russell. *Affliction*. Toronto: McClelland & Stewart, 1989.

Barrie, Doreen and Roger Gibbins. "Parliamentary Careers in the Canadian Federal State." *Canadian Journal of Political Science* XXII.1 (March 1989): 137–45.

Baxter-Moore, Nicolas, Terrance Carroll, and Roderick Church. *Studying Politics: An Introduction to Argument and Analysis*. Toronto: Copp Clark Longman Ltd., 1994.

Belson, William A. *Validity in Survey Research*. Aldershot: Gower Publishing, 1986.

Berg, Bruce L. *Qualitative Research Methods in the Social Sciences*. Boston: Allyn and Bacon, 1989.

Berry, William D. *Understanding Regression Assumptions*. Newbury Park: Sage Publications, 1993.

Bibby, Reginald W. *The Bibby Report: Social Trends Canadian Style*. Toronto: Stoddart, 1995.

Black, Conrad. *Duplessis*. Toronto: McClelland & Stewart, 1977.

Blais, André, Pierre Martin, and Richard Nadeau. "Attentes économiques et linguistiques et appui à la souverainete du Québec: une analyse prospective et comparative." *Canadian Journal of Political Science* XXVIII.4 (December 1995): 637–57.

Bouchard, Lucien. *On the Record* (trans. Dominique Cliff). Toronto: Stoddart, 1994.

Brannen, Julie. "Research Note: The Study of Sensitive Subjects." *Sociological Review* 36 (1988): 552–63.

Broadhead, Robert S. "Human Rights and Human Subjects: Ethics and Strategies in Social Science Research." *Sociological Inquiry* 54 (1984): 107–23.

Brodie, Ian and Neil Nevitte. "Evaluating the Citizens' Constitution Theory." *Canadian Journal of Political Science* XXVI.2 (June 1993): 235–59.

Brodie, M. Janine and Jane Jenson. *Crisis, Challenge and Change: Party and Class in Canada*. Toronto: Methuen, 1980.

Cairns, Alan C. "Political Science in Canada and the Americanization Issue." *Canadian Journal of Political Science* VIII.2 (June 1975): 191–234.

———. "A Defence of the Citizens' Constitution Theory: A Response to Ian Brodie and Neil Nevitte." *Canadian Journal of Political Science* XXVI.2 (June 1993): 261–67.

Callahan, Daniel and Bruce Jennings. *Ethics, The Social Sciences, and Policy Analysis*. New York: Plenum Press, 1983.

Campbell, Angus, Philip E. Converse, Warren E. Miller, and Donald E. Stokes. *The American Voter*. New York: John Wiley and Sons, 1960.

Canadian Press. "Public Jittery About Pensions." *Calgary Herald*. 20 June 1996: A1.

Carroll, James. "Uncle Sam's New Stinginess." *The Boston Globe*. 23 July 1996: A13.

Carroll, Lewis. *Alice's Adventures in Wonderland and Through the Looking Glass*. Notes by Martin Gardner. New York: Random House, 1990: 126.

Chadwick, Bruce A., Howard M. Bahr, and Stan L. Albrecht. *Social Science Research Methods*. New Jersey: Prentice-Hall, 1984.

Chan, Alfred L. and Paul Nesbitt-Larking. "Critical Citizenship and Civil Society in Contemporary China." *Canadian Journal of Political Science* XXVIII.2 (June 1995): 291–309.

Chrétien, Jean. *Straight from the Heart*. Toronto: Key Porter Books, 1994.

Clarke, Harold, Jane Jenson, Lawrence LeDuc, and Jon Pammett. *Political Choice in Canada*. Toronto: McGraw-Hill Ryerson, 1979.

Clarke, Harold D. and Allan Kornberg. "Evaluations and Evolution: Public Attitudes Toward Canada's Federal Parties, 1965–1991." *Canadian Journal of Political Science* XXVI. 2 (June 1993): 287–311.

Clarkson, Stephen and Christina McCall. *Trudeau and Our Times. Volume 1: The Magnificent Obsession*. Toronto: McClelland & Stewart, 1990.

Constantatos, Christo and Edwin G. West. "Measuring Returns from Education: Some Neglected Factors." *Canadian Public Policy* XVII.2 (June 1991).

Dahl, Robert. *Who Governs? Democracy and Power in an American City*. New Haven: Yale University Press, 1961.

———. *Democracy and Its Critics*. New Haven: Yale University Press, 1989.

Davis, James A. *The Logic of Causal Order*. Newbury Park: Sage Publications, 1985.

DeKeseredy, Walter. "Addressing the Complexities of Woman Abuse in Dating: A Response to Gartner and Fox." *Canadian Journal of Sociology* 19.1 (1994): 75–80.

DeKeseredy, Walter and Katherine Kelly. "The Incidence and Prevalence of Woman Abuse in Canadian University and College Dating Relationships." *Canadian Journal of Sociology* 18.2 (1993): 137–59.

Dolence, Michael G. and Donald M. Norris. *Transforming Higher Education: A Vision for Learning in the 21st Century.* Ann Arbor, MI: Society for College and University Planning, 1995.

Downs, Anthony. *An Economic Theory of Democracy.* New York: Harper and Row, 1957.

Driscoll, Kathleen and Joan McFarland. "The Impact of a Feminist Perspective on Research Methodologies: Social Sciences." In Winne Tomm, ed. *The Effects of Feminist Approaches on Research Methodologies.* Waterloo: Wilfrid Laurier University Press, 1989.

Duelli-Klein, R. "How to Do What We Want to Do: Thoughts About Feminist Methodology." In G. Bowles and R. Duelli-Klein, eds. *Theories of Women's Studies.* London: Routledge and Kegan Paul, 1983.

Duffy, Andrew and Brad Evenson. "Canadians Seek Truth, Integrity from Leaders." *Calgary Herald.* 29 June 1996: A8.

Duverger, Maurice. *Political Parties.* London: Methuen and Co., 1964.

Eagles, Munroe. "Money and Votes in Canada: Campaign Spending and Parliamentary Election Outcomes, 1984 and 1988." *Canadian Public Policy* XIX.4 (December 1993): 432–49.

Edwards, Allen L. *Statistical Analysis.* New York: Holt, Rinehart and Winston, 1969.

Edwards, Allen L. *Statistical Analysis,* 3rd ed. New York: Holt, Rinehart and Winston; McGraw-Hill, 1990: 235–38.

Elifson, Kirk W., Richard P. Runyon, and Audrey Haber. *Fundamentals of Social Statistics,* 2nd ed. New York: McGraw-Hill, 1990.

Elkins, David J. "Party Identification: A Conceptual Analysis." *Canadian Journal of Political Science* XI. 2 (June 1978): 419–21.

Eulau, Heinz. *The Behavioral Persuasion in Politics.* New York: Random House, 1964 (c. 1963).

Finch, Janet. "'It's Great to Have Someone to Talk To': The Ethics and Politics of Interviewing Women." In Colin Bell and Helen Roberts, eds. *Social Researching: Politics, Problems, Practice.* London: Routledge and Kegan Paul, 1984: 70–87.

Flanagan, Tom. *Waiting for the Wave: The Reform Party and Preston Manning.* Toronto: Stoddart, 1995.

Fox, Bonnie J. "On Violent Men and Female Victims: A Comment on DeKeseredy and Kelly." *Canadian Journal of Sociology* 18.3 (1993): 321–24.

Frohlich, Norman and Irvin Boschmann. "Partisan Preference and Income Redistribution: Cross-National and Cross-Sexual Results." *Canadian Journal of Political Science* XIX.1 (March 1986): 53–69.

Gadd, Jane. "AIDS Spreading Among Canadians." *The Globe and Mail.* 3 July 1996: A6.

Gartner, Rosemary. "Studying Woman Abuse: A Comment on DeKeseredy and Kelly." *Canadian Journal of Sociology* 18.3 (1993): 313–20.

Gibbons, Jean Dickinson. *Nonparametric Methods for Quantitative Analysis.* New York: Holt, Rinehart and Winston, 1976.

Gidengil, Elisabeth. "Canada Votes: A Quarter Century of Canadian National Election Studies." *Canadian Journal of Political Science* XXV.2 (June 1992): 219–48.

Glaser, Barney G. *Emergence vs. Forcing: Basics of Grounded Theory Analysis.* Mill Valley, CA: Sociology Press, 1992.

Goldberg, Michael A. and Maurice D. Levi. "Growing Together or Apart: The Risks and Returns of Alternative Constitutions of Canada." *Canadian Public Policy* XX.4 (December 1994): 341–52.

Grant, Judith. *Fundamental Feminism: Contesting the Core Concepts of Feminist Theory.* New York: Routledge, 1993.

Griffin, John Howard. *Black Like Me,* 2nd ed. Boston: Houghton Mifflin, 1977.

Hartz, Louis. *The Founding of New Societies: Studies in the History of the U.S., Latin America, South Africa, Canada and Australia.* New York: Harcourt, Brace, and World, 1964.

Hayslett, H.T., Jr. *Statistics Made Simple.* New York: Doubleday, 1968.

Heard, Andrew D. "The Charter in the Supreme Court of Canada: The Importance of Which Judges Hear an Appeal." *Canadian Journal of Political Science* XXIV.2 (June 1991): 289–307.

Hill, Carey Anne. *New Technologies and Territorial Identities in Western Canada.* Unpublished M.A. thesis. Department of Political Science, University of Calgary, 1998.

Hite, Shere. *The Hite Report: A Nationwide Study of Female Sexuality.* New York: Macmillan, 1976.

———. *The Hite Report on Male Sexuality.* New York: Ballantine Books, 1981.

Horowitz, Gad. "Conservatism, Liberalism and Socialism in Canada: An Interpretation." *Canadian Journal of Political Science and Economics* 32.2 (1966): 143–71.

Jackson, Winston. *Methods: Doing Social Research.* Scarborough: Prentice-Hall, 1995.

Jahoda, Marie. "To Publish or Not to Publish?" *Journal of Social Issues* 37 (1981): 208–20.

Jenson, Jane. "Party Loyalty in Canada: The Question of Party Identification." *Canadian Journal of Political Science* 8 (1975): 543–53.

———. "Comment: The Filling of Wine Bottles Is Not Easy." *Canadian Journal of Political Science* XI. 2 (June 1978): 437–38.

Johnston, Richard, André Blais, Henry E. Brady, and Jean Crête. *Letting the People Decide: Dynamics of a Canadian Election.* Montreal: McGill-Queen's University Press, 1992.

Kay, Barry J. "By-Elections as Indicators of Canadian Voting." *Canadian Journal of Political Science* XIV.1 (March 1981): 37–52.

Kelly, Katherine D. "The Politics of Data." *Canadian Journal of Sociology* 19.1 (1994): 81–85.

Key, V.O. *The Responsible Electorate.* Cambridge, MA: Harvard University Press, 1966.

Kimmel, Allan J. *Ethics and Values in Applied Social Research.* Newbury Park: Sage Publications, 1988.

Kuhn, Thomas S. *The Structure of Scientific Revolutions,* 2nd ed., enlarged. Chicago: University of Chicago Press, 1970.

Lane, Robert E. *Political Ideology: Why the American Common Man Believes What He Does.* New York: The Free Press, 1962.

Lanoue, David J. "Debates That Mattered: Voters' Reaction to the 1984 Canadian Leadership Debates." *Canadian Journal of Political Science* XXIV.1 (March 1991): 51–65.

Lather, Patti. "Feminist Perspectives on Empowering Research Methodologies." *Women's Studies International Forum* 11 (1988): 569–81.

Lazerwitz, Bernard. "Sampling Theory and Procedures." In Hubert M. Blalock Jr. and Ann B. Blalock, eds. *Methodology in Social Research.* New York: McGraw-Hill, 1968: 278–328.

LeDuc, Lawrence, Harold Clarke, Jane Jenson, and Jon Pammett. "Partisan Instability in Canada: Evidence from a New Panel Study." *American Political Science Review* 78 (1984): 470–83.

Lee, Raymond M. *Doing Research on Sensitive Topics.* London: Sage Publications, 1993.

Lee, Raymond M. and Claire M. Renzetti. "The Problems of Researching Sensitive Topics." *American Behavioral Scientist* 1:33 (May–June 1990): 510–28.

Liemohn, Wedell. "Research Involving Human Subjects." *Research Quarterly* 50.2 (1979): 157–63.

Lipset, Seymour Martin. *Continental Divide: The Values and Institutions of the United States and Canada.* New York: Routledge, 1990.

Lowe, Graham S. and Harvey Krahn. "Job-Related Education and Training Among Younger Workers." *Canadian Public Policy* XXI.3 (September 1995): 362–78.

Mackie, Richard. "Quebeckers Feel Sovereignty Will Bring Greater Prosperity." *The Globe and Mail.* 24 August 1996: A5.

Maclean's. "False Positive and False Negative." 17 February 1997: 70.

Manheim, Jarol B. and Richard C. Rich. *Empirical Political Analysis: Research Methods in Political Science.* Englewood Cliffs, NJ: Prentice-Hall, 1981.

McCall, Christina and Stephen Clarkson. *Trudeau and Our Times. Volume 2: The Heroic Delusion.* Toronto: McClelland & Stewart, 1994.

McCall, Robert B. *Fundamental Statistics for Behavioral Sciences,* 4th ed. New York: Harcourt Brace Jovanovich, 1986.

McIlroy, Anne. "Dingwall Pledges Tests Will Include Women." *The Globe and Mail.* 10 August 1996: A1.

Michels, Robert. *Political Parties: A Sociological Study of the Oligarchical Tendencies of Modern Democracy.* New York: The Free Press, 1962.

Milbrath, Lester. *Political Participation.* New York: Rand McNally, 1965.

Milgram, Stanley. "Behavioral Study of Obedience." *Journal of Abnormal and Social Psychology* 67 (1963): 371–78.

MRC, NSERC, and SSHRC. *Integrity in Research and Scholarship: A Tri-Council Policy Statement.* January 1994.

Nachmias, David and Chaua Nachmias. *Research Methods in the Social Sciences,* 3rd ed. New York: St. Martin's, 1987.

Neuman, W. Lawrence. *Social Research Methods: Qualitative and Quantitative Approaches,* 2nd ed. Boston: Allyn and Bacon, 1994.

———. *Social Research Methods: Qualitative and Quantitative Approaches.* 3rd ed. Boston: Allyn and Bacon, 1997.

Nevitte, Neil and Roger Gibbins. *New Elites in Old States: Ideologies in the Anglo-American Democracies.* Toronto: Oxford University Press, 1990.

Nie, Norman, Sidney Verba, and John Petrocik. *The Changing American Voter.* Cambridge, MA: Harvard University Press, 1976.

Norusis, Marija J. *SPSS Introductory Statistics Student Guide.* USA: SPSS Inc., 1990.

Ornstein, Michael D. and H. Michael Stevenson. "Elite and Public Opinion Before the Quebec Referendum: A Commentary on the State in Canada." *Canadian Journal of Political Science* XIV.4 (December 1981): 745–74.

Pedhauser, Elazar J. *Multiple Regression in Behavioural Research,* 2nd ed. USA: Harcourt Brace, 1982.

Reinharz, Shulamit. *Feminist Methods in Social Research.* New York: Oxford University Press, 1992.

Roberts, Alasdair and Jonathan Rose. "Selling the Goods and Services Tax: Government Advertising and Public Discourse in Canada." *Canadian Journal of Political Science* XXVIII.2 (June 1995): 311–30.

Roberts, Helen. "Putting the Show on the Road: The Dissemination of Research Findings." In Colin Bell and Helen Roberts, eds. *Social Researching: Politics, Problems, Practice.* London: Routledge and Kegan Paul, 1984: 199–212.

Roethlisberger, F. J. and W. J. Dickenson. *Management and the Worker.* Cambridge: Harvard University Press, 1939.

Seidman, I.E. *Interviewing as Qualitative Research*. New York: Teachers College Press, 1991.

Shapiro, D.M. and M. Stelcner. "The Persistence of the Male-Female Earnings Gap in Canada, 1970–1980: The Impact of Equal Pay Laws and Language Policies." *Canadian Public Policy* XIII.4 (10 December 1987): 462–76.

Shea, Christopher. "Psychologists Debate Accuracy of 'Significance Test.'" *The Chronicle of Higher Education*, 16 August 1996: A12, A17.

Sieber, J.E. and B. Stanley. "Ethical and professional dimensions of socially sensitive research." *American Psychologist* 43 (1988): 49–55.

Sieber, Sam D. "The Integration of Field Work and Survey Methods." *American Journal of Sociology* 78: 1335–59.

Simon, Julian. "Earth's Doomsayers Are Wrong." *The Next City* 1.2 (1995): 10–11.

Singer, Eleanor. "Informed Consent: Consequences for Response Rate and Response Quality in Social Surveys." *American Sociological Review* 43 (1978): 144–62.

———. "Informed Consent Procedures in Surveys: Some Reasons for Minimal Effects on Response." In Robert F. Boruch and Joe E. Cecil, eds. *Solutions to Ethical and Legal Problems in Social Research*. New York: Academic Press, 1983: 183–211.

Singleton, Royce, Jr., Bruce C. Straits, Margaret M. Straits, and Ronald J. McAllister. *Approaches to Social Research*. New York: Oxford University Press, 1988.

Skocpol, Theda. *States and Social Revolutions: A Comparative Analysis of France, Russia, and China*. Cambridge: Cambridge University Press, 1979.

Smiley, Donald. *Canada in Question: Federalism in the Eighties*, 3rd ed. Toronto: McGraw-Hill Ryerson, 1980.

Smith, Denis. *Rogue Tory: The Life and Legend of John G. Diefenbaker*. Toronto: Macfarlane, Walter & Ross, 1995.

Soderlund, Walter C., Ronald H. Wagenberg, and Ian C. Pemberton. "Cheerleader or Critic? Television News Coverage in Canada and the United States of the U.S. Invasion of Panama." *Canadian Journal of Political Science* XXVII.3 (September 1994): 580–604.

Statistics Canada. *The Labour Force* (71-001, December 1989).

Steinem, Gloria. *Outrageous Acts and Everyday Rebellions*. New York: Holt, Rinehart and Winston, 1983.

Strauss, Stephen. "Landmark Male Bisexuality Survey Seeks Basic Truths." *The Globe and Mail*. 2 April 1996: A6.

Studlar, Donley T. and Richard E. Matland. "The Growth of Women's Representation in the Canadian House of Commons and the Election of 1984: A Reappraisal." *Canadian Journal of Political Science* XXVII.11 (March 1994): 53–79.

Tavris, Carol. *The Mismeasure of Woman*. New York: Touchstone, 1992.

Tocqueville, Alexis de. *Democracy in America*. New York: Amereon House, 1863.

Verba, Sidney and Norman Nie. *Participation in America: Political Democracy and Social Equality*. New York: Harper and Row, 1972.

Walker, James. "Charest Would Boost Merged Reform, Conservative Parties: Poll." *The Financial Post*, 18 May 1996: 5.

Warwick, Donald P. and Thomas F. Pettigrew. "Towards Ethical Guidelines for Social Science Research in Public Policy." In Daniel Callahan and Bruce Jennings, eds. *Ethics, the Social Sciences, and Policy Analysis*. New York: Plenum Press, 1983: 335–69.

Watts, Ronald L. "Executive Federalism: The Comparative Context." In David P. Shugarman and Reg Whitaker, eds. *Federalism and Political Community: Essays in Honour of Donald Smiley*. Peterborough: Broadview Press, 1989: 439–59.

Wente, Margaret. "The Feminine Olympics." *The Globe and Mail*. 3 August 1996: D7.

White, Louise G. *Political Analysis*. 3rd ed. Belmont: Wadsworth Publishing, 1994.

Wright, R.L.D. *Understanding Statistics*. New York: Harcourt Brace Jovanovich, 1976.

York, Geoffrey. "Russian Media Accused of Bias." *The Globe and Mail*. 6 July 1996: A1, A12.

Index

Abstract, 363–64
Academic freedom, 69
Accidental sampling, 227
Accuracy, 189
   See also Reliability; Validity
Action research. *See* Applied research
Alpha levels. *See* Confidence levels
Alternative explanations, 49, 58, 96
   See also Hypothesis testing
Alternative hypothesis, 51, 53
Analysis of variance, 253–56, 344
Animal testing, 68
Anonymity, 73–77, 80
ANOVA. *See* Analysis of variance
Appendices, 360–61
Applied research, 37–39, 72, 85
Averages. *See* Central; Mean; Median;
   Mode; Tendency

Background noise. *See* Noise
Bandwagon effect, 86
Basic research, 37, 39
Before–after study, 101–2
   See also Experimental research
Bias, 93–95, 103, 135, 197, 226
Bibby Reports, 109–10
Bibliography. *See* References
Bivariate relationship, 57, 256, 292,
   298, 300, 310, 318

Canadian National Election Study
   (CNES), 106, 112, 120, 181, 247
   See also Survey research
Case studies, 97, 114–15
Categorical concept, 41, 153–54, 183,
   298
   See also Nominal; Ordinal variables
Causal models, 56–57, 149, 181,
   318–20, 322, 324, 348
   voting and, 158–60
Causal relationship, 11, 13, 15, 22–23,
   28–29, 96, 102, 150–51, 156–60
Cells, 51, 312–13
Central-limit theorem, 250–53
Central tendency (measures of), 232,
   232–42, 253, 255–56
   See also Mean; Median; Mode
Charts, 368

Chi-square, 275, 277–84
   distribution, 273–74
   See also Cramer's V
Citations. *See* References
Class. *See* Social class
Cluster sampling, 225–26
Coding, 144–45
Column, 51
   marginals, 52, 257–59
   percentages, 258–60
Comparative research, 96, 100, 136–44
   See also Survey research; System-
   level analysis
Concepts, 25–26, 40–43, 93, 150, 172
   See also Categorical concept;
   Continuous concept;
   Multidimensional concept;
   Typology
Conceptualization, 152–68, 170
Concordant pairs, 311–14
Confidence interval, 218
Confidence levels, 82, 102, 227,
   267–72
   See also Type I error; Type II error
Confidentiality, 73–77, 80
Conflict of interest, 84
Content analysis, 96, 112–14, 145
Contingency tables, 51–54, 256–61,
   298, 310–12, 323, 344–45
   with controls, 325–29
   See also Cells; Column; Row
Continuous concept, 41–42, 153–54,
   183, 298
   See also Interval variable
Control group, 98, 102
Controls, 10, 58–60, 96, 100, 260
   See also Causal models
Convenience sampling. *See* Pilot studies
Convergent validity, 190–91
Correlation, 23, 43, 50, 102, 347
   moderate, 53–55
   negative, 44
   perfect, 52–55
   positive, 44
Correlational analysis, 256, 260
Correlation coefficient, 298–304, 368
   See also Interval levels of
   measurement; Nominal; Ordinal

Covariance, 44
Covert participant observation, 78
Cramer's V, 304, 306–9
Cross-tabulation tables. *See* Contingency tables
Cumulative percentages, 233–34
Curvilinear relationship, 260, 310–11

Data
    grouping, 188–89
Data analysis
    ethical considerations, 82
    qualitative, 144–45
Data collection, 26, 124
Data distribution, 272
    chi-square, 273–74
    f, 274
    Student's t, 273
    z-scores, 273
Data matrix, 145
Deductive reasoning, 166–67, 46–47
Degree of freedom, 280–81
Dependent event, 21–23, 149
Dependent variable, 21–22, 26, 298, 313
Descriptive research, 96, 297
Descriptive statistics, 232
    See also Central tendency; Variation
Determinism, 15, 31, 56
Deviation. *See* Range; Standard deviation; Variation
Difference of means, 284
Disclosure of findings, 87
Discordant pairs, 311–14
Discriminant validity, 191
Discussion, 268–69
Dispersion, 232, 243, 253–56
Dissemination, 85–87
Divergent validity. *See* Discriminant validity
Double-blind experiment, 98
Downs, Anthony, 42, 166
Dummy variable, 187–88, 344, 352
Dummy variable analysis, 351–52

Ecological fallacy, 60
Education, 153–58
Elite interviewing, 73, 123–28
    framework, 126–28
E-mail surveys, 77
Empirical analysis, 5–9, 20, 25, 31–32
Empirical methodologies, 93, 95
Empirical research, 36, 146
    quantitative approach, 36, 37, 92–117

qualitative research, 36, 118–47
Endogenous variance, 149
Equivalent measures, 142
Errors. *See* Nonrandom errors; Random errors
Ethnography. *See* Observation research
Evidence, 2
    hard, 95
Executive summary. *See* Abstract
Exogenous variance, 149
Experimental analogy, 100
Experimental research, 96, 98–103
    steps of, 99
    See also Posttest; Pretest; Treatment
Explanatory research, 96, 297
Exploratory research, 95, 227, 269
External validity, 96, 100, 102, 109, 115, 120
Extrapolation, 165–67

Face validity, 190
False negative. *See* Type II error
False positive. *See* Type I error
Falsifiable, 27
Feasibility, 97, 102
Feeling thermometer, 186–87, 346
Feminism, 178, 190, 191, 201–2, 321
Feminist research, 18, 32, 38, 72, 81, 83, 123
    See also Applied research
Field experiment, 101–2
    See also Before–after study; Non-equivalent comparison study
Field notes, 133
Field research. *See* Observation research
Figures, 367–68
Flynn Effect, 97
Focus groups, 116
Footnotes, 360–61
F-ratio, 292–94
Frequencies, 277
Frequency distribution, 232–34
    See also Mean; Median; Mode; Normal curve
Funding (financial support), 69, 72, 72, 97, 111

Galton's problem, 142–43
Gamma, 311, 314–15, 317
    See also Cells; Concordant; Discordant pairs
Generalizations, 13, 29–31, 37, 40, 46, 93, 96, 102, 114–16, 144, 148, 151
    See also Theory

Grant application. *See* Funding; MRC; NSERC; SSHRC
Graphs, 367–68
Groups. *See* Control groups; Self-assigned groups; Treatment groups

Hard evidence. *See* Evidence
Hawthorne effect, 130–31
Heteroskedastic, 345
Historical research, 137
Homoskedastic, 345
Human subjects, 67
    See also Research subjects
Hypothesis, 40, 44, 47–48, 51, 153, 172, 180, 299, 324, 367, 368
    scientific method and, 4, 13, 22, 26, 27–28
    testing, 46, 48–55, 265
    See also Alternative hypothesis; Null hypothesis
Hypothesized cause, 23, 149–50, 153
Hypothetical. *See* Mind experiment

Independent concept, 22–23, 149
Independent variable, 22–23, 26, 298, 313–14
Index, 201–2
Indicators, 131–32, 180–81, 194
    See also Survey questions
Inductive reasoning, 45–47, 122–24, 165
Inferential statistics, 264, 275, 294
    See also Chi-square; Difference of means; *F*-test; Mann-Whitney *U*-test; *t*-test
Informed consent, 75–78, 80
Integrity, 84
Intercept, 333, 335
Internal validity, 96, 99–100, 102, 120, 109
Internet, 77
    See also Content analysis; Popular media
Intersubjectivity, 7
Interval level of measurement, 41, 182
    See also *F*-ratio; Mean; Median; Mode; Parametric statistics; Range; *R*-square; *t*-test
Interval-level variable, 193, 185–88, 198–99, 292
Intervening variable, 26, 319–21
Interviewer effect, 105
Interviews, 66, 73, 80–82, 98, 103–5, 107, 109

personal, 107–8
telephone, 107–8
See also Elite interviewing; Questionnaires; Survey research
Intuition, 167
IQ test, 97, 193–94

Journalist's credo, 95–96

Lambda, 304–6
    limitations of, 305–6
Lawlike generalizations. *See* Generalizations
Leadership assessment, 347–51, 352–56
    See also Feeling thermometer
Levels of measurement, 182–83, 198, 298, 300, 324
    See also Interval levels of measurement; Nominal; Ordinal
Likert scales, 238
Linear relationship, 260, 292, 309–10, 331–32
Literature review, 165, 167–68, 365–66, 368

Mailed surveys, 107–8
Mann-Whitney *U*-tests, 288, 291
Marginals. *See* Column; Row
Margin of error, 218–22, 226–27, 266
Mean, 216–18, 237–42, 245–48, 250, 333
    See also *t*-test
Media. *See* Popular media
Median, 237–42, 250
Medical research, 66–68, 102–3, 270
Milbrath, Lester, 166
Milgram studies of obedience, 70–71
Mind experiment, 101
Missing data, 200
Mode, 234–42, 250, 304
Most-similar-systems design, 138–40
MRC (Medical Research Council), 84
Multicollinearity, 345
Multidimensional concept, 160, 163–64
Multiple regression analysis, 344–47
Multivariate relationship, 57, 177–78, 192–93, 321–23

Negative findings, 86–87, 368
Negative relationship, 310–13, 47
    See also Correlation
Noise, 102, 200
Nominal data

graphics, 367
Nominal-level data
measures for, 304
See also Cramer's V; Lambda
Nominal levels of measurement, 182,
232–33, 236, 299–301
See also Cramer's V; Lambda
Nominal-level variables, 183, 187
Nonequivalent comparison study, 102
Nonlinear relationship, 310
Nonparmetric statistics, 299, 275
See also Chi-square; Mann-Whitney
U-test
Nonprobability sampling, 212, 226–29
See also Purposive; Quota; Snowball
sampling
Nonrandom errors, 193
Normal curve, 216, 232, 250–53, 273
Normal distribution. *See* Normal curve
Normative analysis, 5–9
NSERC (Natural Sciences and
Engineering Research Council), 84
Null hypothesis, 28, 49–51, 53, 87,
144, 261, 265, 268–70, 272

Objectivity, 7, 31–32, 123
Observation research, 96, 128–36
direct, 130
participant, 131–36
schedule, 130, 132
Operationalization, 26–27, 132,
141–42, 171, 181, 188, 267, 367
Ordinal levels of measurement, 182,
300–1, 309–11, 317
See also Concordant; Discordant
pairs; Gamma; Tau-b
Ordinal-level variables, 183–85, 187,
198–99
Ordinary least squares (OLS), 333–38,
343

Pairs. *See* Concordant pairs; Discordant
pairs
Panel studies, 108
See also Bibby Reports; Interviews;
Survey research
Paradigm, 18–19, 32
Parametric statistics, 275, 299, 309, 331
See also t-tests
Participation, 166, 175–76
Partisanship, 106
Party identification, 158–64, 319
Pearson's r, 341–342
Percentage tables, 257–61

See also Contingency tables
Permission, 80, 84
Piggy-backing
in survey research, 108
Pilot studies, 111, 195
Placebo, 98
Plagiarism, 83
Political analysis. *See* Empirical
analysis; Normative analysis
Political philosophy. 20
Polls, 86, 101, 105, 221, 271–72
See also Bandwagon effect; Survey
questions; Underdog effect
Popular media, 85, 94, 103, 361
See also Content analysis
Population, 109, 206, 207
See also Sample size
Population parameter, 217, 218
Positive findings, 87
Positive relationship, 56, 310–13, 447
See also Correlation
Positivism, 14, 31
See also Science
Postmodernism, 12, 32
Posttest, 98–99
Precision (in measurement), 93, 152,
182, 194
See also Interval; Nominal; Ordinal
Prediction, 13, 298–99
See also Proportional reduction in
error
Predictor validity, 191
Pretest, 98–99
Privacy, 80, 81
Probability, 212–18
sampling, 212, 213
theory, 213–15, 261
Proportional reduction in error
measures, 302–3, 332
See also Gamma; Lambda; Tau-b
Proposition, 44
Protocols
in research, 66
Psychological cost, 66
Psychology
research and, 102–3, 114
Public opinion, 105
Public opinion polls. *See* Polls
Purposive sampling, 228–29

Qualitative research. *See* Comparative
research; Elite interviewing;
Empirical research; Observation
research

Quantitative research. *See* Case studies; Content analysis; Empirical research; Experimental research; Focus groups; Secondary analysis; Survey research
Questionnaire, 81, 86, 103–4
    See also Interviews; Polls; Survey questions
Quota sampling, 229
Quotations, 82

R-square, 292–94, 342, 347
Random errors, 193
Random sampling. *See* Probability sampling
Range, 243
Raw data, 257, 259
Raw scores. *See* New data
Reactivity, 78, 125
Reconceptualization. *See* Inductive reasoning
References, 369–70
Region, 319
Regression
    basic linear, 331, 343–44
    coefficient, 347, 349
    See also Dummy variable regression analysis; Multiple regression analysis; Ordinary least squares
Regression line, 332–38, 345–46
    See also Intercept; Slope
Reinforcing variable, 321, 322
Relationship measures. *See* Correlation coefficients
Relevance. *See* Social relevance
Reliability, 93, 121, 193–95
Religion, 318–19
Replication, 7, 11, 20, 30, 195
Research
    applied. *See* Applied research
    basic. *See* Basic research
Research design, 366–67
    ethical considerations, 80
    validity, 96
Research environment, 104
Research report, 359–70
    See also Appendix; Footnotes
Research subjects 200
    rights of, 75–80
    variation, 102
    See also Sampling
Research topic, 69–73
Residual, 17
Resources, 97

Respondents. *See* Research subjects
Response rates, 76
Risk, 66–70, 74
Row marginal, 258, 52

Sample, 207
    quota, 229
    snowball, 229
Sample size, 212, 218–22, 252–53, 265–66, 269
    heterogeneity, 219, 220
    homogeneity, 219, 220
    margin of error, 219–22
Sampling, 86, 107, 109, 207–9
    accidental, 111
    convenience, 111
    distribution, 216–17
    error, 218–22
    frame, 209–12
    purposive, 138, 228–29
    random, 137–38, 213, 219
    representative, 209, 211, 265
Sampling techniques, 212
    See also Cluster sampling; Non-probability; Probability; Stratified Systematic selection
Scatter plots, 55, 331–32
Science
    hard, 10–11, 35
    postulates of, 15–19
    soft, 10–11
    spirituality and, 17
Scientific approach, 213–14
Scientific method, 11–14, 20, 38, 297
    steps of, 21–30
Scientific revolution, 19–20
Secondary analysis, 112
Self-assigned groups, 102, 228
Sensitive topics, 69–70, 74
Significance, 265–67
    statistical, 102, 251, 265, 349–50
    substantive, 266, 272
    tests, 276
Simple random, 216, 222, 223
Slope, 333–34, 335–37, 338
Snowball sampling, 229
Social class, 179–80
Social relevance, 69, 72
Spurious relationship, 26, 58, 96, 260, 318–19
SSHRC, 72, 73, 84, 111
Standard deviation, 244, 245–48
Standard error of the estimate, 338, 347

Standardized scores, 247–49
Statistic, 207, 218
Statistical correlation. *See* Correlation
Statistics. *See* Inferential; Multivariate;
    Nominal and ordinal data;
    Univariate
Stereotype. *See* Generalization
Stigmatization, 71–72
Stratified sampling, 222, 223–24
Strength of a relationship. *See*
    Correlation coefficient; Regression
    line
Student's *t,* 342
    See also *t*-tests
Subjectivity, 144–45
    See also Objectivity
Subjects. *See* Research subjects
Sum of the squares, 244
Survey questions, 196
    closed, 196–97
    designing, 197–200
    open, 196–97
Survey research, 74, 77, 78, 81, 96,
    100, 101, 103–10, 118, 252
    See also Interviews; Polls;
        Questionnaires
Systematic selection, 223
System-level analysis, 136
    See also Most similar-systems-
        design; Most-different-systems
        design

t-tests, 284–88, 292–94
    one-tailed, 287
    two-tailed, 287
Tau-b, 311, 314–16, 317
Telephone survey, 197
Temporal order, 56, 59–60, 100
Theory, 23–24, 40, 43, 44–46, 150,
    172, 320
    development, 45
    testing, 47
Theory-oriented research, 39, 96

Thesis (statement), 362, 364, 369
Topic. *See* Research topic
Treatment, 98–99
Treatment condition, 100
Treatment group, 98, 100
Triangulation, 120
Type I error, 269–71
Type II error, 269–71
Typology, 42–43

Underdog effect, 101
Univariate analysis, 232
Univariate statistics, 284
    See also Central-tendency; Mean;
        Median; Mode; Range; Standard
        deviation; Variable; Variation

Validity, 32, 96, 121, 189–92
    See also External validity; Internal
        validity
Values, 172
Variability, 245
Variables, 41, 150–52, 172, 175–76,
    180, 297, 300
    See also Control; Dependent;
        Dummy; Independent;
        Intervening; Multiple;
        Reinforcing variables
Variance, 12, 22, 149, 232, 244–47,
    337
    explained, 338–39
    unexplained/residual, 337–38, 346
    See also Endogenous; Exogenous
Variation (measures of), 150, 243
Voting behavior, 72, 151, 153–63,
    321–23
    polls and, 86

women
    drug testing and, 99

z-scores. *See* Standardized scores

To the owner of this book

We hope that you have enjoyed *Explorations: A Navigator's Guide,* and we would like to know as much about your experiences with this text as you would care to offer. Only through your comments and those of others can we learn how to make this a better text for future readers.

School _____ Your instructor's name _____

Course _____ Was the text required? _____ Recommended? _____

1. What did you like the most about *Explorations?*

_____
_____
_____

2. How useful was this text for your course?

_____
_____
_____

3. Do you have any recommendations for ways to improve the next edition of this text?

_____
_____
_____

4. In the space below or in a separate letter, please write any other comments you have about the book. (For example, please feel free to comment on reading level, writing style, terminology, design features, and learning aids.)

_____
_____
_____
_____

Optional

Your name _____ Date _____

May ITP Nelson quote you, either in promotion for *Explorations* or in future publishing ventures?

Yes _____ No _____

Thanks!

You can also send your comments to us via e-mail at
college_arts_hum@nelson.com

PLEASE TAPE SHUT. DO NOT STAPLE.

TAPE SHUT

TAPE SHUT

- - - - - - FOLD HERE - - - - - -

Nelson

MAIL ➤ POSTE
Canada Post Corporation
Société canadienne des postes
Postage paid   Port payé
if mailed in Canada   si posté au Canada
Business Reply   **Réponse d'affaires**
0066102399   **01**

TAPE SHUT

TAPE SHUT

0066102399-M1K5G4-BR01

ITP NELSON
MARKET AND PRODUCT DEVELOPMENT
PO BOX 60225 STN BRM B
TORONTO ON M7Y 2H1